JUSTICE: CONTINUITY AND CHANGE

This selection of essays, speeches and personal reflections, draws on the analysis of one of the leading lawyers of a generation. Lord Dyson, as Master of the Rolls and Head of the Civil Justice System, oversaw a period of reform of both law and legal process. This collection discusses some key themes of, and challenges faced during, his tenure as one of the most senior lawyers in England and Wales. Through these insightful, engaging and compelling pieces, a picture emerges of a robust system of law whose core values can be plotted back to the Magna Carta, but which is flexible enough to respond to current changes without fracturing. A truly compelling exploration of continuity and change in the law by one of its key jurists.

Justice

Continuity and Change

Lord Dyson

·H A R T·
PUBLISHING

OXFORD AND PORTLAND, OREGON
2018

Hart Publishing

An imprint of Bloomsbury Publishing Plc

Hart Publishing Ltd
Kemp House
Chawley Park
Cumnor Hill
Oxford OX2 9PH
UK

Bloomsbury Publishing Plc
50 Bedford Square
London
WC1B 3DP
UK

www.hartpub.co.uk
www.bloomsbury.com

Published in North America (US and Canada) by
Hart Publishing
c/o International Specialized Book Services
920 NE 58th Avenue, Suite 300
Portland, OR 97213-3786
USA

www.isbs.com

**HART PUBLISHING, the Hart/Stag logo, BLOOMSBURY and the
Diana logo are trademarks of Bloomsbury Publishing Plc**

First published 2018

British Library Cataloguing-in-Publication Data
A catalogue record for this book is available from the British Library.

ISBN: HB: 978-1-50991-880-5
ePDF: 978-1-50991-882-9
ePub: 978-1-50991-881-2

Library of Congress Cataloging-in-Publication Data

Names: Dyson, Lord, author.

Title: Justice : continuity and change / Lord Dyson.

Description: Oxford [UK] ; Portland, Oregon : Hart Publishing, 2018. | Includes bibliographical
references and index. | Description based on print version record and CIP data provided by publisher;
resource not viewed.

Identifiers: LCCN 2017045283 (print) | LCCN 2017045672 (ebook) | ISBN 9781509918812 (Epub) |
ISBN 9781509918805 (hardback : alk. paper)

Subjects: LCSH: Justice, Administration of—Philosophy. | Jurisprudence—Philosophy. |
Justice, Administration of—England. | Justice, Administration of—Wales. | Magna Carta. |
Due process of law. | Judges.

Classification: LCC K240 (ebook) | LCC K240 .D97 2018 (print) | DDC 340/.114—dc23

LC record available at https://lccn.loc.gov/2017045283

Typeset by Compuscript Ltd, Shannon
Printed and bound in Great Britain by CPI Group (UK) Ltd, Croydon CR0 4YY

To find out more about our authors and books visit www.hartpublishing.co.uk. Here you will find extracts,
author information, details of forthcoming events and the option to sign up for our newsletters.

To Jacqueline

Acknowledgements

I enjoyed writing these lectures and speeches. Most of them are entirely the product of my own work. But I wish to express my gratitude to Dr John Sorabji, who was my legal secretary when I was Master of the Rolls, in particular for the assistance that he gave me with the lectures and speeches on Civil Justice and Magna Carta. I also wish to thank my wife, Jacqueline, for her assistance in carefully reading many of them in advance and making helpful suggestions for their improvement and then loyally listening to me deliver most of them. This taxed her patience at times, but she never complained.

I was delighted when Sinead Moloney, the Publisher and General Manager at Hart Publishing, expressed an interest in publishing some of my lectures and speeches. She has been extremely encouraging and helpful throughout the gestation process. It has been a novel and enjoyable experience for me and I am delighted with what she and her team have produced. The most difficult part of the whole exercise was choosing the cover for the book. Various ideas were proposed. None of them survived the testing scrutiny of my family. But my good friend, Dr Lyn Rodley, Byzantine Art historian, made various excellent suggestions one of which was the one I finally chose. This is the beautiful Jaccobello del Fiore from the Accademia, Venice.

Contents

Introduction

AUTOBIOGRAPHICAL BACKGROUND

I HAVE INCLUDED in this book a selection of the many lectures and speeches that I gave during my career as a judge. The majority were given while I was a Justice of the Supreme Court (2010–12) and Master of the Rolls and Head of Civil Justice (2012–16). Although they were not given as part of a series and they cover quite a range of subjects, I believe that it is possible to discern in them a number of themes. These include: the shaping of our law on human rights; the importance of access to justice and the need to improve procedural civil justice; and the role of the judiciary in protecting the citizen against the might of the state and developing the common law. Before I say a little more about each of these themes in this introduction, I would like to say something about my personal background.

I do so because my worldview, like that of everyone else, bears the imprint of my upbringing and early formative experiences. Although anyone who rises to the Supreme Court and a senior judicial position such as the Master of the Rolls is likely to be regarded as an Establishment figure, I have never thought of myself in that way. It is true that, during my judicial career, I have met many important people who have helped to shape our society. They have included senior judges and politicians. And in my own small way, I have had some influence on the development of our law. But it was very far from obvious when I was young that such a destiny was likely, or even possible, for me. As a young person, I had no idea what I wanted to do in my life. None of my family had been lawyers or indeed practised any other profession. My parents ran a successful dress shop.

I was born in Leeds. My mother was Bulgarian. My father's parents had come to this country from Lithuania at the turn of the twentieth century. I went to Leeds Grammar School which at the time was a Direct Grant Grammar School. It was a good school after the nineteenth century fashion. Latin was taught from an early age. At the age of 12, I had to choose between Greek and German

(I chose Greek). More importantly, I had to choose between a science education and an education in what we now call the humanities. In the result, I stopped studying physics and chemistry at the ripe age of 12. And in the 6th form, I was strongly urged to study classics for my A levels and did so. It was the obvious choice for clever boys who were not studying science and maths. In one of the lectures included in this book (No 29), I describe how my classical education has influenced my life. The result of this choice was that my education became narrowly specialist at a ridiculously early age. I have always regretted my poor understanding of statistics. My lack of physics and chemistry was to make dealing with certain types of expert evidence in litigation very hard work.

I was the first member of my family to go to university. I was awarded a scholarship to read Law at Wadham College, Oxford. The Warden Sir Maurice Bowra, who was a famous classicist, advised me to read classics rather than law. If you are going to spend your life as a lawyer, why read law? Broaden your mind! As a naïve, rather immature young man, I felt that I was in no position to reject this advice. Anyway, I was not even sure that I wanted to become a lawyer. So I read classics and much enjoyed doing so.

It was only at the end of my time in Oxford that I decided to read for the Bar. I joined Middle Temple, ate my interminable dinners and took a dreary correspondence course, studying just enough to scrape through the Bar examinations.

I had no contacts at the Bar. The sponsor to whom I was allocated by Middle Temple introduced me to someone in his chambers (Patrick Garland, who was later to become Mr Justice Garland). After the most cursory of meetings, he offered me a six-month pupillage. Towards the end of my pupillage, I was offered a second pupillage by Derek Hyamson. I had to pay 50 guineas for each of these pupillages. Pupillage awards were made by the Inns of Court, but not by chambers at that time (I was fortunate to be awarded a Harmsworth pupillage award as well as a Harmsworth scholarship). Towards the end of my second pupillage, I was offered a seat in chambers. In 'Changes in the Law in the last 50 Years' (No 31), I describe some of the changes that have taken place during my professional life. One of these is the way in which pupillages are awarded. No longer is pupillage regarded as a private matter between pupil and pupilmaster (or supervisor as they are now called). Chambers now rightly recognise that they as a whole have an interest in attracting pupils of the highest quality. In the result, for many years now they have been making generous awards to those whom they choose to be pupils.

The chambers which I joined in 1969 were at 11 King's Bench Walk North. We did a mix of general common law, crime and family work. There were no Silks. The de facto head of chambers was Donald Keating. In my early years, I survived on a diet of matrimonial cases (mainly in Grays' magistrates' court) and small criminal and civil cases (mainly possession actions in the county court). I can still recall my weekly visits to Grays to represent wives who were seeking separation and maintenance orders from their feckless husbands. I was grateful for the work at the time. The advisory work that I did consisted mainly of 'devilling' ie doing work for other members of chambers on a quasi sub-contracting basis. But within about five years, I was building up a substantial practice mainly in the field of construction law. In the early 1970s, there was an explosion of litigation in this field and work started to flood into chambers. This was largely as a result of the success of Donald Keating's book on Building Contracts and his and Patrick Garland's taking Silk. I had no idea when I joined chambers that my practice would move in this direction. I had never been particularly interested in technology and my lack of science hardly equipped me well to deal with complex technical issues. But a combination of hard work and basic intelligence usually sufficed to see me home.

The diet of work was fairly limited, but the steady flow of large construction disputes was more than enough to keep me busy. I took Silk in 1982. At the time, that felt like a very big step to take. I can still recall the thrill of receiving my first set of papers with the magical letters QC after my name. In fact, taking Silk made little difference to my practice. My occasional foray into other areas of the law made me realise that there was a large territory for me to explore outside the world of construction cases. I particularly enjoyed doing two cases in the field of medical negligence (now called clinical negligence) which one of my regular construction law solicitors was brave enough to entrust to me. But I do not want to suggest that I did not enjoy doing construction cases. It is true that some were (and still are) rich in boring detail. But many involve interesting issues of fact and law. A significant number of important construction cases went to the House of Lords in the 1970s and 1980s. These included ones which helped to shape the modern law of tort. One of the lectures that I have included in this book discusses the contribution of construction cases to the development of the common law (No 11).

In 1986, I was tempted away from the secure and lucrative pastures of construction law to become Head of Chambers at 2 Garden Court. It was more unusual for a barrister with a successful practice to move chambers at that time than it has since become. My move was described by some as brave. I did it because I had come to appreciate that the only way to diversify my practice (which is what I wanted to do) was to join a set of chambers which had a broader spread of work. Although I continued to do construction cases, after a while I started to be instructed in other areas of work too. I did some general common law and commercial, some football litigation and a little public law work.

We expanded the size of chambers and eventually we moved to 39 Essex Street. By the time I left to become a judge in 1993, there were 33 members (there had been 17 when I joined) and chambers was flourishing.

I took up office as a high court judge in the Queen's Bench Division. In the final lecture in this book, I refer in the barest outline to the huge change in the process by which judges are now appointed. Prior to my appointment, I had had one interview with the permanent secretary of the Lord Chancellor on whose advice the Lord Chancellor (Lord Mackay of Clashfern) made senior judicial appointments. My interview with Sir Thomas Legg in 1992 was a rather strange affair. After a number of questions about my interest in music and my family which I have no doubt were intended to put me at ease, I was asked whether I had given any thought to how I would like my career to develop. I was told that I was too young for a judicial appointment, but was asked whether I would let the Department know if I contemplated doing something drastic like moving to Hong Kong! The next link in this bizarre chain of events was that the private secretary of the Lord Chancellor telephoned one evening to say that the Lord Chancellor wanted to see me the following morning. When I met him (a few days later), he offered me the job. There had been no competition and no interview (except for the one I have described) and no other apparent effort to test my judicial qualities. Nor had there been any lay involvement in the process. The appointment was the product of secret soundings taken by the Department of persons whose identity was not disclosed to me. I have to concede that this secret process was effective in unearthing and winkling out practitioners who, like myself, had not spent their careers doing cases in front of influential heavy-weight judges. Most of my advocacy had been before arbitrators and judges who were then called Official Referees (later judges of the Technology and Construction Court). My appearances in the House of Lords and Court of Appeal (and even in the High Court) were occasional and all the more stressful for being such rarities. Another practitioner who was dug out of his specialist lair was David Neuberger QC who was to become the President of the UK Supreme Court.

This is not the place to give a detailed description of my judicial career. I regard myself as having been immensely privileged to have had such a fascinating life as a judge. As a high court judge, I tried heavy and often interesting criminal and civil cases. I went on circuit and enjoyed the work there, although most of it was in crime. I particularly enjoyed sitting in my home city and staying in the lodgings at Carr Manor. I enjoyed a stroke of early good fortune in 1994 when Lord Taylor, then Lord Chief Justice, was looking for a judge to add to the small group of judges who sat in what was called 'the Crown Office List'. This was the forerunner of the Administrative Court of the Queen's Bench Division. He seemed to think that I was experienced in judicial review and I did not disabuse him: I have always found interesting challenges irresistible. That was how I started doing judicial review cases. I found this area of law absolutely fascinating.

In 1998, I was asked by Lord Bingham, who was then Lord Chief Justice, to become the Head of the official referees' court (then situated in St Dunstan's House on a site in Fetter Lane which has since been demolished). It now seems extraordinary that I should have been the first high court judge ever to have sat in that court. There was a wide misconception (still current in some circles) that construction disputes are all about nuts and bolts and Scott Schedules. In fact, they often involve difficult and important questions of law and fact. I was responsible for changing the title 'official referee' to 'judge of the Technology and Construction Court' or TCC for short. Eventually (after my time in the court) all the judges who sat in the TCC were high court judges. I am pleased to say that the court now has a standing and status which is the equal of the Commercial Court and the Chancery Division in the Rolls Building.

In the TCC, I decided the first cases on the enforceability of awards made by adjudicators under the scheme established by the Housing Grants, Construction and Regeneration Act 1996. I held that an award could only be challenged on the grounds that it had been made without jurisdiction or in breach of the rules of natural justice. I refer to this in my lecture 'Time to call it a day' (No 8).

My early decisions were upheld in our appellate courts. Had the position been otherwise, the adjudication scheme would have foundered. Defendants (often large contractors who raise arguments in an attempt to deprive their usually smaller sub-contractors of cash-flow) would have forced claimants to go through a long expensive trial or arbitration process (which many could not afford) if they wanted their money. In this way, the policy underlying the statute would have been frustrated and the sub-contractors would, in effect, have been denied access to justice. I believe that the adjudication scheme is widely regarded as having been a real success.

After more than seven years in the High Court, I was promoted to the court of appeal. Once again, there was no open competition and no lay involvement. I remained in the Court of Appeal until 2010. During this period, I heard many appeals across a wide area of law. I presided over criminal appeals in the Court of Appeal Criminal Division and sat from time to time in the Divisional Court. Between 2003 and 2006, I was Deputy Head of Civil Justice (deputy to the Head of Civil Justice who was the Master of the Rolls). In that capacity, I become involved in all aspects of civil justice and heard many appeals concerning civil procedure. This was the period when the Woolf Civil Justice reforms were bedding down. It was also a period during which cuts in funding led to a reduction in the availability of legal aid and, later, to an increase in court fees.

By 2010, the appointment of judges had become more open, but also more bureaucratic. Although still done formally by Her Majesty The Queen on the recommendation of Ministers, in reality it was done on the recommendation of the Judicial Appointments Commission, a body independent of government. In that year, I was appointed as a Justice of the UK Supreme Court. In 2012, I successfully applied to become Master of the Rolls in succession to Lord Neuberger of Abbotsbury. This is not the place to give a narrative account of my time in the Supreme Court and back in the Court of Appeal as Master of the Rolls. It is sufficient to say that I greatly enjoyed my work as an appellate judge and having the opportunity with colleagues to interpret, shape and apply our law.

THE PACE OF DEVELOPMENT OF OUR LAW DURING MY PROFESSIONAL CAREER

A number of the speeches and lectures that I have given demonstrate the pace and intensity of the development of both our substantive and procedural law during my professional career. This is the context in which many of my speeches and lectures should be read. I believe that there are a number of reasons for this hectic activity in our law. First, the influence of the European Convention on Human Rights has been huge. Even before its incorporation into our domestic law in 2000 by the Human Rights Act 1998, the Convention was having an effect on the development of the common law in relation to human rights. Once the 1998 Act came into force, the pace at which human rights law developed was remarkable. In the first few years after the incorporation of the Convention, the House of Lords (under the brilliant leadership of Lord Bingham) decided many important cases which set out the relevant principles and showed how they were to be applied. But it soon became apparent that this area of law was not going to settle down quickly. And so it has proved to be. There are many reasons for the growth in the number of human rights challenges in our courts. I would single out two.

The economic crash in 2008 and the so-called age of austerity led the government to make massive cuts to many public services, such as benefits and legal aid. These had seriously adverse effects on the lives of those affected. The result was that many challenges have been made in the courts based on allegations of violations of their human rights. If framed as allegations of breach of common law principles, such challenges would almost certainly fail. Although the draconian common law *Wednesbury* test has been softened to some extent in recent years (in my view under the influence of the Convention), it continues to be a test that is difficult to satisfy. But when framed as alleged violations of Convention rights, challenges have more prospects of success.

The other reason for the increase in the number of human rights challenges that I would highlight is the growth of terrorism. This has proved to be a particularly difficult challenge for our courts to address. I touch on it in my lecture 'Human Rights in an Age of terrorism' (No 13). It is entirely understandable that, conscious of their paramount duty to protect the safety of their citizens, governments have introduced legislation and regulations whose object is to protect the citizens of our country from the scourge of terrorism. It is not surprising that they have been as tough as they dare to be, consistent with a reasonably defensible position on compatibility with the Convention. In this context, a cautious governmental approach is not politically wise. Inevitably, such measures affect individuals' rights. The question of whether the infringements are justified (which is the essential question in many cases) is often difficult to determine. This is proving to be fertile ground for legal challenges.

In addition to the explosion of human rights law, I must also mention two other areas which have engaged much of the attention of our courts during my professional life: immigration and European Union law. There has been a massive growth in immigration in recent years. So long as the United Kingdom remained in the EU, there was little that governments could do to stem the flow of immigration from that source. But approximately half the migrants did not originate from the EU. Successive governments have sought to control this flow of immigration by rushing through ever more complex regulation. Much of this has been poorly drafted and unclear. Legal challenges have inevitably followed.

And there has been a deluge of legislation from Brussels and consequently a massive amount of regulations by which this legislation has been transposed into our domestic law. This too has given rise to a great deal of activity in our courts. Lord Denning MR was right when he said in *Bulmer v Bollinger* of the treaty by which the UK became bound by EU law 'it flows into the estuaries and up the rivers. It cannot be held back'.[1] See again the last chapter in the book. The influence of EU law has been great. Initially, it focussed on economic issues such as competition, patents and consumer protection. But it has now extended much further. Environmental protection law is largely the product of EU law as is the modern law of discrimination. Employment law is now largely regulated by EU law as is much else besides. A great deal of this law as well as the relevant jurisprudence of the Court of Justice of the EU is difficult and obscure. All of this has inevitably led to litigation in our courts, often at the highest level.

THEMES OF THE LECTURES AND SPEECHES AND EXPLANATION OF THE TITLE OF THE BOOK

I should try to identify the broad themes that are covered in this book. I have grouped them under a number of headings. Before expanding a little on each of them, I should explain the title.

Most of the lectures and speeches are concerned with an aspect of justice in the widest sense of that word. I am not a philosopher. It is therefore not surprising that none of them contains any discussion

---

[1] *Bulmer v Bollinger* [1974] Ch 401 at 418.

about theories or the meaning of justice. Most judges are intensely practical and in my view so they should be. They are not academic lawyers. They decide the cases that are before them for determination. In the highest appellate courts, they expound and clarify the law. Their objective should be to find the facts by a fair process and apply the law to the facts as they find them to be. They may consider that the substantive law is not 'just' in the sense that it is not fair. But the ability to change the law so as to make it fair or fairer is usually limited to judges of the highest appellate courts. And even at that level, judges should be cautious about changing the law.

So my reflections are not on the philosophical underpinning or the fairness of our laws. Like most judges, I have taken the existing law as my starting point and have applied it to the letter unless there are cogent reasons for changing it. There are circumstances in which it is permissible and right for a court at the highest level to change the common law so as to reflect changes in social and economic conditions. Hence the title 'Continuity and Change'. Continuity in the law is important because it provides stability and a solid foundation on which people can base their behaviour. Frequent changes give rise to instability and, at worst, chaos. In my view, judges (as opposed to Parliament) should not change the law unless there is a compelling need to do so. But sometimes even judge-made law has to change. As so often happens in our law, the competing arguments between continuity and change have to be weighed and choices made. Making the choice can be one of the most difficult challenges facing an appellate judge. Similar choices are made more often by Parliament and Government.

REFLECTIONS ON THE COMMON LAW AND THE POWER OF THE JUDGES

It is trite to say that judges have very considerable power over the individuals whose cases they determine and in setting precedents for other similar cases. Fortunately, although I took a great deal of care over my judgments, I did not reflect on the enormity of the responsibility that was entrusted to me. I suspect that, if I had done so, I would have frozen and never decided anything. One of the issues that has particularly interested me is that of where the boundary lies between what is for a judge and what should be left for Parliament. I discuss this issue in 'Are the Judges Too Powerful?'

(No 3) and 'The Duty of Care of Public Authorities' (No 6). This is an important issue which will not go away.

A related question is whether the exercise of the jurisdiction to grant judicial review has gone too far and is undermining democracy. This has been the work of the judges who have to decide in what circumstances to declare unlawful decisions of public bodies. I discuss this issue in 'Does Judicial Review Undermine Democracy?' (No 5).

One consequence of the fact that huge power is vested in our judges and that the issues that they decide are so important, both for individual litigators and for society as a whole, is that they are, and in my view should be, susceptible to criticism like any other public servant. Fair criticism of their judgments is commonplace, whether it is by other judges, the media, academics, lawyers or anyone else. That is as it should be. A subject of particular interest to me has been the relationship between judges and the academic community: see my speech 'Academics and Judges' (No 2). On the whole, criticism of judges by public authorities and central government in particular tends to be fair and restrained: the Government's fury at losing a case usually surfaces as an expression of 'disappointment'. Personal abuse is not acceptable, if for no other reason than that the judges cannot answer back and become engaged in slanging matches. My sense is that the standing of judges in our society is currently very high, probably higher than it was when I first became a judge. This may be because today the public seems to have little respect for politicians or journalists. But there have been some egregious examples of unfair criticism of judges. I discuss these issues in the paper entitled 'Criticising Judges' (No 1).

HUMAN RIGHTS

As I have said, there has been an explosion of human rights law during my professional life. It gathered speed after the incorporation of the Convention by the 1998 Act and is showing no sign of abating. In 'What is Wrong with Human Rights?' (No 12), I discuss the issue of why there has been so much criticism of human rights in this country by our media and our politicians. I give my reasons for repudiating much of that criticism and concluding that there is much to celebrate in the Convention and the way in which it has been interpreted by the Strasbourg court. Sometimes Strasbourg does know best. I have always deprecated the xenophobic criticism by some of everything that comes out of Europe.

The question of the application of the Convention outside the area of the territories of the Council of Europe has proved to be very controversial. Many consider that the Strasbourg court has adopted an unwarranted imperialistic interpretation of the scope of the Convention. This is not a view I share. I have attempted to explain why in 'The Extraterritorial Application of the European Convention on Human Rights' (No 15).

The UK and the Strasbourg courts are increasingly having to grapple with and delineate the contours of the right to freedom of religion accorded by article 9 of the Convention. In 'Religion and the Law' (No 14), I discuss some of the jurisprudence on article 9, including cases on the banning of religious symbols and clothing.

In 'Human Rights in an Age of Terrorism' (No 13), I discuss the challenge facing our courts to strike the right balance between doing everything possible to reduce the threat to our security and safety posed by terrorists and the need to protect the human rights of individuals potentially affected by those threats.

MAGNA CARTA AND THE RULE OF LAW

As Head of Civil Justice, I was also *ex officio* Chairman of the Magna Carta Trust. It was my good fortune that the 800th anniversary of the sealing of Magna Carta at Runnymede occurred during my term of office. I gave a number of lectures broadly on a Magna Carta theme which I have included in this book: 'Magna Carta—Liberties, Customs and the Free Flow of Trade' (No 16); 'Delay too often defeats Justice' (No 17); and 'Magna Carta and Religion' (No 18).

On 15 June 2015, approximately 4,000 people converged on the field at Runnymede where the sealing took place. The guests included Her Majesty The Queen, other members of the Royal Family; the Prime Minister, David Cameron MP; Justin Welby, the Archbishop of Canterbury and many other notable people. I was master of ceremonies and was instructed to speak for no longer than 3 minutes. The Prime Minister and the Archbishop were each allowed 4 minutes. My speech 'Runnymede' is at No 19.

I have included my lecture 'Magna Carta and the Compensation Culture' (No 4) in the group entitled 'Reflections on the common law and the power of judges'. It is unquestionably more about the compensation culture than about Magna Carta. For the reasons that I give, I was prevailed upon to knit a Magna Carta piece into the lecture.

ACCESS TO JUSTICE AND CIVIL PROCEDURE

Access to justice is a cornerstone of democracy and the rule of law. It has engaged my attention for much of my judicial life. It should be beyond argument that the citizen is entitled to have access to a court to vindicate his or her legal rights. But there is much scope for argument as to the content of the right of access to justice and the conditions for its exercise. Working this out can raise difficult policy issues. But there must be an irreducible minimum content of the right of access to justice if it is not to be an empty vessel.

Thus if court fees are so high that all but the very rich are unable to get through the court door, that is a denial of access to justice at the most basic level. It is difficult to envisage any circumstances in which that could be regarded as satisfying the rule of law. But views change over time in response to changing social and economic conditions as to what restrictions on access to the courts are acceptable. For example, subject to a means and merits test, legal aid was freely available in most classes of civil and family litigation when I started at the Bar. The result was that litigants in person were rare. Legal aid has gradually been withdrawn from many categories of case. Alternative methods of funding are now available, but there are problems which I touch on in my lecture 'Threats to Justice in the 21st Century' (No 24). And the rise of the litigant in person has presented huge problems for the courts and the litigants themselves. This is deeply troubling. I discuss this issue in 'Litigators—Survive and Thrive' (No 21) and 'Advocates as Protectors of the Rule of Law' (No 20).

The increasing complexity and cost of civil litigation is potentially a form of denial of access to justice. If litigants cannot afford to litigate because the cost of complying with the court processes (for example, disclosure of documents) is so expensive that a would-be litigant cannot afford it, that is a form of denial of access to justice. If a litigant cannot afford to wait the months or years that will pass before his case comes on before a judge and a judgment is given, that too is a denial of justice.

But there are other restrictions on a person's access to justice which are justified in the public interest. Limitation periods are necessary to ensure that defendants are not harassed by stale claims. The power to strike out/stay abusive proceedings is another restriction on access to justice which is necessary in the public interest. I discuss some of these issues in 'Time to call it a day' (No 8).

If litigants are able to get through the court door, the system should not place obstacles in their path by imposing conditions for the conduct of their litigation which unreasonably prevent them from having their claims determined by a judge. That is why the rules of civil procedure are so important. It is only in recent times that civil procedure has become established in the UK as a respectable academic subject. Rules of civil procedure play a crucial role in ensuring that courts control and regulate the exercise of the right of access to justice. Thus the scale of disclosure of documents has become a real impediment to being able to conduct litigation at reasonable cost. I discuss this in 'The Jackson Reforms and Civil Justice' (No 22). And I discuss the approach that the courts have adopted to the imposition of sanctions on parties who fail to comply with court orders and rules in that same lecture. My first attempt as Master of the Rolls to give guidance on this issue was in the case of *Mitchell*.[2] I was heavily criticised for being too tough. My second and slightly gentler attempt was in *Denton*.[3] This seems to have been accepted by the profession. I regarded these two cases as among the most important that I decided in my judicial career.

The increasing sophistication and complexity of commercial life and advances in technology have made litigation more complicated than it used to be. Our procedural rules must adapt to take account of these changes if the courts are not to be overwhelmed with cases that will take longer and longer to be heard. The answer is not inexorably to increase the number of judges. The resources are not available for that solution even if it were thought desirable. So the court processes have to be streamlined to accommodate the changes. And it may be necessary to deliver faster and perhaps less thorough justice.

Other topics related to civil procedure that are covered in this book are: the relationship between litigation and arbitration (No 3); arbitration after the Brussels 1 Regulation (as amended) (No 27); and the place of mediation in our system of dispute resolution as discussed in the case of *Halsey* (No 25).

---

[2] *Mitchell v News Group Newspapers Ltd* [2013] EWCA Civ 1537, [2014] 2 All ER 430.
[3] *Denton v TH White* [2014] EWCA Civ 906, [2015] 1 All ER 880.

OVERVIEW

I gave many speeches during my judicial career which I have not included in this collection. I hope the ones I have selected give a fair idea of my worldview and the kind of lawyer I am. As a judge, I tried to make decisions which were clear, humane and sensible. Inevitably, from time to time I found in favour of the individual against the Executive. But I hope that I always kept firmly in mind the practicalities of governing and the difficulties facing Government and other public bodies. I also hope that the approach that I tried to bring to bear in my decision-making as a judge is reflected in the speeches that I have included in this book.

Part I

Reflections on the Common Law and the Power of Judges

1

Criticising Judges: Fair Game or Off-limits?*

INTRODUCTION

MY CHOICE OF subject this evening is prompted by a personal experience when I was a High Court judge. I had decided a case about the release of six IRA members, all of whom had been sentenced to life imprisonment.[1] In anticipation of lengthy delays which were blighting the Parole Board at the time, the prisoners submitted their applications for release six months early. The Home Secretary refused to refer their cases to the Board until their minimum tariffs expired, and the prisoners applied for judicial review.

I held that the Home Secretary's decision was unreasonable on ordinary public law grounds. Leading counsel for the Home Secretary told me that he was instructed not to seek to appeal the decision. And that, I assumed, was that.

But my ruling had clearly struck a political nerve, and a media storm ensued. Michael Howard, who was Home Secretary at the time, was interviewed by John Humphreys the following day on Radio 4's Today programme. He criticised my judgment in no uncertain terms. But most striking was his comment about my record as a High Court judge. He said this:

> ... we'll have to see what the outcome is if indeed we do appeal. The last time this particular judge found against me ... the Court of Appeal unanimously decided that he was wrong. So we'll have to see what happens if we do appeal. These things are quite difficult to predict ...

The tone of Michael Howard's attack was probably unremarkable to regular listeners of the Today programme. After all, animated

---

* The Third Annual Bailii Lecture, 27 November 2014.
[1] *R v Home Secretary, ex p Norney* [1996] COD 81.

political debate on the radio is commonplace. But for lawyers and judges who are accustomed, to borrow the words of former New South Wales Chief Justice Gleeson, to 'deciding [cases] in the peaceful and calm atmosphere of court, not under surroundings of ... infuriated party politics',[2] this was a shock.

In the event, there was no appeal and my record therefore escaped further scrutiny on this occasion (!).[3] When interviewed some time later by Joshua Rozenberg, the Home Secretary appeared to step back from his personal criticism of me. He insisted that his comments had been intended to highlight the unpredictability of judicial review, rather than question my character or competence as a judge.[4] However, an anonymous senior judge dismissed Mr Howard's interview as 'dreadful', 'outrageous' and 'a complete breach of the conventions'.[5]

It is this final criticism which leads me to the subject of this evening's lecture. I wish to deal with two questions. First, what conventions (if any) govern the criticism of judges? Secondly, when (if ever) may a judge respond to criticism? In an age of rapid technological development, changing media culture and constitutional evolution, I think that these questions deserve urgent attention. If there are conventions, they need to be justified and defended for the twenty-first century, not just asserted or assumed.

What Conventions Govern the Criticism of Judges?

Conventions are difficult to pin down. A great deal of academic ink has been spilt on formulating a test to identify them. But a basic definition will suffice for present purposes. I will proceed on the basis that a convention has two core components: first, a degree of consensus between the relevant actors; and secondly, a degree of convergence in their practices. There is a further complication in our country, in that several conventions go beyond custom and practice, and fill the interstices in our uncodified constitution. The convention that judges are not criticised at all is essentially a social

---

[2] Chief Justice Gleeson, 'High Court Anniversary Speech' (Banco Court, Supreme Court of Victoria, 6 October 2003) (citing Edmund Barton, first Prime Minister of Australia).

[3] For a full account of the episode see J Rozenberg, *Trial of Strength* (Richard Cohen 1997) 2–6.

[4] Rozenberg, *Trial of Strength* 5–6.

[5] Rozenberg, *Trial of Strength* 4.

convention. The convention that the executive does not criticise judges is rooted in the separation of powers and the independence of the judiciary. It is part and parcel of the convention that judges do not speak out extra-judicially against the legislation it is their constitutional role to interpret.

Writing in 1966, Sir Louis Blom-Cooper claimed that there was indeed a convention that judges should not be criticised in public at all. He wrote:

> Criticism of the judiciary over the last fifty years has been confined to conversations over the coffee cups and to the seclusion of private solicitors' offices and barristers' chambers ... The English have cloaked their judges with an immunity from public criticism ...[6]

On Sir Louis Blom-Cooper's thesis, a convention against publicly criticising judges had existed at least since the early 1900s.

I will argue that this convention in the wide sense defined by Sir Louis no longer exists, if it ever did. For quite some time now, judges have faced unprecedented scrutiny by politicians and the public, particularly in the media. Modern history is laced with examples of criticism from both quarters. The social conventions that used to regulate such conduct have, in my opinion, disappeared. A few examples of modern criticism, first from politicians and secondly from and in the media, will suffice to make my point.

Criticism by Politicians

I begin with criticism from politicians. My first example is the fierce criticism targeted at Collins J in 2003. The judge had handed down a decision about the provision of support to destitute asylum seekers.[7] The judgment was an unappetising read for Ministers, who wished to restrict the circumstances in which asylum seekers could access state support.

David Blunkett, the Home Secretary, articulated his disagreement in no uncertain terms. He told the *News of the World* that he was 'personally fed up' with judges overturning decisions made by politicians. 'It's time', he said, 'for judges to learn their place'.[8] Most

---

[6] L Blom-Cooper, 'The Judiciary in an Era of Law Reform' (1966) 37 *Political Quarterly* 378.

[7] *R (Q) v Secretary of State for the Home Department* [2003] EWHC 195 (Admin), [2003] 15 LS Gaz R 26.

[8] *News of the World* (23 February 2003).

disturbingly, there were allegations that the press had been briefed against Collins J by Whitehall.[9]

This was, perhaps, a sign of things to come. My second example took place in 2006. Judge John Griffith Williams Q.C. was called upon to sentence a man who had been convicted of sexually assaulting a three-year-old girl. He handed down a life sentence with a five-year minimum tariff. This was in accordance with the then applicable guidelines. Dr John Reid, the Home Secretary at the time, was quick to express his dissatisfaction. He said that the sentence was unduly lenient and implied that the Attorney General, who had the power to refer the sentence to the Court of Appeal, should think the same. A battery of further criticism followed. Alun Michael MP invited judges to 'wake up and smell the coffee' because they 'simply [weren't] getting it', and Vera Baird QC (a junior minister) told Radio 4 listeners that she thought the judge had 'got the [sentencing] formula wrong'.[10] Dr Reid's comments drew sharp criticism from the Attorney General, Lord Goldsmith, who promised to make an independent decision on the merits of the case, 'not in response to political or public pressure'.[11] Ms Baird subsequently issued a public apology, but only after discussion with the Lord Chancellor, Lord Falconer.[12]

My third example concerns criticism that was delivered by a Prime Minister. In 2006, Sullivan J gave judgment in a case concerning six Afghani nationals who had hijacked a plane to escape the Taliban. Contrary to the ruling of a panel of immigration adjudicators, the Secretary of State refused to allow the men to remain in the UK. Sullivan J held that the Secretary of State's decision was an abuse of power and violated Article 8 of the European Convention on Human Rights.[13] Tony Blair was not of the same opinion. He saw an opportunity to turn the rhetoric of the judge's decision around when he said that 'it's an abuse of common sense frankly to be in a position where we can't [deport these men]'.[14] The Court of Appeal disagreed. It dismissed the Home Secretary's appeal against

---

[9] A Bradley, 'Judicial Independence under Attack' [2003] PL 397, 400–401.

[10] For a full account, see HL Select Committee on the Constitution, *Relations between the executive, the judiciary and Parliament*, 6th Report of Session 2006–07, paras 45–49.

[11] *The Guardian* (14 June 2006).

[12] *BBC News* (19 June 2006), available at news.bbc.co.uk/1/hi/uk_politics/5096266. stm.

[13] *R (S) v Secretary of State for the Home Department* [2006] EWHC 1111 (Admin).

[14] *BBC News* (10 May 2006), available at news.bbc.co.uk/1/hi/uk/4757523.stm.

the ruling and commended Sullivan J's 'impeccable judgment' at first instance.[15]

My final example is from 2012. It is striking because, like my personal anecdote from 1995, it involved a measure of *personal* criticism aimed at a judge. In January 2012 Peter Hain MP, who had previously served as Secretary of State for Northern Ireland, published an autobiography.[16] As one might expect of publications of this kind, it did not pull its punches. Girvan J, who was at the time a High Court judge in Northern Ireland, was described as 'high-handed', 'idiosyncratic' and 'off his rocker'.

Prime Minister David Cameron supported Mr Hain's right to express himself in these terms. In the House of Commons he said this:

> ... there are occasions, as we all know, when judges make critical remarks about politicians; and there are occasions when politicians make critical remarks about judges. To me, that is part of life in a modern democracy ...[17]

But Mr Hain was prosecuted for scandalising the court (about which more later), and the prosecution was only withdrawn after he issued a full apology. Girvan J was subsequently appointed as a Lord Justice of Appeal in Northern Ireland.

What observations can we make on the basis of examples such as these? I suggest there are five, some of which are more profound than others. First, the source of criticism is more likely than not to be the Home Secretary. That is undoubtedly because Home Secretaries are regularly on the receiving end of judicial review challenges, and their decisions tend to engage contentious issues of public policy. Tension is therefore inevitable.

Secondly, the subject-matter of the vast majority of criticisms is the Human Rights Act 1998 and the European Convention on Human Rights.

Thirdly, most if not all of the criticisms have been prompted by rulings which uphold the interests of individuals over those of the government. It would appear that Lord Irvine's invective against the government 'cheer[ing] the judges when a win is secured and boo[ing] them when a loss is suffered' still has mileage.

---

[15] *R (S) v Secretary of State for the Home Department* [2006] EWCA Civ 1157, para 50.
[16] Peter Hain, *Outside In* (Biteback, 2012).
[17] HC Deb 18 April 2012, vol 543, col 317.

Fourthly, all but one of the recent criticisms has been directed at the judge's *decision*, rather than his personal abilities or motivations. And in the exceptional case, the critic apologised.

Fifthly, despite occasional lapses, the convention remains that while Cabinet ministers may disagree with a judgment, it is still off-limits for them to criticise the motives or probity of the judge who made the decision. The point is neatly illustrated by a news report in the *Sun on Sunday*[18] of a ruling by Judge Bernard Dawson sitting in the Upper Tribunal of the Immigration and Asylum Chamber, that a drug dealer could not be deported to his native United States on his release from prison, because he would not be able to receive treatment there for his diabetes and high blood pressure. The Home Office official statement said: 'We are disappointed by the tribunal's decision and we have appealed against it'. On the other hand, Philip Davies MP felt no such constitutional constraint, and told the newspaper: 'This is a perverse decision which highlights the idiocy of the judges who determine these cases.'

I am not alone in reaching this fifth conclusion. In its 2007 Report on relations between Parliament, the executive and the judiciary, the House of Lords Select Committee on the Constitution concluded that there was 'widespread agreement' on the limits of what ministers should and should not say.[19] 'It is acceptable', according to the Report, 'for Ministers to comment on individual cases'.[20] What remains unacceptable, however, is an express or implied statement that there is something wrong with the judge who reached the decision.[21] This appears to be all that is left of the convention.

Before I leave my domestic examples I pause to note, with some relief, that ministerial criticism is not reserved for judges in this jurisdiction. For example, in late 2010 Prime Minister David Cameron told the House of Commons that the ruling of seventeen Strasbourg judges against our blanket ban on prisoner voting made him feel 'physically ill'.[22]

Further, Justice Kirby, then Justice of the Australian High Court, has observed that incidents of political criticism against British

[18] 13 July 2014.

[19] HL Select Committee on the Constitution, *Relations between the Executive, the Judiciary and Parliament*, 6th Report of Session 2006–07, para 42.

[20] ibid para 41.

[21] ibid, citing with approval the oral evidence of Lord Falconer.

[22] HC Deb 3 November 2010, vol 517, col 921, referring to *Hirst v United Kingdom (No 2)* (2006) 42 EHRR 41.

judges 'seem positively genteel by comparison to those which have engaged the Australian judiciary'(!).[23] A notable example is the criticism prompted by a case in 1996 about indigenous title to land.[24] The Premier of Western Australia dismissed the High Court's decision on this subject as 'rantings and ravings',[25] whilst the Premier of Queensland dismissed some of the High Court judges as 'dills about history'.[26] More recently, Prime Minister Julia Gillard launched what was described as an 'extraordinary' attack against Chief Justice Robert French.[27] The Chief Justice had quashed a controversial arrangement for returning asylum seekers to Malaysia.[28] The Prime Minister personally accused Chief Justice French of inconsistency between his High Court ruling and decisions that he had made earlier in his judicial career about government immigration policies.

Criticism in the Media

What, then, of the media? There is, of course, an important difference between media criticism and political criticism. The media and all the commentators who are given air time or space on television, radio and newspapers are not a limb of government or Parliament. Unlike the executive, they cannot be governed by 'constitutional' conventions against criticising judges, although in my view they should comply with their own professional rules and conventions.

There is nonetheless a close relationship between media criticism and political criticism of judges. A media uproar is liable to prompt political criticism of judges, and vice versa. Furthermore, and most importantly for present purposes, there has been a parallel decline of the convention against media criticism of judges. Let me illustrate this.

I begin with the last successful prosecution for the (now abolished) offence of scandalising the court. In 1900 the editor of the

---

[23] M Kirby, 'Attacks on Judges—A Universal Phenomenon' (1998) 72 *Australian Law Journal* 599, available at www.hcourt.gov.au/assets/publications/speeches/former-justices/kirbyj/kirbyj_maui.htm.

[24] *Wik Peoples v Queensland ('Pastoral Leases Case')* [1996] HCA 40, (1996) 187 CLR 1.

[25] Kirby, 'Attacks on Judges—A Universal Phenomenon'.

[26] B Horrigan, *Adventures in Law and Justice: Exploring Big Legal Questions in Everyday Life* (UNSW Press, 2003) 208.

[27] *The Australian* (1 September 2011), available at www.theaustralian.com.au/national-affairs/dennis/story-fn59niix-1226127337399.

[28] *Plaintiff M70/2011 v Minister for Immigration and Citizenship* [2011] HCA 32.

Birmingham Daily Argus published a scathing article about Darling J. He said this:

> No newspaper can exist except upon its merits, a condition from which the Bench, happily for Mr Justice Darling, is exempt. There is not a journalist in Birmingham who has anything to learn from the impudent little man in horsehair, a microcosm of conceit and empty-headedness.[29]

These uncharitable criticisms were, according to later analyses, not entirely misplaced.[30] But they nonetheless attracted a criminal sanction of £100, and the editor was forced to issue a public apology.

Secondly, the *Spycatcher* episode. In 1986 the House of Lords ruled that an injunction should be granted against the publication of Peter Wright's *Spycatcher* book, which had already been published to a global audience outside our jurisdiction.[31] The *Daily Mirror* reacted to the ruling by publishing front-page photographs of Lords Brandon, Templeman and Ackner. The photographs were rotated upside down and the headline set out in capital letters read 'YOU FOOLS!'.[32] *The Mirror's* criticism was to some extent vindicated when the House of Lords reversed its ruling several years later.[33]

Thirdly, the wrongful conviction of the 'Birmingham six' in the late 1980s. This inevitably generated media hostility. Lord Chief Justice Lane, who had presided over the men's unsuccessful appeal in 1988, became the target of acute criticism. *The Times* published an article about Lord Lane which deprecated the 'narcissistic arrogance' of his 'worthless certainty' about the correctness of the jury's verdict.[34] It called for him to step down. Lord Donaldson, Master of the Rolls, later criticised the media response as a scapegoating exercise, but only after Lord Lane had retired.[35]

My final example is the most recent and shows the link between media criticism and disapproval of judges in Westminster or Whitehall. The criticism concerned Collins J, who you will recall had attracted criticism from David Blunkett for his 2003 ruling on destitute asylum seekers. The Home Secretary's broadside inevitably

---

[29] See (1900) 82 LT Reports 534.
[30] D Pannick, *Judges* (Oxford University Press, 1987) 111–112.
[31] *Attorney General v Guardian Newspapers (No 1)* [1987] 1 WLR 1248 (HL).
[32] See Law Commission Report No 335, para 70.
[33] *Attorney General v Guardian Newspapers Ltd (No 2)* [1990] 1 AC 109 (HL).
[34] *The Times* (18 March 1991).
[35] S Shetreet and S Turenne, *Judges on Trial: The Independence and Accountability of the English Judiciary*, 2nd edn (Cambridge University Press, 2013), 388.

spilled over into the media, and *The Daily Telegraph* carried this comment noting that:

> One man's rulings have thwarted all moves meant to stem the tide of refugees ... Whenever the Government has been on the wrong end of an asylum ruling in recent years, Collins J has often been the villain of the piece ... This particular judge is considered a serial offender in Whitehall.[36]

So, there you have four examples of media criticism. They all concern newspaper articles. But the contemporary picture is, of course, more complex. Thanks to the proliferation of online forums, criticism is no longer confined to established media outlets such as newspapers and television channels. Everybody is now a potential critic. It is therefore unsurprising that judges have been targeted by sharp criticism and outright abuse on the internet. As early as 1999 the Lord Chancellor's Office successfully requested an internet service provider to remove a website that was considered to be inappropriately offensive towards judges.[37]

What observations, then, may be drawn from these examples of media criticism, and how does it differ from criticism by politicians? The first is that media criticism is framed in less inhibited language than political criticism. In response to *The Mirror's* *Spycatcher* headline in 1986, Sedley LJ observed that 'not only deference but civility towards the bench has become unmodish'.[38]

Secondly, the boundary between personal and professional criticism is less well-respected in the media than by politicians. Even where the subject of criticism is an individual decision, the judge is unlikely to escape from a degree of character assassination. A good example is the vilification of Lord Lane after the release of the 'Birmingham six' in the early 1990s.

Thirdly, there is little evidence of a convention against criticising judges' decisions in the media. Quite the contrary. Media outlets are prepared to voice their opinions on judgments which they consider engage important public interests and favour and quote commentators or interest groups of their choice who do the same. Even if the views quoted are not explicitly endorsed by the newspaper itself, the commentators are often selected to promote and favour an agenda or world view supported by that newspaper and presumably most of its readers.

---

[36] *The Daily Telegraph* (20 February 2003).
[37] I Cram, *A Virtue Less Cloistered: Courts, Speech and Constitutions* (Hart, 2002) 209.
[38] Sedley LJ, 'Foreword' in I Cram (ed), *Borrie and Lowe: The Law of Contempt*, 4th edn (LexisNexis Butterworths, 2010).

Fourthly, and in my opinion most significantly, the popular image of the judge as expressed through media criticism is in a state of flux. Potter J captured this process of transformation colourfully when he said extra-judicially:

> ... the High Court judge was, in the late 1980s, typically portrayed in some parts of the media as a port soaked reactionary, still secretly resentful of the abolition of the birch and hostile to liberal influences of any kind. The same judge is now, in the same parts of the media, an unashamedly progressive member of the chattering classes, spiritually if not actually resident in Islington or Hampstead, out of touch with 'ordinary people', and diligently engaged in frustrating the intentions of Parliament with politically correct notions of human rights.[39]

I agree with this observation. The tenor of much media criticism against judges has moved away from complaining that judges have *too much* sympathy for the interests of government and the Establishment, towards judges being *too disruptive* of those interests. The contrast between the *Daily Mirror's* reaction to the *Spycatcher* decision in the late 1980s and the *Daily Telegraph's* reaction to Collins J's ruling on destitute asylum seekers in 2003 illustrates this point neatly. If the judges are to come to terms with media criticism, this is a point that must be grasped.

Before I move on, I pause again to note that we must maintain a sense of proportion. Much of the criticism administered in the media in this country is positively inhibited compared to the criticism levelled against our Australian counterparts. Justice Kirby, for example, has recorded examples of judges being described as 'bogus', 'pusillanimous', 'evasive', 'feral', 'pathetic' and 'self-appointed Kings and Queens'.

EXPLANATIONS

How, then, can we explain this decline of the social convention against criticising judges? As Chief Justice McLachlin of the Canadian Supreme Court said, '[t]his is not the world we judges thought we knew, comfortable and secure. What, we are driven to ask, is happening?'.[40]

---

[39] Shetreet and Turenne, *Judges on Trial* 388.
[40] B McLachlin, 'The Role of Judges in Modern Commonwealth Society' (1994) 110 *LQR* 260, 261.

Let me begin by saying where I think the explanation does not lie. It is true that the offence of scandalising the court was abolished last year. That offence criminalised '[a]ny act done or writing published calculated to bring a court or a judge of the court into contempt, or to lower his authority'.[41] The potential chilling effect of this offence was clear. But in my judgment the proliferation of criticism against judges cannot be attributed to this change in the law for two reasons. First, and most obviously, the offence was only abolished last year and all of my examples of criticism predate that event. Secondly, the last successful prosecution of scandalising the court was in 1931,[42] and the chilling effect of the offence has therefore been minimal in recent years.

In my opinion, the true explanation lies elsewhere.

There has been a change in popular culture. Deference towards people who occupy positions of authority has 'become more unfashionable [since] the 1980s'.[43] As Munby LJ observed in a case about a litigant who had conducted protests outside the doors of a court:

> Society has in large part lost its previous habit of deferential respect. Much of what might well, even in the comparatively recent past, have been considered by the judges to be scurrilous abuse of themselves or their brethren has today, as it seems to me, to be recognised as amounting to no more than acceptable if trenchant criticism.[44]

I think, however, that Lord Taylor of Gosforth (former Lord Chief Justice) took this social explanation too far when he argued that:

> As personal and political expectations have risen, people have become more determined to realise them. If things do not go their way, they are not prepared, as our forbears often were, to accept disappointment philosophically.[45]

In my opinion, this unfairly trivialises the genuine opinions that are expressed by politicians and in the media about judges' decisions. Taken to extremes, it would reduce every criticism of a judge to a crude expression of self-interest by the losing party. That is not, I think, what any growth in criticism of judges is about.

So, with that qualification, my first explanation is a change in popular culture. My second explanation is a closely related change

---

[41] *R v Gray* [1900] 2 QB 36 at 40 (QBD).
[42] *R v Colsey* (1991) Times, 9 May.
[43] Shetreet and Turenne, *Judges on Trial* 387.
[44] *Harris v Harris* [2001] 2 FLR 895 (FD), para 372.
[45] Lord Taylor, 'Justice in the Media Age' (1996) 24 *Arbitration* 258, 259.

in media culture. We are all aware, post-Leveson, of the pressures that face the modern media industry. In its 2012 Report, the Law Commission attributed an erosion of the convention against criticising judges to changes in journalistic practices.[46] The pressure to produce stories which sell newspapers has undoubtedly led to more aggressive reporting techniques, from which judges are not immune. In a recent speech, for example, Lord Judge LCJ highlighted the media practice of 'door-stepping' judges and their family members, which has mercifully died down in recent years.[47] They cannot comment on decisions outside court, and the regulators' guidelines recognise that fact.

But it would be wrong, I think, to attribute the decline of conventions against criticising judges purely to cultural changes. There is an important constitutional narrative here, too.

My third explanation is therefore the enactment by Parliament of the Human Rights Act 1998. Professor Shetreet and Dr Turenne make this point in their fascinating book about judicial independence. They argue that:

> There is less criticism of the competence and integrity of the English judges [than previously] ... However, the advent of the Human Rights Act ... calls for judgments of a more 'evaluative' kind, prompting complaints that judges are striking down policies of the democratically elected.[48]

Judges are now required to make difficult decisions as to the proportionality of the acts of public authorities and to conduct assessments about the fairness of policy decisions which affect the lives of large numbers of their fellow citizens. What is more, the policy decisions often raise issues which ordinary people (as well as politicians and the media) can understand and on which they have opinions which they express freely. That is how it should be in a free democratic society.

Theresa May's speech to last year's Conservative Party Conference about Article 8 rights which cited Maya the cat and the case about the American diabetic I mentioned earlier, are two of many examples that support this thesis. Indeed, it is the enactment of the Human Rights Act that has, in my opinion, had the greatest influence

---

[46] Law Commission Report No 335, para 70.
[47] Lord Judge LCJ, 'The Judiciary and the Media' (28 March 2011), available at www.bfhu.org/images/download/lcj-speech-judiciary-and-the-media.pdf.
[48] Shetreet and Turenne, *Judges on Trial* 388.

on the re-definition of judges' popular image as anti-establishment, anti-democratic figures.

My fourth explanation is also related to the Human Rights Act. It is the growing currency of freedom of expression as a political and constitutional value in this country. Although the Strasbourg authorities have equivocated about whether Article 10 protects writers who criticise judges,[49] there can be no doubt that politicians and the media have been emboldened in their criticism by the principles of transparency and accountability that have swept across our governmental landscape. As Lord Pannick observes, 'Judges, like other public servants, must be open to criticism because in this context, as in others, freedom of expression helps to expose error and injustice and it promotes debate on issues of public importance'.[50]

How Should Judges Respond?

How, then, should judges respond to criticism from politicians and from others in the media or elsewhere?

'No Well-tuned Cymbal'—The Traditional Policy of Silence

In 1995 I chose not to respond to the criticisms levelled against me on the *Today* programme. That was consistent with the policy of judicial silence that prevailed at the time. In 1625 Sir Francis Bacon, then Lord Chancellor, wrote in an essay that 'an overspeaking judge is no well-tuned cymbal'.[51] That opinion has prevailed for more than three centuries.

It found currency, for example, in what Lord Kilmuir said in 1955: 'so long as a judge keeps silent his reputation for wisdom and impartiality remains unassailable'.[52] Indeed, Chief Justice McLachlin built this quality into her popular stereotype of a judge who 'decides only what is necessary, says only what is necessary, and on no account ever talks to the press'.[53]

---

[49] See J McBride, 'Judges, politicians and limits to critical comment' (1998) 23 *EL Rev (Supp)* 76, 82–85.

[50] D Pannick, '"We do not fear criticism; nor do we resent it": abolition of the offence of scandalising the judiciary' [2014] *Public Law* 5, 9.

[51] J Spedding, RE Ellis and DD Heath (eds), *Works of Francis Bacon*, vol VI (Hurd and Houghton, 1861) 3.

[52] See AW Bradley, 'Judges and the Media—The Kilmuir Rules' [1986] *Public Law* 383, 385.

[53] B McLachlin, 'The role of judges in modern Commonwealth society' (1994) 110 *LQR* 260, 260.

But this proclivity to remain absolutely silent began to be broken down in the 1980s under Lord Mackay, Lord Chancellor, and Lord Taylor as Lord Chief Justice. In my view, this was a welcome development. Unchecked public criticism of judges undermines confidence in the judiciary. This, in turn, has deleterious consequences for the administration of justice. As Lord Judge CJ said in a recent lecture about judges and the media:

> ... it does matter to the welfare of the community, and the preservation of the independence of the judiciary, that the confidence of the community in its judiciary should not be undermined.[54]

Inaccuracies and misunderstandings are particularly conducive to undermining confidence

The Alternatives to Silence—Three Parameters

But this does not mean we should open the floodgates to uninhibited dialogue between judges and critics. I think Lord Hope struck the right balance when he said in a recent lecture at Birmingham University that:

> There will, no doubt, be times when it is best to keep silent. But reticence, not absolute silence, is what the judicial office requires.[55]

It is therefore necessary to set some parameters within which judges may respond to criticism without doing violence to the nature of their office. In my view, there are three important limitations.

The first is impartiality. Responses to criticism pose a threat to judicial independence on two fronts. A response may give the appearance of the judge stepping into the political arena. In turn, this may raise doubts about the judge's ability to make objective judgements about the relevant legal issue. If judges comment on cases outside court, they undermine the integrity of what they (or their colleagues) have said in court. The spectre of a press conference on the steps of the court to explain and justify a long or short sentence handed down from the bench is inconceivable, but would be the logical extension of any comment beyond re-stating what has been said in open court already. As Lord Woolf observed, a cosy

---

[54] Judge, 'The Judiciary and the Media'.
[55] Lord Hope of Craighead, 'What happens when the Judge speaks out?' (19 February 2010) 11, available at www.birmingham.ac.uk/Documents/college-artslaw/law/holdsworth-address/holdsworth09-10-hope.pdf.

relationship with the politicians or the press is equally liable to prompt suspicions of dependence upon the media, and therefore partiality.[56]

The second parameter is professionalism. A judge must not respond to critics in a way which imperils his own professionalism or that of his or her fellow judges. Indeed, conduct which is inconsistent with the 'dignity of the judicial office' is prohibited by the Lord Chief Justice's *Guide to Judicial Conduct*.[57]

The third parameter is tolerance. As the *Guide to Judicial Conduct* says: 'As a subject of constant public scrutiny, a judge must accept personal restrictions that might be viewed as burdensome by the ordinary citizen'.[58] Sachs J once made a related point in the South Africa Constitutional Court when he observed that:

> ... as the ultimate guardians of free speech, the judiciary [should] show the greatest tolerance to criticism of its own functioning.[59]

A judge must therefore be more tolerant of criticism than a member of the public. Every decision will produce winners and losers. It will upset some parties, and please others. That is simply the nature of the judicial office, and judges must be prepared to accept that.

Responding to Criticism—Individual and Institutional Solutions

Judicial responses to criticism must therefore be acutely measured. They must comply with all three parameters. But what is the best solution?

There are, I think, two potential approaches. The first is to allow judges to respond personally. The second is to set up an institutional framework for responding to criticism. For reasons which I will set out, I favour the institutional solution.

Let us first consider the personal response. This would involve a judge striking back against criticism which has been levelled against him by a minister or a journalist. The response could take the form of a press release or, far more riskily, a media interview.

In my view, there are a number of hazards associated with personal responses. Understandably, unfair criticism is liable (in rare

---

[56] Lord Woolf, 'Should the media and the judiciary be on speaking terms?' (2003) 38 *Irish Jurist* 25, 30.
[57] *Guide to Judicial Conduct* (2013) paras 5.1(2) and (6), available at www.judiciary.gov.uk/wp-content/uploads/JCO/Documents/Guidance/judicial_conduct_2013.pdf.
[58] ibid para 5.1(2).
[59] *The State v Mamabolo* (2001) 3 SA 409 at para 78.

cases) to produce intemperate responses from judges. As Lord Pannick observes:

> Perhaps because cogent criticism of the judiciary is now so rare, its appearance causes disproportionate excitement and leads otherwise sensible people to act in irrational ways.[60]

Such excitement must of course be avoided at all costs. It tarnishes the judge's appearance of impartiality. It also has the potential to imperil the professionalism of the judicial office as a whole.

But even well-measured personal responses are troublesome. They give the appearance of the judge being an active participant in a political conversation, rather than a neutral administrator of the law. A judicial response might invite a counter-response, and what then? As soon as the judge enters the arena of political discussion, the boundary between his personal politics and his status as an impartial administrator of justice begins to break down.

The institutional solution, which invites a collective response to criticism, avoids these problems. An institutional approach would nominate an individual or an organisation to respond on behalf of judges whose decisions have been targeted for criticism.

In this jurisdiction the Lord Chief Justice has been given the role under the 2005 Constitutional Reform Act as head of the judiciary, of official mouthpiece for judges, in succession to the Lord Chancellor; and in parallel the judiciary has its own (small) press office.

The Press Office Solution

The Press Office solution was commended by Lord Woolf in 2003, when he said that:

> We have been greatly helped by the Lord Chancellor's Press Office and, when the office of Lord Chancellor is abolished, I am sure the judiciary must have a Press Office of our own. Not, I emphasise, to spin, but to provide the media with the basic facts they need.[61]

I am pleased that Lord Woolf's prediction came to pass under the Constitution Reform Act. The Judicial Press Office now carries out excellent work on behalf of judges up and down the country. I expect the Office's excellent support to continue.

The use of modern technology, such as the Judicial Office Twitter account, should be encouraged in this respect. It has already

---

[60] Pannick, *Judges*, 121.
[61] Wolff, 'Should the media and the judiciary be on speaking terms?' 33.

improved the Office's ability to pre-empt inaccurate reporting by distributing faster and greater quantities of accurate information (such as full transcripts of a judgment or a judge's sentencing remarks) ahead of the next news cycle.[62] Fire-watching, not fire-fighting, must be the aim of the game. With the full remarks available, the news stories, the commentary and the follow ups are in the context of the full facts.

The Lord Chief Justice

The Lord Chief Justice is also well-placed to offer an institutional response to criticism. In 2009 Lord Hope said that primary responsibility for defending judges against criticism should rest with the Lord Chief Justice.[63] He regretted, however, that the Chief Justice's ability to discharge this function had been compromised by the disqualification of senior judges from sitting in the House of Lords.[64]

I am more sanguine about that. Paragraph 6.40 of *The Cabinet Manual* confers on the Chief Justice the important right to 'make written representations to Parliament on matters which he or she believes are of importance relating to the judiciary or the administration of justice'. This reflects the power provided by section 5 of the Constitution Reform Act 2005. He and other judges give evidence to Select Committees, and he sends an annual written report to Parliament.

The Chief Justice also enjoys a valuable opportunity to respond to critics through the medium of an annual Press Conference. For example, earlier this month Lord Thomas CJ, whilst making clear he could not comment on any actual cases, expressed his support for the naming of defendants in secret terrorist trials; in November 2013 he responded to criticism about the over-zealous application of Article 8 in deportation cases; and in 2012 Lord Judge commented on concerns about the length of the proceedings which preceded the deportation of Abu Hamza.[65]

I hope that, if the noise of criticism from ministers and the press becomes louder, the Judicial Press Office and the Lord Chief Justice will continue to serve as important correctives to unfair comment and misinformation about judges.

---

[62] twitter.com/JudiciaryUK.
[63] Lord Hope of Craighead, 'What happens when the Judge speaks out?'.
[64] ibid.
[65] See www.judiciary.gov.uk/wp-content/uploads/JCO/Documents/News+Release/lcj-press-conference-270912.pdf.

CONCLUSIONS

To conclude, the convention against criticism of judges' *decisions* has been eroded, even if it remains in place, albeit sometimes precariously, for government ministers. Uncertain and testing conditions therefore lie ahead.

In my opinion, it is time for judges (if they have not already done so) to accept these changes that have been brought about by shifts in our culture, our Constitution, and our technology. In my view it is right that judges' reasoned decisions should be open to public debate and scrutiny. Our courts are open and free, and the media perform a valuable job in our democracy of reporting the courts and the justice system to the wider public. What I hope is that the debate should be reasoned and based on the evidence. And what is not fair or reasonable is to impugn the motives of judges, or ascribe them to prejudices.

Judges must expect criticism and, where appropriate, they must offer a robust response. This response should take the form of a well-organised, measured, institutional reply.

We must, however, maintain some perspective. Judges' primary responsibility is judging, not public relations. I therefore conclude with the ringing words of my predecessor Lord Denning, who had this to say about the criticism of judges:

> We do not fear criticism, nor do we resent it ... Exposed as we are to the winds of criticism, nothing which is said by this person or that, nothing which is written by this pen or that, will deter us from doing what we believe is right; nor, I would add, from saying what the occasion requires ... Silence is not an option when things are ill done.[66]

Finally, I wish to express my gratitude to Mr Tom Pascoe, my former judicial assistant, for his considerable assistance in preparing this lecture.

---

[66] *R v Commissioner of Police of the Metropolis, ex p Blackburn (No 2)* [1968] 2 QB 150 at 155 (CA).

2

*Academics and Judges**

T HE RELATIONSHIP BETWEEN judges and academic lawyers
is complex and fascinating. We have a symbiotic co-existence.
As I shall explain, we need each other. For some of us, the
need is so intense that we actually decide to co-habit with each
other. There are a number of cohabiting couples here tonight and
my wife Jackie and I are one of them. She is a tax lecturer at UCL.
A few years ago, I was involved in a tax case in the Court of Appeal.
It raised the question of whether a payment was to be regarded as
capital or income. I asked my wife for a matrimonial view. Surely,
I could make the most of the advantage that I had over my colleagues
and indeed the advocates in this case. She said that the question
was very difficult and that no clear statement of principle could
be derived from the cases. I regarded this answer as very clear, but
deeply unsatisfactory. This was the first time I had asked her advice
on a question of tax law and it was disappointing that this was the
best that my in-house academic could do. So I set about trying to
work out some principles for myself and set these out in my judgment. I felt quite pleased with myself. Things got even better when
the draft judgment that I circulated persuaded one of my colleagues
(but not the other) to agree with me and the House of Lords dismissed a petition for leave to appeal. What could be better?

Well a few months later, I read an article in the *British Tax Review*
about the case by a distinguished academic. The writer, who was
not my wife, did not think much of my judgment and said so in
fairly trenchant terms. He showed with devastating cogency that
one of the principles of which I was so proud was plainly wrong. I
hasten to say that this did not impose undue strains on the safety of
my marriage.

So what light does this experience shed on the relationship
between judges and academics? First, if you are lucky enough to

* Speech in Middle Temple, Dinner for members and academics.

be married to an academic lawyer, listen to her (or him). Secondly, it demonstrates the value to academics of having court decisions to criticise. If you academics agreed with every judgment that we judges wrote, what would there be for you to write about? And these days, you have to admit that we give you much grist for your mill. I am afraid to say that the judgments are becoming longer and longer (although perhaps, to some extent at least, this tendency is also being replicated in academic writings); and, in the Supreme Court (but not, of course, the Court of Appeal), there is a multiplicity of judgments such that there is much scope for arguing about what the case actually decided. All of this provides a diet rich in nutrients for the academic community. You really need us to feed you with material for learned books and articles.

But thirdly (and more seriously), my little experience also shows the value of academic writings to judges. If only I had had the benefit of the *British Tax Review* article *before* I had written my judgment, I would have been saved from error. But my judgment in that case was a relatively meagre offering. Let me come to something altogether meatier.

In a postscript to his masterly judgment in *The Spiliada* case, Lord Goff said:

> 'I feel that I cannot conclude without paying tribute to the writings of jurists which have assisted me in the preparation of this opinion. Although it may be invidious to do so, I wish to single out for special mention articles by Mr Adrian Briggs ... Miss Rhona Schuz ... They will observe that I have not agreed with them on all points; but even when I have disagreed with them, I have found their work to be of assistance. For jurists are pilgrims with us on the endless road to unattainable perfection; and we have it on the excellent authority of Geoffrey Chaucer that conversations among pilgrims can be most rewarding'.[1]

Lord Goff's image of pilgrims journeying together along the road marked a distinct shift in attitude. The conventional approach— which to a great extent prevailed until at least the mid-1970s—had kept the pilgrims at more than arms' length from each other. The distance was so great in fact that judges were only able to entertain conversation of sorts once the jurists had long since stopped their journey. The conventional approach was, as I am sure you know, known as 'better read when dead'.

---

[1] *Spiliada Maritime Corpn v Cansulex Ltd, The Spiliada* [1987] AC 460 at 488 (HL).

To our eyes, this convention was as ridiculous as many of the other conventions with which the legal profession was encrusted until fairly recently. The convention was circumvented by some extraordinarily disingenuous practices. Counsel were permitted to adopt as part of their submissions the views of academics taken directly (even verbatim) from their articles and textbooks, so long as they did not attribute them to the academic or the book from which they were taken. Even worse, even if counsel did not adopt the views of academics in this way, judges would surreptitiously adopt them and, without acknowledgement, parade the academic writing as if it were the product of their own brilliance.

These days, judges are far more open about these things. Judgments are peppered with references to and quotations from academic writings. That is, of course, how it should be.

The influence of academic writings on judicial decision-making is considerable. I wish to give only two examples. My first example concerns the House of Lords decision in *Anderton*.[2] In an article, which was famously toned down on editorial advice, Glanville Williams noted how the House failed to keep out of the 'intellectual minefield' of the law regarding attempts to commit an offence which it is impossible to commit. Their Lordships had, in his words, failed to 'heed the "Keep out" notice' which Parliament had erected through section 1 of the Criminal Attempts Act 1981; a notice which was intended to ensure that the courts did not keep making 'asses of themselves'. As John Smith rather laconically put it, the Lords in *Anderton* ignored the warning notice and 'obligingly [provided] their critics with ample ammunition to demonstrate the morass in which they ... landed us'. They had done so, as he put it, by substituting 'confusion and uncertainty' for Parliament's 'orderly and simple solution'.

Within a year of the decision in *Anderton*, and as Lord Bridge acknowledged, in no small part owing to Glanville Williams' criticism and relying to a large part on points Professor Smith had made, the House of Lords in *Shivpuri* overturned its earlier decision.[3]

The academics had spoken and the judges had listened. A real conversation between pilgrims took place.

My second example is the detailed analysis carried out by the late Peter Birks and the collaborative work of Lord Goff and Gareth Jones

---

[2] *Anderton v Ryan* [1985] AC 560 (HL).
[3] *R v Shivpuri* [1987] AC 1 (HL).

(a paradigm case of the good which comes from judges and academics working together), without which it is doubtful whether the law of restitution would have developed as it has.

In the case of *Re OT* (2004),[4] Master Longmore famously said: 'nowadays judges read academic articles as part of their ordinary judicial activity'. Well 'famously' may be stretching things a little and I am not sure which judges he had in mind (perhaps Master Moses) or what his evidence was for this sweeping statement. I am sure that judges do read academic articles if they are cited to them; and some even find time to read them in their so-called free time. Many of us are rather overwhelmed with all this learning, but it is good to know that it is there for us.

At all events, I think we can all agree that these days our symbiotic relationship is flourishing. One characteristic that we all seem to share is a love of gossip. An event like this dinner (and the fact that it has been so well attended) is the best possible evidence of the success of our relationship. It certainly gives us all ample opportunity to gossip. I am sure that I speak on behalf of us all when I express my gratitude to the Inn for organising this wonderful dinner.

---

[4] *Re OT Computers (in administration); First National Tricity Finance Ltd v OT Computers Ltd (in administration)* [2004] EWCA Civ 653, [2004] Ch 317.

3

*Are the Judges Too Powerful?**

I
T IS A huge honour for me to be here tonight. As many of you
know, UCL occupies a special place in my heart. I have attended
more Bentham Presidential lectures than I care to think about.
My first one was in 1986 and I have missed very few since then. Last
year I received an honorary LLD from this wonderful institution
and now it is my turn to give this prestigious lecture. Conscious of
the glittering roll call of past presidents, I am faced with a daunting
task.

As I said, I have been coming here for many years. So too has
my dear friend Edwin Glasgow QC. He has been chairman of the
Bentham Association and its predecessor for 15 years. He has
chaired these annual events with consummate elegance and wit.
He is a brilliant advocate. I owe a great debt to him for his irresistible advocacy which as long ago as 1986 persuaded me to move and
become head of his chambers. This was a career move from which
I benefited greatly.

The departure of Edwin is a big loss to Bentham. But the arrival
of another good friend, Nigel Pleming QC, is a great coup. He is one
of the outstanding public law barristers of his generation. Bentham
is lucky to have him.

Mr Bentham was no great admirer of the judiciary. He once said
'the same fungus, which when green, is made into Bar, is it not,
when dry, made into Bench?' He distrusted the judges. When drafting a 'New Plan for the organisation of the Judicial Establishment
in France' in the 1820s, he was adamant that judges should not be
permitted to legislate:

> Appointed for the express purpose of enforcing obedience to the laws,
> their duty is to be foremost in obedience. Any attempt on the part of
> the judge to frustrate or unnecessarily to retard the efficacy of what he
> understands to have been the decided meaning of the legislature, shall be
> punished with forfeiture of his office.

* Bentham Lecture, University College London, 2013.

The proper role of the judge in a democratic society continues to excite much interest and to provoke differences of opinion. Lord Sumption contributed to the debate in his recent Sultan Azlan Shah lecture delivered in Kuala Lumpur. He asked: what kinds of decisions should properly be taken by the judges and the courts, as opposed to other agencies of social control? He suggested that there is or may be an excess of judicial law-making. In this lecture, I intend to consider two distinct questions. The first is whether, on the purely domestic front, our courts are trespassing into areas which should not be their preserve. The second is whether the European Court of Human Rights is overstepping the mark in imposing political and social values on the UK for which it has no democratic mandate. Both questions raise big issues on which many have expressed views in recent years.

I start with the domestic scene. The topic has become of more interest to the general public in recent times because of the rise of judicial review. But before we come to judicial review, we should not lose sight of the fact that the general problem of the boundary separating the legitimate development of the law from legislation is not new. In *Omychund v Barker*,[1] the question before the court was whether the testimony of a witness who refused to swear a Christian oath could be admitted in evidence in an English trial. Several witnesses who were called by the plaintiff swore an oath in the manner of their Gentoo (ie Hindu) religion. You may know that Mr Bentham wanted to get rid of all religious oaths. There was no binding authority on whether this kind of oath was sufficient. Counsel for the plaintiff was William Murray (later the great Chief Justice Lord Mansfield). He submitted to the judge, Lord Chancellor Hardwicke, 'the only question is whether upon principles of reason, justice and convenience, this witness ought to be admitted'. He explained the key role of the courts in making law, because the legislature cannot predict all the eventualities that may occur after it enacts a statute:

> all occasions do not arise at once; now a particular species of Indians appears; hereafter another species of Indians may arise; a statute very seldom can take in all cases, therefore the common law, that works itself pure by rules drawn from the fountain of justice, is for this reason superior to an act of parliament.

The Lord Chancellor admitted the testimony of the witnesses who had sworn according to their religion.

---

[1] *Omychund v Barker* 26 Eng Rep 14 (1744).

Now it is true that the Lord Chancellor did not explicitly accept the full floridity of counsel's submissions. It may also be said that the control over the court's processes is classic judicial territory. Nevertheless, it is a striking early example of the court grappling with the legitimate scope of judicial power.

But over the centuries, judges have developed the common law, sometimes in dramatic ways. In *Woolwich Building Society v Inland Revenue Commissioners*,[2] the House of Lords had to decide whether to overturn a longstanding rule that there was no right of recovery of money paid under a mistake of law in response to an ultra vires demand by a public authority.

One argument against the recognition of a right of recovery was that it would overstep the boundary which separates legitimate development of the law from legislation. As to this objection, Lord Goff said:

> I feel bound however to say that, although I am well aware of the existence of the boundary, I am never quite sure where to find it. Its position seems to vary from case to case. Indeed, if it were to be as firmly and clearly drawn as some of our mentors would wish, I cannot help feeling that a number of leading cases in your Lordships' House would never have been decided the way they were.

One of the arguments advanced against changing the law was that it was accepted that some limits (in addition to the usual six-year time bar) had to be set to such claims and that the selection of such limits, being essentially a matter of policy, was one which the legislature alone was equipped to make. But Lord Goff did not accept that this was persuasive enough to deter him from recognising in law the force of the justice underlying the claim. He gave a number of reasons. These included that the opportunity to change the law would never come again; and however compelling the principle of justice might be, it would never be sufficient to persuade a government to propose its legislative recognition by Parliament. Lord Goff was not prepared to leave it to Parliament to change the law.

The subject matter of the *Woolwich* case was far removed from court processes and the administration of justice. It was firmly in the area of substantive law. But the law of unjust enrichment or restitution was itself a creature of the judges. So why should the judges not sweep away a restriction on the right of recovery which could now be seen to be unjust?

[2] *Woolwich Equitable Building Society v IRC* [1993] AC 70 (HL).

But it was a controversial decision. Lord Keith dissented, saying that what was proposed amounted to 'a very far reaching exercise of judicial legislation' and that the rule that money paid under a mistake of law was not recoverable was 'too deeply embedded in English jurisprudence to be uprooted judicially'. He added:

> formulation of the precise grounds upon which overpayments of tax ought to be recoverable and of any exceptions to the right of recovery, may involve nice consideration of policy which are properly the province of Parliament and are not suitable for consideration by the courts.'

The law was changed by a majority of 3:2.

In *National Westminster Bank v Spectrum Plus*,[3] Lord Nicholls said at para 32:

> The common law is judge-made law. For centuries judges have been charged with the responsibility of keeping this law abreast of current social conditions and expectations. That is still the position. Continuing but limited development of the common law in this fashion is an integral part of the constitutional function of the judiciary. Had the judges not discharged this responsibility, the common law would be the same now as it was in the reign of King Henry II. It is because of this that the common law is a living instrument of law, reacting to new events and new ideas, and so capable of providing the citizens of this country with a system of practical justice relevant to the times in which they live.

As always, Lord Nicholls expressed himself with consummate elegance. But there is no real clue here as to the limits of legitimate development of the common law by the judges. On the whole, the judges seek to identify and distil from precedents the principles already inherent in the common law. As Parke J put it in *Mirehouse v Rennell*,[4] at 546:

> Our common law system consists in the applying to new combinations of circumstances those rules of law which we derive from legal principles and judicial precedents; and for the sake of attaining uniformity, consistency, and certainty, we must apply those rules, where they are not plainly unreasonable and inconvenient, to all cases which arise; and we are not at liberty to reject them, and to abandon all analogy to them, in those to which they have not yet been judicially applied,

---

[3] *National Westminster Bank plc v Spectrum Plus Ltd* [2005] UKHL 41, [2005] 2 AC 680.
[4] *Mirehouse v Rennell* (1833) 1 Cl & F 527.

because we think the rules are not as convenient and reasonable as we ourselves could have devised. It appears to me to be of great importance to keep this principle of decision steadily in view, not merely for the determination of the particular case, but for the interests of law as a science.

Even this early statement recognises that the common law does not require precedent to be followed where it is plainly unreasonable and inconvenient to do so. Most judges are supporters of the 'never say never' school of thought. But some are bolder than others. That fact of human nature alone explains why some are more likely to leave change to Parliament than others.

But over the centuries, the law has developed incrementally in response to changing social and economic conditions and changing moral values. From time to time, the law has taken a big step forward. More usually, the steps are small and barely noticed. *Woolwich* is an example of a big step taken in the field of substantive law. The fact that the House was split 3:2 on the issue of whether it was proper for the courts to make the change suggests that this was a case near the boundary to which Lord Goff referred. And indeed it was. There were powerful arguments for saying that the proposed change should be left to Parliament. Of these the most important was that, as even Lord Goff recognised, there had to be limits to the right to recovery. He said that legislative bounds could be set to the common law principle and he plainly envisaged that they would be.

An important principle is that the common law should not be developed where the courts are not equipped to decide whether the development is in the interests of justice or to define the parameters of the development. But where the court feels that it is equipped to develop the law, sometimes radically, it can and in my view it should be willing to do so. As Lord Goff said, *Donoghue v Stevenson*[5] is a good example of this. Another good example is *Hedley Byrne & Co Ltd v Heller & Partners Ltd*.[6] In that case, Lord Reid said that, apart altogether from authority, the law should treat negligent words differently from negligent acts. The law ought so far as possible to reflect the standards of the reasonable man and that is what *Donoghue v Stevenson* set out to do. Lord Reid then identified

[5] *Donoghue v Stevenson* [1932] AC 562 (HL).
[6] *Hedley Byrne & Co Ltd v Heller & Partners Ltd* [1964] AC 465, [1963] 3 WLR 101 (HL).

the relevant differences between acts and words and said that there was 'good sense' behind the then existing law that in general an innocent but negligent misrepresentation gave no cause of action. Something more was required than mere misstatement. As is well known, building on what Lord Haldane said in earlier cases, he said that what was required was a relationship where it was plain that the person seeking information or advice was trusting the other to exercise such a degree of care as to the circumstances required and where the other knew or ought to have known that the inquirer was relying on him. So here the law (the embodiment of the reasonable man) was being developed in these terms. This is a classic example of the law being developed incrementally. The courts were well equipped to make such a development. The development was a reflection of the standards of the reasonable man, no more and no less. The courts are at least as well able to state what the standards of the reasonable man are as Parliament. This is an example of what Lord Reid referred to as 'lawyer's law' in *Pettitt v Pettitt*,[7] where he said:

> Whatever views may have prevailed in the last century, I think that it is now widely recognised that it is proper for the courts in appropriate cases to develop or adapt existing rules of the common law to meet new conditions. I say in appropriate cases because I think we ought to recognise a difference between cases where we are dealing with 'lawyer's law' and cases where we are dealing with matters which directly affect the lives and interests of large sections of the community and which raise issues which are the subject of public controversy and on which laymen are as well able to decide as are lawyers. On such matters it is not for the courts to proceed on their view of public policy for that would be to encroach on the province of Parliament.

Before I go any further, I need to say something about the limitations of our judicial law-making system. This is discussed in detail by Justice Heydon in his excellent *Law Quarterly Review* article 'Limits to the powers of ultimate appellate courts' (1996).[8] As he says, our legal system prizes answers to problems thrashed out in adversary argument. But the process of adversary argument is not directed to abstract inquiries, but to providing answers which it is necessary to

---

[7] *Pettitt v Pettitt* [1970] AC 777 at 794–5 (HL).

[8] JD Heydon, 'Limits to the Powers of Ultimate Appellate Courts' (2006) 122 *Law Quarterly Review* 299.

give to live questions having a direct impact on the interests of the parties in the particular case. In my experience, advocates faithfully respect their duty to assist the court by bringing to its attention all relevant authorities of which they are aware, including those which are unhelpful their client's case. But the adversary nature of the process inevitably shapes the way in which submissions are made. The principal goal of the advocate is to win the case. Any interest the advocate may have in helping the court to develop the law is bound to be subordinate to that primary objective. Even if he wishes to do so, the advocate in our adversarial system is unlikely to be well placed to draw to the court's attention the wider ramifications of a possible development of the law. It is true that interveners give valuable assistance by providing a broader view. But they appear in a small number of cases (mainly in the Supreme Court) and they tend to represent a particular group of interests or a particular viewpoint and to adopt something of an adversarial position even though they do not make submissions on the facts. Good adversarial argument is an effective way of solving most disputes. But where what is at issue is whether and, if so, how to develop the law, this may not be as effective as, say, a thorough examination of the problem by the Law Commission.

There is also the problem of decisions in which one party, though present and opposing the other, is either unrepresented or badly-represented. The danger of reaching conclusions which are adverse to a badly represented loser is clear. Inequality of arms can lead to decisions which are bad for the losing party, but also bad for the development of the law. The attractions of the argument presented by an outstanding advocate may seduce the court into error which an effective opponent would have been able to expose.

There is a further danger inherent where judges decide a point on which they have not heard sufficient argument. Points can occur to a judge after the completion of oral argument. He may conduct his own research and find authorities to which reference was not made in the oral argument or in the written submissions placed before the court. It is not usual for a court to acknowledge that the case has been decided on a point on which the parties were not heard. In *Smith v Smith*,[9] Scrutton LJ opened a judgment with the words 'I ... regret that counsel who argued this case would probably not

---

[9] *Smith v Smith* [1923] P 191 at 202 (CA).

recognise any part of the judgments as having any relation to the arguments they addressed to us'. That is an engaging, but unusual admission. In *Miliangos v George Frank (Textiles) Ltd*[10] Lord Simon of Glaisdale said: 'where a court does its own researches itself as it often will and sometimes must, it should proceed with special caution since it is thereby acting without the benefit of adversary argument'. It is sometimes a difficult question for a court to decide whether to ask for further submissions on a point on which there has been no argument. If the point is relatively peripheral, there is no need. Certainly, natural justice does not require it. But where the point is important and, particularly where it is decisive, to deny the parties the opportunity to make submissions on it is not only to deny natural justice, but is also to throw away one of the advantages of the adversarial system as a means of propounding and developing the law.

After that detour into the strengths and weaknesses of the adversarial system for the development of our law, I need to give examples of situations in which judges have recognised the limitations on their ability to decide what the law should be. There is an analogy here with the so-called 'deference' that judges show to the decisions of the Executive in public law proceedings. Much has been written on this subject. The generally-held view is that judges tend not to uphold challenges to decisions of the Executive which fall within its (rather than the courts') constitutional or institutional competence. Thus certain decisions require a legitimacy which can be conferred only by entrusting them to persons responsible to the community through the democratic process. But of perhaps greater relevance in the present context is the fact that the courts will also refuse to interfere with decisions of the Executive if they consider that they are institutionally incompetent to do so. In the case of *R v Cambridge Health Authority, ex p B*[11] the Court of Appeal was concerned with the allocation of resources by a health authority for medical treatment. The court said that difficult judgments had to be made as to how a limited budget would be best allocated: 'that is not a judgment which a court can make' said Sir Thomas Bingham MR. But, no doubt, if the court had been provided with all the material which was before those who made the decision that was under challenge in that case, it would have been able to make a

---

[10] *Miliangos v George Frank (Textiles) Ltd* [1976] AC 443 at 478 (HL).
[11] *R v Cambridge Health Authority, ex p B* [1995] 1 WLR 898 (CA).

sensible decision, and no less rational and sensible than that made by the health authority. I do not think that the court was saying that the court *could not* make such a judgment. Clearly, it was not impossible for the court to do so, especially if it was provided with all the material that was available to the original decision-maker. But it was not the normal function of courts to make such judgments, and they were less well-equipped than health authorities to make them.

For similar reasons, the courts will in some circumstances say that they are less well equipped than Parliament to decide whether to develop the law in a certain direction. I have already referred to the distinction made by Lord Reid in *Pettit v Pettit*. In *Morgans v Launchbury*[12] the issue was whether a wife could be vicariously liable for the negligent driving of a person to whom she had given permission to drive her husband. Lord Denning in the Court of Appeal had sought to extend the liability of a car owner for the negligent driving of his car by others, because the car was the family car and the car owner was the person who had or ought to have had a motor insurance policy. The House of Lords held that the driver was not the wife's agent in driving the car and that to hold the wife liable for the negligence of the driver would involve a substantial extension of the doctrine of vicarious liability which was a matter for the legislature and not the courts. Lord Wilberforce[13] said that he was willing to assume (although more evidence was needed to prove the point) that traditional concepts of vicarious liability may be inadequate to reflect the problems created by the growing numbers of cars on the roads, their increasing speed and the severity of the injuries they cause. He also accepted that some adaptation of the common law rules to meet these problems was capable of being made by the judges. Indeed, that is what had been done in the United States. But he concluded that this could not be done here. His reasons are interesting. First, he said that, assuming that it was desirable to fix liability in such cases on the owner, at least three different systems could be adopted: (i) the 'matrimonial' car theory advocated by Lord Denning, ie that all purposes for which the car was used by either spouse were to be presumed to be matrimonial purposes; (ii) the 'family' car theory, ie that any user by any member of the family was the owner's 'business'; and (iii) any owner who permitted another to use his car should be liable by the fact of the permission, a theory adopted by statute in certain Australian states.

---

[12] *Morgans v Launchbury* [1973] AC 127, [1972] 2 WLR 1217 (HL).
[13] [1972] 2 WLR 1217 at 1222A.

Lord Wilberforce said that he did not know on what principle the House of Lords acting judicially could prefer one of these systems to the others or on what basis any one of them could be formulated with sufficient precision or its exceptions defined. The choice was one of social policy. The second reason he gave was that liability and insurance were so intermixed that for the judiciary to alter the basis of liability without adequate knowledge (which they did not have the means to obtain) as to the impact this might make on the insurance system would be dangerous and 'irresponsible'. Thirdly, to change the law might inflict great hardships on a number of people and at least would greatly affect their assumed legal rights.

Lord Pearson said:[14]

> these innovations, whether or not they may be desirable, are not suitable to be introduced by judicial decision. They raise difficult questions of policy, as well as involving the introduction of new legal principles rather than extension of some principle already recognised and operating. The questions of policy need consideration by the government and Parliament, using the resources at their command for making wide enquiries and gathering evidence and opinions as to the practical effects of the proposed innovations.

It is tempting to say that, since the doctrine of vicarious liability is a creature of the common law, it was for the judges to determine its metes and bounds. After all, the scope of vicarious liability has been subject to modification by the courts over time. As we have seen, Lord Wilberforce acknowledged that there was no objection in principle to the judges modifying the doctrine. But he was unwilling to countenance such a modification unless it was made on a rational and informed basis and without giving rise to undesirable unintended consequences. To do otherwise would be to take a leap into the dark and that would be irresponsible. My own view is that the second and third reasons given by Lord Wilberforce should not have been given much weight. If it was thought to be just to extend vicarious liability to car owners for loss caused by the negligent driving of their cars, then the court should not have been deflected from extending this judge-made doctrine by a concern as to how the insurance industry would react. And the concern about the effect on assumed legal rights should not have been a matter of great moment. That would be an argument against any common law extension of liability. If that were a powerful argument, it would have presented

---

[14] [1972] 2 WLR 1217 at 1228D.

an insuperable obstacle to the removal by the courts of immunity from suit of advocates and expert witnesses.

But what about the choice of *how* to extend the doctrine of vicarious liability in this situation? On the one hand, it could be said that over the years the judges have shown far more innovative boldness than would have been required simply in order to choose one of the systems on offer. If the judges did not shrink from devising the doctrine of vicarious liability in the first place, why should they shrink from deciding on how far it should be extended? That is a legitimate question to ask. Why should the fact that there are various possible extensions mean that the courts should not choose the one that seems to them to be the most suitable?

A similar problem arose in the different context of listing people considered unsuitable to work with vulnerable adults under the Care Standards Act 2000: see *R (Wright) v Health Secretary*.[15] The Secretary of State had provisionally included the claimants' names in the list. In the Court of Appeal, we held by a majority that the denial of the right to make representations before a name was so included was a breach of Article 6 of the ECHR. We gave effect to section 3(1) of the HRA 1998 and interpreted the 2000 Act as requiring the Secretary of State to give a care worker an opportunity to make representations before being included in the list, unless such an opportunity would expose vulnerable adults to the risk of harm. The House of Lords was unable to accept this solution. They said that the problem could not be cured by offering some of the care workers an opportunity to make representations in advance, while denying that opportunity to other workers who may have been just as unfairly treated by their former employers. They held that no other solution could properly be adopted by way of the interpretative obligation in section 3(1) of the HRA. It was not for the House to rewrite the legislation. A delicate balance had to be struck and it was for Parliament to strike it.

I think that the answer to the question that I have posed is that the law should not be developed by the judges in an arbitrary way. In *Launchbury*, the court considered that it had no rational basis for choosing one solution in preference to another. It did not have the requisite institutional competence to make a choice. It was unable to consult interested parties such as insurers and lawyers and take into account their views as to the likely impact of the various

---

[15] *R (Wright) v Secretary of State for Health* [2009] UKHL 3, [2009] AC 739.

options. It would no doubt do its conscientious best to arrive at what it considered to be the best solution, but it is probably not an overstatement to say that this would be a stab in the dark. For the reasons already mentioned, the adversarial system of advocacy is not well suited to assisting the court to arrive at the best solution in such circumstances, although the problem could be alleviated by suitably responsible interveners.

A good example of the judges developing the common law in response to what they perceive to be the changing needs of contemporary society is from the field of marital rape. It had long been part of our common law that a husband could not be guilty of the rape of his wife: see Sir Mathew Hale *History of the Pleas of the Crown*.[16] In 1991 Lord Keith in the House of Lords said that the common law was capable of evolving in the light of changing social, economic and cultural developments.[17] Hale's proposition reflected the state of affairs at the time it was enunciated. Since then, the status of women, and in particular married women, had changed out of all recognition in various ways. In modern times, marriage is regarded as a partnership of equals. Any reasonable person must regard as quite unacceptable the proposition that by marriage a woman gives her irrevocable consent to sexual intercourse with her husband in all circumstances. Lord Keith also said, perhaps imaginatively, that the decision would not involve the creation of a new offence, but the removal of a common law fiction which had become anachronistic and offensive. This is another example of the court developing the common law by reference to what it conceives to be the view of the reasonable person in contemporary circumstances.

But there were those who, although delighted with the decision, felt that it was a matter for Parliament. Jo Richardson, Labour spokeswoman on women's affairs said: 'it's fine and very welcome to have case law like this. But it still leaves it to the whim of the court and the whim of the judges. We need to make women feel secure and know that if they take a case they have got a reasonable chance of getting through with it'.[18] Lord Denning made a similar point: 'the law was ripe for change, but it was not for the Law Lords to do it'. That was perhaps a surprisingly conservative thing for Lord Denning to say, but he was very old and long since retired.

This change did not require any difficult policy choices to be made. It was uncontroversial, widely welcomed and long overdue.

---

[16] *History of the Pleas of the Crown* (1736) Vol 1 ch 58 p 629.
[17] *Regina v R* (1992) Cr. App. R. 216.
[18] *The Times* (24 October 1991).

Ms Richardson's unkind reference to judicial whimsy seems ungracious. It is and was inconceivable that Parliament would reverse this decision. Parliament had had plenty of opportunity to legislate for an amendment of the law. It seems that the political call for change was not sufficiently compelling. The judges were surely right to step in.

Let me consider two further areas where the judges have felt able to develop the law boldly, unconstrained by lack of research or evidence about the likely impact of the development. The first concerns the important question of immunity from suit. I shall start with the issue of the liability of advocates for negligence. For many years, advocates had blanket immunity for everything that they did in connection with litigation. As the House of Lords explained in *Rondel v Worsley*,[19] the immunity was based on the public policy grounds that the administration of justice required that a barrister should be able to carry out his duty to the court fearlessly and independently, and that actions for negligence against barristers would make retrying the original actions inevitable and so prolong litigation, contrary to the public interest. In *Saif Ali v Sydney Mitchell & Co*[20] the immunity was limited (again on grounds of public policy) to what barristers did in court and to work which could fairly be said to affect the way that the case would be conducted if it came to a hearing. The court had a choice as to how far to go and it made that choice without the benefit of research or consultation of those likely to be affected by the change. If it had applied the approach of Lord Wilberforce in *Launchbury*, the House might have said that all three of his reasons militated against modifying the immunity. Why limit the immunity to what was done in court? Why make that choice? Could it not be said that the impact of so limiting the immunity was uncertain and therefore dangerous and irresponsible? And could it not be said to be unfair on advocates who had acted on the basis of the law as it was previously understood to be to impose liabilities on them for what they did outside court? The immunity was finally swept away altogether in *Hall (Arthur JS) & Co v Simons*,[21] when it was decided that the policy grounds previously relied on were no longer sufficient to justify a departure from the general rule that where there was a wrong there should be a remedy.

---

[19] *Rondel v Worsley* [1969] 1 AC 191 (HL).
[20] *Saif Ali v Sydney Mitchell & Co (a firm)* [1980] AC 198 (HL).
[21] *Hall (Arthur JS) & Co v Simons* [2002] 1 AC 615 (HL).

Which brings me to the immunity accorded to expert witnesses. In *Jones v Kaney*[22] the Supreme Court had to decide whether to abolish the rule that a witness could not be sued in negligence by his client. The justification for the immunity accorded to lay witnesses is long-standing and is based on policy considerations which are well understood. The immunity enjoyed by expert witnesses from liability to their clients had also been established, although it was a less well-entrenched principle. The majority of the Supreme Court held that the immunity could no longer be justified, particularly in view of the abolition of the immunity of advocates. The immunity could no longer be justified in the public interest. They were not persuaded that, if experts were liable to be sued for breach of duty, they would be discouraged from providing their services at all; or that immunity was necessary to ensure that expert witnesses give full and frank evidence to the court; or that diligent expert witnesses would be harassed by vexatious claims for breach of duty; or that the removal of the immunity would engender a risk of multiplicity of suits. And all of this without the benefit of research as to the possible or likely results of removing the immunity.

The dissentients took a less adventurous line. Lord Hope said that the lack of a secure principled basis for removing the immunity from expert witnesses; the lack of a clear dividing line between what is to be affected by the removal and what is not; the uncertainties that this would cause; and the lack of reliable evidence to indicate what the effects might be, all suggested that the wiser course would be to leave matters as they stood. Lady Hale saw the proposed abolition of immunity as an exception to the general rule that witnesses enjoy immunity from suit. She asked rhetorically how far the exception should go. Did it cover all classes of litigation? In particular, how far beyond ordinary civil litigation did it go and did it cover all or only some of the witness's evidence? It was impossible to say what effect the removal of immunity would have, either on the care with which the experts give their evidence, or on their willingness to do so. It was not self-evident that the policy considerations in favour of introducing the exception to the general rule were so strong that the court should depart from previous authority to make it. It was 'irresponsible' to make such a change on an experimental basis. This was a topic more suitable for consideration by the Law Commission

---

[22] *Jones v Kaney* [2011] UKHL 13, [2011] 2 AC 398.

and reform, if thought appropriate, by Parliament than by the court. It is interesting to see how the charge of irresponsibility recurs in this context. The majority were not exactly thrilled to be described as 'irresponsible'.

As one of the majority in this case, I accept that I may not be best qualified to express an objective view about it. But I remain unrepentant. I fail to see how it was 'irresponsible' and off-limits to remove the immunity. This was classic 'lawyer's law' territory. The immunity was a creature of the common law in the first place. Having given birth to this child, it was the duty of the judges to decide whether it had outlived its useful life. Did the circumstances which were thought to have justified the immunity in the first place still exist? To apply the terminology of public law, it was for the judges to decide whether the court was institutionally competent to decide this question. Although there are obvious differences between the position of advocates and that of expert witnesses, there are striking similarities too. It seems to me that, as an institution, the court was as well equipped to decide whether to retain the immunity of expert witnesses as it had been to decide whether to retain the immunity of advocates. The court abolished advocates' immunity without the benefit of any survey or consultation of interested parties as to the likely effect of the abolition. It is difficult to see what value such a survey or consultation would have had even if it were placed before the court. Those who act as expert witnesses might well have said that, if the immunity were abolished, they would think twice before giving evidence. They might also have said that their fees would have to rise in order to pay for insurance premiums. But responses of this kind are hardly likely to have affected the court's decision. It should be noted that the question facing the court in *Jones v Kaney* was a simple yes/no question: should the immunity from suit of an expert witness to his own client be abolished? The court did not even have to grapple with the difficulty that arose in *Morgans v Launchbury* where a decision had to be made as to the *extent* of the abolition and where the House said that it was not able to decide *that* question. I should point out that the rise and stepped fall of the advocate's immunity shows that the court did not feel institutionally incompetent to make choices as to the *extent* of an immunity in that context.

The second concerns the scope of legal professional privilege. In *R (Prudential plc) v Special Commissioner of Income Tax* the issue under appeal was whether legal advice given by an accountant

regarding a tax avoidance scheme was privileged.[23] The general
principle the court had to consider in determining this question was
whether and, if so, how far it could extend the privilege at common
law to accountants, and other professionals, who were able to give
legal advice. The UK Supreme Court refused to extend the privilege.
Again by a majority—Lords Clarke and Sumption dissented—the
court held that such an extension would go beyond long-established
precedent. It would lead to uncertainty. There was no apparent
pressing need for such an extension. Lord Neuberger PSC, in the
majority, was particularly concerned that this was a question for
Parliament as,

> the consequences of allowing [the] appeal [were] hard to assess and
> would be likely to lead to what is currently a clear and well understood
> principle becoming an unclear principle, involving uncertainty ... [it]
> ... raises questions of policy which should be left to Parliament ... [and]
> Parliament had enacted legislation relating to [it, through the Legal
> Services Act 2007], which, at the very least, suggests that it would be
> inappropriate for the court to extend the law ...[24]

The minority view was that legal advice privilege was a judge-
made creature of the common law. No question arose of social or
economic or other issue of macro-policy which are classically the
domain of Parliament. There was no reason in principle why legal
advice privilege should not be accorded to legal advice given by
non-lawyers. There was no logical basis for distinguishing between
legal advice given by a lawyer and an accountant and any other professional person. What the majority considered would have been an
extension of the common law was, for Lord Sumption, necessarily
inherent in the existing law. I think that the minority view is to be
preferred. Clarifying the nature of the common law and drawing out
what is necessarily inherent in it is very much within the limits of
the court's proper role. This was not something that needed to be
deferred to Parliament.

So to return to the beginning, can we say with any degree of confidence where Lord Goff's boundary lies? The fact that our highest
court has been split on the issue (for example the Supreme Court in
Jones v Kaney and the *Prudential* case) shows how difficult it is to
answer this question. In his recent lecture 'Developing the Common

---

[23] *R (Prudential plc) v Special Commissioner of Income Tax* [2013] UKSC 1, [2013]
2 AC 185.
[24] [2013] 2 AC 185 at 222.

Law: how far is too far?', Lord Walker said that it was not easy to discern from the pronouncements of the House of Lords and the Supreme Court any clear policy as to what is, and what is not, off-limits for the development of the common law by a court of last resort. A lot seemed to depend on judicial intuition. But the cases suggested that it is common law rules which might be described as 'lawyer's law'—such as witness immunity or mistake of law—that judges are most ready to develop. I agree with this assessment, but would add the development of the law of negligence as being another area of 'lawyer's law'.

The law reports are replete with examples of important judicial law-making in diverse areas affecting many aspects of our national life. Some of the decisions have been bold and creative and have involved difficult policy choices. My few (inevitably highly selective) examples may give an impression of randomness which suggests that the Labour spokeswoman was right after all. But she was not. It is true that, in deciding whether to develop the common law or to leave any change to Parliament, the courts do not apply some overarching principle. That is not how our unwritten constitution works. But there is nothing whimsical about this.

In his essay 'The Judge as Lawmaker: An English perspective in the Struggle for Simplicity in Law: Essays for Lord Cooke of Thoroton',[25] Lord Bingham identified a number of situations in which most judges would shrink from making new law. These were: (i) where reasonable and right-minded citizens have legitimately ordered their affairs on the basis of a certain understanding of the law; (ii) where, although a rule of law is seen to be defective, its amendment calls for a detailed legislative code, with qualifications, exceptions and safeguards which cannot feasibly be introduced by judicial decisions, not least because wise and effective reform of the law calls for research and consultation of a kind which no court of law is fitted to undertake; (iii) where the question involves an issue of current social policy on which there is no consensus within the community; (iv) where an issue is the subject of current legislative activity; and (v) where the issue arises in a field far removed from ordinary judicial experience. This is not an exhaustive list.

As a statement of the general approach of the courts to this issue, as so often, I doubt whether it is possible to improve on Lord

---

[25] (1997), in Tom Bingham, *The Business of Judging: Selected Essays and Speeches* (Oxford University Press, 2000).

Bingham's masterly summary. As I have said, I think the analogy with the test for what is often called 'judicial deference' in the context of public law challenges may also be useful. Just as a court will be reluctant to strike down a decision in an area into which it is institutionally ill-equipped to go, so too it will be reluctant to develop the law in an area in which it is institutionally ill-equipped to assess the implications of the development. The wisdom of the proposed development cannot be properly determined without research and consultation of a kind which, to use Lord Bingham's words, no court of law is fitted to undertake.

But there is surely another factor at work too, one to which Lord Bingham did not refer. That is judicial temperament. It is an escapable fact that some judges are more conservative than others. Some are cautious and prefer to paddle in the warm and safe shallows of clear precedent. Others are more adventurous and are prepared to give it a go in the more treacherous waters of the open sea. Fortunately for them, the worst fate that they can suffer is to be overturned, unless they are in the Supreme Court. But history has shown that the product of today's buccaneer sometimes becomes tomorrow's orthodoxy. That is what makes the law endlessly fascinating.

The judges have great power in shaping the common law and, therefore, influencing the lives of all of us. The existence of this power is, of course, always subject to Parliament. If Parliament wishes to change the common law, it can do so. But, despite some notable exceptions (for example, the change to the law on causation in asbestos-related disease cases), Parliament rarely shows any appetite for changing the common law. So far as I am aware, the manner in which the judges develop the common law has not excited much political comment or given rise to a demand to clip the wings of the judges. I would like to think that this is because, on the whole, the judges have done a good job in this area and no-one has suggested a fundamentally different way of doing things that would command popular support.

It may have been noticed that, so far, I have steered clear of judicial review.

I must now turn to judicial review. The government says that it acknowledges the importance of judicial review. In its Consultation Paper dated December 2012, the Secretary of State for Justice said: 'Judicial Review is a critical check on the power of the State, providing an effective mechanism for challenging decisions of public bodies to ensure that they are lawful' (para 1.2). As I said in

R (Cart) v Upper Tribunal[26] 'Authority is not needed (although much exists) to show that there is no principle more basic to our system of law than the maintenance of the rule of law itself and the constitutional protection afforded by judicial review'. It is the courts that are the guardians of the rule of law.

I do not believe that any of this is now controversial. But whereas judicial development of private law seems to have gone largely unnoticed except by lawyers, the same cannot be said for judicial review. In his FA Mann Lecture (2011), Lord Sumption expressed a concern that judges are tending to intervene in decisions of public authorities which they should leave well alone. He revisited the issue in his recent Kuala Lumpur lecture. He referred to the statement by Lord Diplock in *R v Inland Revenue Commissioners, ex p National Federation of Self-Employed and Small Businesses*[27] that Parliament is sovereign and has the sole prerogative of legislating; officers or departments of central government are accountable to Parliament for what they do as regards efficiency and policy and of that Parliament is the only judge; they are responsible to a court of justice for the lawfulness of what they do, and of that the court is the only judge. Lord Sumption said that this statement, though neat and elegant, is 'perfectly useless' because it begs all the difficult questions, in particular: what is a question of law and what is a question of policy? Lord Diplock would not have been amused.

Lord Sumption illustrated the inadequacy of Lord Diplock's analysis by a detailed consideration of the decision in *R v Lord Chancellor, ex p Witham*.[28] Section 130 of the Supreme Court Act 1981 empowered the Lord Chancellor to fix the level of court fees in the most general language: 'The Lord Chancellor may by order under this section prescribe the fees to be taken ...'. In 1997, the Lord Chancellor introduced new regulations providing for an increase in the court fees, but omitting provisions in the previous regulations which had exempted people on income support. They had to pay the court fee like everyone else. Mr Witham was a man on income support. He wanted to bring a libel claim but could not afford the fee. So he applied for judicial review of the new regulations.

The application came before the Divisional Court, which quashed the regulations. Laws J delivered the leading judgment. He said that

---

[26] *R (Cart) v Upper Tribunal* [2011] UKSC 28, [2012] 1 AC 663 at para 122.
[27] *R v Inland Revenue Commissioners, ex p National Federation of Self-Employed and Small Businesses* [1982] AC 617 (HL).
[28] *R v Lord Chancellor, ex p Witham* [1998] QB 575 (DC).

access to justice at an affordable price was a constitutional right. It was a basic or fundamental right which could not be abrogated unless specifically permitted by Parliament. The general words of section 130 of the 1981 Act were not sufficiently specific to author-ise the Lord Chancellor to make the new regulations.

In my view, the analysis of Laws J was entirely orthodox and should not have caused great surprise. Indeed, Lord Sumption him-self referred in his earlier FA Mann lecture to the statement by Lord Hoffmann in *R v Home Secretary, ex p Simms*[29] that fundamental rights cannot usually be overridden by general or ambiguous statu-tory words or, usually, without explicit provision. As Lord Sumption said, this principle had been applied in both private and public law cases for many years before Lord Hoffmann articulated it. He added that he doubted whether anyone would seriously quarrel with it. It did beg the question what rights and principles are to be regarded as so fundamental that a power to depart from them cannot be conferred by general words; but, he said, access to justice would probably figure in anyone's list of fundamental rights.

He criticised the reasoning in the *Witham* case. He said that Laws J was 'exercising a purely judicial authority when he declared this constitutional right [of access to justice at an affordable price] to exist'. That is, of course, true. But he was merely following well-trodden ground. And surely if (as Lord Sumption appeared to accept) there is a fundamental right of access to justice, that right is breached if the state imposes a charge on access to the court which the would-be litigant cannot afford to pay so that he cannot get his case before a court and the right cannot be overridden by general or ambiguous words. The right of access to the court is useless if it cannot be exercised whether on grounds of cost or for any other rea-son. I confess that I have difficulty in seeing what was wrong with the decision of the Divisional Court, still less how it illustrates the inadequacy of Lord Diplock's statement. There could be no doubt as to the question of law that the Divisional Court had to resolve. It was whether the new regulations were permitted or empowered by section 130 of the 1981 Act. This was a question of statutory interpretation. It was undoubtedly a question of law and one which under our constitution only a court could determine. The court decided it by applying conventional principles. I do not regard this as evidence that judges are exercising too much power. Who else

---

[29] *R v Secretary of State for the Home Department, ex p Simms* [2000] 2 AC 115 (HL).

should decide the meaning of statutes and other issues of interpretation of documents?

It is time to move away from the *Witham* case and widen the scope of the discussion. A theme that is present in both of Lord Sumption's lectures is that parliamentary scrutiny is generally perfectly adequate for the purpose of protecting the public interest in the area of policy-making. It is the only way of doing so which carries any democratic legitimacy. For those who are concerned with the proper functioning of our democratic institutions, the judicial resolution of inherently political issues is difficult to defend. It has no legitimate basis in public consent, because judges are quite rightly not accountable to the public for their decisions.

I accept that it is not always easy to draw the line between a policy's lawfulness and an assessment of its merits. But as Lord Goff said in the *Woolwich* case, the boundary between what is and what is not legitimate for the development of the common law in the context of private law is not always easy to find either. In some respects, it is easier to find in judicial review. If a regulation or policy is not authorised by the statute under which it is purportedly made, then it is unlawful. As Lord Diplock said, this is a matter for the courts and for them alone to determine. The courts are all too conscious of the need for restraint when faced with a judicial review challenge which seeks to impugn what may loosely be called the 'merits' of an executive policy or decision. Lord Sumption acknowledges that the courts do not examine the merits of decisions on foreign affairs and national security and they seek to avoid imposing on the executive duties which have significant budgetary implications. I am sure that he would accept that there is an extensive body of judicial authority which recognises the impermissibility of adjudication on political issues. The more purely political a question is, the greater the likelihood is that the courts will say that it is a matter for political resolution and the less likely it is to be appropriate for judicial decision.

So what is all the fuss about as regards judicial review in our domestic law? I am not aware of a widespread sense of unease that judges are routinely overstepping the mark and impermissibly quashing executive decisions. In its two consultation papers proposing reform of judicial reform, the Ministry of Justice did not suggest that judicial review is being granted inappropriately by the courts. The main thrust of the papers was that the judicial process is too slow and that time and money is being wasted in dealing with unmeritorious cases which may be brought by applicants simply in order to generate publicity or to delay implementation of a decision that was properly made.

And yet Lord Sumption states in his Kuala Lumpur lecture that

> judicial resolution of major policy issues undermines our ability to live together in harmony by depriving us of a method of mediating compromises between ourselves. Politics is a method of mediating compromises in which we can all participate, albeit indirectly, and which we are therefore more likely to recognise as legitimate.

If the European Convention on Human Rights is disregarded, I am unaware of any major policy issue whose merits which have been resolved judicially. The only example given by Lord Sumption is the *Witham* case. Most successful challenges succeed on the grounds that there has been some important procedural flaw in the decision-making process. Successful challenges to major decisions on the grounds of irrationality are very rare in my experience. Judges are only too aware of the need for judicial restraint in this area.

I am conscious that, so far, I have given a wide berth to Europe. This has become a toxic and highly-political subject. I regret that judges have descended into the arena. An impression has been created that the entire judiciary is critical of the European Court of Human Rights. I believe that this impression has been created by a small number of lectures given by a few senior judges. They have not claimed to speak on behalf of their colleagues or, so far as I am aware, anyone else. I believe that, as one would expect, there is a wide range of judicial views on this subject.

I propose to say very little about EU law and the power of the CJEU in Luxembourg. It is, however, striking that so much of the criticism of European decisions that is made by the media and the government is directed to the decisions of Strasbourg rather than Luxembourg. It is true that our Parliament remains sovereign. But it has given EU law supremacy in increasing areas of our national life. I note that in his lecture 'Constitutional Change: Unfinished Business',[30] Lord Judge downplayed the significance of the rulings of the Luxembourg court (which we are bound to observe) when he said that it is a court 'giving rulings about the workings of a common market' in relation to 'economic matters'. We should be under no illusions: the jurisdiction of the Luxembourg court covers far more than economic matters. It affects many parts of our national

[30] 4 December 2013.

life. The EU Charter of Fundamental Rights covers much of the same ground as the European Convention on Human Rights.

Much has been said about the relationship between our courts and Strasbourg. Even the most vociferous critics of the Strasbourg court agree that the text of the Convention is admirable. The human rights enshrined in it are important and need to be protected. Two principal complaints are levelled at Strasbourg. First, in the course of interpreting the text of the Convention, the court has considerably extended its scope. This it has done in the light of what it perceives to be evolving social conceptions common to the democracies of Europe so as to keep it up to date. This is analogous to the evolution of the common law by our judges to which I have earlier referred. The second complaint is that the court's approach to judicial law-making is anti-democratic. This is a particular problem given the inherently political character of many of the issues that the court decides. A number of the most important human rights recognised by the Convention are qualified by express exceptions for cases where what is complained of is 'necessary in a democratic society'. The Strasbourg case law provides guidance as to how these qualifications are to be applied. The court must decide whether the measure being challenged is necessary; whether it has a 'legitimate aim'; and whether the measure is proportionate to that aim. I entirely accept that these questions raise policy issues. Sometimes, they raise issues which are acutely controversial and on which passions run high. Two current such examples are the question whether the blanket ban on prisoners' voting rights is lawful and whether it is lawful to pass a whole life sentence of imprisonment. I should say at once that I have no intention of expressing my view on either of these topics.

It is undoubtedly true that, because some provisions of the Convention are expressed in rather unspecific terms, it was inevitable that the Strasbourg court would fill in the interstices by case law. The fact that it did this can have caused no surprise. The precise interpretation of the law has followed processes analogous to those employed by our judges in developing the common law. But the big difference is that, because of the range of application of Convention rights and the standards that they impose, they cover far wider areas of public policy and demand a more intrusive review of administrative and legislative action than our common law courts adopted before the incorporation of the Convention by the Human Rights Act 1998. Even if the Strasbourg court had adopted a less expansionist approach to the interpretation of the Convention, it is inevitable that it would have been drawn into adjudication on policy issues. That is what the signatories to the Convention must have intended. Their vision was that the values of the Convention should be adopted by all contracting states in the Council of Europe and that the court should apply a pan-European human rights law.

It must have been obvious that the court would not be able to engage in a process of dialogue with the legislatures of all these states, which will adopt different policy positions reflecting the interests and demands of very disparate national populations. Recognising this difficulty, the court sets out common ground rules of acceptable political practice. Sometimes (particularly in relation to require-ments of equal treatment of women, racial groups and homosexuals) the rules have a strong substantive content, but more usually they allow a significant margin of appreciation to contracting states.

The margin of appreciation is an inherent part of the balancing framework deployed by the Strasbourg court. There are, however, limits to the margin of appreciation. Some risk of affecting the polit-ical culture of contracting states is inherent in having an enforce-able human rights instrument in place. Nevertheless, the margin of appreciation is an important mechanism by which the court pro-vides for the accommodation of democratic ideology. The flexibil-ity inherent in the doctrine of the margin of appreciation allows the court to adjust the intensity of its supervision by reference to common European standards articulated by the court, depending on its perception of the value of the individual rights at stake and the importance of uniform enforcement of such standards. The current position is well summarised by Philip Sales in his article 'Law and Democracy in a Human Rights Framework':

> But [the margin of appreciation] has also assumed far greater prominence in the case law of the ECtHR as well, reflecting the court's increasing engagement with the detailed constitutional position within states as it examines the precise facts of particular cases before it in order to arrive at an acceptable balance of individual and public interests. The margin of appreciation will generally be found to be wider where the court is examining a choice made by a democratically elected legislature in rela-tion to a topic which is the subject of public debate and one on which opinions may reasonably differ in a democracy. Similarly, where com-pliance with a Convention right depends on a balance being struck by the national authorities by reference to some consideration of the public interest, the ECtHR will often give particular weight to their view because they are best placed to assess and respond to the needs of society.[31]

---

[31] P Sales, 'Law and Democracy in a Human Rights Framework' in D Feldman (ed), *Law in Politics, Politics in Law* (Hart Publishing, 2013).

It is well known that there have been calls from some of the media and some government ministers for the UK to withdraw from the Convention. This has usually been in response to a particular decision of the Strasbourg court with which its critics disagree. In a spirited response to these attacks, Sir Nicolas Bratza, then President of the court, pointed out that the court's judgments are replete

> with statements that customs, policies and practices vary considerably between Contracting States and that we should not attempt to impose uniformity or detailed and specific requirements on domestic authorities, which are best positioned to reach a decision as to what is required in the particular area.

The court is acutely aware that it is not a representative or democratically accountable body. That is why it recognises the importance of according a margin of appreciation to the Contracting States. But as Lord Mance has recently pointed out,[32] the potential for good in fundamental rights provisions at a European level should not be ignored. Nor should we make the mistake of thinking that the UK is alone in being critical of some of the Strasbourg jurisprudence. But Strasbourg has led the way in a number of important areas. For example, it has led to the removal of sentencing discretion from the executive; the lifting of the ban on homosexuals in the armed forces; the ending of detention without trial of aliens suspected of terrorist activity; and the prevention of deportation of aliens who, if deported, would face a real risk of torture or inhuman treatment. The changes to our domestic law which resulted from these decisions of the Strasbourg court have been accepted and, I believe, are now regarded by many people in this country as welcome. The court emphasises in its case law that the Convention is intended to promote a pluralist, tolerant and broadminded society. As a general statement, it is surely difficult to quarrel with this. It is in the application of this general approach in particular cases that the court sometimes makes decisions which are controversial and which the Contracting States find objectionable. But the court is aware that it is not democratically accountable. In interpreting and applying the Convention, it seeks to give effect to its fundamental principles in a way which respects the views of the Contracting States without undermining the very essence of those principles.

Finally, I must briefly look at the way in which the Convention has been incorporated into our domestic law and the role that our own

---

[32] Lord Mance, 'Destruction or Metamorphosis of the Legal Order' (World Policy Conference, Monaco, 14 December 2013).

courts are required to perform. Section 2(1) of the Human Rights
Act 1998 provides that a court determining a question in connection with a Convention right 'must take into account' any judgment
of the Strasbourg court. Section 3 provides that legislation must be
read and given effect so far as possible in a way which is compatible
with the Convention rights. Section 4(2) provides that, if a provision
is incompatible with a Convention right the court may grant a declaration of incompatibility. Section 6(1) provides that it is unlawful
for a public authority (which includes a court) to act in a way which
is incompatible with a Convention right.

There has been much debate in the literature and case law as to
what is meant by the requirement to 'take into account' any judgment of the Strasbourg court. But what is more important for present
purposes is that the effect of these provisions is to require our judges
to apply the Convention and to decide Convention issues for themselves. There is no doubt that many of these involve policy questions of a kind which, before the enactment of the 1998 Act, judges
would not have been called upon to make. This is the inevitable
consequence of the decision of Parliament in 1998 to bring Convention rights home. Lord Sumption in his Kuala Lumpur lecture says
that the development of the Convention by the Strasbourg court
was not foreshadowed by the language of the Convention and could
not have been anticipated by Parliament when it passed the Act.
But many of the developments of the Convention pre-date 1998.
Parliament knew that Strasbourg regarded the Convention as a
'living instrument' when it passed the Act. It is wholly unrealistic to
suppose that Parliament believed that the Convention would remain
immutable as at 1998. It follows that a political choice was made to
give judges a power which they had not previously enjoyed and
to impose an obligation on them to take into account decisions of
the Strasbourg court. This was no grab for power by the judges. The
whole point of the 1998 Act was to bring Convention rights home
and to reduce the need for litigants to go to Strasbourg for a vindication of those rights. Just as Parliament gave the courts this power,
so it can take it away. No-one denies that. I would merely say that,
as the Strasbourg court seeks to make up for its democratic deficit
by liberal recourse to the margin of appreciation which it accords to
the institutions of the Contracting States, so too (for similar reasons)
do our judges accord to domestic policy-makers an area of discretionary judgment in relation to the making of their decisions.

To conclude. I have tried to explain why I do not consider that
judges are too powerful in the purely domestic sphere. They continue

to perform their vital historic role of developing the common law responsibly, making changes incrementally only where these are considered to be necessary to respond to changing social conditions, values and ideas. Judges shrink from altering the law in certain areas for a variety of reasons which are now well understood and some of which I have summarised. They do not apply a single overarching principle. But they do apply a number of well-established norms and the system works tolerably well. Only occasionally do judges disagree on the question whether they should move the common law in a certain direction or whether it is more appropriate to leave it to Parliament. Even if it were possible or desirable to devise a single overarching principle, it is inevitable that judges would not always agree as to how it should be applied. I have also tried to explain that our judges exercise their judicial review power in a careful and measured way. They are mindful of the existence of territory into which they should not enter. In exercising this power, they seek to uphold the decisions of the legislature and to respect the sovereignty of Parliament and the rule of law.

The position with regard to the Convention on Human Rights is different. The effect of the Human Rights Act is that Parliament has given judges a power that they did not previously possess. It requires them to make value judgments which are different from those which, as custodians of the common law, they have been accustomed to making. My own view is that they are exercising this power responsibly and carefully. It can, of course, be removed by Parliament taking away what it gave by the 1998 Act. That, however, is a matter for politicians, not judges. It is a striking fact that, in the debate about the Convention, it seems that the real complaint of those who wish to sever our links with Europe is not that our judges are too powerful. Their objections are directed at Strasbourg, not at our judiciary. That is why they would like to see a UK Bill of Rights interpreted by our judges. The oft-heard cry 'let our Supreme Court be supreme' is a ringing vote of confidence in our judges.

4

*Magna Carta and Compensation Culture**

INTRODUCTION

MY FIRST IDEA was to give a lecture about the so-called compensation culture: what is it and should we be concerned about it? That is a topical subject which the organisers of the lecture thought would be of interest. But as we all know, 2015 is the 800th anniversary of Magna Carta and it was pointed out to me that the Bodleian Library has no fewer than four of the 17 surviving pre-1300 engrossments of Magna Carta. So I was asked whether I could introduce a Magna Carta theme into my lecture. I did not want to give up on Compensation Culture. Hence the somewhat Delphic title of the lecture 'Magna Carta and the Compensation Culture'. The title was the easy bit.

On Christmas Eve 1166, Henry II's youngest son John was born at Beaumont Palace in this great city. The Palace no longer exists, but set into a pillar on the north side of Beaumont Street is a stone which bears the inscription 'near to this site stood the King's Houses later known as Beaumont Palace'. John was not a good king. According to one historian he was 'not even a good "bad" king'. Unlike his Angevin predecessors who were 'effective tyrants', John did not even qualify to earn that doubtful accolade. As we approach the end of 2015, we do not need to be reminded that the most enduring consequence of John's reign is Magna Carta.

Magna Carta, or—as it was originally known—the Charter of Runnymede, started life as a peace treaty between John and his barons, a significant number of whom could no longer tolerate the way in which he abused his powers as king. A particularly egregious example was his misuse of the justice system. In the words of

* The High Sheriff of Oxfordshire's Annual Law Lecture, 13 October 2015.

McKechnie, he used it to satisfy 'his lust and greed'.[1] The machinery of justice was nothing more than 'instruments of extortion and outrage'[2] by which he could channel the flow of ever increasing amounts of money into the royal coffers.

One of the ways in which John achieved this was by selling justice to the highest bidder. Since 1209, the Court of Common Pleas had followed the King around the country. Cases were decided by the King's Court. In addition to John, it included 'the whole body of counsellors, ministers, knights, clerks and domestic servants who (accompanied the King).' Not an independent court, as we would know it.[3] Decisions were made either by the King himself or, if by others, they were heavily influenced by him.

This system provided the perfect environment for the making of what were known as 'proffers'. Proffers were payments of money made by litigants to the King in order to obtain favourable decisions. And if one litigant was willing to make a proffer, his opponent might consider that he had to make a higher proffer in order to win the case. In other words, justice was sold to the highest bidder on the basis that they would receive a pay-out if judgment was obtained in their favour.[4] Money was not only paid to secure favourable decisions at the end of a hearing. It was also paid to halt justice in its tracks. In order to secure support for his war efforts, in 1206 John offered the incentive to his knights that, if they joined the army, claims against them would be stayed.[5]

In view of John's predilection for deciding disputes involving his barons which would previously have been dealt with by a Court of Barons—that is by the barons' peers—it is hardly surprising that in 1215 abuse of justice featured prominently in the list of the barons' grievances and consequently in the clauses of Magna Carta.

Thus Chapter 17 provided: 'ordinary lawsuits shall not follow the royal court around, but shall be heard in a fixed place'. The Court of Common Pleas was to resume sitting at Westminster Hall. Chapter 45 guaranteed that the King would only appoint 'such men that know the law of the realm and are minded to keep it well' as judges. No longer were claims to be decided by those unqualified in the law. Chapter 39 provided that 'No free man shall be taken,

---

[1] Cited in JC Holt, *Magna Carta* 2nd edn (Cambridge University Press, 1992) 179.
[2] ibid.
[3] D Carpenter, *Magna Carta* (Penguin, 2015) 157.
[4] Cited in Holt, *Magna Carta*, 179.
[5] Holt, *Magna Carta*, 84.

imprisoned, disseised, outlawed, banished, or in any way destroyed, nor will we proceed against or prosecute him, except by lawful judgment of his peers or by the law of the land.' The barons were to be judged by their peers in the Barons' Court or by the law of the land. No longer were they to be subject to the capricious rulings of the King and his court. And Chapter 40 guaranteed that 'To no one will we sell, to no one will we deny or delay, right or justice.' The age of the proffer, of abuse of the justice system as a means of swelling the Exchequer's coffers, was to be brought to an end.

FROM MAGNA CARTA TO COMPENSATION FOR HARM

Chapters 39 and 40 are famous to this day. They have a resonance which continues to thrill. They remain on the statute book, in slightly revised language, as section 29 of the 1297 version of Magna Carta. While they were born out of the barons' immediate concerns to put an end to John's abuse of the justice system at their expense and to restore their privileges,[6] they have, over the centuries, taken on a life far beyond that narrow self-interest. They stand today as a symbol of our commitment to equality before the law, access to justice and the rule of law. In the seventeenth century they were an inspiration for Lord Coke CJ and the Parliamentarians in the struggle between the Stuart Kings and Parliament. Later they inspired the American revolutionaries in their battle against the English.

One tenet of Magna Carta that remains as valid now as it was in 1215 is its statement that justice shall be done by 'the law of the land'. It is not surprising that our view of what the law of the land should be today differs markedly from what the barons thought it should be in 1215. But the principle that justice should be done according to the law of the land is as important today as it was in 1215. Establishing and preserving the rule of law is a vital pillar of our democratic system. To use the language of a later version of Magna Carta, justice must be determined according to 'the due process of law'.[7]

Our common law has developed over the centuries in response to changing social and economic circumstances. Sometimes it has

---

[6] W McKechnie, *Magna Carta*, 2nd edn (Maclehose & Sons, 1912) 449.

[7] Magna Carta 1354, 28 Edw 3, c 3, '... no man of what estate or condition that he be, shall be put out of land or tenement, nor taken, nor imprisoned, nor disinherited, nor put to death, without being brought in answer by due process of law.'

developed slowly and almost imperceptibly; sometimes it has taken large strides forwards. All of this is entirely consistent with the rule of law provided that the developments are visible, applicable to all who wish to have access to the law and disputes as to the application of the law continue to be determined fairly by independent judges.

A well-known example of a giant leap forward of the common law in this country is the famous 1932 case of *Donoghue v Stevenson*.[8] The alleged facts are probably well known to many of you. Two people went into a café in Paisley, near Glasgow. One bought the other a bottle of ginger beer. Half the contents of the bottle were poured into a glass and consumed. The rest of the ginger beer was then poured into the glass. A rather strange-looking object fell out of the bottle. On close inspection it appeared to be the decomposing body of a snail. Shortly afterwards the woman who drank the ginger beer developed a severe stomach upset. She started proceedings claiming compensation from the manufacturer of the drink.

She could not claim damages for breach of contract because she had no contract with the manufacturer or with the owner of the café. She framed her claim in tort. But at that time it had not been established that such a claim could be made. In one of the most far-reaching and important cases in the development of our law, the House of Lords decided that such a claim could in principle be brought in the tort of negligence. Thus, provided that the manufacturer owed the woman a duty of care and she had suffered loss as a result of a breach of that duty, she would be entitled to compensation for her loss. The House formulated the rule for determining whether a duty of care was owed. The essence of the rule was enshrined in the 'neighbour principle'. This was a far cry from simply asserting that, provided that the woman had suffered loss as a result of consuming the ginger beer, she would be entitled to compensation. This was a principled development by our independent judges of the law of the land as expressed in our common law. It was made in response to the perceived social and economic needs of the time. In its essentials, it was a natural application of the principles of Magna Carta.

It is time to turn to the issue of compensation which lies at the heart of this lecture. The so-called compensation culture has been criticised as a form of abuse with as much passion as the barons

---

[8] *Donoghue v Stevenson* [1932] AC 562 (HL).

complained of John's abuses. An article by Professor Frank Furedi in 2012 complained about it 'poisoning our society'.[9] A number of academic, government and parliamentary studies have made recommendations as to how it should be tackled.[10] Parliament has twice passed legislation aimed at eliminating or at least reducing it: the Compensation Act 2006 and the Social Action, Responsibility and Heroism Act 2015.

There is nothing new in the idea that, where a right is infringed, monetary compensation is the primary means by which the law makes good any loss caused by the infringement. It was present in the first English law code, issued by King Æthelberht, King of Kent, in about 602 CE.[11] It set out a detailed set of fines and compensation. If, for example, a freeman was found to have committed adultery he would be required to pay the injured party a '*wergeld*'—the value of the injured party's life. He would also have to 'provide another wife with his own money, and bring her to the other.'[12] More prosaically: loss of an eye required payment of fifty shillings compensation;[13] loss of a thumb, twenty shillings;[14] and loss of the shooting finger—the one needed to use a bow and arrow effectively—eight shillings.[15] If you cut someone's ear off you were required to pay compensation of twelve shillings.[16] If you merely mutilated it, you would only have to pay six shillings.[17] If, however, you cut the ear off and your victim was deaf in the other ear, you would have to pay twenty-five

---

[9] F Furedi, 'The compensation culture is poisoning our society' *Daily Telegraph* (9 September 2012).

[10] F Furedi and J Bristow, *The Social Cost of Litigation* (Centre of Policy Studies, September 2012); Better Regulation Task Force, *Better Routes to Redress* (2004); Lord Young, 'Common Sense, Common Safety' (Cabinet Office, 2010); *Compensation Culture*, House of Commons, Constitutional Affairs Committee (Third Report of Session 2005–06) (HC 754–I); Ministry of Justice, *Legal Aid Reform in England and Wales: the Government Response* (The Stationery Office, 2011); Ministry of Justice, *Reducing the number and costs of whiplash claims—A consultation on arrangements concerning whiplash injuries in England and Wales* (The Stationery Office, 2012).

[11] The Laws of Æthelberht, available at legacy.fordham.edu/halsall/source/560-975dooms.asp#The%20Laws%20of%20%C3%86thelberht.

[12] ibid cl 31, 'If a freeman lie with a freeman's wife, let him pay for it with his wergeld, and provide another wife with his own money, and bring her to the other.'

[13] ibid cl 43, 'If an eye be (struck) out, let bot be made with fifty shillings.'

[14] ibid cl 54 'If a thumb be struck off, twenty shillings. If a thumbnail be off, let bot be made with three shillings. If the shooting [i.e. fore] finger be struck off, let bot be made with eight shillings. If the middle finger be struck off, let bot be made with four shillings. If the gold [ie ring] finger be struck off, let bot be made with six shillings. If the little finger be struck off, let bot be made with eleven shillings.'

[15] ibid.

[16] ibid cl 39, 'If an ear be struck off, let bot (reparation) be made with twelve shillings.'

[17] ibid cl 40, 'If the other ear hear not, let bot be made with twenty-five shillings.'

shillings.[18] Compensation was proportionate to the harm, a requirement that was later echoed in Magna Carta's treatment of criminal offences: it required punishments to fit the crime—to be proportionate to the offence.[19]

By the nineteenth century, the idea of compensation for harm was as well established as it had been in the seventh century. Records held by Aviva, the insurance company, provide some fascinating detail. A grocer who slipped while playing blind man's buff was awarded the equivalent of £724 compensation. A travelling salesman who was watching an accident, while on the top deck of an open-topped tram and was hit by a pole received the equivalent of £401 compensation. A wedding guest who was hit in the eye with rice thrown presumably over the happy couple received the equivalent of £2,994. And, for slipping on orange peel whilst shopping, a bank clerk received the equivalent of £8,901 compensation.[20]

The level of compensation may have changed over time, but the principle underpinning the Anglo-Saxon and Victorian approaches was the same: if one person was legally responsible for causing harm to another, he was required to pay the victim compensation to vindicate his rights and make good the harm caused.[21] This principle continues to apply today. We have our own version of Æthelberht's code which indicates the level at which compensation should be awarded. *The Judicial College Guidelines for the Assessment of General Damages in Personal Injury Cases* is a distillation of typical awards of damages made by judges for various personal injuries. For example, it states that loss of an eye now attracts between £40,300 and £48,200 compensation; and minor or transient eye injuries, such as that which the Victorian wedding guest suffered, would attract compensation of between £1,620 and £6,400.

---

[18] ibid cl 42, 'If an ear be mutilated, let bot be made with six shillings.'

[19] Magna Carta 1215, Ch 20, 'For a trivial offence, a free man shall be fined only in proportion to the degree of his offence, and for a serious offence correspondingly, but not so heavily as to deprive him of his livelihood. In the same way, a merchant shall be spared his merchandise, and a villein the implements of his husbandry, if they fall upon the mercy of a royal court. None of these fines shall be imposed except by the assessment on oath of reputable men of the neighbourhood.'

[20] All as detailed in J Insley, 'Compensation culture: a history of bizarre personal injury claims in Britain' *The Guardian* (14 July 2011), available at www.theguardian.com/money/blog/2011/jul/14/compensation-culture-personal-insurance-claims.

[21] *Clerk & Lindsell on Torts*, 21st edn (Sweet & Maxwell, 2014) 1–12.

FROM COMPENSATION TO COMPENSATION CULTURE

There is therefore nothing new about the idea that the law requires the payment of fair compensation for harm which results from civil wrongs. It is long established. It is one of the hallmarks of the rule of law and of the law of our land. But what is compensation culture and how does it fit in to all of this? Lord Falconer, who was Lord Chancellor at the time, gave an apt definition in 2005. He put it this way:

> 'Compensation culture' is a catch-all expression ... It's the idea that for every accident someone is at fault. For every injury, someone to blame. And, perhaps most damaging, for every accident, there is someone to pay.[22]

It is the idea that for every accident and every resultant injury or loss, someone other than the victim of the accident is to blame. The victim must, therefore, always be compensated. It is important not to confuse compensation culture with no-fault compensation. No-fault compensation is a legal principle according to which a person (C) is entitled to compensation for loss caused by another person (D) regardless of whether D was in any way at fault. This is an intellectually respectable principle which society may choose to embrace. But in doing so, it must face up to its costs and economic consequences.

On the other hand, the compensation culture is not a legal principle at all. It has not displaced the principles of the law of negligence, whose essential elements remain as they were propounded in *Donoghue v Stevenson*. Rather, to the extent that it exists, it is evidence of an attitude borne of an expectation as to how in particular defendants will behave in their approach to the application of the principles of the law of negligence. In short, an expectation that defendants will pay up rather than fight and risk losing. This has led to the idea that the compensation culture implies that there is no need to establish that a duty of care was owed to the injured party by whoever is viewed as being responsible; and there is no need to establish a breach of duty and causation of loss. All that the injured person has to do is to litigate (or even merely threaten to litigate) irrespective of the legal merits of the claim, and compensation will follow.

---

[22] Lord Falconer, 'Compensation Culture' (22 March 2005) 1–2.

One consequence of this is the view that as a society we have undergone a cultural shift. No longer is British society characterised by a somewhat philosophical and accepting approach to life. On the contrary, the view is taken that we are becoming more American in our approach; more ready to rush into litigation. To borrow from Tony Weir, we have become a 'wondrously unstoical and whinge-ing society with (an) endemic compensation neurosis', and which rather than see us 'grin and bear it' sees us 'grit (our) teeth and sue'.[23]

Perhaps even more dangerously, this shift in approach has been accompanied by a growing concern that an unjustified burden is now being placed on employers, businesses, schools, the NHS and local and central government (as regards payment of compensation and, even worse, legal costs which often substantially exceed the amount of compensation). To make matters worse, all of this is said to be giving rise to defensive practices on the part of such bodies. It is said that, as a consequence of the compensation culture, schools now ban conker fights on health and safety grounds;[24] and school trips no longer take place. I should say that the conker story rests on a misunderstanding of the law by a no-doubt well-meaning head-teacher and has been described by the Health and Safety Executive as 'a truly classic myth.'[25]

Media stories to this effect are commonplace. They tend to be about payments of large amounts of money for seemingly trivial injuries; not unlike those mentioned in Aviva's records from the nineteenth century. In June 2011 a school pupil was reported as hav-ing received nearly £6,000 in compensation. He had burnt his hand at school during his lunch break. Spilt custard was the cause.[26] In 2013 a police officer was reported to have received £10,000 in com-pensation for injuries caused by a fall from a chair.[27] More recently, a payment of £12,000 was reported to have been made to some-one who was injured by a 'toilet lid while flushing'.[28] Someone else

[23] T Weir, 'Governmental Liability' (1989) *Public Law* 40, 76.
[24] See   www.dailymail.co.uk/news/article-1378251/One-schools-ban-conkers-elf-n-safety-fears--leapfrog-marbles-threat.html;   www.telegraph.co.uk/education/education-news/8458526/Schools-banning-conkers-and-leapfrog-over-safety-fears.html.
[25] www.hse.gov.uk/myth/september.htm.
[26] See www.mirror.co.uk/news/uk-news/schools-hand-out-cash-for-classroom-134505; www.dailymail.co.uk/news/article-2011131/Pupil-awarded-6-000-custard-splash-play-ground-compensation-culture-costs-taxpayers-2million.html.
[27] See www.dailymail.co.uk/news/article-2308088/Compensation-culture-gone-mad-Police-officer-claims-10-000-compensation-falling-chair-London-Underground.html.
[28] See   www.lincolnshireecho.co.uk/1-800-payout-hit-market-stall-pole-Lincolnshire-s/story-27448276-detail/story.html.

was apparently paid £12,566 compensation for injuries caused as a result of a foot becoming stuck in a Henry Hoover.[29] A Google search will no doubt reveal many more such stories, each of which furthers the perception that something has gone badly wrong with civil justice in this country.

Compensation culture does not simply exercise the media. It has featured in two government studies: 2004's *Better Routes to Redress*[30] by the Better Regulation Task Force (the BRTF Report) and 2010's *Common Sense, Common Safety*[31] by Lord Young. It was the title, and subject of one Parliamentary Report[32] and was the impetus behind the Compensation Act 2006. It was also the subject of a critical study published last year by the Centre of Policy Studies, entitled *The Social Cost of Litigation.*[33] That study formed the basis of more newspaper column inches through a follow-up article by one of the study's authors, Professor Frank Furedi, in *The Daily Telegraph.* The article's title, 'The compensation culture is poisoning our society',[34] leaves no room for doubt about the view taken in the study. Most recently it has featured as an underpinning to the government's consultation on whiplash claims which arise from road traffic accidents.[35]

All of this acts as a spur to enterprising solicitors to encourage clients to launch speculative claims on a no-win no-fee basis. Clinical negligence claims are a good example. Some solicitors advertise their services on boards close to hospitals informing patients that, if they have not been satisfied with their treatment, they can sue the hospital authority at no cost to themselves. But many unsuccessful treatments are not the result of negligence. Patients may die despite the best possible surgery. The harsh commercial reality is that the legal costs to the NHS of defending a clinical negligence claim are often out of all proportion to the amount of damages that it will have

[29] ibid.

[30] Better Regulation Taskforce (May 2004).

[31] A Report by Lord Young (October 2010).

[32] *Compensation Culture,* House of Commons, Constitutional Affairs Committee (Third Report of Session 2005–06) (HC 754–I).

[33] F Furedi and J Bristow (September 2012), available at www.cps.org.uk/files/reports/original/120905122753-thesocialcostoflitigation.pdf.

[34] F Furedi, 'The compensation culture is poisoning our society' *Daily Telegraph* (9 September 2012), available at www.telegraph.co.uk/comment/9530139/The-compensation-culture-is-poisoning-our-society.html.

[35] Ministry of Justice, *Reducing the number and costs of whiplash claims—A consultation on arrangements concerning whiplash injuries in England and Wales* (December 2012) at 8 and 22, available at www.justice.gov.uk/news/press-releases/moj/government-action-on-whiplash-claims.

to pay if the claim is successful. For this reason, the NHS is often willing to pay a claimant a sum to buy off a claim, even one which it considers is likely to fail. Claimant solicitors are only too aware of this.

I should make particular mention of whiplash claims. These are claims for damages for whiplash injuries usually sustained in motor accidents. It has been said that whiplash is a peculiarly UK disease. It accounts for about 80 per cent of car accident injury claims. In other countries, the figure is far lower. There is no doubt that there has been something of a whiplash industry in our country in recent years and our government is rightly trying to do something about it. The problem is that insurers usually pay up because the cost of contesting the claims is simply too high. All of this would tend to suggest that litigation is out of control and that we are in the grips of compensation fever. Is this really the case? As I shall now explain, the situation is not straightforward.

COMPENSATION CULTURE—PERCEPTION AND REALITY

Let us take the case of the school child who was reported as having received almost £6,000 for the burn that he sustained from hot custard. It is easy to see how this could be portrayed by the media as an example of the compensation culture running riot. £6,000 may seem a ridiculous amount of money to pay by way of compensation for a burn caused by custard. But how hot was the custard and how serious the burn? If it caused no real pain or lasting harm, then the payment was clearly exorbitant. But if the burn was severe and painful and left permanent scarring, the position would have been quite different. In other words, one's perception of the reasonableness of compensation is coloured by the way in which the story is presented.

The difference between perception and reality is well illustrated by two famous examples drawn from America. They were relied on by Anthony Hilton in an article he wrote in the *Daily Mail* in 2003. He said:

> The claims culture and the compensation culture have taken root [here] ...

> It is not as bad yet as in the United States, for which we should be grateful. McDonald's had to pay out for not telling a customer the coffee she bought and then spilled was hot, but a similar claim here was tossed out because coffee is meant to be hot. That is as nothing, however, when compared with the Winnebago case where the driver left the wheel of

his mobile home while his vehicle was speeding down the freeway and went into the back to brew a coffee. With no-one steering, the vehicle crashed, but the owner sued successfully because no-one had told him it was unsafe to leave the driver's seat when doing 70mph.[36]

The facts alleged in the Winnebago case were that a woman was awarded $1.7m in compensation after putting her motor vehicle on cruise control at 70 mph, and then getting up to make herself a cup of coffee in the back of the vehicle. She claimed that Winnebago (the manufacturer) should have warned her that she could not leave the driver's seat after putting the cruise control on. The basis of the claim was that it had failed to put a warning in the driver's manual explaining that cruise control was not an auto-pilot device. This is an extraordinary tale and, if true, would have been a good example of the wilder excesses of the compensation culture. But the problem with the story is that it is simply not true. As the *Los Angeles Times* described it, it was 'a complete fabrication'.[37]

As portrayed by the media, the spilt coffee case involved a woman who foolishly placed a cup of hot coffee between her legs while she was driving a car. She had bought the coffee from a drive-thru McDonalds. She had to brake the car suddenly and the coffee spilt over her legs. She sued McDonalds. They were to blame for her burnt legs. A court agreed and she was awarded many millions of dollars in damages. That is the story; the reality is rather different.

Unlike the Winnebago story, this is based on a real case, namely *Lieback v McDonald's Restaurant*.[38] Stella Liebeck, the injured party, was in a car. But she was not driving. She was a passenger. And the accident did not occur when the car suddenly stopped. It happened when it was stationary. She had not placed the coffee between her legs because that was convenient whilst she was driving. She placed it there to hold it still while she tried to take the lid off. The coffee was extremely hot. In fact, it was between 180–190°F. It did spill and burn her. It caused third-degree burns to various parts of her body, resulting in a hospital stay of eight days

---

[36] A Hilton, 'Reforms the Insurers Must Risk' *Daily Mail* (10 September 2003) www.dailymail.co.uk/money/news/article-1520339/Reforms-the-insurers-must-risk.html; see also Vanessa Feltz, *Daily Star* (15 November 2003), cited in Better Regulation Taskforce (May 2004) at 13.

[37] M Levin, 'Legal Urban Legends Hold Sway' *LA Times* (14 August 2005) articles.latimes.com/2005/aug/14/business/fi-tortmyths14.

[38] *Lieback v McDonald's Restaurant* No 93-02419 (1995 WL 360309) (DNM 18 August 1994); see further C Forell, 'McTorts: The Social and Legal Impact of McDonald's Role in Tort Suits' (2011) 24(2) *Loyola Consumer Law Review* 105 at 134ff.

for treatment, skin grafts. It caused her to suffer permanent scarring and two years' partial disability. She did not rush to the courts. She only sued McDonalds after it had rejected her request for payment of her medical expenses and her daughter's lost wages (her daughter had had to take time off work to look after her). In total she had asked for $10,000 to $15,000. In the face of that refusal, she issued proceedings not in negligence, but under a certain strict liability statutory provisions.[39]

The claim went to trial before a civil jury. Jurors can comment on their experience in the US. Some of them were reported as having commented that they were 'insulted' to be asked to hear such a case, that it 'sounded ridiculous', and that it was a waste of time over a 'cup of coffee'.[40] It seems that these jurors thought that this was a case of compensation culture run wild. But their view changed during the trial. The evidence showed that between 1982 and 1992, more than 700 claims had been brought against McDonalds arising out of coffee burns, some of them third-degree burns. McDonalds knew that the coffee, which it insisted on serving at a temperature of between 180 and 190 degrees, was dangerous. Its quality assurance manager admitted that the coffee was not 'fit for consumption' and that it would scald the throat. Its expert witness accepted that coffee served at more than 130 degrees could produce third degree burns, and that coffee served at a temperature of 190 degrees would burn skin in two to three seconds. It is, therefore, not surprising that the jury was willing to find that the coffee was a defective product, and that McDonalds had sold it in breach of the implied warranty of merchantability and of fitness for purpose.[41]

The jury found in Ms Liebeck's favour, albeit with a reduction of 20 per cent for contributory negligence on her part. She was awarded $160,000 for the injuries and $2.7 million in punitive damages, which was intended to represent two days' profits earned by McDonalds from coffee-related sales. The judge reduced this aspect of the award to $480,000. Despite the judgment, the claim was subsequently settled for an undisclosed sum, no doubt in the face of a possible appeal. It can therefore be seen that the portrayal of this case by Mr Hilton in his article was a caricature. This was a serious claim which amply justified an award of compensation.

---

[39] Forell, 135–136.

[40] Forell, 136–137.

[41] K Cain, 'The McDonald's Coffee Lawsuit' (2007) 11(1) *Journal of Consumer and Commercial Law* 15, 15–17.

COMPENSATION CULTURE IN ENGLAND AND WALES

So what is the position in England and Wales? The perception is clear: compensation culture has taken firm root here and unwarranted and excessive compensation is routinely paid to claimants. This perception seems to persist despite studies and reports showing, as a parliamentary inquiry put it, that the 'evidence does not support the view that increased litigation has created a "compensation culture"'.[42] It is worth asking whether the behaviour of our courts has contributed to this perception. Let me give you some examples which show that our judges are astute not to do anything to encourage the bringing of unjustified claims.

In *Bogle v McDonald's* Field J dealt with a series of preliminary issues arising out of a number of claims that were being dealt with under a Group Litigation Order. There were a total of 36 claimants. The majority were children between the ages of 4 and 16. While they had each brought separate claims against McDonald's arising from distinct incidents in which they had suffered personal injuries in the form of burns caused by spilt hot drinks, specifically hot coffee sold by McDonald's at around the same temperature as the coffee sold in the *Lieback* case. Factually then the claims were similar to the *Lieback* claim. The claims also raised similar legal issues to those in issue in the US claim. One issue, for instance, was whether the coffee cup lids were a poor fit, such that McDonald's had been negligent in using them. Another was whether McDonald's had sold a defective product under the terms of the Consumer Protection Act 1987. The claims also raised the question of whether McDonald's were negligent in dispensing and serving hot drinks at the temperature at which they were served. Just as in the *Lieback* case, so here it was clear, as Field J put it, that there 'was a risk that a visitor might be badly scalded and suffer a deep thickness burn by a hot drink that is spilled or knocked over after it has been served'.[43]

If, as was suggested in the media a year after this case was decided, we were in the grips of a compensation culture, the claims would surely have succeeded. But the claimants failed on all issues. McDonald's was held not to have been negligent in serving coffee

---

[42] *Compensation Culture*, House of Commons, Constitutional Affairs Committee (Third Report of Session 2005–06) (HC 754–I) at 13; and see, for instance, Better Regulation Taskforce, *Better Routes to Redress* (2004) at 3; Lord Young, 'Common Sense, Common Safety' (Cabinet Office, 2010).

[43] *Bogle v McDonald's Restaurants Ltd* [2002] EWHC 490 (QB) at [16].

at high temperatures. Its cups and their lids were held not to have been manufactured negligently. The judge held that there had been no breach of consumer protection law. On this basis it ought to be reasonably clear that, if the *Lieback* claim had been brought in our courts, it too would have failed.

So far as I am aware, our media did not make much, if anything, of the *Bogle* case. They could have made the point that, whereas in the US this type of claim tends to succeed, in our courts it is likely to fail; and that, whereas in the US there is a rampant litigation culture (although as we have seen even there the media reports are not always accurate), that is not the case in our country. Surely there was scope for a positive story to be told about the robustness of our legal system and our substantive law. But that is not the way the media operates, because such a measured and accurate good news story would be unlikely to appeal to them.

My second example is *Tomlinson v Congleton Borough Council*,[44] which was decided by the House of Lords in 2003. One hot bank holiday in 1995, the claimant decided to go for a swim. He and friends were in the local park. They had been there many times before. In the park there was a flooded sand quarry, which had been made into a place for families to sunbathe and paddle in the water. As it was such a nice day and he was hot, the claimant decided to dive into the water to cool off. This was not the first time he had done this. Tragically however he hit his head on the bottom of the quarry. He broke his neck and, as a consequence was left a tetraplegic. He sued the local council. The House of Lords rejected the claim. In doing so Lord Hoffmann reiterated a principle that is entirely at odds with the idea that our courts are promoting a compensation culture. He said:

> ... the law does not provide such compensation simply on the basis that the injury was disproportionately severe in relation to one's own fault or even not one's own fault at all. Perhaps it should, but society might not be able to afford to compensate everyone on that principle, certainly at the level at which such compensation is now paid. The law provides compensation only when the injury was someone else's fault.[45]

The law is fault-based. It requires a claimant to establish a duty of care, breach and causation of loss. These are not always straightforward matters and if a claimant fails to establish any one of them, his

---

[44] *Tomlinson v Congleton Borough Council* [2003] UKHL 47, [2004] 1 AC 46.
[45] [2003] UKHL 47, [2004] 1 AC 46 at [4].

claim fails. The courts have not in recent years lowered the hurdles that a claimant must surmount.

My next example concerns occupiers' liability as well as negligence. It is the case of *West Sussex County Council v Pierce*,[46] which I heard in the Court of Appeal, and which the *Daily Telegraph* reported could have led to water fountains being 'banished' from schools.[47] The claimant was a nine-year-old boy. He and his seven-year-old brother were in the school playground. They went over to the newly-fitted stainless steel water fountain. It was of a type that is common throughout schools in England and Wales. The younger brother sprayed the claimant with water from the fountain. He retaliated and tried to punch his brother, who was cowering underneath the fountain. He missed, and his punch hit the underside of the fountain. He sustained 'a laceration to the dorsal aspect of his right thumb and associated tendon damage.'[48] Apart from a small scar to his thumb, he made a full recovery. The claim was brought against the school on the basis that the water fountain had a sharp underside edge, which posed a 'real and foreseeable risk of children coming into contact' with it. It was said that the school had failed to consider the risk or take steps to mitigate it. At trial, having examined the water fountain, the judge held that it was sharp and that the school was liable for failing to consider the risk. The Court of Appeal overturned the decision. It too examined the water fountain, but did not agree that it could properly be described as sharp. It also held that the wrong legal test for liability had been applied by the judge. The legal question was whether, viewed objectively, the school was reasonably safe to those on the premises bearing in mind that children 'are inclined the lark around.' It was, and as Sharp LJ put it,

> The School was not under a duty to safeguard children against harm under all circumstances. Each case is of course fact sensitive, but as a matter of generality, the School was no more obliged as an occupier to take such steps in respect of the water fountain than it would be in respect of any of the other numerous ordinary edges and corners or surfaces against which children might accidentally injure themselves whilst

---

[46] *West Sussex County Council v Pierce* [2013] EWCA Civ 1230.

[47] 'Water fountains may be banned in schools as "unsafe"' *Daily Telegraph* (10 October 2013)   www.telegraph.co.uk/news/uknews/law-and-order/10369098/Water-fountains-may-be-banned-in-schools-as-unsafe.html.

[48] [2013] EWCA Civ 1230 at 3.

on the premises. The law would part company with common sense if that were the case, and I do not consider that it does so.[49]

Espousal of the compensation culture might suggest that any injury caused in the course of games or sporting activities ought to result in an award of damages. If correct, this would have a seriously adverse effect on professional sport as well as school and amateur sports. In 2004 in the case of *Blake v Galloway*,[50] if you will forgive reference to another case in which I was involved, the Court of Appeal was asked to consider the question of liability for such injuries in a somewhat unusual context. The claimant was with a group of friends practising as part of a jazz quintet. They decided to take a break from their rehearsal. They went outside and started playing a rather bizarre impromptu game. It involved picking up and throwing twigs and bark at each other. The claimant picked up and threw a four-centimetre piece of bark at one of the others which hit him on the leg. His friend picked it up and threw it back at the claimant. It hit him in the right eye and caused a significant injury. The claimant issued proceedings alleging that the injury was caused by the defendant's negligence and/or battery. The defendant, amongst other things, contended that the fact that they were playing a game meant that any liability was vitiated by the claimant's consent.

To rely on a consent-based defence it is, however, necessary first to establish liability. The Court of Appeal held that liability had not been established. In an informal game such as that in which the claimant and his friends had engaged (like in organised sport), liability was not established unless the offending conduct amounted to either reckless conduct or exhibited a very high degree of carelessness.[51] If the defendant had, for example, chosen to throw a stone rather than a twig (contrary to the conventions of the informal game in which they were involved), that might have been reckless and sufficient to amount to a breach of duty of care. But what happened in this case was simply an unfortunate accident. There was no actionable negligence. What about the claim in battery? The general rule in sporting activities that involve the risk of physical contact is that the participants impliedly consent to such contact as can reasonably be expected in the course of the game. There was such implied consent here, as long as the participants did no more than

[49] [2013] EWCA Civ 1230 at [17]–[18].
[50] *Blake v Galloway* [2004] EWCA Civ 814, [2004] 1 WLR 2844.
[51] ibid at [16].

throw twigs according to the tacit rules of their informal game. The defendant had done no more than this. The claimant accordingly had given his consent and could not establish liability for battery either. His claim was, therefore, rejected. This is another example of our courts adopting a robust, common sense approach to claims for compensation which is inconsistent with the idea that they are giving encouragement to the advancement of a compensation culture.

CONCLUSION: COMPENSATION CULTURE—PERCEPTION AND THE LAW'S SHADOW

What do these four cases illustrate? I think one answer is that our courts are well aware of the dangers of contributing to the idea that all injuries should result in compensatory awards. They are decisions that cannot be seen as encouraging the idea that anyone who suffers an injury has a remedy in damages. The judgment of Field J in the *Bogle* case applied conventional, well-known and well-understood principles of law. The *Tomlinson* case underscored the necessity of establishing fault. The *Pierce* case showed that the risk of injury has to be real and foreseeable; remote or fanciful risks will not suffice. And *Blake* emphasised the need for culpability to the requisite standard as a condition of liability. A common theme is that accidents can and do happen and that the law does not compensate for accidents in the absence of legal responsibility.

Thus the reality of what goes on in our courts does not match the perception that we are in the grip of a compensation culture. The difference between the reality and the perception is problematic. In 1979 two US scholars wrote a famous article entitled 'Bargaining in the Shadow of the Law: the case of divorce'.[52] It considered the effect that the framework provided by the law had upon divorce or rather the impact that legal framework had upon 'on negotiations and bargaining that occur *outside* the courtroom.'[53] The essential point that has been repeated by a number of scholars, including recently by Professor Dame Hazel Genn, is that the law casts a shadow far beyond the courtroom. It guides conduct. It provides the framework within which businesses operate, schools organise activities for pupils, doctors operate within hospitals, local authorities

---

[52] R Mnookin and L Kornhauser, 'Bargaining in the Shadow of the Law: the case of divorce' (1978) 88 *Yale LJ* 950.
[53] ibid at 950.

maintain pavements and so on. Moreover, it helps to create as Professor Genn puts it, 'the credible threat of litigation if settlement is not achieved.'[54] We act in the shadow of the law.

What if the shadow is a false one? If, for instance, we have a false perception that the law prohibits certain activities or requires certain steps to be taken, we are likely to act in accordance with this perception. A perception that the law requires compensation for any accident regardless of the circumstances is likely to lead individuals, businesses and governments to act on the basis that the perception is true. This might have the consequence that nobody apologises for bumping into another person in case that is taken as an acknowledgement that an accident has occurred which attracts legal liability. Another consequence might be that schools ban certain activities as a result of their misperception of the law. More significantly perhaps, a false shadow of the law might lead to threats of litigation and then to settlements that would not have been made if the law had been properly understood. This last concern is particularly worrying. As I said earlier, defendants are probably often induced to make what they refer to as 'commercial' settlements for reasons which have little, if anything, to do with their assessment of the likely outcome of a court hearing. Litigation is inherently uncertain. The behaviour of witnesses and, dare I say it, judges is unpredictable. Most troubling of all is the fact that the cost of litigation is so high. Legal fees are exorbitant. The laws of competition and the market place seem to be helpless in resisting the rising tide of the cost of litigating. Many would-be litigants simply cannot afford to go to court. The obvious solution is to introduce reasonable and proportionate fixed legal costs. Our government is taking a long time to grasp this nettle.

Meanwhile, the perception that we are in the continuing grip of a compensation culture casts its false shadow. It is a shadow that should vanish if the litigation landscape is surveyed properly in the bright light of the cases that have been, and I trust will continue to be, decided in this country. I have only mentioned four such cases. There are many more. They do not attract media publicity. That is because they are balanced and sensible and therefore do not make for a good story. They do not support the existence of a compensation culture. They are applications of 'the law of the land', that precious gem which shines in Clause 39 of Magna Carta and which,

---

[54] H Genn, *Judging Civil Justice* (Cambridge University Press, 2010) 21.

800 years later, continues to be rightly valued as essential to the well-being of our system of justice.

The link between the compensation culture and Magna Carta may not be immediately obvious. The existence of the link would certainly not have occurred to King John and the barons. Indeed, I am certain that I would not have chosen the title of this lecture if I had not been delivering it in 2015. But perhaps the link becomes a little less Delphic when one focuses on the significance of the phrase 'the law of the land'. In this year when we celebrate the 800th anniversary of Magna Carta, just as the barons demanded their right to receive justice according to the law of the land, we should remind ourselves of what the law actually requires and do what we can to explode the false perception of compensation culture.

5

*Does Judicial Review Undermine Democracy?**

Y OUR ROYAL HIGHNESSES, distinguished guests, ladies and gentlemen, it is an enormous pleasure and privilege to deliver the 29th Sultan Azlan Shah Lecture and a great honour for me to be added to the roll call of distinguished jurists who have given this prestigious lecture since 1986. The undoubted brilliance of the previous lecturers is daunting for those who have to follow. It is a striking feature that almost all of them have been UK jurists. This undoubtedly reflects the international reputation of UK judges. But, perhaps even more importantly, it also betokens the closeness of the bond between our two countries. We share many traditions. Personal friendships abound. Long may that continue.

Before I address the question raised by the title of this lecture, I need to say something about the scope of judicial review in England and Wales. This is a huge subject which I can only touch on in the barest of outlines. But it is necessary to do this before considering whether in the twenty-first century judicial review poses a threat to our parliamentary democratic system.

As I said in *R (Cart) v Upper Tribunal*:[1] 'Authority is not needed (although much exists) to show that there is no principle more basic to our system of law than the maintenance of the rule of law itself and the constitutional protection afforded by judicial review'. In his Consultation Paper dated December 2012, the Secretary of State for Justice said: 'Judicial Review is a critical check on the power of the State, providing an effective mechanism for challenging decisions of public bodies to ensure that they are lawful'.[2] Statements at this high level of generality are not controversial. But what has

---

* The Sultan Azlan Shah Lecture, Malaysia, November 2015.

[1] *R (Cart) v Upper Tribunal* [2012] 1 AC 663 at para 122.

[2] *Judicial Review: proposals for reform*, Consultation paper CP25/2012 (December 2012) para 2.

proved to be problematic has been fleshing them out. In the same Consultation Paper, the Secretary of State invited comment on various proposed measures which were intended to curb what he claimed to be an unacceptable growth in the incidence of judicial review proceedings.

There is no doubt that in my country in the past few decades there has been a massive increase in the number of applications for judicial review. There have been several reasons for this. These include first that, as I shall explain, the standard of review has been relaxed. This may in part be because our judges are no longer as executive-minded as they once were.

Secondly, there has been an explosion of legislation, much of it rushed through without sufficient consideration. This has given rise to uncertainty, which generates litigation. Thirdly, under the pressure of major national and international challenges, executive public bodies take risks and make decisions which are, at least arguably, of doubtful legality. Thus, for example, they have made controversial decisions to safeguard national security from the threat of terrorism, to maintain an effective immigration policy and to cut costs in order to reduce the national debt. Decisions in these (and other) areas inevitably involve making political judgements and promoting the interests of one group of individuals against those of others.

How active should judges be in intervening in the business of elected government? Those who would espouse a minimalist approach have remarked on the social exclusivity of the judges and their supposed isolation from the real world as well as on their non-accountability to the electorate. There is the further and perhaps more important point that an adversarial judicial process is not the most effective means of resolving problems that need often to be considered having regard to wider considerations of public policy, which lie beyond the boundaries of particular litigation. Courts decide issues that are raised before them by the parties. Occasionally, they have the benefit of representations by interveners who have a particular knowledge about, and interest in, the subject of the dispute before the court. But the nature and quality of the evidence and submissions made to a court in litigation varies greatly. It is not always calculated to assist the court to arrive at the best solution to the problem.

The questions which have particularly troubled our courts include: (i) what is the correct standard of review; and (ii) to what extent and in what circumstances should the court examine and determine the merits of the decision under challenge for itself? These are fundamental questions.

A useful starting point is Lord Diplock in 1984. He said in *Council of Civil Service Unions v Minister for the Civil Service*[3] that judicial review had developed to the stage when, without reiterating any analysis of the steps by which the development had come about, one could conveniently classify under three heads the grounds on which administrative action is subject to control by judicial review. The first ground he called 'illegality'; the second 'irrationality'; and the third 'procedural impropriety'. He recognised that further development on a case-by-case basis might add further grounds. Presciently, he had in mind particularly the possible adoption in the future of the principle of 'proportionality' recognised in the administrative law of several Member States of the European Economic Community.

By 'irrationality', Lord Diplock was referring to '*Wednesbury* unreasonableness', ie a decision which is so outrageous in its defiance of logic or of accepted moral standards that 'no sensible person who had applied his mind to the question to be decided could have arrived at it'. He was confident that 'whether a decision falls within this category is a question that judges by their training and experience should be well equipped to answer, or else there would be something badly wrong with our judicial system'. That was said only 30 years ago. A great deal has happened since then. I shall not attempt to produce a Diplockian synthesis of the current state of the law. I suspect that Lord Diplock would have been less reticent: he probably have found the challenge irresistible.

His statement of principle underlined the fact that the court was not concerned with the question of whether the decision-maker reached the 'correct' decision, but rather with the question of whether sensible decision-makers, properly directed in law and properly applying their minds to the matter, could have regarded the conclusion under review as a permissible one.

But even before the Human Rights Act 1998 came into force in 2000, judges did not always apply the harsh and austere irrationality test in the most rigorous way. Very few decisions are illogical or immoral in the sense that Lord Diplock probably intended the irrationality test to be understood. If that principle, understood in

---

[3] *Council of Civil Service Unions v Minister for the Civil Service* [1985] AC 374 at 410 (HL).

that way, had stood the test of time, judicial review would probably have stayed relatively unnoticed in a quiet backwater of our law.

The edges of 'irrationality' have, however, undoubtedly been softened during the past 30 years and a far more nuanced approach has emerged. This has not been the direct result of any legislation. It has been the product of judicial activity in developing the common law. As we shall see, this development has gained momentum under the influence of the European Convention on Human Rights and its incorporation into our domestic law by the Human Rights Act.

Perhaps the most important and clearest example of a more nuanced and sophisticated approach is to be found in *R v Ministry of Defence, ex p Smith*.[4] This was considered to be a hugely important case at the time. By a statement made in 1994, the Ministry of Defence reaffirmed its policy that homosexuality was incompatible with service in the armed forces and that personnel known to be homosexual would be discharged from service. The policy had been considered by both Houses of Parliament in debate and by select committees of the House of Commons and was consistent with advice received from senior members of the services. The four applicants were serving members of the armed forces who had been administratively discharged on the sole ground that they were of homosexual orientation. They challenged the decisions to discharge them and the policy on which it was based on the grounds that they were irrational and contrary to Article 8 of the European Convention on Human Rights ('the Convention'). The Divisional Court dismissed the applications. The court approached the case on the conventional *Wednesbury* basis adapted to a human rights context and asked whether the Secretary of State could show an important competing public interest which he could reasonably judge sufficient to justify the restriction. The primary judgment was for him. Simon Brown LJ said 'only if his purported justification outrageously defies logic or accepted moral standards can the court, exercising its secondary judgment, properly strike it down'. The court had a duty to remain within its constitutional bounds. Only if it were plain beyond sensible argument that no conceivable damage could be done to the armed forces as a fighting unit would it be appropriate for the court to remove the issue entirely from the hands of the military and of the government. If the Convention were part of our law, the primary judgment would be for the court and the constitutional balance would shift.

---

[4] *R v Ministry of Defence, ex p Smith* [1996] QB 517 (CA).

In the Court of Appeal, Sir Thomas Bingham MR accepted that irrationality was the test for judicial review, but adopted the approach proposed by Mr Pannick QC that the court may not interfere with the exercise of an administrative discretion on substantive grounds save where the court is satisfied that the decision is 'unreasonable in the sense that it is beyond the range of responses open to a reasonable decision-maker'. In judging whether the decision-maker has exceeded the margin of appreciation the human rights context is important. And then this important statement: 'The more substantial the interference with human rights, the more the court will require by way of justification before it is satisfied that the decision is reasonable in the sense outline above'.

Having considered the facts, the Master of the Rolls concluded that the policy could not be stigmatised as irrational. As he said. it was supported by both Houses of Parliament and by those to whom the ministry properly looked for professional advice. There was no evidence before the ministry which plainly invalidated that advice. It was true that changes had been made by other countries, but the ministry did not have the opportunity to consider the full range of arguments that had been deployed before the court. Major policy changes should be the product of mature reflection, not instant reaction. The threshold of irrationality was a high one. It had not been crossed in this case.

The applicants took their case to Strasbourg and were successful.[5] It was accepted by the government that the policy involved interferences with the applicants' right to respect for their private lives protected by Article 8 of the Convention. The principal issue was whether the interferences were justified. The court found the interferences with the applicants' private lives to be 'especially grave'. It followed that, whilst taking account of the margin of appreciation open to the State in matters of national security, the court had to consider whether 'particularly convincing and weighty reasons exist by way of justification for the interferences with the applicants' right to respect for their private lives'. The government's case (supported by the professional advice of the military) was that the presence of open or suspected homosexuals in the armed forces would have a substantial and negative impact on morale and, consequently, on the fighting power and operational effectiveness of the armed forces. The court scrutinised the government case critically

---

[5] *Smith and Grady v UK* (1999) 29 EHRR 493 (ECtHR).

and in a degree of detail eschewed by our domestic courts. It was not persuaded by the evidence that the policy was justified. But it went further in the light of the strength of feeling aroused by the issue in military circles and 'the special, interdependent and closely knit nature of the armed forces' environment' and proceeded on the basis that it was reasonable to assume that some difficulties could be anticipated as a result of any change in what was now a long-standing policy. The court said that it had not been shown that codes of conduct and disciplinary rules could not adequately deal with any behavioural issues on the part either of homosexuals or heterosexuals. The court, therefore, concluded that convincing and weighty reasons had not been put forward by the government to justify the policy and consequently the discharge of the applicants from the armed forces.

I shall have to come back to the Convention. Meanwhile, it is right to record that the approach to the test adopted by the Court of Appeal in *Ex p Smith* was routinely applied in our courts. Thus in *R (Mahmood) v Secretary of State for the Home Department*[6] Laws LJ said that, in addition to the traditional *Wednesbury* test, in fundamental rights cases, a court could 'insist that that fact be respected by the decision-maker, who is accordingly required to demonstrate either that his proposed action does not in truth interfere with the right, or, if it does, that there exist considerations which may reasonably be accepted as amounting to a substantial objective justification for the interference'. This approach and the basic *Wednesbury* rule are 'by no means hermetically sealed one from the other'. Rather, he said, there is a sliding scale of review; the graver the impact of the decision in question upon the individual affected by it, the more substantial the justification that will be required.

In *R (Q) v Secretary of State for the Home Department*[7] the Court of Appeal explicitly recognised that the law had moved on. It said:

> Starting from the received checklist of justiciable errors set out by Lord Diplock in [*CCSU*] the courts, as Lord Diplock himself anticipated they would, have developed an issue-sensitive scale of intervention to enable them to perform their constitutional function in an increasingly complex polity. They continue to abstain from merits review—in effect, retaking the decision on the facts—but in appropriate classes of case they will

[6] *R (Mahmood) v Secretary of State for the Home Department* [2001] 1 WLR 840 (CA).
[7] *R (Q) v Secretary of State for the Home Department* [2003] EWCA Civ 364, [2004] QB 36, para 112.

today look very closely at the process by which facts have been ascertained and at the logic of the inferences drawn from them.

So on the eve of the coming into force of the Human Rights Act, the common law was no longer insisting on the uniform application of the rigid test of irrationality. The nature of judicial review in every case depended on the context and on factors including the gravity of the issue which was the subject of the decision under challenge. Thus, quite apart from modern international human rights law, there were certain rights which were regarded by our domestic common law as so fundamental that interference with them was difficult to justify before the courts. This gave rise to the use of 'anxious scrutiny' as a technique for reviewing decisions in fundamental rights cases. Lord Sumption has recently criticised this as a catch phrase with little or no legal content: see his Administrative Law Bar Association Lecture November 2014. He is right to insist on intellectual rigour in the use of such a phrase.

This is just another facet of our common law feeling its way towards a more just and proportionate solution. The trouble with the original formulation was that it was too blunt an instrument.

It is time to come back to proportionality. This is a concept that has become increasingly important in UK public law over recent years. In *R (ABCIFER) v Defence Secretary*,[8] the Court of Appeal noted that there was growing support for the recognition of proportionality as part of English domestic law in cases which do not involve EU law or the Convention on Human Rights and said that the case for this was a strong one. Trying to keep the *Wednesbury* principle and proportionality in separate compartments was unnecessary and confusing. The criteria of proportionality were more precise and sophisticated. The *Wednesbury* test was moving closer to proportionality and in some cases it was not possible to see any daylight between them. The court said that it had difficulty in seeing what justification there now was for retaining the *Wednesbury* test. Nevertheless, it was not for the Court of Appeal to perform its burial rites.

There is no doubt that the incorporation of the Convention (which affects so many areas of our domestic law) has led to the routine application of the doctrine of proportionality in many judicial review cases. It has led to a further relaxation of the rigours of the *Wednesbury* principle in its original manifestation and as explained

---

[8] *R (ABCIFER) v Secretary of State for Defence* [2003] EWCA Civ 473, [2003] QB 1397.

by Lord Diplock. As currently understood, four questions generally arise where the court applies the principle of proportionality. These are: (i) is the objective of the measure under challenge sufficiently important to justify limiting a fundamental right? (ii) are the measures which have been designed to meet it rationally connected to it? (iii) are they no more than are necessary to accomplish it? (iv) do they strike a fair balance between the right of the individual and the interests of the community? The fourth question is often the most difficult and controversial. It is at this stage of the analysis that the court decides the proportionality question in the strict sense. Although the first three questions require the court to make value judgements to a certain extent, it is the fourth question which calls for the ultimate judgement of the proportionality of the measure.

R (SB) v Governors of Denbigh High School[9] provides a good illustration of the problems raised by the fourth question. The claimant, a schoolgirl who professed the Muslim faith, sought judicial review of the decision of the school governors not to admit her to school wearing a jilbab and claimed that it was contrary to her right to manifest her religion under Article 9(1) of the Convention. Her claim failed. Lord Bingham said that the court's approach to an issue of proportionality under the Convention must go beyond that traditionally adopted to judicial review in a domestic setting. The inadequacy of that approach had been exposed in *Smith and Grady v UK*.[10] He said: 'there is no shift to a merits review, but the intensity of the review is greater than was previously appropriate, and greater even than the heightened scrutiny test adopted by the Court of Appeal in [*Ex p Smith*]'. He continued: 'The domestic court must now make a value judgment, an evaluation, by reference to the circumstances prevailing at the relevant time ... Proportionality must be judged objectively, by the court ... the court must confront these questions, however difficult'.

In rejecting the challenge, Lord Bingham said that the school was fully justified in acting as it did. It had taken immense pains to devise a uniform policy which respected Muslim beliefs. There was no evidence that the school's policy was opposed by anyone other than the claimant. Different schools had different policies, no doubt influenced by the composition of their pupil bodies and a range of other matters. Each school had to decide what uniform,

---

[9] *R (SB) v Governors of Denbigh High School* [2007] 1 AC 100.
[10] *Smith and Grady v UK* (1999) 29 EHRR 493 (ECtHR).

if any, would best serve its wider educational purposes. It would in any event be irresponsible of any court, lacking the experience, background and detailed knowledge of the head teacher, staff and governors to overrule their judgement on a matter as sensitive as this: the power of decision had been given to them for the compelling reason that they were best placed to exercise it. There was no reason to disturb their decision.

In his Administrative Bar Association Lecture, Lord Sumption has commented with reference to this authority that the Convention asks whether the decision under challenge was actually proportionate and not whether the decision-maker could rationally have thought that it was. He questions whether you can address the questions posed by the doctrine of proportionality without accepting some shift to a merits review. I agree. He made a similar point judicially in the recent case of *Phom v Secretary of State for the Home Department*.[11]

On the face of it, the fourth question appears to require a full merits review. The question 'do the measures strike a fair balance' is categorically different from the question 'could the decision-maker reasonably have decided that the measures strike a fair balance?' Despite his clear statement that there has been no shift to a merits review, part of Lord Bingham's reasoning strongly suggests that he was indeed undertaking a merits review. What else is the statement that the court must make a value judgement and that proportionality must be judged objectively by the court by reference to the circumstances prevailing at the time? On the other hand, the statement that it would be irresponsible of the court to overrule the judgement of the school suggests that, if this was a merits review, it was one which allowed a generous area of judgement to the decision-maker. It is plain that the outcome would have been the same if the court had applied the heightened scrutiny test adopted by the Court of Appeal in *Ex p Smith*. In other words, despite the rhetoric, it is questionable whether there are many cases where the outcome will differ according to which approach is adopted by the court.

After a good deal of uncertainty and shifting about, we seem to have reached the position where there has been a degree of assimilation of the domestic and European tests of judicial review. The speed of the changes that have taken place since Lord Diplock

---

[11] *Phom v Secretary of State for the Home Department* [2015] UKSC 19, [2015] 3 All ER 1015.

spoke in the *CCSU* case in 1984 has been remarkable. The incorporation of the Convention has played an important part in this. But
I suspect that, even if the Convention had not been incorporated,
the influence of the Convention and of the jurisprudence of the
Strasbourg court on the development of our common law would
have been huge. Our common law would have looked rather as it
looks today. Lord Mance helpfully summarised the present position in *Kennedy v The Charity Commissioners*.[12] He said that both
a reasonableness review (ie the current version of the *Wednesbury*
test) and proportionality involve considerations of weight and balance by the court, with the intensity of the scrutiny and the weight
to be given to a primary decision-maker's view dependent on the
context. The advantage of the terminology of proportionality is that
it introduces an element of structure into the exercise, by directing
attention to factors such as suitability or appropriateness, necessity and the balance or imbalance of benefits and disadvantages.
There seems no reason why such factors should not be relevant in
judicial review even outside the scope of the Convention and EU
law. The right approach is that it is inappropriate to treat all cases
of judicial review together under a general but vague principle of
reasonableness. It is preferable to look for the underlying principle
which indicates the basis on which the court should approach any
administrative law challenge in a particular situation.

Having described in the barest of outlines what the test for
judicial review on substantive grounds now is, I need to address
the question raised by the title to this lecture. In one sense, it is
obvious that judicial review is a valuable tool for the safeguarding
of democracy. It is an effective means of ensuring that executive
public bodies do not act illegally. It will be recalled that illegality
was Lord Diplock's first head of review. It includes ensuring that
these bodies comply with their statutory obligations. Since these
obligations are the result of the democratic process, their enforcement is an essential handmaiden to democracy itself. It is the very
antithesis of something that undermines or constitutes a threat to
democracy. It is true that the interpretation of statutes is undertaken by judges and, as we are frequently reminded, judges in the
UK at any rate are not elected by the people and are not accountable

---

[12] *Kennedy v The Charity Commissioners* [2014] UKSC 20, [2015] AC 455.

to Parliament. But that should not be a cause for concern, since the aim of the interpretative process undertaken by the judges is to ascertain and give effect to the will of Parliament. Someone has to undertake this (sometimes difficult) task. In our system, I believe that there is a consensus that independent judges, skilled in the exercise, are best qualified to undertake it. This may seem fairly trite and obvious. But it needs to be said, because many judicial review challenges are based on the complaint that the decision-maker failed to comply with his statutory obligations. Insisting on the performance of these obligations is one of the hallmarks of any truly democratic system. There is no point in having carefully drafted legislation enacted by a democratically elected body if there is no effective mechanism for ensuring that public bodies faithfully comply with it. But the illegality head of review goes much further than this. It also includes unlawful delegation or divestment of the decision-making power; fettering of discretion in the sense of imposing limits on the decision-maker's future freedom of action; and the taking into account of irrelevant considerations, including the distinction between those considerations to which regard must be had and the relative weight to be attached to each consideration, and the purposes for which a power may or may not be exercised, including the concept of bad faith. I would suggest that most fair-minded people would agree first that any fair and rational system of justice requires a mechanism for striking down decisions of public bodies which are illegal in any of these senses, and secondly that adjudications on illegality should be made by independent judges.

But what about judicial review challenges to policies or decisions which are not founded on complaints that the decision-maker acted illegally in the sense that I have just explained? I have already outlined the contours of judicial review and the scope of the reasonableness and proportionality tests. Our courts are sensitive to the limitations in their competence to make normative judgements in certain contexts. Thus, for example, they are reluctant to investigate pure questions of policy. They do not examine the merits of decisions on foreign policy and national security. They seek to avoid imposing duties on the executive which have significant budgetary implications. They avoid adjudicating on political issues. The boundaries of this judicial self-restraint are not the product of legislation. They have been gradually worked out by the judges themselves through case-law in the way that the common law typically develops. As Lord Bingham put it in *A v Secretary of State for the Home Department*:[13]

> ... Great weight should be given to the Home Secretary, his colleagues and Parliament on this question, because they were called upon to exercise a pre-eminently political judgment ... The more purely political (in a broad or narrow sense) a question is, the more appropriate it will be for political resolution and the less likely it is to be an appropriate matter for judicial decision. The smaller, therefore, will be the potential role for the court. It is the function of political and not judicial bodies to resolve political questions ... The present question seems to me to be very much at the political end of the spectrum.

The case, in fact, concerned national security.

The academics have a field day debating whether the rationale for this self-restraint on the part of the courts is their lack of constitutional competence or their relative lack of institutional competence. Lord Bingham was inclined to think that it was better to approach the question in *A* as one of relative institutional competence. Although he did not describe the rationale for his decision in these terms in the *Denbigh* case, it seems clear enough that Lord Bingham based his conclusion in that case, at least in part, on the fact that the court was less well equipped than the school authorities to make a judgement on what would best serve the wider educational purposes of the school. They were the experts and had the practical experience of the likely impact on the running of the school of taking one decision rather than another. Similarly, the court is less well equipped to make judgements on issues of foreign policy, national security, economics and so on than those who have the experience and expertise to make them.

In my view, lack of institutional competence and lack of constitutional competence often complement each other. The decision-makers who are expert in making decisions in these areas are usually democratically accountable to the electorate, whether it is local or national. That is why the court lacks the necessary constitutional competence to make judgments as to the reasonableness or proportionality of decisions of this kind.

In *Mahmood,* the challenge was to a decision of the Secretary of State refusing a citizen of Pakistan leave to remain in the UK on the

---

[13] *A v Secretary of State for the Home Department* [2004] UKHL 56, [2005] 2 AC 68 at para 29.

ground of his marriage to a British citizen. The reason for the refusal was that the marriage did not pre-date the enforcement action by at least two years as required by the relevant policy. One of the issues was whether the decision was contrary to Article 8 of the Convention. It was argued (and accepted) that the court in that case was in as good a position as the Secretary of State to decide whether Article 8 was fulfilled on the facts of that case. The court was not, therefore, institutionally incompetent to review the merits of the decision under challenge. But Laws LJ said that the judges were not authorised to stand in the shoes of Parliament's delegates. The arrogation of such a power to the judges would usurp those functions of government which are controlled and distributed by powers whose authority is derived from the ballot box. In that case, therefore, the court dismissed the challenge because it considered that it did not have the constitutional competence to substitute its view for that of the Secretary of State.

This approach is similar to that applied by the courts in relation to qualified rights under the Convention on Human Rights. The courts have recognised in a wide range of different types of case the need for deference to decisions of the executive.

I accept at once that the ambit of the self-restraint that I am describing is not clear-cut or hard-edged. It is inevitable that some judges will be more deferential to decision-makers than others. But on the whole, I believe that our judges are acutely conscious of the need for caution. As I shall shortly explain, our government has recently sought to rein in judicial review to some extent. It has not, however, based its concerns about the rising tide of judicial review applications on a complaint that judges are striking down decisions by unwarrantably entering into the arena of merits reviews. In short, therefore, I do not consider that our judges are showing a predilection for granting judicial review in circumstances which constitute a threat to our democracy. In any event, it is always open to the government to introduce legislation which has the effect of overturning a particular judicial decision which it considers to be creating difficulties and it does so from time to time. The fact that this occurs comparatively rarely suggests that, generally speaking, our judges steer a responsible course. I recognise, of course, the practical problems of finding parliamentary time to introduce legislation. It would probably also be open to Parliament to pass legislation which had the effect of amending the judge-made law as to the grounds for judicial review. That would be a drastic step to take.

So far as I am aware, there is no pressure to take it. But the sovereignty of Parliament is such that I can see no constitutional impediment to such a course.

Thus far, I have concentrated entirely on judicial review on substantive grounds and sought to explain why I do not consider it to be a threat to our democracy. In fact, however, the majority of judicial review challenges are based on what Lord Diplock described as procedural impropriety. The most common are the failure of the decision-maker to comply with certain procedural rules which have been propounded and refined by the courts over many years. They are all designed to secure fairness in the decision-making process. They include the requirement to consult those who are likely to be affected by the proposed decision; the rules of natural justice (including that decision-makers should not be judges in their own cause and that there should be no appearance of bias); where Article 6 of the Convention applies, decision-makers must be independent; and in all cases, they must not have such preconceived views as amount to an unlawful fettering of discretion.

This is not the place to explore these rules. They are to be found in a huge body of case-law both domestically and in Strasbourg (as well as in other jurisdictions). What is relevant for today's purposes is that in my view they do not pose any threat to democracy. The body of case-law developed by the courts is the product of long experience of judges as to the requirements of a fair process. I do not believe that any reasonable person would dispute that decisions should be taken fairly by public bodies or that the broad elements of what fairness requires are as I have summarised them to be. The application of the rules of procedural fairness in individual cases often calls for a difficult exercise of judgement. Someone has to perform this exercise. Competent individual judges are the obvious candidates to perform it.

What I have said in relation to the grounds of substantive judicial review applies with equal force in relation to the rules of procedural fairness. If Parliament wishes to change the judge-made law in this area, it is free to do so. But it should be alive to the fact that Article 6 and the Strasbourg jurisprudence on it has much to say on the subject. Our government has recently attempted to tackle what it perceives as the problem of a rising tide of judicial review applications. In the consultation paper to which I referred earlier, the Secretary of State for Justice proposed a number of procedural reforms to judicial review proceedings. The paper noted that proceedings create delays and add to the costs of public services 'in some cases stifling innovation and frustrating much needed reforms, including those aimed at stimulating growth and promoting economic recovery.' The declared intention of the reforms was 'not to deny, or restrict, access to justice, but to provide a more balanced and proportionate approach'. The paper noted that in 1974 there were 160 applications for judicial review, but by 2000 this had risen to nearly 4,250 and by 2011 had reached over 11,000. The increase had been mainly the result of the growth in the number of challenges made in immigration and asylum cases. In 2011, these represented more than 75 per cent of all applications for permission to apply for judicial review. In order to tackle the problem, the government proposed some fairly modest reductions in the time limit for bringing judicial review proceedings in cases involving challenges to public procurement and planning application decisions. It made further proposals which included, for example, (i) the introduction of a fee for an oral renewal hearing of an application for permission to seek judicial review following a refusal on the papers; and (ii) some proposals in relation to legal aid which were widely criticised.

Since the 1960s, public law has become prominent in the landscape of UK public administration and judicial review decisions have begun to have a real impact on the daily work of administrators. An indication of this is the fact that in 1987 the Cabinet Office issued guidelines on judicial review to civil service administrators, prepared by the Treasury Solicitor's Department. The book bears the Orwellian title *The Judge over Your Shoulder*. The most recent edition was issued in 2006. As one would expect, it is a balanced and careful summary of the relevant legal principles. It explains that its purpose is not 'How to survive Judicial Review'. Rather, it says, it is 'to inform and improve the quality of administrative decision-making—though, if we are successful, that should have the incidental effect of making decisions less vulnerable to Judicial Review'. The Preface continues: 'We have always tried to emphasise what is best practice in administrative decision-making, rather than what you can get away with: see, for example, on the recording and giving of reasons'. What better evidence could there be of the importance of judicial review and its role in the public life of our country? Judges must be constantly vigilant to make sure that the remedy is not abused. I believe that they are only too aware of this responsibility. They know that many individuals who are the subject of adverse administrative decisions are desperate people who will leave no stone unturned in their attempts to mount a legal challenge. Many of these challenges are dismissed. Indeed, many are hopeless. A high percentage of them are made by unsuccessful asylum seekers or other would-be immigrants. The stakes raised by these cases are often very high indeed. That is why they are considered so carefully by the judges. I do not believe that any fair-minded person would say that the judges adopt an approach to these cases or to judicial review more generally which undermines our democracy.

6

*Liability of Public Authorities in Negligence**

T
O BE ASKED to give this lecture in memory of Richard Davies
was, for me, a truly poignant honour. An honour, because it
has become established as one of the most prestigious annual
lectures on the legal scene. And poignant, because Dickie welcomed
my arrival at what is now 39 Essex Street in 1986 with all the warmth
and commitment for which he was well known and for which he
was loved by so many of his friends and admirers. He was a brilliant advocate. He had huge expertise in the field of personal injury
law. His early death was a terrible loss to the legal profession. He is
greatly missed to this day.

Personal injury law has become increasingly complex in recent
years. Some of the issues that have troubled the courts have been
peculiar to personal injury litigation. The law reports are replete
with tricky points relating to the assessment of damages in that area
of the law. But questions of wider application have also arisen in
personal injury litigation. For example, the vexed issue of causation, which was once thought of as being essentially one of fact, otherwise known as a 'jury question'. Some of the most teasing of the
cases on causation in recent times have been decided in personal
injury cases. And of perhaps even more general importance is the
fundamental issue of whether a duty of care is owed and the whole
question of immunity from suit. I wish to devote my lecture to this
topic, with particular reference to the circumstances in which a
public authority owes a duty of care in negligence in relation to the
manner in which it discharges its public functions. This is a huge
subject in a developing area of the law. There are many cases, and
many of them cannot be reconciled with each other.

I shall take as my starting point the Bar Council Law Reform
Lecture given by Lord Hoffmann on 17 November 2009 entitled

---

* Richard Davies Lecture for the Personal Injuries Bar Association, 27 November 2012.

'Reforming the Law of Public Authority Negligence'. I start here because this characteristically brilliant polemic encapsulates the arguments in favour of limiting the duty of care owed by public authorities. The lecture was written as a vigorous riposte to the Law Commission Consultation Paper No 187 entitled 'Administrative Redress: Public Bodies and the Citizen'. A central proposal was that a person who had suffered loss in consequence of the act or omission of a public body would be able to claim compensation if it had been seriously at fault in the exercise of its powers. Lord Hoffmann said that this was 'an absolutely terrible idea' and he hoped that it would be quietly dropped.

Time does not permit me to do justice to his lecture. He said that the concept of the duty of care, whose moral basis had been the Aristotelian concept of corrective justice, did not fit well upon questions involving the administration of public bodies. Unlike individuals, such bodies often have no choice as to whether to provide a service or not; their funds are limited and, in a democratic country, they have choices about their spending priorities. So the question of whether they have acted reasonably in matters of administration cannot be equated with whether a plumber or doctor has exercised reasonable care. He criticised as hopelessly question-begging the well-known quotation from Lord Bingham: 'the rule of public policy which has first claim on the loyalty of the law [is] that wrongs should be remedied.' And then there was the question of democracy. Was it right for judges to create a duty of care in private law when Parliament had omitted to do so? Creating such a liability means adding to the financial burdens on the public body: to defend actions or to pay compensation. Was it not better for Parliament to decide whether resources should be used in this way? The courts are ill-equipped to assess the effect of the introduction of new causes of action on the behaviour of public bodies. Lord Hoffmann had conducted some empirical research on the effect of the House of Lords decision in *Phelps v Hillingdon Borough Council*,[1] which created a cause of action against a local education authority for negligence in failing to diagnose dyslexia in school children. He had conducted some empirical research which revealed that 58 claims had been made at the time of the *Phelps* decision. Almost all of the claims failed. At considerable expense, the local education authorities succeeded in defending themselves. These cases are very difficult to prove both on liability and causation. Lord Hoffmann had been able

---

[1] *Phelps v Hillingdon Borough Council* [2001] 2 AC 619 (HL).

to find only three cases in which such claims had succeeded and in those the amounts recovered were relatively trivial. As against that, the local authorities had been required to spend large amounts of scarce public resources to defend themselves, almost always successfully.

All of this seems convincing enough at a fairly high level of abstraction. Lord Hoffmann acknowledged, rightly, that there are circumstances where the law recognises that a public body owes a duty of care. He explained his approach as follows:

> Of course, if Parliament creates statutory powers or duties which enable public authorities to do things which create a duty of care in private law, Parliament must be taken to have accepted that if the public body is in breach of that duty of care, it will be liable to pay compensation just as a private body would have been liable. You cannot set up a National Health Trust which treats patients as in a private hospital and then claim that public funds should not be used in paying compensation for medical malpractice. But when Parliament has created a purely public power or duty and the public body has done nothing which would generate a duty of care in private law, the question is a very different one.

Phelps v Hillingdon was not contrary to these general principles, because it did not use the authority's statutory powers to generate a duty of care at common law. Rather, the authority's educational psychologist, who examined the child, had assumed a duty similar to that which would be undertaken by a private medical adviser and there owed a duty of care.

I doubt whether it is any longer controversial that you cannot get a common law duty of care simply out of a statutory power or public law duty. A common law duty is created, if at all, by what the public body actually does: whether it assumes responsibilities or does acts which, if they had been done by a private body, would have given rise to a duty of care. This explains why an NHS Trust owes a duty of care to its patients in relation to the care they receive from its doctors, nurses and other staff; and the Prison Service owes a duty of care to prison inmates in relation to the manner in which they are treated whilst they are in prison. But it also explains why a duty of care is not owed to patients and inmates in relation to the taking of policy decisions at the macro-level. It will be recalled that in *Anns v Merton London Borough Council*[2] (much criticised in this jurisdiction, but not in other jurisdictions), Lord Wilberforce drew the distinction between policy and operational areas.

---

[2] *Anns v Merton London Borough Council* [1978] AC 728 (HL).

In *Caparo v Dickman*[3] the House of Lords laid down the famous threefold test for determining when a duty of care is owed. It applies equally in cases involving public and private defendants alike. In *Van Colle v Chief Constable of the Hertfordshire Police*[4] (a public authority case) Lord Bingham said at para 42 that the threefold test laid is currently the most favoured test of liability. The application of the third test (whether it is fair, just and reasonable that the law should impose a duty of a given scope) has proved particularly problematic. It is applied in personal injury cases no less than it is in cases like *Caparo*, which was a case of pure economic loss: see *Mitchell v Glasgow City Council*[5] para 24.

Lord Hoffmann criticised as question-begging the dictum of Lord Bingham to which I have already referred and which was approved by the House of Lords in *X (Minors) v Bedfordshire County Council*[6] and elsewhere. In a sense, I agree that the dictum is question-begging, since rights and wrongs are only such if they are so recognised by the law. But it is clear what is meant here. It is that prima facie if A foreseeably suffers harm as a result of the careless acts of B and there is a relationship of sufficient proximity between the two of them, then A should be compensated by B for the harm he has caused. That seems to me to be a good working principle. But it is no more than that. It requires a good deal of fine tuning. The third *Caparo* test provides the filter by which a duty of care may not be recognised even though the tests of foreseeability and proximity are satisfied. The fair, just and reasonable test is famously uncertain and difficult to apply. But the cases show that a number of factors militate against a duty of care.

The *Bedfordshire* case is a good place to start. The court was concerned with five cases which fell into two groups: two were child abuse cases, and three were education cases. I shall summarise the reasoning which led Lord Browne-Wilkinson to hold that in the child abuse cases, the policy considerations which militated against there being a duty of care on the part of the local authority outweighed those which favoured the existence of a duty. In the first case, a child sued the local authority for failing adequately to investigate allegations of parental neglect and abuse, and failing to exercise

---

[3] *Caparo v Dickman* [1990] 2 AC 605 (HL).
[4] *Van Colle v Chief Constable of the Hertfordshire Police* [2008] UKHL 50, [2009] AC 225.
[5] *Mitchell v Glasgow City Council* [2009] UKHL 11, [2009] AC 874.
[6] *X (Minors) v Bedfordshire County Council* [1995] 2 AC 633 at 749 (HL).

its powers to institute care proceedings and protect the child from harm. In the second case, the child and her mother brought proceedings against inter alia the local authority alleging that it had carried out its investigation into allegations of child abuse by the mother's cohabitee incompetently and had negligently obtained a court order removing the child from her mother, placing her in a foster home and restricting the mother's contact with her.

A number of reasons were given to support the conclusion that it was not just and reasonable to superimpose a common law duty of care on the local authority in relation to the performance of its statutory duties to protect children. First, such a duty would cut across the whole statutory system set up for the protection of children at risk. This is inter-disciplinary, involving the participation of the police, educational bodies, doctors and others. It would be almost impossible to disentangle the respective liability of each for reaching a decision found to be negligent. But this is hardly a convincing reason. Courts are well familiar with the task of having to disentangle the liability of several defendants each of which is alleged to have caused or contributed to the loss for which a claimant seeks compensation. Multi-partite litigation is common enough. Claims for contribution between defendants and allegations of contributory negligence may be difficult to resolve. But that is all part of the rich pattern of the complexities of contemporary litigation. None of these difficulties should be a reason for denying compensation to a claimant who has suffered loss as a result of what would otherwise be the actionable acts or omissions of a public authority. It is noteworthy that this consideration was not accepted as a reason for excluding liability in *Phelps v Hillingdon.*

The second reason was the fact that the task of the local authority in dealing with children at risk is extraordinarily delicate. But that is not a good reason for denying the existence of a duty of care, although it is a good reason for being slow to find a breach. All professional persons have to assess fraught and difficult situations from time to time. Take the surgeon who has to make a potentially life-threatening decision at the operating table or the advocate who has to make a snap decision in the heat of battle in court. They respectively owe their patient and client a duty of care, but the bar of liability is raised to reflect the exigencies of professional life.

The third reason was that, if there were potential liability for damages, it might well mean that local authorities would adopt a more cautious and defensive approach to their duties. This consideration was subsequently discounted by the House of Lords in

Barrett v Enfield Borough Council[7] as well as in *Phelps.*[8] A similar argument has been deployed in other contexts and I shall revert to it later in this lecture.

The fourth reason was that the relationship between the social worker and the child's parents is often one of conflict. This would be likely to breed ill-feeling and often hopeless litigation which would divert money and resources away from the performance of the social services for which they were provided. I shall come back to this too.

Fifthly, there were other remedies for maladministration of the statutory system for the protection of children in statutory complaints procedures and the power of the local authorities' ombudsman to investigate cases. I shall come back to this too.

The final reason was that the development of novel categories of negligence should proceed incrementally and by analogy with decided categories: there were no close analogies. The court should proceed with great care before holding liable in negligence those who have been charged by Parliament with the task of protecting society from the wrongdoing of others.

So to come back to the consequentialist arguments that are deployed against the imposition of a duty of care. I shall concentrate on two of these. The first of these is that imposing a duty of care may cause public officials to respond in an unduly risk averse or 'defensive' manner. In the *Bedfordshire* case, it was said that if social workers were made liable for wrong decisions in respect of removing children at risk, they might hesitate when it came to making such decisions in the future. The delay would prejudice the child who was actually being abused, as well as other children who would suffer as a result of slower decision-making by individuals.[9] To take a different example, it has been suggested that highway authorities should not be held liable for failing to improve road safety, in case they overdo it and thereby 'debase the currency' of road safety signs.[10] In another case, it was suggested that, if local authorities were to owe duty of care in their supervision of building construction, then building inspectors might be overcautious in their enforcement of building regulations and insist on higher

---

[7] *Barrett v Enfield Borough Council* [2001] 2 AC 550 at 568 (HL).
[8] [2001] 2 AC 619 at 672.
[9] [2001] 2 AC 550 at 750.
[10] *Gorringe v Calderdale Metropolitan Borough Council* [2004] UKHL 15, [2004] 1 WLR 1057 at para 103.

standards than are actually required under the regulations. This would come at a considerable cost to those constructing buildings.[11] This view is in sharp contrast to that expressed by Lord Denning MR as long ago as 1971 when in *Dutton v Bognor Regis UDC*,[12] he considered whether there were any policy reasons for not holding a local authority liable for loss caused by the negligent inspection of building foundations. He asked whether, if liability were imposed on the council, it would have an adverse effect on the work. Would it mean that the council would not inspect at all, rather than risk liability for inspecting badly? Would it mean that inspectors would be harassed in their work or be subject to baseless charges? Would it mean that they would be extra cautious and hold up work unnecessarily? He noted that such considerations had influenced cases in the past, as in *Rondel v Worsley*.[13] But, he said 'I see no danger. If liability is imposed on the council, it would tend, I think, to make them do their work better, rather than worse.' Lord Denning had no more empirical evidence to support this confident assertion than do have those who rely on the risk of cautious or defensive practice as a reason for *not* imposing a duty of care.

Policy arguments based on the risk of cautious or defensive practice have been criticised by academic commentators on the basis that they are unsupported by empirical evidence: see, for example, Duncan Fairgrieve, *State Liability in Tort*.[14] Moreover, in foreign jurisdictions, including US states, France and Germany, the presence of a legal duty to compensate has not induced a risk-averse culture.[15] Nevertheless, despite the absence of empirical evidence to support it, the argument still carries weight in our jurisprudence. A good example is the immunity enjoyed by the police.

In *Hill v Chief Constable of West Yorkshire*[16] the House of Lords held that as a matter of public policy the police were immune from actions for negligence in the investigation and suppression of crime. Lord Keith wrote the main opinion. He said rather cautiously that 'in some instances the imposition of liability may lead to the exercise of a function being carried on in a detrimentally defensive frame of

---

[11] Per Lord Keith in *Rowling v Takaro Properties Ltd* [1988] AC 473 at 502 (PC).

[12] *Dutton v Bognor Regis UDC* [1972] 1 QB 373 (CA).

[13] *Rondel v Worsley* [1969] 1 AC 191 (HL).

[14] (Oxford University Press, 2003) 130–131.

[15] See Law Commission Consultation Paper No 187 'Administrative Redress: Public Bodies and the Citizen' (2008) para 3.150.

[16] *Hill v Chief Constable of West Yorkshire* [1989] AC 53 (HL).

mind. The possibility of this happening in relation to the investiga-
tive operations of the police cannot be excluded'. He then gave other
reasons for holding that no duty of care was owed. These included
that, if actions were instituted arising from a police investigation,
it would be necessary to examine the manner of the conduct of the
investigation. This would entail scrutinising a variety of decisions
on matters of policy and discretion, for example as to which particular line of inquiry is most advantageously to be pursued, and what
is the most advantageous way to deploy the available resources.
A great deal of police time, trouble and expense might be expected
to have to be put into the preparation of the defence to the action
and the attendance of witnesses at the trial. The result would be a
significant diversion of police manpower and attention from their
most important function, that of the suppression of crime.

A similar approach to public policy was applied in *Calveley
v Chief Constable of the Merseyside Police*,[17] where it was held
that no duty of care was owed by the police in the conduct of disciplinary proceedings against a police officer. In *Elguzouli-Daf
v Metropolitan Police Commissioner*,[18] the issue was whether the
CPS owed a duty of care to those whom it was prosecuting. Relying
in large measure on the reasoning in *Hill,* the Court of Appeal held
that there was no such duty. Lord Bingham said[19] that the interests
of the whole community were better served by not imposing a duty.
Such a duty would tend to have an inhibiting effect on the discharge
by the CPS of its central function of prosecuting crime. It would
in some cases lead to a defensive approach by prosecutors to their
multifarious duties and a risk that prosecutors would act so as to
protect themselves from claims of negligence. There was the further familiar point that the CPS would have to spend valuable time
and use scarce resources in order to prevent law suits against themselves. It would generate a great deal of paper to guard against the
risks of law suits; and the time and energy of CPS lawyers would be
diverted from concentrating on their prime functions of prosecuting
offenders.

Many may think that, at least in the context of the police and the
CPS, these are powerful reasons for not imposing a duty of care.
But this approach has not been followed in Canada or South Africa.
Moreover, in *Hill* the House of Lords relied on the barrister's

---

[17] *Calveley v Chief Constable of the Merseyside Police* [1989] AC 1228 (HL).
[18] *Elguzouli-Daf v Commissioner of Police of the Metropolis* [1995] QB 335 (CA).
[19] At 349–50.

immunity enunciated in *Rondel v Worsley*[20] and that immunity no longer exists. It was in these circumstances that in *Brooks v Commissioner of Police of the Metropolis*[21] the House of Lords was asked to look at the question of police liability for the treatment of victims or witnesses in respect of their activities when investigating suspected crimes.

Lord Steyn gave the leading speech. He endorsed the main thrust of the approach enunciated in *Hill.* The police must concentrate on preventing the commission of crime; protecting life and property; and apprehending criminals and preserving evidence. A retreat from the principle in *Hill* would have detrimental effects for law enforcement. The police would in practice be required to ensure that in every contact with a potential witness or a potential victim, time and resources were deployed to avoid the risk of causing harm or offence. Such legal duties would tend to inhibit a robust approach in assessing a person as a possible suspect, witness or victim. By placing general duties of care on the police to victims and witnesses, the ability of the police to perform their public functions in the interests of the community, fearlessly and with despatch, would be impeded. It would be bound to lead to an unduly defensive approach in combating crime. There is nothing tentative about this. Unlike Lord Keith in *Hill* who spoke of the possibility of defensive police practice, Lord Steyn confidently predicted that a defensive culture of policing would be the result.

Moving away from the world of crime, I return to the land of child abuse. In *D v East Berkshire Community Health NHS Trust*[22] the parents of young children brought actions for negligence against healthcare authorities and, in one case, a local authority for alleged psychiatric harm caused as a result of unfounded allegations made by healthcare and child care professionals, that the parents had abused their children. The House of Lords (Lord Bingham dissenting) upheld the decision of the judge on a preliminary issue that no duty of care was owed to the parents by any of the defendants on the ground that it was not fair, just and reasonable to impose such a duty. Lord Bingham welcomed what he perceived as a shift of emphasis from consideration of duty to consideration of breach. He thought that the concept of duty had proved to be a blunt

---

[20] [1969] 1 AC 191.
[21] *Brooks v Commissioner of Police of the Metropolis* [2005] UKHL 24, [2005] 1 WLR 1495.
[22] *D v East Berkshire Community Health NHS Trust* [2005] UKHL 23, [2005] 2 AC 373.

instrument for dividing claims which ought reasonably to lead to recovery from claims which ought not. But the reasoning of the majority was very much in line with that of Lord Browne-Wilkinson in *X v Bedfordshire*. Lord Nicholls emphasised the conflict of interests point. Where a doctor suspected that a child might have been abused by a parent, there was, potentially at least, a conflict between the interests of the child and those of the parent. Lord Nicholls said at para 85 that when considering whether something does not feel 'quite right', the doctor must be able to act single-mindedly in the interests of the child. He ought not to have at the back of his mind an awareness that if his doubts about abuse prove unfounded he may be exposed to claims by a distressed parent. The seriousness of child abuse as a social problem demands that health professionals acting in good faith in what they believe are the best interests of the child should not be subject to potentially conflicting duties when deciding whether a child may have been abused. Lord Brown referred to the appalling prevalence of child abuse in our society and said that doctors (and presumably other health professionals) have a vital part to play in combating the risk of child abuse. Nothing must be done to discourage them in that task. Then at para 137, he said that there is always a temptation to say in all these cases that no-one will ever in fact be held liable unless he has conducted himself manifestly unreasonably; it is unnecessary, therefore, to deny a duty of care, better rather to focus on the appropriate standard by which to judge whether it is breached. But Lord Brown rejected this solution, which commended itself to Lord Bingham, because it overlooked two fundamental considerations: (i) the insidious effect that his awareness of the proposed duty would have on the mind and conduct of the doctor (subtly tending to the suppression of doubts and instincts which in the child's interests ought rather to be encouraged); and (ii) the need to protect him against the risk of costly and vexing litigation, by no means invariably soundly based. This latter consideration would seem to be a real risk in the case of disgruntled parents wrongly suspected of abuse.

I would draw attention to two features of the reasoning of the majority. First, they reached their conclusion without any empirical evidence as to the likely effect of imposing a duty of care. Lord Brown felt that he had a sufficient understanding of the psychology and motivation of professional men that he was able to say with confidence what the effect of the existence of a duty of care would be. I am bound to say that I find this surprising. Lord Nicholls put the point in a rather more restrained way. He said in terms that he was not suggesting that doctors or other health professionals would be consciously swayed by the conflict of interests. As he put it: 'these professionals are surely made of sterner stuff'. After all, doctors often owe duties to more than one person. An analogous situation is faced by advocates and expert witnesses who owe duties both to their clients and the court. But the existence of divided loyalties is usually not a sufficient reason for denying the existence of a duty of care. So why did the House feel able to reach its conclusion? It is the second feature of their reasoning which provides the answer. This is that the scourge of child abuse was considered to be so great and the need to protect children from it so compelling that health care professionals should not be placed in a position where they *might* put the interests of children at risk. It is in the interests of society as a whole that, so far as possible, children are protected from abuse. There is an analogy with the police and the prosecuting authorities here. As we have seen, one of the reasons why no duty of care was imposed in those cases was that nothing should be done which might deflect those authorities from the activities which they perform in the interests of society as whole.

The cases show that, in deciding whether it is fair, just and reasonable to impose a duty of care on a public authority, the courts tend to adopt a multi-factorial approach. A good example of this is to be found in *Rowley v Secretary of State for Work and Pensions* [2007] 1 WLR 2861. The question there was whether the Child Support Agency which had the responsibility for the assessment, collection and enforcement of child support maintenance payments from non-residence fathers for qualifying children owed a duty of care to those children. The claim included a claim for psychological injury by one of the claimants. The Court of Appeal held that a common law duty would be inconsistent with the statutory scheme which gave a right of appeal against a refusal to make a maintenance assessment and the amount of the assessment. The court went on to give two further reasons why it would not be fair, just and reasonable to impose a duty of care. First, complaints about maladministration by the CSA could be referred to the ombudsman. Secondly, the sums at stake where there were complaints of incompetence on the part of the CSA would usually be small relative to the cost of recovering them as damages for negligence. Litigation was likely to be complex, protracted and expensive. Having held that it would not be fair, just and reasonable to impose a duty of care to pure economic loss, the court considered whether there should be a duty of care to avoid personal injury, such as the psychological harm that was alleged by one of the claimants. The court decided that, although, in many contexts, different considerations are applicable in relation to personal injury claims from those applicable in relation to other claims, this was not the case here. I have to confess that I was the author of the main judgment in this case.

The cases show that whether it is fair, just and reasonable to impose a duty of care on a public authority depends on various factors. The open-textured nature of the test is such that, to some extent, its application is likely to vary according to the philosophy of the judge. Some, like Lord Hoffmann, believe that litigation against public authorities is a bad thing. The authorities are hard-pressed, strapped for cash and often have to perform difficult and sensitive functions. They should not be diverted from performing the important functions that they perform in the public interest. They should not be distracted by fear of the possibility of facing costly (and usually unsuccessful) litigation. Such judges tend to apply the third *Caparo* test in a way which favours public authorities. For them, the suggestion that there should be a shift of emphasis from a consideration of duty to a consideration of breach (in other words, raising the bar for breach) is an unsatisfactory answer. It is unsatisfactory because it does not remove the spectre of potential litigation; public authorities will continue to perform their functions defensively; they will have to make and keep detailed records of everything they do; and they will have to incur great expense in unwelcome and usually unsuccessful litigation from which only lawyers will benefit.

But even Lord Hoffmann accepts that you cannot set up a National Health Trust which treats patients as in a private hospital and then claim that public funds should not be used in paying compensation for medical malpractice. As I said earlier, there is something of a tension between (i) his accepting that a public authority owes a duty of care for acts which, if done by a private person, would give rise to a duty of care and (ii) his statement that the *Phelps* decision has been an unqualified disaster.

It seems to me that one of the conclusions that one can draw from an examination of the cases is that it is very difficult to predict how the third *Caparo* test will be applied in any given situation. Much depends on the subject-matter and the mind-set of the judges to it. Even where the question appears to have been settled by a decision of the highest court in the land, a different answer to the same question may be given later even if circumstances do not appear to have changed materially or at all. This makes life difficult for those giving legal advice and for judges in the lower courts. That is not because judges have been behaving capriciously in this area. It is because the test is not hard-edged and the answers are inherently difficult to predict. This is an area of the law which, I suspect, will never settle down completely, particularly in the area of public authority liability. That may be a source of joy to academics who are assured of constant food supply sufficient for a veritable and moveable feast. I fear that what I have had to say this evening amounts to the most meagre of hors d'oeuvres. I dearly wish that I could have discussed it with Richard Davies. Of one thing I am certain, he would have had very strong views about it and would not have hesitated to express them with vigour and passion.

7

The Shifting Sands of Statutory Interpretation[*]

M ANY MONTHS AGO, I was asked by Lord Rodger to give this address. There were three features of the request that made it irresistible. First, it was made many months before I had to speak. The future would take care of itself. Secondly, the request was made with Lord Rodger's characteristic charm. Thirdly, he said that I could talk on any subject that I fancied. It was, I suppose, a reasonable inference that the subject had to be related in some way to statutes, but otherwise I believed that I had a free hand. Later in the year, he pressed me gently for a title. I was rather busy adapting to my new life in Parliament Square and had not decided what to talk about. So I chose a title that gave me maximum room for manoeuvre. When I started to think about what I wanted to say, I looked at the Statute Law Society's website and found to my dismay that the theme of this year's conference is 'Legislation and the Supreme Court'. What did that mean? It obviously did not mean 'legislation about the Supreme Court'. 'The attitude of the Supreme Court to statutory interpretation' seemed a more likely candidate. There are those who believe that in time the Supreme Court will become more bold in its approach to constitutional and human rights issues. That is, of course, possible. Time will tell. But at the present time, there is no evidence to suggest that the Supreme Court will adopt a different approach from that which would have been adopted if the Appellate Committee of the House of Lords had continued in being. And why should the Supreme Court have a different attitude to statutory interpretation from, say, the High Court or the Court of Appeal?

I could, I suppose, have enquired whether there were any *travaux preparatoires* of the decision to choose the theme of the conference.

---

[*] Lecture for the Statute Law Society, 9 October 2010.

But I decided to let sleeping dogs lie and rely on my broad title. As will become apparent, I have devoted a significant part of this lecture to an analysis of a recent decision of the Supreme Court on a pure question of statutory interpretation. To that extent at least, I am faithful to the theme of today's conference. But I confess at the outset that I shall not be suggesting that the Supreme Court does have a different approach to statutory interpretation except in the mundane sense that it is not bound by earlier court decisions as to the true meaning of any particular statute.

Looked at very broadly, I do not think that the current approach to statutory interpretation in a purely domestic context without regard to the European Convention on Human Rights is any longer in doubt. The days when the literalists held sway are long gone. As so often, Lord Bingham, whose death we all mourn, has encapsulated the modern approach with beautiful simplicity. For example, in *R (Quintavalle) v Secretary of State for Health* he said:

> The basic task of the court is to ascertain and give effect to the true meaning of what Parliament has said in the enactment to be construed. But that is not to say that attention should be confined and a literal interpretation given to the particular provisions which give rise to the difficulty. Such an approach not only encourages immense prolixity in drafting ... It may also (under the banner of loyalty to the will of Parliament) lead to the frustration of that will. Because undue concentration on the minutiae of the enactment may lead the court to neglect the purpose which Parliament intended to achieve when it enacted the statute ... The court's task, within the permissible bounds of interpretation, is to give effect to Parliament's purpose. So the controversial provisions should be read in the historical context of the situation which led to the enactment.[1]

This is the general approach that is adopted by the courts today. These days, the problems are almost always of how to apply this general approach and it is striking how often judges can differ in their application of it. But this was not always the general approach. Statutory interpretation has undergone many twists and turns over the centuries. As I shall explain, changes have sometimes been introduced as a response to changes in external circumstances; sometimes as a response to the problem raised by a particular case; and sometimes as the individual response of a particular strong-minded judge who happens to believe that a change of approach is necessary. It may be surprising, but occasionally we need to remind

---

[1] *R (Quintavalle) v Secretary of State for Health* [2003] UKHL 13, [2003] 2 AC 687 at para 8.

ourselves that judges are human beings. They respond to problems in different ways. Some are cautious and acutely conscious of precedent and the need for certainty. Others have an altogether more adventurous spirit, although one might be hard-pressed to name a judge who could fairly be described as 'swashbuckling'. But this is not the place to embark on a psychological study of judges. Nor is it possible even to begin to conduct a comprehensive review of the changes over time in the approach of the courts to statutory interpretation. I shall, however, pick out a few landmark stages along the way before I examine two modern cases in a little detail.

The approach of the judges to statutory interpretation in the first half of the fourteenth century has been the subject of a fascinating and erudite study by Theodore Plucknett.[2] As he points out, the formal side of judicial interpretation at that time was so little developed that the courts themselves had no ordered ideas on the subject and were apt to regard each case purely on its merits, without reference to any other case, still less to any general canon of interpretation. But cases and decisions began to repeat themselves. It was only gradually that the courts made a practice of examining the intention of a statute in order to find a clue to its interpretation. Until the early years of Edward II's reign, the approach to interpretation was informed by the fact that, although statutes were the acts of the 'King in Parliament', they were generally framed by the King's justices. The judges had inside information as to what the statutes were intended to mean. It was entirely natural, therefore, for judges to interpret statutes on the basis of what had been discussed and agreed in Parliament. Thus, for example, in one case Hengham J settled a matrimonial dispute ruling that: 'We agreed in Parliament that the wife if not named in the writ, should not be received.' He is reported as having said to counsel: 'Do not gloss the statute for we know better than you, we made it'.[3] There were also occasions when judges decided that consultation with their legislator brethren was appropriate in order to ascertain the meaning of the statute. Thus in *Bygot v Ferrers*,[4] Brabazon CJ had cause to consider the nature of *Scire Facias* in the Statute of Westminster II, c 45 and simply said: 'We will advise with our companions who were at the making of the statute.' Another striking example is to be found in *Belyng v Anon*.[5]

---

[2] *Early English Legal Literature* (Layston, 1980).
[3] *Aumeye v Anon* YB 33 & 35 Edw I 82 (1305–1307).
[4] *Bygot v Ferrers* YB 33 & 35 Edw I 585 (1305–1307).
[5] *Belyng v Anon* YB 5 Edw II, I 176–177 (1311–1312).

The statute *De Donis* enacts that lands given upon 'condition', that is entailed, cannot be alienated by the donee to the disinheritance of his issue. The statute provided that the word 'issue' did not extend beyond the first generation. Bereford CJ agreed that this was the literal meaning of the statute, but said:

> He that made the statute meant to bind the issue in fee tail as well as the feoffes until the tail had reached the fourth degree, and it was only through negligence that he omitted to insert express words to that effect in the statute; therefore we shall not abate by this writ.

So at this early stage, what we would describe as a purposive approach to interpretation, and an exorbitant one at that, was applied. The judges had inside knowledge as to what was intended (or could get it from their brethren) and saw no reason not to use it.

But there came a time when the judges of Edward I's day were no longer living, and the new generation of judges could only learn the intentions that produced his epoch-making statutes from the tradition preserved among themselves. Later still, the court gradually started to infer the intention of the law-maker from the statute without the aid of personal knowledge, or professional tradition.

Thus it was that a more literal approach to statutory interpretation began to take root. Indeed, Bereford CJ himself adopted this approach on occasions. Thus in *Stirkeland v Brunolfshed* he said:

> You allege a Statute for the case, and the words of the Statute do not accord with your case, whereas they and your writ should be accordant … No writ is maintainable outside of the course of the common law [and] 'by the form of the Statute' unless it be expressly given by the Statute.[6]

Another example is *Waughan v Anon*, a case on whether an amendment to a writ should be allowed. Shareshulle J said:

> [T]he statute says only that the process shall be amended in respect of such mistakes and it does not say that mistakes in writs are to be amended in such manner, and therefore we cannot carry the statute further than the words expressed in it.[7]

This literal approach was fortified by later developments. The introduction of the printing press and the replacement of manuscript statute-books after 1480 meant that there was a single authoritative and carefully printed text of current statutes. As Sir John Baker has

---

[6] *Stirkeland v Brunolfshed* YB 3 Edw II, 108 (1310).
[7] *Waughan v Anon* YB 20 Edw III, ii, 198 (1346–1347).

said in Volume VI of *The Oxford History of the Laws of England* at p 76, proposed legislation now started life as a draft statute, the exact wording of which could be debated and amended, usually with the combined legal expertise of judges, law officers and legally qualified members of the lower house. As a consequence, the finished product could be regarded as of considerable textual significance. The printed text created a culture of draftsmanship, where, as Sir John Baker has said (p 77), the draftsman would take 'increasingly elaborate care to furnish bills with preambles setting out their objects, and to ensure that they provided for every contingency in the operative provisions, piling clause upon clause, qualifying them with provisos, savings and exceptions'.

Thus, Fyneux CJ advocated a strict literal construction wherever this could be sensibly achieved. In difficult cases, however, he said that there were three relevant factors, namely: (i) the words of the statute; (ii) if the words were difficult 'the mind of those who made it'; and (iii) previous interpretation by 'wise men' all of which should be combined with 'good reason'.[8] It was therefore understood that a strict literal interpretation should not be adopted if this produced a result which was not sensible. A basic interpretative theory was implemented. 'Negative' statutes (ie ones which were penal or in derogation of common right or in abridgement of the common law) were interpreted strictly and 'affirmative' or beneficial statutes (which 'enlarged' the common law or remedied a mischief at common law) were interpreted generously 'for the common profit of the realm'.[9] But the distinction between abridgment and enlargement statutes became difficult to apply. Thus the attempt to create a hybrid literal and purposive approach to statutory interpretation gave rise to problems. In *Marmyon v Baldwin*,[10] for example, Shelley J said: 'a statute is always taken as it has been applied, and is not taken strictly [even] if it is penal. For no statute is more penal than the *praemunire*, and yet no statute has been more largely construed. Thus the intention of the makers [is paramount]'. And a little later: 'the sense and intent of the makers of any statute, and the mens statuti, should alone lead a judge to an upright judgment in construction of any statute.'

---

[8] See *Anon* (1516) Chaloner 278 no 1.

[9] See J Baker *The Oxford History of the Laws of England*, vol VI (Oxford University Press, 2003) 77–78.

[10] *Marmyon v Baldwin* (1527) 120 Selden Soc 61 at 63.

By the middle of the sixteenth century, the shift away from literalism and towards parliamentary intention was well established. Thus, for example, in *Partridge v Straunge*, Serjeant Saunders said:

> [T]he efficacy of statutes is not solely in the wording of the statutes but in the intent of the statutes, which ought always to be greatly weighed, and the words ought to be bent thereto; and upon like reason a penal statute shall be extended by the equity if the makers thereof may be so perceived.[11]

In *Heydon's Case*,[12] at the instance of the King, the Barons of the Exchequer amplified the purposive approach by introducing what we now call the 'mischief rule'. In the seventeenth century, Coke was to say that the court's duty was to interpret an Act 'according to the true intent of them that made it',[13] a dictum which has been judicially approved many times.

During the seventeenth, eighteenth and first half of the nineteenth centuries, there was an explosion of legislation, much of it complex and badly drafted. Public law statutes were drafted by committees of the House of Commons that met in Middle Temple Hall. They at least had the benefit of the expertise of lawyers. Private bills were drafted by their promoters without the benefit of the same expertise. As Holdsworth has described in his *History of English Law*:

> Thus the style in which the statutes were drawn became more and more variegated. The result was increased difficulty in interpreting them, and sometimes in ascertaining their relations to one another. And since, during this period, the style of legal draftsmanship, which was used in the drawing of pleadings, conveyances, and other documents, was tending to become more verbose, the statutes which these lawyers drew exhibited the same quality: and so the difficulties of understanding and applying the growing body of statute law were increased.[14]

By the nineteenth century, the prevailing state of affairs led Jeremy Bentham to observe characteristically: 'The English lawyer, more especially in his character of parliamentary composer, would, if he were not the most crafty, be the most inept and unintelligent, as well as unintelligible of scribblers'.[15] As Holdsworth notes (p 377), in 1838, Arthur Symonds of the Board of Trade wrote to CP Thomson, the President of the Board of Trade, complaining that 'during the

---

[11] *Partridge v Straunge* (1553) Plowd 77v at 82.
[12] *Heydon's Case* (1584) 3 Co Rep 7a.
[13] 4 Inst 330.
[14] 1924, XI 370.
[15] J Bowring (ed), *The Works of Jeremy Bentham*, vol 3 (1843) 242.

last 250 years our statute law has been a topic of ridicule and sarcasm' and that its quality had been condemned by 'statesmen, judges, lawyers, wits, poets and public writers of all kinds'. The voices of dissatisfaction grew ever louder until 1869 when the office of Parliamentary Counsel was established. From then onwards, public Acts were (on the whole) drafted with precision and in a uniform style. Thus it is not surprising that the courts started to adopt an approach to interpretation which, although still seeking to reflect the intention of Parliament, paid more respect to the literal language of the text. Jessel MR put it this way in *Lowther v Bentinck*:

> Now in construing instruments, I have always followed the rule laid down by the House of Lords in *Grey v Pearson* which is to construe the instrument according to the literal import, unless there is something in the subject or context which shows that that cannot be the meaning of the words.[16]

In *Eastman Photographic Material Co Ltd v Comptroller-General of Patents, Designs and Trademarks*, Lord Halsbury LC approved this statement:

> We have therefore to consider not merely the words of this Act of Parliament, but the intent of the Legislature, to be collected from the cause and necessity of the Act being made, from a comparison of its several parts, and from foreign (meaning extraneous) circumstances so far as they can justly be considered to throw light upon the subject.[17]

At the risk of gross over-simplification, it can be fairly said that for the most part this approach has been followed ever since, although it has been amplified and elaborated upon. Hence the many so-called canons of construction so helpfully and comprehensively described and analysed by Francis Bennion in his magisterial tome on *Statutory Interpretation*. Of course, there have been deviations from time to time. The most obvious example was the excursion taken many times by Lord Denning and heavily criticised by some judges, of whom perhaps Lord Simonds was the most vehement. In *Magor and St Mellons RDC v Newport Corpn*,[18] Denning LJ had said: 'We sit here to find out the intention of Parliament and of Ministers and carry it out, and we do this better by filling in the gaps and

---

[16] *Lowther v Bentinck* (1874) LR 19 Eq 166 at 169.
[17] *Eastman Photographic Material Co Ltd v Comptroller-General of Patents, Designs and Trademarks* [1898] AC 571 at 575.
[18] *Magor and St Mellons RDC v Newport Corpn* [1950] 2 All ER 1226 (CA).

making sense of the enactment than by opening it up to destructive analysis'. In the House of Lords,[19] Lord Simonds said that:

> [T]he general proposition that it is the duty of the court to find out the intention of Parliament—and not only of Parliament but of ministers also—cannot by any means be supported. The duty of the court is to interpret the words that the legislature has used; those words may be ambiguous, but, even if they are, the power and duty of the court to travel outside them on a voyage of discovery are strictly limited.

As for Denning LJ's statement about filling in gaps, Lord Simonds said that this could not be supported.

> It appears to me to be a naked usurpation of the legislative function under the thin disguise of interpretation. And it is the less justifiable when it is guesswork with what material the legislature would, if it had discovered the gap, have filled it in. If a gap is disclosed, the remedy lies in an amending Act.

How Lord Simonds must have enjoyed writing this piece.

When he became Master of the Rolls, Lord Denning continued to express an 'expansive' approach to interpretation. But it was roundly rejected by the House of Lords in a number of decisions. It is perhaps sufficient to refer to what Lord Salmon said in *Buchanan (James) & Co Ltd v Babco Forwarding and Shipping (UK) Ltd*:

> For a court to construe a statute is one thing but to graft a provision on to it on the ground that the court thinks it is reasonable to do so would bring the law into chaos ... For the courts to graft a provision on to a statute or a contract is a practice which is entirely foreign to our jurisprudence and, as far as I know, to any other.[20]

The extreme positions adopted by Lord Denning on the one hand and Lord Simonds on the other were more in the nature of personal deviations from the conventional approach than part of a general trend. They do, however, indicate that judges have idiosyncratic views. The different approaches of Lord Denning and Lord Simonds were the product of different world views of the role of a judge. That judges do so differ may be as welcome to academics as it is unwelcome to those who believe that the law should be certain. But it is a fact of life.

I have attempted to show in this extremely superficial survey that there have been dramatic shifts in the approach of the courts to

---

[19] *Magor and St Mellons RDC v Newport Corpn* [1952] AC 189 at 190 (HL).
[20] *Buchanan (James) & Co Ltd v Babco Forwarding and Shipping (UK) Ltd* [1978] AC 141 at 160H (HL).

statutory interpretation from time to time. There have been various explanations for this, including the fact that the judges drafted some of the most important early legislation; the advent of the printing press; improvements in the quality of the drafting; and the gradual realisation that the intention of Parliament would not always be reflected in a strict literal interpretation of the words used. And that is to say nothing of the fascinating voyages of adventure undertaken by some individual judges and the deprecation of them by others.

Moving from the general to the particular, I would now like to consider the shifting attitude of the courts to the question of whether it is permissible to refer to parliamentary material in order to interpret a statutory provision. Prior to *Pepper (Inspector of Taxes) v Hart*,[21] the general rule was that references could not be made to parliamentary material as an aid to statutory construction. This was a judge-made rule. As Lord Reid explained in *Beswick v Beswick*:

> For purely practical reasons we do not permit debates in either House to be cited: it would add greatly to the time and expense involved in preparing cases involving the construction of a statute if counsel were expected to read all the debates in Hansard, and it would often be impracticable for counsel to get access to at least the older reports of debates in Select Committees of the House of Commons; moreover, in a very large proportion of cases such a search, even if practicable, would throw no light on the question before the court.[22]

The facts in *Pepper v Hart* are probably well known, but I need to summarise them. The taxpayers, who were members of the staff of a fee-paying public school, were higher-paid employees for the purposes of section 61 of the Finance 1976 Act. The school operated a concessionary fees scheme that enabled the taxpayers, as members of staff, to have their sons educated at one fifth of the fees charged to parents of other pupils. During the relevant years, the school had surplus pupil capacity and was therefore able to take the sons of the taxpayers without turning away other boys. The taxpayers were assessed to tax on the basis that they had received benefits that were to be treated as 'emoluments' of their employment under section 61, the cash equivalent of the benefits being chargeable to income tax in accordance with section 63. On appeal, the taxpayers contended that the cash equivalent of the benefit had to be determined under the principle of marginal costing to the school.

---

[21] *Pepper (Inspector of Taxes) v Hart* [1993] AC 593 (HL).
[22] *Beswick v Beswick* [1968] AC 58 at 74A (HL).

The special commissioner found that the school incurred no additional expenditure in educating the taxpayers' sons other than on some minor items and allowed the appeals.

The judge allowed an appeal by the Crown, holding that the cash equivalent of the benefit was a rateable proportion of the overall expenditure incurred by the school on providing its facilities to all of the pupils. The Court of Appeal dismissed the appeals by the taxpayers.

The taxpayers appealed to the House of Lords. The committee, comprising Lord Bridge, Lord Emslie, Lord Griffiths, Lord Oliver and Lord Browne-Wilkinson heard the appeals. At the conclusion of the argument which lasted one day, three members of the committee, Lord Bridge, Lord Oliver and Lord Browne-Wilkinson were subsequently to say that they were in favour of dismissing the appeals. Although no judgments were delivered at that time, in their judgments they were later to make it clear that, adopting well-established and orthodox principles of statutory interpretation, they were of the view that the words in section 63(2) 'the cost of a benefit is the amount of any expense incurred in or in connection with its provision' referred to the average cost of the provision of the benefit to all pupils and not to the marginal cost of providing the benefit to the sons of the taxpayers. Alan Moses QC (now Moses LJ), who represented the Revenue, has told me that at the end of the first hearing it was plain that the appeal would be dismissed. In fact, he had only been called upon to address the House in what he has described as a 'desultory way'. Importantly, everybody (including the courts at each level) had been aware of the parliamentary material which was to assume such significance. At no stage did the taxpayers submit that it was permissible to use it in order to construe the statute. The point was raised by nobody.

As for the other two members of the committee of the House, Lord Griffiths was to explain in his judgment that he considered the language of section 63(2) to be ambiguous. He saw the strength of the linguistic argument in favour of the average cost construction. Nevertheless, he said: 'I could not believe that Parliament intended such a construction because it will produce what I regard as such unfair and absurd results'. I have not been able to discover what Lord Emslie thought. Perhaps it does not matter since, unlike the others, he was not a member of the committee that sat when the House reconvened for further argument.

As is well known, after several months, the parties, no doubt to their great surprise, were told to return for further argument on the question whether the parliamentary material could be used as an aid to construction. Their Lordships had decided of their own motion to revisit the long-standing exclusionary rule and to sit in a constitution of seven. The excerpts from Hansard included material which showed that during the debate in committee, the Financial Secretary to the Treasury (who was promoting the Bill), when responding to a question about the impact on the children of staff at fee-paying schools of clause 54(4), which was to become section 63 of the Act, said: 'The removal of clause 54(4) will affect the position of a child of one of the teachers at the child's school, because now the benefit will be assessed on the cost to the employer, which would be very small indeed in this case'. In other words, the Financial Secretary was saying that the effect of the statutory provision would be that the cost of the benefit would be the marginal cost of the benefit to the employer and not the average cost of the provision of the benefit.

After six days of further argument, judgment was reserved for a further few months. In the event, by a majority of 6:1 (Lord Mackay of Clashfern LC dissenting), the House decided that the rule excluding reference to parliamentary material as an aid to statutory interpretation should be relaxed so as to permit such reference where: (i) legislation was ambiguous or obscure or led to absurdity; (ii) the material relied on consisted of one or more statements by a minister or other promoter of the Bill together with such other parliamentary material as was necessary to understand such statements and their effect; and (iii) the statements relied on were clear. Lord Mackay dissented primarily on the ground that legal advisers would require to study Hansard in many cases and that as a result there would be a significant increase in the cost of litigation. This was no more than a restatement of what Lord Reid had said in *Beswick v Beswick.* Perhaps this could be called 'the Scottish objection'.

It is not my aim in this lecture to add to the litany of writings on the question of whether *Pepper v Hart* was a good decision. It has been subject to great scrutiny and criticism and, I think, the general view now is that the majority opinions were seriously flawed not least because they mistakenly equated the intention of government spokesmen in the House of Commons with the intention of Parliament. Rather, I have referred to the case because it is an interesting example of a decision where a long-standing judge-made rule was revised, albeit in carefully circumscribed terms. Why did the House do it? As Francis Bennion says in *Statutory Interpretation* at p 635:

> *Pepper v Hart* was an unsuitable vehicle for a major change in the law governing resort to Hansard in relation to statutory interpretation. It was

not the ordinary case where the court simply has to decide on the disputed legal meaning of an enactment. It was an income tax case that had unusual background features.

The main background feature was that the Board of Inland Revenue managed the income tax legislation under its control in a special way. It exercised a discretion as to how its statutory powers would be employed. It also operated a complex and extensive system of extra-statutory concessions. Prior to the introduction of the Finance Bill 1976, the Inland Revenue never conceded that the marginal cost was the appropriate measure, but had acquiesced in what Alan Moses QC has described as a 'practice of compromise or fudge and muddle'.[23]

In view of the position taken by the majority after the conclusion of the first hearing, it is worth asking why they decided to abrogate the long-standing rule against the use of parliamentary material in this case. Lord Bridge said:

> I should find it very difficult, in conscience, to reach a conclusion adverse to the appellants on the basis of a technical rule of construction requiring me to ignore the very material which in this case indicates unequivocally which of the two possible interpretations of section 63(2) of the Act of 1976 was intended by Parliament. But for all the reasons given by my noble and learned friend, Lord Browne-Wilkinson, with whose speech I entirely agree, I am not placed in that invidious situation.

Lord Griffiths said that the object of the court was to give effect so far as the statutory language permitted to the intention of the legislature. 'Why then cut ourselves off from the one source in which may be found an authoritative statement of the intention with which the legislation is placed before Parliament?'

Lords Keith, Ackner and Oliver also agreed with Lord Browne-Wilkinson who gave the most comprehensive speech. He said that as a matter of principle, although the court could not attach a meaning to words which they could not bear, if the words were capable of bearing more than one meaning, the court should be able to look at all available materials to ascertain the true intention of Parliament and this should include a ministerial statement made in Parliament. He considered all the practical and constitutional objections that had been advanced against this innovation and rejected them one by one.

So why was the rule changed in this case? The basic rule of interpretation was well established and was not in issue. Put very

---

[23] '*Pepper v Hart:* Why it happened', unpublished talk 15 and 16 April 1994, referred to in *Bennion* at p 634.

simply, as Lord Browne-Wilkinson recognised, it was to interpret the language of the statute in such a way as to give effect to the intention of Parliament. In most cases, this involved giving the words used their ordinary and natural meaning when read in their context. But in some cases, the language was ambiguous, obscure or produced absurdity. In those cases, Lord Browne-Wilkinson said, principle required the court to take account of what was said during the passage of the Bill thorough Parliament as evidence of Parliament's intention. But why was it in this case (and no earlier case) that the House of Lords decided to find a new principle and depart from the long-established rule against using such material as an aid to construction? Could the answer be no more complicated than that the majority were of the view that an application of conventional principles of statutory interpretation was bound to produce a result which was contrary to the meaning which the promoter of the Bill said he intended and that such a result was simply so unjust and unfair to the taxpayers that it could not be accepted?

Lord Griffiths was not prepared to adopt what he called the linguistic argument since it produced a result that was so unfair and absurd that it could not have been intended by Parliament. But surely it did not produce an absurd result. And it was not inherently unfair. It would not have been unfair if nothing had been said during the course of passage of the Bill through Parliament. It was only unfair because of what the Finance Secretary had said in committee. Lord Bridge agreed that it should be possible to have recourse to Hansard, subject to the conditions proposed by Lord Browne-Wilkinson, because in that way he avoided being placed in the 'invidious situation' of ignoring the material which indicated which interpretation was intended by Parliament. But that situation was only invidious because of the clear promise that had been made by the Financial Secretary. It was not inherently invidious to be called upon to ascertain the intention of Parliament without recourse to what was said during the passage of the Bill. Courts had been doing that for centuries, apparently without turning a hair or at least without turning too many hairs. They were quite accustomed to interpreting obscure and arguably ambiguous provisions. The fact that a provision was obscure or ambiguous had not previously caused the court to abandon the well-established exclusionary rule. It is, however, fair to say that in *Pickstone v Freemans plc*,[24] the House of

---

[24] *Pickstone v Freemans plc* [1989] AC 66 (HL).

Lords, in construing a statutory instrument, did have regard to what was said by the Minister who initiated the debate on the regulations. But that seems to have been in support of a conclusion reached on other grounds. At all events, there was no reasoned analysis of the exclusionary rule or the reasons why or the circumstances in which it was legitimate to depart from it.

I should add that the judge-made tests of 'obscurity' and 'ambiguity' as pre-conditions for the application of the new principle are in any event not easy to apply. What do they mean? Once a judge decides on the meaning of a statutory provision, however difficult it may be to do so, he usually reaches the peaceful haven of believing that any obscurity that he may initially have thought to exist has been replaced by clarity and any possible ambiguity resolved. It is curious that, at the close of the first hearing in *Pepper v Hart*, Lords Bridge, Oliver and Browne-Wilkinson were all of the view that, applying orthodox principles of statutory interpretation, section 63(2) of the 1976 Act bore the meaning for which the Revenue contended. They were so sure of their ground that, as I have said, counsel for the Revenue was scarcely troubled in argument. The statutory words were not so obscure or ambiguous that it was not possible for their Lordships to arrive at what they considered to be the correct meaning. And yet Lord Browne-Wilkinson was able to say in his speech (p 640G) that he had no hesitation in holding that section 63 was ambiguous and obscure. In saying that the section was ambiguous, he was clearly using the word 'ambiguous' in the sense that it was *possible to argue* that the section 63 was capable of two meanings, rather than that, applying orthodox principles of interpretation, it was capable of two meanings between which it was impossible to choose.

But I have not come here to praise or to criticise *Pepper v Hart*. As regards why the House changed a long-established rule of statutory interpretation in this case, it is surely because, as I have suggested, the Crown's position was so unattractive and so unjust in the particular circumstances of the case. On any view, the State (through the Revenue) was reneging on the promise it had made (through the Financial Secretary) as to how it intended the statutory provision to be interpreted. If the majority had felt able to agree with Lord Griffiths that the taxpayers' interpretation was correct, it is clear that the case of *Pepper v Hart* would have been of interest only to lawyers and accountants practising in the field of tax and would have not have aroused any general interest at all. I expect that it would have been reported in *Simon's Tax Cases*, but I suspect nowhere else.

As it is, the case is an interesting recent example of a shift in the sands of statutory interpretation. Only time will whether it proves to be an important and enduring shift. The signs are not propitious.

I would now like to spend a little time considering the recent decision in *R (Electoral Commission) v City of Westminster Magistrates' Court*.[25] A little detail is necessary. A donor who was entitled to be registered as an elector made 69 donations to a registered political party of which he was a member in a period when he was not registered in an electoral register and therefore did not qualify as a permissible donor within the meaning of section 54 of the Political Parties, Elections and Referendums Act 2000. Section 54 identifies those who are permissible donors. They include an individual registered in an electoral register and registered companies carrying on business in the UK. The party failed to make any of the relevant checks and did not return any of the donations. Section 56(2) provides that if the party receives a donation which it is prohibited from accepting, it must be sent back to the donor within 30 days of the date of receipt. Section 56(3) provides that, if the party fails to return an impermissible donation within 30 days, the party and its treasurer are each guilty of an offence. The Commission applied to the magistrates' court for a forfeiture order under section 58 in the sum of circa £350,000, which represented all the impermissible donations over £200 made by the donor to the party during the relevant period.

Section 58 provides:

(1) This section applies to any donation received by a registered party—
   (a) which, by virtue of section 54(1)(a) or (b), the party are prohibited from accepting, but
   (b) which has been accepted by the party.
(2) The court may, on an application made by the Commission, order the forfeiture by the party of an amount equal to the value of the donation.'

It is sufficient to say that the Court of Appeal concluded that section 58(2) conferred a narrow discretion, that there was a strong presumption in favour of forfeiture which was only displaced by exceptional circumstances and that an order for forfeiture, if made, was to be made in the full amount and not for a lesser sum.

The party's appeal was allowed by the Supreme Court by a majority of 4:3 (Lord Rodger, Lord Walker and Lord Brown dissenting).

---

[25] *R (Electoral Commission) v City of Westminster Magistrates' Court* [2010] UKSC 40, [2010] 3 WLR 705.

It was common ground that: (i) the primary object of the Act was to prohibit the receipt of foreign funding by a political party; and (ii) section 58(2) gave the court a discretion to forfeit an amount equal to the value of an impermissible donation. The members of the court were divided as to the nature of the discretion. Was it a broad discretion or was there a strong presumption in favour of forfeiture exercisable in all but exceptional circumstances?

Lord Phillips (with whom Lord Clarke agreed) reviewed the legislative history. The Committee on Standards in Public Life under the chairmanship of Lord Neill of Bladen QC produced a report in 1998 recommending that only those who live, work and carry on business in the United Kingdom should be entitled to give financial support to the operation of the political process here. Foreign donations were to be outlawed. They recommended that political parties should be able to receive donations from: (i) people who are registered voters in the UK; and (ii) those who are eligible to be put on an electoral register in the UK. In due course, the government issued a White Paper in which they accepted the committee's recommendations on foreign donors, but they introduced a significant modification: only individuals who were registered voters should be permitted to make donations to political parties. Lord Phillips said that, if Parliament had enacted the Neill Committee scheme, there would have been a strong presumption in favour of forfeiting the whole of a donation from an impermissible source: it would be, or would be likely to be, a foreign source and objectionable as such. But Parliament adopted a scheme under which impermissible donations may or may not be foreign. It made the power to forfeit discretionary with the intention that the magistrates' court should discriminate between cases where forfeiture was warranted and cases where it was not. Proof of acceptance of a donation from an impermissible source should raise a presumption that the donation is foreign. If the party cannot rebut that presumption, forfeiture should follow. If the party succeeds in showing that the donor was entitled to be placed on an electoral register, forfeiture should depend on whether it is an appropriate sanction for such shortcomings as led to the acceptance of the donation. Lord Phillips considered that, where the donor is shown not to be foreign, 'Parliament would have intended, by conferring a discretion whether or not to forfeit, that there would be a careful evaluation of all the circumstances in order to decide whether the draconian step of forfeiture was justified'. In other words, a proportionate response. He then addressed the question whether the power to forfeit was an all or nothing power. That raised the question of the true meaning of the words 'an amount equal to the value of the donation' in section 58(2). Having regard inter alia to the fact that the Neill Committee contemplated that the amount to be forfeited would be variable, Lord Phillips held that the better interpretation was to treat the power to order forfeiture of an amount equal to the value of the impermissible donation as implicitly including the power to order forfeiture of a lesser sum.

Lord Mance said that the discretion introduced by section 58(2) was on its face an open discretion capable of responding to different circumstances, in particular the difference between foreign donations and donations made irregularly by a person who was entitled to be on a register, but who by mistake was not. He also agreed with Lord Phillips that section 58(2) permits partial forfeiture. A conclusion that partial forfeiture is possible and that the discretion is broad is more consistent with the policy of the legislation than that adopted by the minority, the policy being the elimination of inappropriate 'foreign' donations.

Lord Kerr said that the critical question was whether forfeiture of a sum of less than the full amount of the donation was possible. If it was, the discretion was wide; if it was not, the discretion was not. If one concentrated exclusively on the language of section 58(2), it was difficult to resist the conclusion that partial forfeiture was not possible. But there were strong policy reasons for interpreting section 58(2) as permitting partial forfeiture. The culpability of the offender is more easily reflected in the penalty if one has a calibrated reaction to the gradations of impermissibility that will arise; the impact on the party of the proposed forfeiture order can be assessed; whether it is a foreign donation can be taken into account; and the inaction of the Electoral Commission after it has discovered the impermissible donation can also weigh in the balance. Lord Kerr said that the most convincing argument, however, was that it was never intended that there be forfeiture where the donor was someone who was entitled to be on the electoral register, but was not registered because of an administrative error. There was no sign of this in the Neill Report, which spoke of the courts taking into account the degree of culpability in setting the level of forfeiture. And there was nothing in the White Paper that signalled a movement by the government away from the essential purpose identified by the Neill Report. It was therefore possible to hold that,

> since the primary function of the Act was to ban foreign donors, Parliament must have intended that where others were caught because of the simplicity and breadth of the provision that was actually adopted

to achieve that aim, it cannot have been intended that they would be subject to the same draconian penalty as those to whom the legislation was principally directed.

Lord Rodger started by observing that nothing could be clearer than the intention behind the language of section 54 of the Act: political parties were not to accept donations from any individual who was not registered on an electoral register. He agreed with Lord Phillips that the ultimate aim of the Act was to catch foreign donors. But Parliament had chosen to pursue that aim by prohibiting parties from accepting donations from all except a narrowly-defined class of permissible donors. That class excludes foreign donors who are not entitled to be registered, but it also excludes donors who are entitled to be, but are not, registered. As the White Paper explained, there were good practical reasons for adopting this legislative approach. Lord Rodger said that section 58(2) did not permit partial forfeiture. The plain meaning of the language could not be displaced by reference to the Neill Report which stood at two removes from the statute. Nor was there the slightest hint in the wording of the statute of the elaborate scheme for the exercise of the discretion that had been constructed by Lord Phillips. In a case, like the present, where the party had held on to the donations which section 56 required it to return to the donor, it was difficult to see how the court could properly do other than make an order for forfeiture, since forfeiture so clearly promoted the statutory object of preventing parties from accepting donations from individuals who were not permissible donors.

Lord Brown gave a judgment essentially agreeing with Lord Rodger. As he trenchantly asked: how could a court properly allow a party to retain the value of a donation which Parliament has plainly ordained that it should never have accepted? Lord Walker agreed with both Lord Rodger and Lord Brown.

I have set all of this out at some length partly because it is a very recent case on statutory interpretation and the commentators have not yet had time to get their sharp teeth into it; and because it contains judgments by Lord Rodger and Lord Brown with which I entirely agree. It shows the court at work uninhibited by human rights considerations or by the constraints of EU law. All members of the court seem to have been of the view that their task was the orthodox one of ascertaining the intention of Parliament and giving effect to the true meaning of what Parliament had said. In a sense, therefore, the decision is unremarkable. No member of the court identified a novel principle of statutory interpretation.

Nevertheless, the differences of approach to the ascertainment of the true meaning of section 58 were striking. I cannot help thinking that what drove the majority to their conclusion was their belief that the result that had been reached by the Court of Appeal on the facts of the present case was so draconian, disproportionate and unfair that it could not have been intended by Parliament. But none of the judges in the majority put it quite like that. It will be recalled that this is precisely how Lord Griffiths reached his conclusion as a matter of construction without reference to the parliamentary material in *Pepper v Hart.* But in view of the fact that the discretion is exercisable only where a party has received a donation from an impermissible donor and the party has not discharged its statutory obligation to return the donation within 30 days, it is surely impossible to argue realistically that it is so unfair and disproportionate to order forfeiture of the donation save in exceptional circumstances that this cannot have been intended by Parliament.

Rather, the majority derived their conclusion as to what Parliament intended mainly from the Neill Report. I find this rather surprising. As Lord Browne-Wilkinson said in *Pepper v Hart* at 630G, it is permissible to have regard to reports such as the reports of commissioners, including law commissioners, and white papers, but only for the purpose of ascertaining the mischief which the statute is intended to cure, and not for the purpose of discovering the meaning of the words used by Parliament to effect such cure. It is true that in *R v Secretary of State for Transport, ex p Factortame Ltd*,[26] the House of Lords went further and had regard to a Law Commission report not only for the purpose of ascertaining the mischief, but also for the purpose of drawing an inference as to the intention of Parliament from the fact that it had not expressly implemented one of the Law Commission's recommendations.

But I am not aware of any case where the court has used a report to construe the meaning of a statutory provision in the way that the majority did in this case. It was a particularly striking case because, as Lord Rodger said, the Neill Report stood at two removes from the statute and the statute radically changed the scheme envisaged by the report. Clearly, the report could be looked at in order to identify the mischief which the Act was intended to cure, namely foreign donations to UK political parties. So much was common ground. But it is difficult to see what else could be gleaned from the report

---

[26] *R v Secretary of State for Transport, ex p Factortame Ltd* [1990] 2 AC 85 (HL).

as an aid to the ascertainment of the true meaning of its provisions. All the more so, since Parliament made such important changes to the scheme recommended in the Neill Report. The majority did not explain why it was permissible to look at the report for an altogether more exorbitant purpose.

The court disagreed on the question whether section 58(2) permits a partial forfeiture. It seems to me that it was (as most of their Lordships said) to regard the question of whether partial forfeiture is possible as central to the enquiry whether the discretion to order forfeiture was broad or narrow. A power to forfeit either all or nothing does not sit happily with the notion of a wide discretion. The majority (certainly Lord Phillips and Lord Kerr) considered that the natural and ordinary meaning of the words 'an amount equal to the value of the donation' was 'the full amount of the donation' and not the strained meaning of 'an amount up to the full amount of the donation'. That was obviously right. As Lord Brown pointed out, there is a variety of other phrases that could have been used if the strained meaning had been intended. But the majority felt able to adopt the strained meaning mainly because the Neill Committee contemplated that the amount to be forfeited would be variable and *therefore* Parliament must have so intended. The objection to this course is the one I have already mentioned. In this context too it is surprising that the majority relied on the Neill Report in view of the fact that the White Paper and then the Act radically changed the scheme envisaged by the report. Surely, Lord Rodger was right to say that in these circumstances the report could not displace the plain meaning of Parliament's words.

I cannot leave this case without wondering, no doubt disrespectfully, whether the decision of the majority would have been the same if the amount forfeited had been £350, not £350,000. On any view, it is a striking modern example of a case where judges have taken different views as to the true meaning of a statute whose subject-matter is straightforward and which is expressed in simple words.

I return to almost where I started. The general approach to statutory interpretation is today not in doubt. But if this brief and inevitably superficial survey achieves anything, it surely demonstrates that it would be a mistake to think that there is no room for further development in the area of statutory interpretation. After all, *Pepper v Hart* was something of a bolt out of the blue. Nothing is fixed. I do not believe that the sands have necessarily ceased to shift forever.

8

*Time to Call it a Day: Some Reflections on Finality and the Law**

THE ORIGINAL TITLE of this lecture was simply 'Time to call it a day'. But on reflection, it seemed to me that such a Delphic title might mislead people into thinking that I was going to use this occasion as a platform to make an hour-long announcement of my retirement from the Supreme Court (which would be of no interest whatsoever to anybody and would be a hoax in any event); or, perhaps more interestingly, to say why, in the light of recent statements by the First Minister of Scotland, I thought that the Supreme Court should cease to have jurisdiction to hear any Scottish appeals. But, rather pusillanimously, I thought it more prudent not to plunge into such treacherous political waters, particularly at this rather febrile time. I therefore thought that I should amplify the title to give something of a clue (but not too much) of the theme of this lecture. My remarks are directed at the position in England and Wales. Anyone who is hoping for some titbits from me on Scottish law will be disappointed.

I should say at the outset that I propose to speak mainly about civil litigation. But I shall say a few words about crime before I move on. With one exception, there is no statutory limitation period for criminal proceedings. The exception is that a magistrates' court may not try an accused for a summary offence unless the information was laid within six months of when the offence was allegedly committed. Subject to that minor exception, so far as I am aware, Parliament has never said that there should come a time when it is too late to prosecute. No statute has imposed a time limit after which a criminal can rest easy in the knowledge that he cannot be prosecuted for a crime that he is alleged to have committed. In this respect,

* Edinburgh University, 14 October 2011.

Parliament has drawn a sharp distinction between crimes and civil wrongs. It has consistently taken the view that it is never time to call it day so far as the prosecution of serious crimes is concerned. This is presumably because, in balancing the interests of alleged criminals on the one hand and those of their victims, as well as the interest that society as a whole has in the prosecution of serious crimes, the scales come down resoundingly in favour of the latter. It would be unfair to the victims of crime and an affront to society to allow a defendant to escape from the criminal process merely because of the lapse of time. But where Parliament has declined to intervene, the courts have stepped in. Under the common law, the court has the inherent power to stay the proceedings as an abuse of process if, by reason of the passage of time, a defendant would not be able to have a fair trial. A person's right to a fair trial is paramount. As a matter of policy, the State will not countenance the possibility of subjecting anyone to criminal proceedings, even an alleged serial murderer, unless he can be given a fair trial.

This is but one of many examples of the law saying that it is time to call it a day because that is what fairness and justice require. Unsurprisingly, fairness and justice are touchstones of our law. They are concepts which are clear enough in general terms, but they are often difficult to apply in particular situations. The power to stay criminal proceedings as an abuse of process by reason of the passage of time is a good example. There is no doubt as to what the relevant principles are. But opinions may reasonably differ in relation to any set of facts on the question whether a defendant will be able to have a fair trial by reason of the passage of time. I suspect that courts are less likely in practice to find that a fair trial will be impossible where the defendant is facing a serious charge than where he is facing a minor one, although it is difficult to see any logical or principled basis for drawing a distinction between the two cases. Understandably, courts are more reluctant to prevent the trial of a murderer than a thief.

So the question whether it is time to call it a day is engaged when the court is called on to decide whether it is too late to prosecute. But it is also engaged when the question of a retrial arises. If a person has been acquitted after a trial, the common law doctrine of *autrefois acquit* may be invoked to prevent a second attempt by the Crown to secure a conviction for the offence of which he has been acquitted, even if fresh and possibly overwhelming fresh evidence is discovered following the acquittal. The common law doctrine of *autrefois convict* protects a person from being tried for a crime in respect of which he has previously been convicted or in respect of which he could on some previous indictment have been convicted. These doctrines are founded on the idea that basic fairness demands that even those alleged to be guilty of crimes need to be protected from oppression at the hands of the State. There are two statutory exceptions to the doctrine of *autrefois acquit*. The first is where the acquittal is 'tainted' within the meaning of section 54 of the Criminal Procedure and Investigations Act 1996. The second (introduced by sections 75 to 97 of the Criminal Justice Act 2003) permits a prosecutor to apply to the Court of Appeal for an order to quash a person's acquittal for a qualifying offence. Qualifying offences are serious offences (which in the main carry a maximum sentence of life imprisonment). The Court of Appeal must order a retrial if there is new and compelling evidence in the case (section 78) and it would be in the interests of justice for an order to be made (section 79).

Where a defendant is convicted and his conviction is quashed on appeal, he may now face a retrial, but only if it appears to the Court of Appeal that the interests of justice so require: see section 7 of the Criminal Appeal Act 1968. Before the enactment of that provision, there could be no retrial.

In outline, this is how the balance between defendant and the State is currently struck in criminal proceedings. However serious the alleged crime, a defendant's right to a fair trial is sacrosanct and if he has been acquitted once, he cannot be prosecuted again for the same offence unless the narrowly circumscribed statutory criteria apply.

What is the position in civil proceedings? I shall suggest that fairness and justice lie at the heart of the law on finality in civil as in criminal proceedings. But two important differences should be noted at the outset. First and obviously, the stakes are different. Society's interest in the prosecution of crime is different from its interest in seeing that civil wrongs are remedied. Secondly, Parliament has not been content to leave it to the courts to develop the law in this area. As we shall see, it has intervened with increasing frequency to prescribe detailed rules. Some of the rules are certain and easy to apply; others call for an exercise of judgement the outcome of which may be difficult to predict. Tempted though I am to do so, I do not intend to explore why Parliament has intervened with careful attention to detail in the arena of civil litigation, but ceded so much territory to the courts in relation to the prosecution of crime.

I doubt whether it is controversial that, although the fundamental aim of any system of justice in a modern democracy is that parties should have their disputes determined fairly and so far as possible correctly, there must be finality at some point. Of course, it hardly needs any longer to be stated that access to justice is a fundamental right both at common law and under the European Convention on Human Rights. But the question arises: when is enough enough? How much time should be allowed to a claimant from the date when his cause of action arises before it becomes too late for him to start proceedings? How many bites of the litigation cherry should he be allowed to have? How many times should a defendant be required to face the same claim in proceedings? How many times should an unsuccessful litigant be permitted to appeal? How long should he be allowed to take the various procedural steps that are prescribed by statutory rules and what sanctions should he face if he fails to observe the time limits imposed by the rules or by court orders?

Any answer to these questions should attempt to strike a fair balance between the interests of claimant and defendant. It is now realised that the State also has an interest in ensuring that litigation is conducted in a responsible and proportionate manner. It is in the public interest that courts are used efficiently, so that litigants do not have to wait any longer than is necessary to have their cases heard. If the courts are clogged up with stale claims which are conducted at a snail's pace, the interests of other litigants will be prejudiced.

A number of different techniques have been developed in England and Wales to strike a fair balance between the twin objectives of: (i) allowing parties to have their disputes determined fairly and, so far as possible, correctly; and (ii) keeping dispute resolution within reasonable bounds. Some of these are statutory; others are by judge-made law. The most obvious area in which Parliament has intervened is in prescribing limitation periods in which proceedings may be brought. The first 'limitation periods' were introduced in the thirteenth century, but these were restricted to land-related actions.[1] The Limitation Act 1623 introduced for the first time limitation periods in relation to non land-related actions: two years for actions on the case for words; four years for actions of assault and false imprisonment; and six years for most other actions. Thereafter, apart from some modification to the limitation periods for

---

[1] F Pollock and FW Maitland, *The History of English Law before the time of Edward I*, vol 2, 2nd edn (Cambridge, 1968) 85.

land-related claims (the Real Property Limitation Act 1833 and the Real Property Limitation Act 1874), Parliament did not turn its attention to the issue of limitation until it enacted the Limitation Act 1939, which provided for a limitation period of six years for all causes of action except actions on a specialty. Since then, there have been further parliamentary interventions further refining the law, including reducing the period to three years for personal injury claims (Limitation Act 1963); making special provisions for the date of knowledge (Law Reform (Miscellaneous Provisions) Act 1971 and Limitation Act 1975)); introducing a judicial discretion to disapply the limitation period in personal injury cases where it is equitable to do so; and so on.

The underlying rationale for these rules is the need to strike a fair balance between the interests of claimants and defendants. Claimants are expected to start proceedings within a reasonable time of the accrual of their causes of action. But where it is not reasonable to expect them to be able to do this, whether because they suffer from a disability or they are not aware that they have a cause of action (whether because the defendant has been guilty of concealment or for some other reason) and they could not reasonably be expected to be so, then the start of the limitation period is postponed. What is remarkable is the extent to which Parliament has regulated this part of the law.

Another area where Parliament has stepped in to secure finality in the interests of fairness and justice is civil procedure. Thus, in England and Wales the Civil Procedure Rules provide that a party who wishes to appeal must in most cases seek permission to appeal and show that an appeal would have real prospects of success or that permission to appeal should be granted for some other reason. Judges in other jurisdictions are surprised that the right of appeal (which they consider to be a fundamental requirement of access to justice) can be restricted in this way. Others view our rather draconian approach with envy. For second appeals, the criteria for permission to appeal prescribed by the Rules are tougher still. It must be shown that the point at issue is one of general importance or that there is some other compelling reason to appeal. Few cases raise a point of general importance. The test of 'some other compelling reason' gives the courts a little more flexibility, but it has been said on a number of occasions that this too is a fairly steep mountain for a would-be appellant to climb. It has been suggested that it might be satisfied where it is strongly arguable that the individual has suffered from a wholly exceptional collapse of fair procedure or that there has been an error of law which has caused truly drastic consequences.[2] Importantly, in a second appeal the mere fact that it is arguable that the decision of the court below is wrong is not enough. The same thinking informs the rules which govern the grant of permission to appeal to the Supreme Court. Paragraph 3.3.3 of the Supreme Court Practice Directions states:

> permission to appeal is granted for applications that, in the opinion of the Appeal Panel, raise an arguable point of law of general public importance which ought to be considered by the Supreme Court at that time, bearing in mind that the matter will already have been the subject of judicial decision and may have been reviewed on appeal.

These restrictions on the right of appeal are the statutory response to the fact that some unsuccessful litigants, if free to do so, would appeal against a decision which they think is wrong and go on appealing, as they would say, 'for as long as it takes'. It seems that litigation can seriously disturb the balance of the mind. Most judges can testify to the truth of this lamentable fact. Many of us have had the experience of dealing with those who have been declared 'vexatious litigants'. But any legal system also has to deal with those who have arguable cases and who, perhaps not unreasonably, believe that they should have won and wish to go on and on until they win. Some cases are intrinsically difficult and could reasonably be decided either way. The propensity of the Supreme Court to reach split decisions (a source of despair in some quarters) provides eloquent testimony of this fact of litigation life. Justice Robert Jackson of the Supreme Court of the USA once famously wrote: 'We are not final because we are infallible, but we are infallible because we are final'.[3]

So any system of justice that is fair to all parties requires that a time should come when it is time to call it a day. Thus the time should come when the losing party must accept an adverse decision for better or worse. The successful party is entitled to nothing less. The more generous the scope for challenging decisions by appeal or review, the greater the chance of eliminating error. But successive proceedings involve delay and additional expense. And the pall of uncertainty continues to hang over the parties until their disputes have finally run their course and an unchallengeable decision emerges. Certainty, even if less than perfect, has great value. At least

---

[2] *R (Cart) v Upper Tribunal* [2011] UKSC 28, [2012] 1 AC 663 at para 131.
[3] *Brown v Allen* 344 US 443, 540 (1953).

the parties can get on with their lives knowing exactly where they stand.

The common law continues to play a part in promoting finality in civil litigation too. The doctrines of acquiescence and laches protect a defendant against the claimant who seeks to make a claim for equitable relief after an unconscionable delay. Further protection to defendants from the attention of unsuccessful claimants who do not call it a day is provided by the doctrines of issue estoppel and res judicata. These are analogous to the doctrines of *autrefois acquit* and *autrefois convict* in the criminal law. Parties are not allowed to reopen issues that have already been decided between them. The case of *R (Coke Wallis) v Institute of Chartered Accountants in England and Wales*[4] is an interesting recent example of the application of the principle of res judicata. The institute preferred a complaint against a chartered accountant alleging a breach of a particular bye-law. The complaint was dismissed. A second complaint was preferred. The substance of the underlying conduct was the same in the case of both complaints, although as a matter of form they were differently expressed. The Supreme Court held that, since the proceedings were not criminal, the doctrines of *autrefois acquit* and *autrefois convict* did not apply. But the principle of res judicata applied because the two complaints were concerned with the same substantive allegations. There was force in the suggestion that, in the context of professional disciplinary proceedings (unlike conventional civil litigation), an exception should be recognised to the strict application of cause of action estoppels. But the Supreme Court held that whether, and in what circumstances, such an exception should be permitted was a matter for Parliament and not the courts.

The court's inherent power to prevent an abuse of process has been invoked to prevent a person from bringing a subsequent claim because he could and should have raised it during previous litigation. This rule is one of public policy based on the desirability in the public interest as well as that of the parties themselves, that litigation should not drag on for ever, and that a defendant should not be oppressed by successive suits when one would do. As Lord Bingham explained in *Johnson v Gore Wood & Co*,[5] there will rarely

---

[4] *R (Coke Wallis) v Institute of Chartered Accountants in England and Wales* [2011] UKSC 1, [2011] 2 AC 146.

[5] *Johnson v Gore Wood & Co (a firm)* [2002] 2 AC 1 (HL).

be a finding of abuse unless the later proceeding involves what the court regards as 'unjust harassment' of a party. It is wrong to hold that, because a matter could have been raised in earlier proceedings, it should have been, so as to render the raising of it in later proceedings necessarily abusive. What is required is a broad merits-based judgement, which takes account of the public and private interests involved and focuses attention on the crucial question whether, in all the circumstances, a party is misusing or abusing the process of the court by seeking to raise the issue which could have been raised before. In other words, a balance has to be struck and a judgement made as to what is required in the interests of fairness and justice.

A recent important example of judicial striking of the balance between the interests of claimants and defendants is in relation to the scope of judicial review of a refusal by an upper tribunal of permission to appeal to itself from a decision of a lower tribunal on a point of law. Judicial review is a judge-made doctrine and it is for the courts to determine its scope. A number of possibilities were canvassed in the recent appeals in *Cart* and *Eba v Advocate General for Scotland*[6] in the Supreme Court. The first possibility was that there should be untrammelled access to judicial review on all the conventional public law grounds where no other remedy is available. This had been the Scottish approach. The second, which found favour with the Court of Appeal in *Cart*, was that judicial review should only lie on grounds of excess of jurisdiction in the sense understood prior to the decision in *Anisminic Ltd v Foreign Compensation Commission*[7] or some serious procedural flaw. The third was that Civil Procedure Rules criteria for second appeals should be adopted by analogy.

The choice could only be taken on policy grounds. The court was given no clue or steer by statute. It was surely uncontroversial that it had to arrive at a reasonable, proportionate and just solution. But there was considerable scope for disagreement as to what that solution should be. This is amply demonstrated by the fact that the Supreme Court adopted a different solution from that adopted by the lower courts. The Supreme Court rejected the Scottish approach essentially on floodgates grounds. A substantial number of the cases would be immigration and asylum cases. Previous experience had shown that, if judicial review on all the conventional public law

---

[6] *Eba v Advocate General for Scotland* [2011] UKSC 29, [2012] 1 AC 710.
[7] *Anisminic Ltd v Foreign Compensation Commission* [1969] 2 AC 147 (HL).

grounds was the criterion, the courts would be likely to face large numbers of applications for judicial review on the basis of alleged errors of law which in truth were complaints about findings of fact. The cost and delay of such (often) hopeless applications was a powerful reason for not adopting that approach. The courts would be clogged up. This would clause delay to public authorities in implementing, for example, decisions to remove failed asylum-seekers. It would also prejudice deserving litigants, who would have to wait longer for their day in court.

The court also rejected the approach of the Court of Appeal for two reasons. First, it was not a good idea to revert to the unsatisfactory Byzantine world of pre-*Anisminic* jurisprudence in order to determine what did and what did not constitute an excess of jurisdiction. Secondly, the Court of Appeal solution to the problem meant that an arguable error of law which did not satisfy the pre-*Anisminic* jurisdictional test could not qualify for judicial review, even if the point at issue was one of considerable importance. To resurrect the test of jurisdictional error in the narrow pre-*Anisminic* sense would be a retrograde step for all the reasons stated by Lord Reid in *Anisminic* itself.

So the Supreme Court decided on the third way and adopted the second appeals criteria approach. It considered that this best struck the balance between the interests of justice and the need for finality.

The general principle that is applied in civil litigation is, therefore, clear enough. A fair balance has to be struck between the interests of claimants and defendants in the interests of justice, but also bearing in mind that the State has an interest in ensuring that its increasingly limited resources are not dissipated in the determining of repeat appeals or hearing of claims which should have been litigated on an earlier occasion. I now wish to look in a little detail at the question of finality in two particular commercial contexts, where special policy reasons have led to a different approach to the balance between the need for a correct decision and the need for finality from that which has been adopted in conventional civil litigation. The first is arbitrations; the second is adjudications under the Housing Grants, Construction and Regeneration Act 1996.

A series of Arbitration Acts (of which the Arbitration Act 1996 is the latest) contain provisions which strike a balance between the interest that the parties have in arbitrators producing correct decisions fairly and justly and their interest in achieving finality and having the arbitral process protected from undue challenges by the losing party. There is also a public interest in having an arbitral system in which parties have confidence. This is achieved by a proportionate degree of regulation and control by the courts, even though individual arbitrations are private and confidential affairs and arbitrators derive their jurisdiction from the consent of the parties. The idea that erroneous decisions and procedural impropriety should be beyond challenge in all circumstances, however egregious the error or impropriety, and however disastrous the consequences for the victim, would strike many as unjust and unacceptable. There is the further point that knowledge by an arbitrator that his or her decision may be challenged in certain circumstances tends to concentrate the mind and to lead to careful and conscientious decision-making. The ability to challenge decisions in tightly circumscribed circumstances should therefore enhance the arbitral process and increase the confidence of businessmen in it. That is obviously in the public interest.

The public interest in limiting the ability to challenge an arbitrator's award by appeal is well demonstrated by a little legislative history. The background to the significant changes that were introduced by the Arbitration Act 1979 is well known. I shall, therefore, deal with it briefly. One of the complaints about the position that existed under the Arbitration Act 1950 was that a nit-picking approach by clever and zealous advocates to awards generated large numbers of appeals. Although there could be no appeal on questions of fact, courts would order arbitrators to state a case on any question of law that was real, substantial and fairly arguable. No distinction was drawn between 'one off' points of law that were of no interest other than to the parties to the arbitration and those that were of general public importance. One of the concerns that inspired the reform of the appeal provisions was a concern that parties (especially foreign parties) were ceasing to arbitrate in London. They did not like the idea of the courts being so ready to hear appeals with all the delay, cost and uncertainty that this entailed. There was a danger that, despite the excellence of the commercial lawyers and arbitrators in London, it would cease to be a pre-eminent centre for international arbitration. There was a real public interest in intervening to stop this trend.

The Arbitration Act 1979 provided that an appeal would lie to the High Court on any question of law arising out of an award: (a) with the consent of all the other parties to the reference; and (b) with the leave of the court. The statute said that leave was not to be given unless the court considered that, having regard to all the circumstances, the determination of the question of law could substantially affect the rights of one or more of the parties to the arbitration agreement. At first sight, there seemed to be nothing in the Act to indicate that the court would be required to apply different criteria from those previously applied when exercising its jurisdiction in relation to the granting of leave to appeal. All that seemed to be required for an appeal was a question of law. But this myopic view of the Act overlooked two things. First, the requirement that, unless both parties consented, the leave of the court was obtained. Secondly, Lord Diplock who was perhaps the most powerful and influential judge of his day. He had very strong views about the 1979 Act and he was determined to see that they prevailed.

In *The Nema*[8] he gave a breathtakingly purposive interpretation of section 1(3) of the 1979 Act. He drew a distinction between: (a) a question of law involving the construction of a 'one off' clause and its application to the particular facts of the case; and (b) a question as to the construction of contracts in standard terms. The test to be applied in the former case was whether it was apparent to the judge on a mere perusal of the reasoned award and without the benefit of adversarial argument, that the meaning ascribed to the clause by the arbitrator was 'obviously wrong'. In the latter case, it was sufficient for the aggrieved party to show that there was a strong prima facie case that the construction favoured by the arbitrator was wrong. He said that, in weighing the rival merits of finality and 'legal meticulous accuracy', there were several indications in the Act that Parliament intended to give effect 'to the turn of the tide in favour of finality in arbitral awards'. He perceived in other provisions of the Act an intention to accord the primacy of the principle of finality less weight where the award dealt with standard forms of contract, than where the subject-matter was a 'one off' clause. On any view, this was a piece of creative purposive statutory interpretation plugging gaps which Lord Diplock clearly felt had to be plugged in the public interest.

He clearly thought that the legal profession had not understood his message, because he returned to the fray in *The Antaios*,[9] where he repeated and reinforced the so-called *Nema* guidelines in rousing terms. His rallying cry was that, unless judges were vigilant in

---

[8] *Pioneer Shipping Ltd v BTP Tioxide Ltd sub nom BTP Tioxide Ltd v Pioneer Shipping Ltd and Armada Marine SA, The Nema* [1982] AC 724 (HL).
[9] *Antaios Cia Naviera SA v Salen Rederierna AB, The Antaios* [1985] 1 AC 191 (HL).

the exercise of their powers under sections 1 and 2 of the 1979 Act, they would frustrate the intention of Parliament

> to promote speedy finality in arbitral awards rather than insistence upon meticulous semantic and syntactical analysis of the words in which business men happen to have chosen to express their bargain made between them, the meaning of which is technically, though hardly commonsensically, classified in English jurisprudence as a pure question of law.

No room for misunderstanding here.

An inevitable (indeed intended) consequence of this approach was that far fewer appeals from arbitrators' decisions would come to the courts. When I started at the Bar, the law reports contained a significant number of reports of commercial cases from the Court of Appeal and House of Lords. Many of these were appeals by way of case stated arising from arbitration awards. A perusal of the law reports over the past 30 years shows that this flow of jurisprudence has largely dried up, no doubt to the relief of the commercial community. Lord Diplock would certainly have been pleased.

But debate continued about the extent of the courts' role. The abolitionists wished to exclude the involvement of the courts altogether and to respect the arbitrator's decision as inviolable. The interventionists considered that there should continue to be a limited right of appeal to correct an arbitrator's error of law. The interventionists considered that failure to apply the law properly would not achieve the result contemplated by the arbitration agreement and that party autonomy does not require the sacrifice of the rule of law on the altar of finality. Lord Saville chaired a Departmental Advisory Committee to investigate the working of the 1979 Act. Its report, which recommended a compromise between the two extremes, was the progenitor of the Arbitration Act 1996. This Act reflects Parliament's latest thoughts on the question of finality and the arbitral process. So far as I am aware, it is working well and there is no pressure for further change.

Section 69 of the 1996 Act introduced a modified right of appeal on a point of law arising out of an award. An appeal may not be brought except with the agreement of all the other parties to the proceedings or with the leave of the court. Section 69(3) provides that leave to appeal shall only be given if the court is satisfied: (a) that the determination of the question will substantially affect the rights of one or more of the parties; (b) that the question is one which the tribunal was asked to determine; (c) that, on the basis of the findings of fact in the award the decision of the tribunal on the question is obviously wrong, or the question is one of general public importance and the decision of the tribunal is at least open to serious doubt; and (d) that, despite the agreement of the parties to resolve the matter by arbitration, it is just and proper in all the circumstances for the court to determine the question.

It will be seen that the *Nema* guidelines have been articulated in section 69(3)(c), although with some modifications. In one respect, the test has been relaxed by the introduction of the requirement that the arbitrator's decision is at least open to doubt (rather than that it is obviously wrong). But in other respects, the requirements have been tightened. It is now necessary to show that the determination of the question *will* substantially affect the rights of one or more of the parties. By section 1 of the 1979 Act, it was sufficient that the determination *could* have that effect. Under the 1996 Act, therefore, a peripheral point of law can no longer be the subject of leave to appeal, even if the arbitrator's decision on it is obviously wrong and even if it is on an issue of general public importance. In effect, leave will be refused unless the point goes to the heart of the dispute.

Finally, there is the interesting requirement in section 69(3)(d) that the court must be satisfied that, despite the agreement to arbitrate, it is just and proper in all the circumstances for the court to determine the question. I am not aware of evidence that applications for leave to appeal are refused on the grounds that they fail to satisfy this additional requirement. It appears to give the court the discretion to refuse leave to appeal, even where the other conditions are satisfied, on the grounds that it is just and proper that the aggrieved party should have to live with the award, simply because he agreed to have the dispute resolved by arbitration. In considering what justice requires, the fact that the parties have chosen to arbitrate rather than litigate is an important factor.

What are the circumstances to which the court should have regard in deciding whether it is just and proper to grant leave to appeal despite the agreement to arbitrate? Section 69 does not provide an answer. They do not include the extent to which the determination of the question will affect the rights of the parties, since that is a distinct factor separately mentioned. Nor do they include the prospect of succeeding in an appeal, since that too is already covered. What is postulated is a question whose determination will substantially affect the rights of the parties, where the decision is either obviously wrong, or (in the case of a question of general public importance) at least seriously open to doubt, and yet which it is unjust and improper that it be considered by the court. It would seem that

section 69(3)(d) is a statutory reminder to the judge who is considering whether to grant leave to appeal that some weight must be given
to the fact that the parties have agreed to resolve their disputes by
arbitration. In theory at least, this goes some way to meeting the
concerns of the abolitionists. But the Act gives no guidance as to
what factors may be taken into account (other than the agreement
to arbitrate itself) in deciding whether it is just and proper to grant
leave to appeal. After all, every case is one in which the parties have
agreed to resolve the dispute by arbitration.

One example of a situation in which I suggest that the court might
invoke section 69(3)(d) to refuse to give leave to appeal is where a
party suspends the performance of a contract pending resolution
of a dispute, and the parties agree to hold a quick arbitration so
that their rights can be determined and performance of the contract
resumed with minimum delay. In the *Nema* (which was a case of
this type), Lord Diplock described the giving of leave in such circumstances as 'an unjudicial exercise of discretion'. Another example may be where, although the issue does substantially affect the
rights of the parties under the contract in question, the amount at
stake is small and of no significance for the paying party. The arbitrator may have made an obvious error, but the court may decide
that the victim of the error should not be allowed to challenge it:
justice in the particular circumstances of the case requires the court
to respect the public interest in the finality of arbitral awards. The
beneficiary of the mistake may have small means and the court may
fix on section 69(3)(d) to say 'enough is enough'. At all events, experience thus far suggests that, if the other conditions of section 69(3)
are met, it will only be in comparatively few cases that leave to
appeal will be withheld on the basis of section 69(3)(d).

To summarise, Parliament has decided that arbitral decisions may
only be challenged in the limited circumstances prescribed by the
1996 Act, principally in order to encourage the use of London as a
centre for arbitration, and in particular international arbitration for
the resolution of commercial disputes. This policy reason has no
application in conventional litigation where, as we have seen, the
balance between the desirability of having decisions made correctly
and fairly on the one hand and of finality on the other hand has been
struck quite differently.

I now turn to the Housing Grants, Construction and Regeneration
Act 1996. The essentials of the statutory adjudication scheme are
as follows. A party to a construction contract is entitled to refer a
dispute arising under the contract for decision by an adjudicator.

The adjudication procedure must either comply with the statutory scheme imposed by regulations made under the Act or with an equivalent voluntary scheme. An adjudicator must be appointed within seven days of a notice of intention to refer a dispute to adjudication, and the adjudicator's decision must be made within 28 days of appointment. This period may be extended with the consent of the referring party for one further period of up to 14 days. For present purposes, the important feature of the scheme is that section 108(3) of the Act provides that the decision of the adjudicator is binding until the dispute is finally determined by legal proceedings, by arbitration or by agreement. The label 'temporary finality' has been used to describe this element of the scheme. Although something of an oxymoron, it captures its essence.

The policy that underpins the scheme is clear enough. It is that a party to a construction contract who wishes to assert a claim should be able to have his claim adjudicated quickly by an independent third person, whose decision will be enforceable and binding until the dispute is finally resolved by litigation, arbitration or agreement. As I said in *Macob v Morrison*,[10] the plain intention of Parliament in enacting this part of the 1986 Act was 'to introduce a speedy mechanism for settling disputes in construction contracts on a provisional interim basis, and requiring the decisions of adjudicators to be enforced pending the final determination of disputes by arbitration, litigation or agreement.' The statutory background was that hard-pressed contractors were being kept out of their money, sometimes for long periods of time, before their claims reached court or a hearing before an arbitrator. Small sub-contractors, in particular, complained of oppressive and cynical behaviour by their more muscular main contractor customers. Parliament recognised that there was force in these complaints. There was a public interest in claimants obtaining a swift decision from an adjudicator that was binding until the dispute could be finally resolved. It must have been appreciated that the speed of the adjudication process would inevitably lead to mistakes. Some of the disputes are extremely complex. The process is bound to be rough and ready and mistakes are bound to occur.

One of the striking features of the Act is that it contains no provisions for challenging decisions of adjudicators. There is no right of appeal and no power to set aside decisions for procedural irregularity

---

[10] *Macob Civil Engineering Ltd v Morrison Construction Ltd* (1999) 64 ConLR 1, [1999] BLR 93 (QBD).

or for any other reason. In this respect, the Act is to be contrasted with the carefully structured and finely balanced provisions for challenging arbitrators' awards that are found in the Arbitration Acts, to some of which I have already referred. So whether, and if so to what extent, decisions of adjudicators could be challenged had to be worked out by the courts themselves. The problem was analogous to that which the court was later to face in *Cart*. The courts had to solve the problem.

It was not long before claimants' attempts to enforce the decisions of adjudicators by summary proceedings were being resisted by their opponents raising all manner of defences. A striking example was the case of *Bouyges (UK) Ltd v Dahl-Jensen (UK) Ltd*.[11] The adjudicator had awarded the claimant approximately £200,000. It was common ground that, in arriving at this figure, he had made a simple arithmetical error and that he should have awarded £140,000. But the adjudicator was not willing to correct the error. I held (and the Court of Appeal agreed) that it was inherent in the scheme that injustices would occur, but these would be subsequently corrected by litigation, arbitration or agreement. If a defendant could resist a claim for summary judgment to enforce an adjudicator's decision by alleging that the decision was arguably erroneous in fact or law, the scheme would fail and the intention of Parliament would be frustrated. It was held, therefore, that the courts would not refuse to enforce an adjudicator's decision on the grounds of error, even an obvious error that was admitted to be such by the defendant. It would only refuse to enforce a decision if it was arguable that there had been a fundamental jurisdictional error or serious procedural unfairness. This approach has been robustly and consistently applied in subsequent case law. As Chadwick LJ said in *Carillion Construction Ltd v Devonport Royal Dockyard Ltd*,[12] it is all too easy in a complex case for a party who is dissatisfied with the decision of an adjudicator to comb through the adjudicator's reasons and find points on which to present a challenge under the labels of 'excess of jurisdiction' or 'breach of natural justice'. But the task of the adjudicator is to find an interim solution which meets the needs of the case. The need to have the correct answer has been subordinated to the need to have an answer quickly. It may be said with some force that to require a defendant to comply with an adjudicator's decision

---

[11] *Bouyges (UK) Ltd v Dahl-Jensen (UK) Ltd* [2000] BLR 49 (TCC).
[12] *Carillion Construction Ltd v Devonport Royal Dockyard Ltd* [2005] EWCA Civ 1358, [2006] BLR 15 at para 86.

that is manifestly incorrect is unfair and produces injustice. It produces injustice which is avoided even by the stringent provisions of the Arbitration Acts of 1979 and 1996. It may be said that this does not sit easily with the broad philosophy of striking a fair balance between the interests of claimants and defendants which I have suggested underpins the statutory and common law rules that deal with the problem of finality in conventional civil litigation. To the extent that this is true, it is because, for policy reasons, the 1986 Act was introduced in order to achieve justice for contractors who were being starved of cash-flow by being force to sue for their money in expensive, drawn-out arbitration and litigation. The statutory solution to this problem was to devise a scheme which provided for decisions by adjudicators which had temporary final effect. But it did not produce true finality. That is why it is not significantly out of harmony with the broad philosophy to which I have referred.

As I have said, the courts had to work out an answer to the question whether and on what grounds an adjudicator's decision could be challenged. Not only are no statutory grounds of challenge identified, but we find an express provision in the statute that a decision is binding until the dispute is finally determined by legal proceedings, arbitration or agreement. This promotes the statutory purpose of protecting contractors from being starved of cash-flow while disputes grind their slow and expensive way through arbitrations or the courts. The courts have decided to limit the ability to challenge decisions severely in order not to frustrate that purpose. They have done all that they reasonably can to discourage challenges to decision of adjudicators. The cases show that the scope for alleging that the adjudicator did not have jurisdiction to make the decision is limited. But where an issue is raised that there has been a breach of natural justice, a defendant may be on more fertile ground. There are many reported cases where a defendant has argued that a decision should not be enforced on the grounds that the adjudicator did not consider all the issues that had been raised; he took into account new material or a new point raised by the referring party which was not raised at the outset and on which the responding party did not have an opportunity to comment or; he failed to consult the parties either about a communication he had received from one party, or about a view that he had formed independently of the parties' submissions. These are points of the kind that are familiar to public law practitioners. The cases show that where points of this kind are raised in answer to a claim to enforce an adjudicator's decision, they are scrutinised most critically. After all, allegations of this kind are easy to make.

Thus, although the courts have interpreted the scheme as providing for temporary finality, subtle and ingenious lawyers continue to attempt to circumvent it in ways that those who decided the early cases (including myself) would not have foreseen. The adjudication scheme was intended by Parliament to be simple and swift. An indication of how far it has fallen short of this aspiration is demonstrated by the fact that in 2007, Sir Peter Coulson published the first edition of his excellent book *Construction Adjudication.* The second edition was published this year. It runs to some 500 pages.

Adjudications are not subject to the Arbitration Act 1996 and an adjudicator's decision is most certainly not the same as an arbitrator's award. An arbitrator's award may be challenged in the limited circumstances prescribed by the 1996 Act. An adjudicator's decision can be challenged only in the limited circumstances that have been explained by the courts. Parliament intended an arbitrator's award to be largely immune from challenge in the courts in order to promote the use of London as an arbitration centre for the resolution of commercial disputes. That purpose would be frustrated if there could be wholesale challenges on the grounds of error of fact or law. Parliament also intended an adjudicator's decision to be largely immune from challenge in the courts in order to ensure that the adjudication scheme was effective and that cash flow was maintained for contractors pending lengthy litigation or arbitration between them and their customers. In these two important areas of commercial life, the balance has been struck between the need for decisions which are made correctly and fairly and the need for finality in a particular way for policy reasons. In this area as in so many others, as Lord Steyn memorably said: 'context is everything'.[13]

The final subject that I wish to discuss can at best be described as a distant cousin of those that I have been discussing so far. It concerns the question: when does a claimant suffer damage for the purpose of completing his cause of action in negligence where his case is that the defendant's negligence has exposed him to a contingent liability to a third party? Is it at the date of the creation of the contingent liability or is it only when the contingency occurs? There have been a number of cases in this area in recent years. The most recent south of the border is the Court of Appeal decision in *Axa Insurance Ltd v Akther & Darby.*[14] The court gave permission to appeal to the

---

[13] *R v Secretary of State for the Home Department, ex p Daly* [2001] UKHL 26 at para 28.
[14] *Axa Insurance Ltd v Akther & Darby Solicitors* [2009] EWCA Civ 1166, [2010] 1 WLR 1662.

Supreme Court on the grounds that the law in this area is difficult. But the case was compromised. Apart from what I concede to be the rather remote consanguinity between this topic and my main theme of finality, I would seek to justify saying something about it on the grounds that it is interesting and continues to puzzle the courts.

In *Forster v Outred*[15] the facts were that, as a result of her solicitors' alleged negligence, Mrs Outred mortgaged her property as security for a loan made to her son. The Court of Appeal held that her cause of action in negligence arose when the mortgage was executed. Although her liability was contingent on her son defaulting on the loan, she had suffered actual damage as soon as she encumbered her property with a charge.

In *Wardley Australia Ltd v State of Western Australia*,[16] as a result of allegedly misleading conduct by Wardley, the State had granted an indemnity in favour of a bank in respect of a facility granted by the bank to a third party. The High Court of Australia held that the State first suffered loss when a call was made on the indemnity and that before then 'the likelihood, perhaps the virtual certainty, that there would be a loss ... did not transform the liability into an actual or present liability at that time'.

In *Law Society v Sephton & Co*[17] an accountant was alleged to have negligently failed to identify fraud by a solicitor, thereby exposing the Society to liability for claims against its compensation fund. The House of Lords held that no loss was suffered by the Society until a claim was actually made on the fund. Even though it was true that, if the claimants had known the truth, they would have exercised their statutory powers of intervention in the practice and prevented misappropriation of funds, there had been no transaction changing their legal position or diminishing their assets. The reasoning in *Wardley* was applied. The solicitor's fraud gave rise to the possibility of a liability to pay a grant out of the fund, contingent on the misappropriation not being otherwise made good and a claim in proper form being made. A contingent liability is not damage until the contingency occurs. The existence of a contingent liability may depress the value of other property (as in *Forster*), or it may mean that a party to a bilateral transaction has received less than he should have done, or is worse off than if he had not entered into

---

15 *Forster v Outred & Co (a firm)* [1982] 1 WLR 86 (CA).
16 *Wardley Australia Ltd v Western Australia* (1992) 175 CLR 514 (Aus HC).
17 *Law Society v Sephton & Co* [2006] UKHL 22, [2006] 2 AC 543.

the transaction. Where any of these things occurs, loss is suffered when the claimant enters into the transaction. But standing alone, the contingency is not damage.

Thus it can be seen that damage is not suffered in respect of advice given on a personal guarantee until the lender makes a call on the guarantee; but where the guarantee is secured on the guarantor's property, it is suffered as soon as the security is given. The intelligent observer of these things might find it difficult to see why the unsecured guarantor should be less vulnerable to the risk of his negligence claim being time-barred than the guarantor who grants security over his property. But that seems to be the law.

In *Axa's* case, the facts were these. The claimant was the assignee of an insurer (NIG) who was in the business of providing after the event (ATE) legal expenses insurance in respect of claims by litigants. Claims would be insured if vetted by certain panel solicitors as being more likely than not to succeed and as being likely to meet a minimum value threshold of £1,000. The claimant brought proceedings against panel solicitors who it alleged had been negligent in their certification of the prospects of success in some cases. Many of the policies were made more than six years before the issue of the proceedings to which the insurance related. As regards the claims made in respect of these policies, the panel solicitors advanced a limitation defence. A preliminary issue was ordered to be tried on the question of when the claimant suffered loss. The majority (Arden and Longmore LJJ) held that loss was suffered when the policies were issued. Lloyd LJ held that it was when NIG first came under an actual liability to make payment under the relevant policy.

From these and other cases, it is clear that a pure contingent liability does not amount to actual damage. The risk of future loss is not enough. Something more is required. There must be a loss which is capable of being measured. The risk of future financial loss is not damage; but where the risk of future financial loss results in an immediate and measurable loss, there is damage. These statements at this level of generality are not controversial. But the problem arises in applying them. The line is difficult to draw. In *Knapp v Ecclesiastical Insurance Group plc*[18] it was held that, where a policy of insurance was voidable for non-disclosure because of the broker's negligence, the cause of action arose when the policy was effected, not at the later stage when it was repudiated. On the other

---

[18] *Knapp v Ecclesiastical Insurance Group plc and Smith* [1998] PNLR 172 (CA).

hand, in *Nykredit Mortgage Bank plc v Edward Erdman Group Ltd*,[19] a valuer was responsible for the claimant having made a loan on the basis of an inadequate security. The issue was not one of limitation, but of when the cause of action accrued for the purpose of interest on damages. On the facts, the borrower defaulted immediately and the cause of action in respect of the inaccurate valuation was held to arise from the time of the transaction or very soon thereafter. However, the House of Lords was of the view that in general the question whether the lender had suffered a loss could not be determined without taking account of the value of the borrower's covenant to repay. It might be worthless or of some (uncertain) value or it might be adequate to protect the lender's interests.[20]

The difficulties in this area provoked something of a cri de coeur from the Court of Appeal in *Axa,* who took the unusual course of themselves giving permission to appeal to the Supreme Court. The majority held that the facts in *Axa* did not reveal a case of mere contingent liability. Arden LJ expressed her conclusions in various ways. The claimants had suffered a loss from the outset because the liabilities under the ATE policies were greater than they should have been (para 60); if as a result of the vetting breaches a policy resulted in loss to the insurer, it carried that risk from inception and a valuation of the policy on inception would always have reflected that inherent risk (para 61); and NIG suffered loss which was to be measured as the difference between its financial position having issued the policies and its financial position if it had not issued them (para 62). Longmore LJ said that the claimants had entered into a flawed transaction which they ought not to have entered into and that there was a measurable relevant loss on the inception of the policies in that any valuation would have to take into account the fact that there had been no proper vetting. Lloyd LJ accepted that the negligence had an adverse effect on NIG's commercial and economic position from the date of the issue of the policies. But he considered that the decision in *Sephton* compelled the conclusion that this was a case of pure contingent liability.

I agree with the majority. It is distinctly odd to say that by issuing the policies the claimant was put in a seriously worse commercial and economic position than it ought to have been, but that it did not suffer any loss until and unless it was called to meet a claim under

---

[19] *Nykredit Mortgage Bank plc v Edward Erdman Group Ltd (No 2)* [1997] 1 WLR 1627 (HL).
[20] See per Lord Nicholls at 1631–32.

a policy. I see no necessity for the law to travel down such a commercially unrealistic route. I suggest that any fair-minded person would say that NIG suffered a loss as soon as it issued the policies which, but for the defendants' assumed negligence, it would not have issued. It was in the business of writing insurance policies. It could have sold some or all of the policies which were vetted by the defendants. Any valuation of the policies on their inception would have to take into account the fact that there had been no proper vetting.

I also see force in the point that NIG suffered damage as soon as the ATE business was written because the liabilities were such as to affect the value of its business or goodwill on the open market. Both the judge and majority in the Court of Appeal did not and did not need to decide the issue on this basis. In taking this course, they were influenced by the statement by Lord Hoffmann in *Sephton* (para 29) that it was irrelevant that a prudent accountant, drawing up the accounts of the compensation fund to give a true and fair view of its assets and liabilities, would have included provision for contingent liabilities. That statement was made in the context of when loss was suffered by the Law Society which is not a commercial body and does not trade. The position of NIG was quite different. It was in the business of writing insurance. It did engage in trade. It had a business which it could sell. The value of that business was affected by the value of its assets, including its portfolio of insurance policies. I cannot see in principle why, if the value of its business is reduced by the issuing of unprofitable policies, it did not suffer a loss which was measurable at the date when the policies were issued.

Lloyd LJ said (para 165) that he found the case far from easy to decide, not least because the application of *Sephton* produced a result which was at odds with what one would anticipate in terms of the commercial and economic reality of NIG's position. *Sephton* is not an easy decision. It is tempting to say that what constitutes damage is essentially a question of fact and that it should not give rise to sophisticated arguments or engage the attention of the higher courts. But that is not how the law has developed. I am sure that we have not read the last word on this difficult subject.

To conclude, I shall return briefly to my main theme. The balance between access to justice and the need for finality is struck in different ways in different contexts. Parliament has intervened in some areas; the common law has set the parameters in others. Special situations call for special treatment. I have identified arbitration and adjudication as two types of dispute resolution procedure where for policy reasons the balance is struck differently from the way in which it is struck in conventional civil litigation. But generally speaking the golden thread that pervades throughout is the quest for fairness and justice. That is a constant. Views change over time as to how the demands of fairness and justice can best be met and how the balance should be struck. The law in this area as in others must always be responsive to developing social and moral values. There have been huge changes during my professional life. I have no reason to suppose that the pace of change will slacken. I would find it interesting to have the opportunity to rewrite this lecture in 25 years' time and see how much, if any of it, would survive in recognisable form. I suspect very little indeed. But rewriting this lecture in 25 years' time seems a rather unrealistic aspiration.

9

*The Globalisation of Law**

INTRODUCTION

I

T IS A great pleasure to have been asked to give the Pilgrim
Fathers Lecture, particularly in a year so rich in anniversaries.
I congratulate Plymouth University on having established this
prestigious annual lecture. The previous lecturers include some of
the most distinguished jurists of our time.

There have been so many anniversaries to choose from this year.
Who can be unaware that it is the 800th anniversary of Magna Carta,
a document that was the product of a local dispute between tyran-
nous King John and his truculent barons, and which has contributed greatly to the development of the rule of law both here and
throughout the democratic world? It is also the 200th anniversary
of the Plymouth Law Society, whose first president was Henry
Woollcombe. It must be particularly satisfying for the Society that
your current President, Charles Parry, is one of his successors in the
firm Woollcombe Yonge.[1] The importance of maintaining a strong
independent legal profession locally cannot be overstated; and a
profession that is strong and independent locally is all the better
equipped to operate effectively on the international stage. I doubt
whether many of you will know that this year is the 100th anniversary of the publication by Patrick Geddes of his book *Cities in Evolution*, in which he advocated the idea 'think globally, act locally'—an
idea which is now generally recognised as being of great importance
for the preservation of our planet.[2]

Plymouth is a city that embodies the idea that what happens on
the local scene can have effects globally. It was their persecution for

---

* Pilgrim Fathers Lecture 2015, Plymouth University, 6 November 2015.
[1] See www.plymouthherald.co.uk/New-Plymouth-Law-Soc-president-mark-organisa-
tion/story-25897856-detail/story.html.
[2] See P Geddes, *Cities in Evolution* (1915) cited at en.wikipedia.org/wiki/Think_
globally,_act_locally.

rejecting the Church of England that impelled the Pilgrim Fathers to sail from Plymouth on 16 September 1620 in search of a better life in what is now known as New England. Nearly four hundred years later, individuals from across the world still move from one place to another in search of a better life, many of them fleeing persecution. 2015 has been a particularly harrowing year for those seeking asylum in safe countries. Who cannot be moved by the daily sight on our television screens of large numbers of civilians seeking to escape from the violence to which they have been subjected in their home countries? The movement of individuals from one country to another is now governed by increasingly complex rules of domestic and international law. The globalisation of the law is a development of the twentieth and twenty-first centuries. It is of importance to all of us. In the light of current events, I propose to start with asylum law.

On 28 July 1951 the United Nations adopted the Convention relating to the Status of Refugees (the Refugee Convention). The inspiration for it was, in the words of Ruud Lubbers and Anders B Johnson, the acknowledgment by the international community of the need to 'deal with the aftermath of World War II' and of 'the strong global commitment to ensuring that the displacement and trauma caused by the persecution and destruction of the war years would not be repeated.'[3] It is a treaty that has 'become known as the Magna Carta of international refugee law'.[4]

The interpretation of the Refugee Convention falls in the first place on the domestic courts of the signatories. There are now almost 150 such parties. They have diverse judicial systems and cultures. It is inevitable that there will be differences of approach between them as to the interpretation and application of the Convention.

There are two principal ways in which the signatories can diverge from each other in their interpretation of it. The first is by their own domestic legislation. The second is by the interpretative process itself. I propose to say nothing about the first of these. But the second lies at the heart of what I want to discuss today.

The rules governing the interpretation of international treaties are to be found in Articles 31 and 32 of the Vienna Convention on the Law of Treaties. The essential rule is contained in Article 31(1),

---

[3] Foreword to *Refugee Protection: A Guide to International Refugee Law*, available at www.ipu.org/pdf/publications/refugee_en.pdf.
[4] Cited by R Wilkinson, (2001) 123(2) *Refugees* 2, available at www.unhcr.org/3b5e90ea0.html.

which provides that a treaty shall be interpreted in good faith in accordance with the ordinary meaning to be given to the terms of the treaty in their context and in the light of its object and purpose. The alluring simplicity and obvious good sense of this are deceptive.

A good example of the problem is to be found in the meaning of the word 'refugee' in Article 1A(2) in relation to persecution by non-state agents. In the case of *Adan v Secretary of State for the Home Department*,[5] the applicants challenged a certificate issued by the Secretary of State authorising their return to Germany or France as safe third counties where their asylum claims would be determined in accordance with the Convention. The basis of the challenge was that Germany and France failed to recognise persecution by non-state agents as qualifying for protection under the Convention, at least if the state was not itself complicit in the persecution. It was contended that the French and German interpretation of a 'refugee' was wrong, so that they were not countries to which the applicants could lawfully be returned. The House of Lords decided that it had to inquire into the meaning of the Convention approached as an international instrument and to determine the 'autonomous' meaning of the relevant provisions of the treaty. It had to be given an independent meaning derivable from the text of the Convention as well as the sources mentioned in Articles 31 and 32 and without taking colour from the distinctive features of the legal system of any individual contracting state. As a matter of principle, there could only be one true meaning of a treaty. It was true that Article 38 provides that, if there is disagreement as to the meaning of the Convention, it can be resolved by the International Court of Justice. That court, however, had never been asked to make such a ruling and the prospect of a reference to it was remote. In practice, therefore, it was left to national courts, faced with a material disagreement on an issue of interpretation, to resolve it. And that is precisely what the House did. It explained why the French and German interpretation was wrong. France and Germany were not, therefore, safe countries where the applicants' claims would be determined in accordance with the Convention.

Another problem area has been the meaning of 'persecuted', which is an integral part of the definition of 'refugee' in Article 1A(2). This has arisen in a significant number of cases. The problem is that the Convention itself does not shed any light on the meaning of

---

[5] *R v Secretary of State for the Home Department, ex p Adan* [2001] 2 AC 477 (HL).

'persecution', but the *UNHCR Handbook* does. In *Adan,* Lord Steyn pointed out that under Articles 35 and 36 of the Convention (and under Article II of the 1967 Protocol), the UNHCR plays a critical role in the application of the Convention. Contracting States are obliged to co-operate with the UNHCR. It is, therefore, not surprising that the *UNHCR Handbook*, although not binding on states, has high persuasive authority and is much relied on by domestic courts and tribunals.

In *Sepet v Secretary of State for the Home Department*,[6] the House of Lords had to consider whether refugee status should be accorded to Turkish Kurds who claimed asylum in the UK on the ground that, if they were returned to Turkey, they would be liable to perform compulsory military service on pain of imprisonment if they refused. The House examined the leading international instruments to see whether they provided any support for the applicants' case. These included the *UNHCR Handbook*, the General Comment No 22 of the UN Human Rights Committee, the 1996 Joint Position Statement, the Charter of Fundamental Rights of the EU and the draft directive of the EU (the forerunner of the Qualifications Directive). This material did not show a clear international recognition of the right for which the applicants contended. The House then considered whether the applicants' case found compelling support in the jurisprudence of other jurisdictions. It concluded that, although there were indications of changed thinking among a minority of members of the European Commission, there was as yet no authority to support the applicants' case. The claim was, therefore, rejected.

Sepet is an interesting example of the techniques deployed by a national court in seeking to find the true interpretation of the Convention. The starting point is the Vienna Convention, but that is only the starting point. It examines relevant international instruments to see whether they provide a clear indication of the answer to the question at issue. Having regard to the central role of the UNHCR, the *Handbook* is of particular importance. It also considers what leading academic writers have to say. Finally, it has regard to the decisions by courts of other jurisdictions. There is a growing corpus of case-law from a significant number of national courts on the interpretation of the Convention. In the UK, we have drawn heavily on the jurisprudence of the courts of Australia, New Zealand and Canada.

---

[6] *Sepet v Secretary of State for the Home Department* [2003] UKHL 15, [2003] 1 WLR 856.

An interesting and difficult question is: by what criteria does a national court decide whether to adopt the views of academic writers or the decisions of other national courts? In our courts at least, a passage from a textbook or a judgment is often cited to reinforce a conclusion that has already been reached by independent detailed reasoning. Sometimes, however, the passage sets out reasoning which the judge considers to be so compelling that he or she simply adopts it. The willingness of judges to borrow from each other is now an accepted and, in my view, welcome fact of judicial life. There is much that we can learn from each other, and not merely in relation to the interpretation of international treaties. In recent years, the development of the common law of England has benefited hugely from decisions of courts of other common law jurisdictions.

But to return to the Convention, what Roger Haines said in a paper in 1995 ('International Judicial Co-operation in Asylum Laws. Suggestions for the future') should surely be of universal application. He said that it is a question of seeking out the best of overseas refugee jurisprudence. He gave as an example the meaning of the requirement that the fear of persecution be 'well-founded' and the standard of proof that an applicant must satisfy. He referred to a number of formulations of the test adopted in different jurisdictions, included 'a reasonable possibility' (US Supreme Court), 'a reasonable degree of likelihood' ((UK House of Lords) and 'a real chance' (High Court Australia). Having reviewed these alternatives, the New Zealand Court of Appeal preferred the 'real chance' test because it considered that it was more readily capable of comprehension and application by sometimes harassed decision-makers.

Mr Haines warned (rightly in my view) that, if we are increasingly to borrow what we perceive to be the best refugee jurisprudence from other states, we must be aware of the domestic law setting and the considerations which may have influenced that state's jurisprudence. For example, there is much in the Canadian cases law which is driven by the imperatives of the Canadian Charter of Rights and Freedoms, especially in relation to procedural fairness.

I would now like to examine two fairly recent and striking decisions of the UK Supreme Court which considered whether the claimants were refugees within the meaning of the Refugee Convention. These are *HJ (Iran) v Secretary of State for the Home Department*[7] and *RT (Zimbabwe) v Secretary of State for*

---

[7] *HJ (Iran) v Secretary of State for the Home Department* [2010] UKSC 31, [2011] 1 AC 596.

the Home Department.[8] As we shall see, in both decisions the Supreme Court drew on comparative jurisprudence on the Convention.

Let me start with *HJ (Iran)*. This appeal concerned two cases. Both appellants were gay men. HJ was an Iranian who arrived in the UK in 2001 and claimed asylum on arrival. HT was a Cameroonian who arrived in the UK in 2007, having travelled on a false passport. He claimed asylum on his arrest at Gatwick airport. Both appellants asserted that they had a well-founded fear that they would be persecuted if they were returned to their countries of origin. The central question in both appeals was whether the claimants were refugees within the meaning of Article 1A(2) of the Convention, which defines a refugee as an individual who:

> owing to a well-founded fear of being persecuted for reasons of race, religion, nationality, membership of a particular social group or political opinion, is outside the country of his nationality and is unable or, owing to such fear, unwilling to avail himself of the protection of that country ...

Both asylum claims were rejected by the Secretary of State. Challenges to these refusals were rejected by our lower courts. The question for the Supreme Court was succinctly stated by Lord Rodger in these terms:

> A gay man applies for asylum in this country. The Secretary of State is satisfied that, if he returns to his country of nationality and lives openly as a homosexual, the applicant will face a real and continuing prospect of being beaten up, or flogged, or worse. But the Secretary of State is also satisfied that, if he returns, then, because of these dangers of living openly, he will actually carry on any homosexual relationships 'discreetly' and so not come to the notice of any thugs or of the authorities. Is the applicant a 'refugee' for purposes of the United Nations Convention relating to the Status of Refugees 1951 ('the Convention')? ...[9]

In other words, can a gay man, who would have a well-founded fear of persecution if he were to live openly as a gay man on return to his home country, be said to have a well-founded fear of persecution if on return he would in fact live discreetly, thereby probably escaping the attention of those who might harm him if they were aware of his sexual orientation? At first sight, it might be thought that, if the

---

[8] *RT (Zimbabwe) v Secretary of State for the Home Department* [2012] UKSC 38, [2013] 1 AC 152.
[9] ibid at [40].

sexual orientation of the asylum seeker would not in fact come to the attention of anyone, it is impossible to see how he could be said to have a fear, let alone a well-founded fear, of persecution on the ground of his sexual orientation.

But the Secretary of State did not go so far as to contend that there are no circumstances in which an asylum-seeker could have a well-founded fear of persecution if he or she were to take measures to avoid detection on return. Her case was that, if the measures that an asylum-seeker would take on return to avoid persecution were not reasonably tolerable, then that of itself would amount to persecution. But provided that the avoiding measures were reasonably tolerable, there could be no well-founded fear of persecution.

The Supreme Court rejected the reasonable tolerability test. It was unworkable and wrong in principle. It was based on a misunderstanding of two previous authorities, one of which was a decision of the High Court of Australia.

It decided that the claimants had a well-founded fear of persecution notwithstanding the fact that they would lead discreet lives if they were returned. The language of Article 1A(2) itself did not provide the answer to the problem. But the court reached its conclusion by interpreting the Convention in a principled way having regard to its purpose and intendment. The key point was that the underlying rationale of the Convention is that gay men should be able to live freely and openly as gay men without fearing that they may suffer harm of the requisite intensity or duration because they are gay. The country of nationality does not meet the requisite standard of protection from persecution simply because conditions in the country are such that a gay asylum-seeker would be able to take, and would in fact take, steps to avoid persecution by concealing the fact that he is gay.

As Lord Rodger put it,

> The underlying rationale of the Convention is ... that people should be able to live freely without fear that they may suffer harm of the requisite intensity or duration because they are, say, black, or the descendants of some former dictator, or gay. In the absence of any indication to the contrary, the implication is that they must be free to live openly in this way without the fear of persecution. By allowing them to live openly and free from that fear, the receiving state affords them the protection which is a surrogate for the protection which their home state should have afforded them.[10]

---

[10] [2010] UKSC 31, [2011] 1 AC 596 at [53].

And as I put it in my judgment,

> The Convention must be construed in the light of its object and purpose, which is to protect a person who 'owing to a well-founded fear of being persecuted ...'. If the price that a person must pay in order to avoid persecution is that he must conceal his race, religion, nationality, membership of a social group or political opinion, then he is being required to surrender the very protection that the Convention is intended to secure for him. The Convention would be failing in its purpose if it were to mean that a gay man does not have a well-founded fear of persecution because he could conceal the fact he is a gay man **in order to avoid persecution** on return to his home country.[11]

The court found support for this approach in some valuable Commonwealth jurisprudence which had considered the very issue that was before the court. The High Court of Australia decision of *Appellant S395/2002 v Minister for Immigration*[12] was the subject of sustained analysis by Lord Rodger[13] and described by him as 'powerful authority'. In that case McHugh and Kirby JJ said that the fact that the applicants would act discreetly did not mean that they did not have a well-founded fear of persecution on their return. Rather, the tribunal had to ask why they would act discreetly. If it was because they would suffer serious harm if they lived openly as a homosexual couple, they would have a well-founded fear of persecution 'since it is the right to live openly without fear of persecution which the Convention exists to protect'.

Asking why an asylum-seeker would act discreetly focuses the court's attention on the reason why the individual has acted discreetly in the past, and would have to do so in the future. As McHugh and Kirby JJ explained,

> In many—perhaps the majority of—cases, however, the applicant has acted in the way that he or she did only because of the **threat** of harm. In such cases, the well-founded fear of persecution held by the applicant is the fear that, unless that person acts to avoid the harmful conduct, he or she will suffer harm. It is the **threat** of serious harm with its menacing implications that constitutes the persecutory conduct.[14]

By asking why he would act discreetly, the attention of the court is focused on what would happen to the individual if he did not act discreetly on his return. Was discretion the means by which he

[11] ibid at [110].
[12] *Appellant S395/2002 v Minister for Immigration* (2003) 216 CLR 473.
[13] ibid at [66]ff.
[14] Cited at ibid [66].

would hope to avoid persecution? If yes, was the fear of persecution that the individual hoped to avoid by so acting well-founded? If yes, the individual had a well-founded fear of persecution within the meaning of the Convention. This leads to a further consideration, also noted by McHugh and Kirby JJ. An individual who dissimulates may successfully avoid coming to the attention of the authorities. But he will still be in fear of persecution, fearfully waiting for a knock at the door.[15] Throughout the period when he is seeking to evade detection, he continues to be in fear of persecution. As Madgwick J said in *Win v Minister for Immigration and Multicultural Affairs*,[16] to say otherwise would stand the Refugee Convention on its head and one would be driven to say: 'Anne Frank, terrified as a Jew and hiding for her life in Nazi-occupied Holland would not be a refugee.'[17]

Lord Rodger noted that the reasoning of McHugh and Kirby JJ had been applied in *NABD of 2002 v Minister of Immigration and Multicultural and Indigenous Affairs*.[18] This case concerned the question whether the appellant who had converted to Christianity would face persecution if he returned to Iran. It had also been applied in *SZATV v Minister for Immigration and Citizenship*,[19] where the appellant, a journalist from Ukraine had been subject to a campaign of harassment on account of his political views. It had been held by the lower court that he could safely return to Ukraine, not as a journalist, but as a construction worker who kept his political beliefs to himself. The High Court of Australia overturned this decision: it had focused on what steps the appellant would take to avoid persecution rather than why he would take them. As Lord Rodger explained, the decision was predicated on the journalist having to give up 'the very right to express his political views without fear of persecution which the Convention was designed to protect.'[20]

The Supreme Court noted that the courts in New Zealand had reached a similar conclusion on the issue, but on the basis of a somewhat different analysis. On this analysis, which is explained in the leading case of *Refugee Appeal No 74665/03*,[21] the emphasis

---

[15] ibid at [116].

[16] *Win v Minister for Immigration and Multicultural Affairs* [2001] FCA 132 at [18].

[17] Cited at *Appellant S395/2002 v Minister for Immigration and Multicultural Affairs* (2003) 216 CLR 473 at [117] (Aus HC).

[18] *NABD of 2002 v Minister of Immigration and Multicultural and Indigenous Affairs* (2005) 79 AJR 1142 (Aus HC).

[19] *SZATV v Minister for Immigration and Citizenship* (2007) 233 CLR 18.

[20] *Appellant S395/2002 v Minister for Immigration* (2003) 216 CLR 473 at [71].

[21] *Refugee Appeal No 74665/03* [2005] INLR 68.

is on the fact that refugee status cannot be denied to a person who on return would forfeit a fundamental human right in order to avoid persecution. As I noted in my judgment, in agreement with Lord Rodger, the attraction of this approach is that it gives due weight to the fact that the Convention must be interpreted

> in accordance with its broad humanitarian objective and having regard to the principles, expressed in the preamble, that human beings should enjoy fundamental rights and freedoms without discrimination and that refugees should enjoy the widest possible exercise of these rights and freedoms.[22]

It can, therefore, be seen that the Supreme Court drew heavily on Commonwealth jurisprudence in determining a difficult question of interpretation which had not been considered at the highest level in the UK courts. In rejecting the reasonable tolerability test which had been proposed by the Secretary of State and accepted by the Court of Appeal, I noted that this test had found no support in other jurisprudence. This was important 'in view of the implicit rejection of it in a number of other jurisdictions, including at least Australia and New Zealand' and 'the fact that it was desirable as far as possible that there should be international consensus on the meaning of the Convention'. Attempting to achieve international consensus is perhaps a more realistic ambition for domestic courts than striving to find the single autonomous meaning of the Convention which, as we have seen, was the goal set by the House of Lords in *Adan*.

The question that arose in *RT (Zimbabwe)* was: is it an answer to a refugee claim by an individual who has no political views and who therefore does not support the persecutory regime in his home country to say that he would lie and simulate loyalty to that regime in order to avoid the persecutory ill-treatment to which he would otherwise be subjected?

RT and KM had no political views. They neither supported nor opposed the Zimbabwean regime. But anyone who was unable to demonstrate loyalty to the regime was at risk of persecution. Their case was that they had a well-founded fear that they would be persecuted, because they would lie and pretend to support the regime solely in order to avoid the persecution that they would suffer if they did not demonstrate their loyalty to the regime. In other words, this was a case analogous to *HJ (Iran)*.

---

[22] *Appellant S395/2002 v Minister for Immigration* (2003) 216 CLR 473 at [113].

There was no doubt that the *HJ (Iran)* principle applies to any person who does have political beliefs and who would be obliged to (and would) conceal them to avoid the persecution that he would suffer if he were to reveal them. The central question was whether the right to hold *no* political beliefs (and say so) attracts Convention protection as much as the right to hold and express political beliefs. The starting point for the analysis was the emphasis placed by the Convention on human rights. The court agreed with the important principle (a point made in the New Zealand authorities by reference to the preamble to the Convention) that human beings shall enjoy fundamental rights and freedoms without discrimination. We noted that this was reflected in European Union legislation, and that the right to freedom of thought, opinion and expression recognised in international and European human rights law protects non-believers as well as believers, and extends to the freedom *not* to hold beliefs as well as to hold them and the freedom *not* to express opinion as well as to express them.[23] The same principled approach had been taken in jurisprudence drawn from the United States and from South Africa.[24]

The Supreme Court referred to Justice Jackson's judgment in *West Virginia State Board of Education v Barnette:*

> If there is any fixed star in our constitutional constellation, it is that no official, high or petty, can prescribe what shall be orthodox in politics, nationalism, religion, or other matters of opinion or force citizens to confess by word or act their faith therein. If there are any circumstances which permit an exception, they do not now occur to us.[25]

This celebrated statement may well have been inspired first by the Mayflower Compact, which foreshadowed the United States' Constitution, and secondly by the fundamental rights expressed in the US Bill of Rights which reflected some of the enduring values enshrined in Magna Carta.

The court also referred to the South African Constitutional Court decision in *Christian Education South Africa v Minister of Education*, where Sachs J said:

> There can be no doubt that the right to freedom of religion, belief and opinion in the open and democratic society contemplated by the Constitution is important. The right to believe or not to believe, and to act or

---

[23] [2012] UKSC 39, [2013] 1 AC 152 at [29]ff.
[24] [2012] UKSC 39, [2013] 1 AC 152 at [37]ff.
[25] *West Virginia State Board of Education v Barnette* (1943) 319 US 624, 642.

not to act according to his or her beliefs or non-beliefs, is one of the key ingredients of any person's dignity.[26]

The various authorities pointed in one direction: the same as that identified in *HJ (Iran)*. As I explained:

> ... the right not to hold the protected beliefs is a fundamental right which is recognised in international and human rights law and ... the Convention too ... Nobody should be forced to have or express a political opinion in which he does not believe. He should not be required to dissemble on pain of persecution. Refugee law does not require a person to express false support for an oppressive regime, any more than it requires an agnostic to pretend to be a religious believer in order to avoid persecution. A focus on how important the right not to hold a political or religious belief is to the applicant is wrong in principle ...

> As regards the point of principle, it is the badge of a truly democratic society that individuals should be free not to hold opinions. They should not be required to hold any particular religious or political beliefs. This is as important as the freedom to hold and (within certain defined limits) to express such beliefs as they do hold. One of the hallmarks of totalitarian regimes is their insistence on controlling people's thoughts as well as their behaviour. George Orwell captured the point brilliantly by his creation of the sinister 'Thought Police' in his novel *1984*.[27]

So *RT (Zimbabwe)* is another example of a case where our court has reached a decision heavily influenced by foreign jurisprudence. It is not at all surprising that it should do this when interpreting an international treaty. The provisions of the treaty have an autonomous and, strictly speaking, single meaning. It is undesirable that national courts of parties to the Convention should produce different interpretations of the same provisions. If there is a more or less consistent interpretation by the domestic courts of other signatory states of a provision of the Refugee Convention, then our court should be very slow to depart from it.

This is not a satisfactory state of affairs. The situation exposed in *Adan* was regrettable. There ought to be an international court whose decisions on questions of interpretation are binding on the signatory states. Meanwhile, it is to be hoped that courts will apply the interpretation that commands majority, if not universal, support.

I would like to conclude this lecture by making some observations about the globalisation of our common law. Our judges are not

---

[26]   (2000) 9 BHRC 53 at [36].
[27]   ibid at [42]–[43].

bound to follow the jurisprudence of the courts of other common law systems. But there is a growing interest in the extent to which the jurisprudence of other common law courts should influence the development of the common law here.

There is nothing new in the idea of our common law being influenced by the law of other jurisdictions. Lord Denning said that advocates ought to draw the court's attention to relevant commonwealth authorities just as they would authorities from England and Wales.[28] This was not a novel idea. Take the phrase 'an Englishman's home is his castle'. It gives expression to the long-established principle that the State cannot enter or deprive someone of his property without either consent or lawful authority. The phrase originated in a case called *Semayne's Case* in 1604.[29] The ratio of the decision was that, although the King's Sheriff could break and enter a property with valid lawful authority to do so, he had first to knock and seek consent to enter. In the course of the proceedings, Sir Edward Coke, who was Attorney-General at the time, said: 'the house of every one is to him as his castle and fortress, as well for his defence against injury and violence as for his repose.' It might be thought that Coke was relying on the famous provision in Magna Carta that no one should be disseised without due process of law. He was well versed in Magna Carta. In fact, the origin of the phrase that he used was far more ancient. The idea came from Roman law, specifically *Gaius's Commentaries on the Twelve Tables*.[30]

Coke was not alone in borrowing from Roman law. Such borrowings were relatively frequent in the formative years of the common law both as regards substantive law[31] and procedure.[32] Equity, the great product of the medieval period, owed much to Europe. Coke's successor as Chief Justice, Lord Mansfield, is famous for having drawn inspiration from Roman law, from mercantile law, and from European jurists, as has been most recently demonstrated by Norman Poser in his excellent biography of Mansfield's life

---

[28] Lord Denning MR cited in *The Supreme Court Practice 1999*, vol 1 (Sweet & Maxwell, 1999) at 1480.

[29] *Semayne's Case* (1604) 5 Coke Rep 91.

[30] J Frank, 'Civil Law Influences on the Common Law—Some Reflections on "Comparative" and "Contrastive" Law' (1955–1956) 104 *University of Pennsylvania Law Review* 887 at 888.

[31] E Re, 'The Roman Contribution to the Common Law' (1961) 29 *Fordham Law Review* 447 at 470.

[32] P Vinogradoff, 'Reason and Conscience in Sixteenth-Century Jurisprudence' (1908) 24 *Law Quarterly Review* 373.

and career.[33] These foreign influences did not come to an end with Mansfield. A more recent example is to be found in the 1984 judgment of Lord Diplock in *Council of Civil Service Unions v Minister for the Civil Service*.[34] This case concerned the question whether civil servants working at GCHQ could lawfully be banned from joining a trade union. The basis of the ban was said to be national security. In the course of his judgment in the House of Lords, Lord Diplock adverted to the 'principle of proportionality'. This is a concept that is well-established in our law today. But it was not so at that time. Lord Diplock presciently said that English law might adopt the principle at some time in the future. He noted that it was recognised in the administrative law of several of our fellow members of the European Economic Community.[35] Since then, under the influence of EU law and the European Convention on Human Rights, the principle has gradually assumed a central position in our law.

In 1962 in *Smith v Leech Brain & Co Ltd* Lord Parker LCJ said that 'it is important that the common law, and the development of the common law, should be homogeneous in the various sections of the Commonwealth.'[36] A good example of a common law decision by a foreign court influencing our law is *Bazley v Curr*,[37] a decision of the Canadian Supreme Court. The issue that arose in *Lister v Hesley Hall*[38] was whether the owners of a boarding house were vicariously liable for the sexual abuse of its residents committed by the warden it had employed. The Court of Appeal had followed a previous English authority and held that the warden's acts could not be regarded as an unauthorised mode of carrying out his authorised duties. His employer was, therefore, not vicariously liable for them. The previous authority was criticised in the Canadian case. The House of Lords in *Lister* agreed. Lord Steyn said that he had been 'greatly assisted by the luminous and illuminating judgments of the Canadian Supreme Court in Bazley'. He said that wherever such problems are considered in the future in the common law world these judgments will be the starting point. The new test was to ask whether the employee's torts were so closely connected with

---

[33] N Poser, *Lord Mansfield: Justice in the Age of Reason* (McGill, 2013).

[34] *Council of Civil Service Unions v Minister for the Civil Service* [1985] AC 374 (HL).

[35] ibid at 410, discussed in J Laws, *The Common Law Constitution* (Cambridge University Press, 2014) 60–61.

[36] *Smith v Leech Brain & Co Ltd* [1962] 2 QB 405 at 415 (QBD).

[37] *Bazley v Curr* 174 DLR (4th) 45.

[38] *Lister v Hesley Hall Ltd* [2001] UKHL 22, [2002] 1 AC 215.

his employment that it would be fair and just to hold the employers vicariously liable. This test has now taken root here. It might not have done so but for the compelling reasoning of the judgments in the Canadian decision.

More recently in *FHR European Ventures LLP v Cedar Capital Partners LLC*, having considered decisions from, for example, Australia, Lord Neuberger noted that, while it was inevitable that the common law would develop in different ways in different common law jurisdictions, it remained 'highly desirable for all those jurisdictions to learn from each other, and at least to lean in favour of harmonising the development of the common law round the world.'[39]

We are living in an increasingly interdependent world. Jurists read each other's judgments with ease on the internet. They meet at international conferences to discuss issues of common interest. The good sense of learning from each other and taking the best that each of us has to offer is now well appreciated. And this is not limited to influencing the development of the common law. In the field of civil procedure, we have borrowed ideas relating to the proper management of expert evidence from Australia and New Zealand. And we have exported to them the principle of proportionality in the conduct of civil litigation. And influences are not limited to common law jurisdictions. Thus, for example, changes to our procedural law here have influenced reform in Norway. In the late 1990s we introduced a process whereby the court, rather than litigants, were responsible for the management of litigation. The Norwegian Dispute Act of 2005 adopted that very approach. They drew their inspiration from our reforms.

There are many other examples of such influences and effects. Many more than I can give this evening. What I hope I have done however is to give a flavour of the relationship between national laws and how national jurisdictions can and have influenced each other.

CONCLUSION

More than 60 years after the Refugee Convention was signed, it continues to give rise to difficult questions of interpretation. In the

---

[39] *FHR European Ventures LLP v Makarious* [2014] UKSC 45, [2015] AC 250 at [45].

absence of a final international court dedicated to giving authoritative decisions on these questions, the courts of the signatories have to do their best to resolve them. As I have shown, they learn from and influence each other. In many areas, a common understanding of the meaning of the principal provisions has been reached. It is to be hoped that in the same way a common understanding of problems not yet resolved will emerge in the future.

As regards the development of the common law, we have seen that our courts are open to the influence of other jurisdictions. This does not mean that we slavishly adopt or follow the decisions of those jurisdictions. We scrutinise and analyse their decisions in the light of our own experience, culture and social and economic conditions. As has been said, 'the common law's genius' is the ability to '(refine) principle over time'.[40] We continue to do so in the light of decisions and developments from abroad, and we continue to influence those developments.

---

[40] Laws, *The Common Law Constitution* 9.

10

*Recent Developments in Commercial Law Conference**

I T IS A great pleasure to be here in my home City to take part in this important conference. I went to Leeds Grammar School, which was just up the road. This university acquired the site some years ago. It now has its magnificent Law School building on the site of the school swimming pool. Two years ago, I was honoured with an honorary LLD here. This was a great moment in my professional career. I rarely refuse an invitation to come back to give a lecture or take part in some other event in Leeds. And when Professor Roger Halson invited me to speak and chair an event today, I had no hesitation in accepting. Sadly, such are the pressures on a Master of the Rolls these days that I could not afford the time to be here for the whole conference, much though I would have liked to do so.

I was asked to say a few words about the nature of the office, although it does not have a great deal to do with the subject-matter of the conference. I am very happy to do this, because our Chinese visitors may find it interesting. But the mysteries of what the Master of the Rolls does are such that any lifting of the curtain seems to be of interest even to law students and lawyers (not to mention the interested layman).

Today, the Master of the Rolls is President of the Court of Appeal of England and Wales and Head of Civil Justice for England and Wales. He is the second most senior judge in England and Wales (after the Lord Chief Justice) and assists him in the running of the justice system in our country. As President of the Court of Appeal, he is responsible for the running of the Civil Division of that court. He decides many of the most important civil cases that are heard by that court. Some of the decisions of the court are appealed to the Supreme Court, but not many.

* Opening Address, University of Leeds, 14 March 2016.

I have many other responsibilities. I chair the Advisory Council which advises the government on public records and archives. Most public records are disclosed to the public after 30 years (now coming down to 20 years). The major task of the Advisory Council is to advise whether to accept requests to keep from public view documents that it would not be in the public interest to disclose. We see, for example, the delightfully uninhibited terms in which the members of the Foreign Office have reported on the personal shortcomings of foreign leaders. Documents which it is thought would be likely to damage foreign relations are on the whole kept from public view until it is thought that their disclosure is no longer likely to cause damage.

I chair the Magna Carta Trust which is charged with the responsibility of promoting the principles of Magna Carta. Last year was a particularly busy year because it was the 800th anniversary of the sealing of Magna Carta. There were many lectures to give and events to attend.

This is the first academic conference held by the China-Britain Joint Research Centre on Commercial Law. I am sure that this will be extremely successful. Co-operation of this kind between our two countries and the exchange of ideas that such conferences generate will, I suggest, help us to learn from each other and improve our approaches to how we should address legal issues. The ever increasing growth of globalisation means that commercial law is perhaps the one area where, above all, such co-operation, and cross-fertilisation, is as desirable as it is necessary. The Joint Research Centre will undoubtedly be at the forefront of such developments.

One of my famous predecessors as Master of the Rolls, Lord Denning, said in 1975 that 'equity (was) not past the age of child bearing'.[1] He was not the first to say so. He may well have borrowed the statement from Mr Justice Harman, who in turn may have borrowed it from Lord Mansfield. The point he was making was simple: equity remained as potentially vibrant a source of legal innovation in 1975 as it had been in its earliest days. There may be less scope or need for innovation in some areas of our law today. That is only to be expected given the maturity of our laws and the growth in modern statute law.

But the common law, commercial law and our approaches to dispute resolution, both in England and Wales and internationally,

---

[1] *Eves v Eves* [1975] 1 WLR 1338 (CA); and see R Evershed MR, 'Equity is not to be presumed to be past the age of child-bearing' (1953–1955) 1 *Sydney Law Review* 1, fn 1.

are all areas where innovation not only remains possible, but is in some ways increasingly necessary. As Mr Justice Blair, the judge in charge of our Commercial Court, noted in a lecture recently, while there are coherent sets of rules governing trade and shipping, such rules have 'yet to emerge' in terms of finance.[2] I think that the Joint Research Centre may have a positive role to play here.

The creation of new rules is the most striking way in which Lord Denning's observation remains of relevance today. Just as importantly, and more subtly, it remains of relevance through the willingness of our courts to develop and adapt the common law in the light of changing social and commercial conditions. For example, in *Jones v Kaney*[3] in 2011, a long-established rule which gave experts immunity from claims by their own clients was abolished by our Supreme Court. Earlier this year, the court changed the criminal law relating to joint enterprise.[4]

In *Woolwich Equitable Building Society v Inland Revenue Commissioners*,[5] the House of Lords set aside the view, generally understood to be the case for two centuries, that there was no right of recovery in restitution of money paid pursuant to an ultra vires demand by a public authority. In *Re Spectrum Plus Ltd*,[6] the House of Lords corrected the law concerning floating charges; a law that had stood—albeit on the basis of a first instance decision—for 25 years.[7] There are other such examples of changes in the common law achieved by court decision rather than legislation.

The willingness of our courts to develop our commercial law is fundamental to its continuing utility, both nationally and internationally. The international plane is of huge importance to us. As was emphasised by Mr Justice Blair in the lecture I referred to a moment ago, 'in the international context, most commercial and

---

[2] W Blair, 'Contemporary Trends in the Resolution of International Commercial and Financial Disputes' (21 January 2016) at 3: 'It is probably true to say that a coherent set of rules governing finance in the same way as applies to trade and shipping has yet to emerge. A significant difference between the sectors is relatively recent in the form of the growing amount of financial regulation. This tends to spill over into private law—anti-money laundering regulations are an example. But more coherence is both possible and necessary, and the courts have a part to play in this', available at www.judiciary.gov. uk/wp-content/uploads/2016/01/blair-durham-iccl-lecture-2016.pdf.

[3] *Jones v Kaney* [2011] UKSC 13, [2011] 2 AC 398.

[4] *R v Jogee and Ruddock v The Queen (Jamaica)* [2016] UKSC 8, [2017] AC 387.

[5] *Woolwich Equitable Building Society v Inland Revenue Commissioners* [1993] AC 70 (HL).

[6] *Re Spectrum Plus Ltd* [2005] 2 AC 680 (HL).

[7] See *Siebe Gorman & Co Ltd v Barclays Bank Ltd* [1979] 2 Lloyd's Rep 142 (ChD).

financial contracts have an express choice of law clause. In many cases, English law continues to provide a suitable vehicle.'[8]

He went on to say that it is of real importance that our courts, appellate and first instance, continue to 'expound the governing principles' of our commercial law. Two recent examples of our contract law being developed by the courts will feature prominently in the discussions at this conference. I refer, of course, to *Cavendish Square Holdings v Makdessi*,[9] on penalty clauses, and *Arnold v Britton*,[10] on contractual interpretation.

Cavendish is a clear example of the courts' willingness to innovate in the field of contract law; to reconsider established principles in changed times. For the first time in over a hundred years, our highest court considered the principles that underpin the law concerning contractual penalty clauses. Some have, perhaps mischievously, queried whether it was worth the wait.[11] No doubt answers to this question will be offered during your discussions today.

The decision raises a number of issues, which I think are relevant to your discussions and the development of the law in the light of increasing globalisation. Let me take one. It concerns the Supreme Court's refusal to abolish the penalty rule. This was despite the fact that, as Lords Neuberger and Sumption noted, if asked to create such a rule today it was unlikely that the courts would do so.[12] Their reasons for retention of the rule were, first, that it was common to 'almost all major systems of law, at least in the western world'. Secondly, that it was also included in such international texts as the *Unidroit Principles of International Commercial Contracts* (2010).[13] Thirdly, it was a rule that had formed part of the common law for 300 years, and it was not for the courts to set it aside. More positively, the rule was consistent with a more general equitable approach by which, through the application of well-established principles, the harshness of the common law was softened. And finally, its anomalies could be cured through a restatement of the law.[14]

I noted a moment ago that the long-established immunity of expert witnesses to claims by their clients was abolished by the Supreme

---

[8] Blair 'Contemporary Trends in the Resolution of International Commercial and Financial Disputes' 5.

[9] *Cavendish Square Holdings BV v Talal El Makdessi* [2015] UKSC 67, [2015] 3 WLR 1373.

[10] *Arnold v Britton* [2015] UKSC 36, [2015] AC 1619.

[11] See, for instance, R Ansell QC, 'Contract Law—2015 Highlights' (TECBAR Annual Conference, 2016).

[12] *Cavendish Square Holdings* at [36].

[13] ibid at [37].

[14] *Cavendish Square Holdings* at [39].

Court. The longevity of the rule did not save it. The Supreme Court was able to point to other common law jurisdictions which had already abolished the rule.[15] Perhaps the first jurisdiction to abolish the immunity felt some reticence about doing so. Nevertheless, following an examination of the relevant policy arguments, it concluded that abolition was justified.

Since the Supreme Court in *Cavendish* acknowledged that the penalty rule was not universally accepted, and some major jurisdictions did not adopt it, might its consideration have benefited from detailed analysis of those other systems, their alternatives to the penalty rule, and the rationale they rely upon to explain the different approach they take? It may be that the alternatives are more appropriate than the penalty rule, even as now reformulated. There is much to be said for comparative law and for developing our law taking what we consider to be the best that other systems have to offer.

Arnold v Britton raises similar issues. It is well-known that the common law's approach to contractual interpretation has waxed and waned. Since the early 1970s the courts have approached it with what might be said to be increasing emphasis on the importance of commercial common sense. From *Prenn v Simmonds*,[16] to Lord Hoffmann's famous statement of principle in *ICS v West Bromwich Building Society*,[17] to *Rainy Sky SA v Kookin Bank*,[18] that has been the distinct direction of travel.

Concerns have been expressed about this trend. Placing such weight on the more flexible, contextual approach has been said to increase uncertainty. It is trite to say that, in contracts, particularly commercial contracts, the need for certainty is usually of crucial importance to the parties. (There are, of course, times when parties want to avoid it.) Importantly, it might be said from the perspective of commercial common sense that there is a need for a certain degree of predictability in the approach that courts will take to contractual interpretation.

The obvious case in point to illustrate this problem is *Chartbrook Ltd v Persimmon Homes*.[19] Applying the contextual approach, Briggs J, at first instance, accepted one interpretation as correct. That interpretation was upheld by the majority in the Court of Appeal: Tuckey

---

[15] *Jones v Kaney* [2011] UKSC 13, [2011] 2 AC 398 at [80] per Lord Collins.

[16] *Prenn v Simmonds* [1971] 1 WLR 1381 (HL).

[17] *Investors' Compensation Scheme v West Bromwich Building Society* [1998] 1 WLR 896 (HL).

[18] *Rainy Sky SA v Kookin Bank* [2011] UKSC 50, [2011] 1 WLR 2900.

[19] *Chartbrook Ltd v Persimmon Homes Ltd* [2009] UKHL 38, [2009] 1 AC 1101.

and Rimer LJJ. Lawrence Collins LJ, dissenting, took another view. The House of Lords set aside the High Court and Court of Appeal's decision, favouring the interpretation Lawrence Collins LJ had held to be correct.

A critic might suggest that an interpretative approach by the courts that can lead to such divergence of view might be one that is a little too flexible, a little too unpredictable. They may take the view, as the courts in Singapore have done, that the contextual approach needs a little refinement. While its courts broadly adopted the approach set out in *IRC v West Bromwich Building Society*, in *Zurich Insurance (Singapore) Ltd v B-Gold Interior Design & Construction Pte Ltd*[20] they introduced a number of additional criteria into the interpretative exercise and emphasised that the traditional canons of interpretation continued to apply. This approach, while offering flexibility, did so within a framework that provided greater certainty than the English approach arguably provided.

By emphasising that commercial common sense enters the frame only where the drafting is unclear or ambiguous, the decision in *Arnold* places greater weight on the words the contract parties have used. The court should not go hunting for ambiguity in order to sidestep the natural meaning of the words used by the parties, and thereby consider which interpretation is the one that makes better commercial common sense. This approach marks an attempt to introduce the greater certainty into the *IRC* test, which Singapore had already attempted to do.

Again we can ask whether the Supreme Court may have benefited from a detailed analysis of the approach taken in Singapore, on how that approach had been applied in subsequent cases there. We could also ask what approaches to contractual interpretation are being adopted in other major legal systems.

Cavendish and *Arnold v Britton* are recent illustrations of how the courts remain open to the idea of refining the law, including in areas that have a significant impact on commerce and finance. I think that our courts (and I suggest other courts in developed legal systems) should take greater account of developments in, and approaches adopted by, other jurisdictions. Your conference today is a prime example of how we can facilitate that learning process, of how we can improve our law through sharing knowledge and insights drawn from differing systems and perspectives. We all gain from that, and I wish you every success.

---

[20] *Zurich Insurance (Singapore) Ltd v B-Gold Interior Design & Construction Pte Ltd* [2008] 3 SLR 1029.

11

The Contribution of Construction Cases to the Development of the Common Law[*]

INTRODUCTION

WHEN I CAME to the Bar in 1968, construction law was regarded as a rather dull, specialist subject, in some respects hardly worthy of being considered as proper law at all. It was all about boring Scott Schedules and claims for damages for defects and disruption and delay claims, otherwise known in the trade as 'buggeration claims'. It was thought of as being all fact and no law. The judges who tried these cases were not called judges at all. They bore the strange title of 'Official Referees'. Although the cases often involved very large sums of money (well in excess of the county court jurisdiction), these judges were not High Court Judges. After the 1971 reforms, they were senior circuit judges. Before that I believe that they were sui generis. They were addressed as 'your honour', not 'my lord'. It is true that the courts in which they sat were in the Royal Courts of Justice. But Official Referees' cases appeared right at the bottom of the Daily Cause List, almost as if they were an afterthought. And you needed an experienced orienteer to find the courts. You took a rickety lift up to the top floor of the West Block of the RCJ and then walked down a long corridor until you arrived at the courts. Hence the name 'the Official Referees' Corridor'.

The first edition of *Hudson Building and Engineering Contracts* was published as long ago as in 1891. But I do not think that it was perceived as a serious specialist area of the law by many people until after World War II. The first edition of *Keating's Building Contracts*

[*] Keating Lecture 2015, 25 March 2015, Assembly Hall, Church House Conference Centre. Reprinted with the kind permission of Keating Chambers.

was not published until 1955. I was in chambers with Donald from 1969 until 1986. He led me many times. His contribution to the development of construction law is well known. I regret that I never asked him why he became interested in the subject. Like me, he started at the Bar doing a bit of this and a bit of that.

The integration of construction law into the mainstream has taken place gradually during my professional life. First, the Official Referees emerged from their lair in the Corridor and moved to St Dunstan's House, Fetter Lane. This was not a wonderful building, but it was important that it was also occupied by the Commercial Court. Next, the name of the court was changed in 1998 to the Technology and Construction Court and Official Referees were given the accolade of the title of 'judge' and were now to be addressed as 'my Lord'. The growing recognition of the court culminated in their inclusion (with the judges of the Commercial Court and the Chancery Division) in the judges who moved to the Rolls Building. The TCC judges in the Rolls Building were now exclusively High Court Judges.

Following the changes in 1998, His Honour Judge Bowsher QC, appointed as an Official Referee in 1987 and a distinguished member of the court, commented:

> The official referees no longer cry in the wilderness: they have been anointed if not priests at least deacons of the established church as judges of the Technology and Construction Court ...[1]

It may have been apt in 2000 to describe the TCC judges as deacons of the established church. I do not think it is apt to so describe them today. They are fully fledged priests, taking their stand alongside the judges of the Commercial Court and the Chancery Division. Construction law has come in from the cold. TCC judges decide important issues of law which are of general application. These include difficult questions of contract, tort, limitation, restitution and damages—indeed the whole gamut of law.

I shall seek to dispel the idea that construction cases are somehow different and apart from the general law and that they only concern Scott Schedules, lists of defects and delay claims. On the contrary, I hope to demonstrate the wide range of issues that arise in construction cases as in any other area of the law and mention a few of

---

[1] HHJ Bowsher QC, 'The Technology and Construction Court before and after the Woolf civil procedure reforms' (2000) 3(1) *International Arbitration Law Review* 19.

the many important cases in the construction field that have found their way into the general law reports.

FORMATION OF CONTRACT

Like Julie Andrews in the Sound of Music, I shall start at the very beginning: formation of contract. It should not be overlooked that, in its essentials, a construction contract is no different from any other contract. It should, therefore, come as no surprise that the principles which determine whether a construction contract has been created are no different from those that govern the formation of any other type of contract.

An issue that commonly arises in construction cases, as in contract cases more generally, is the question of whether a contract was formed at all. Construction contracts more than many tend to be complex and detailed. Negotiations can drag on interminably. Work often starts before all the details have been sorted out. This may be done pursuant to a letter of intent which states that there is an intention to enter into contractual negotiations; or pursuant to an agreement which is said to be 'subject to contract'. Sometimes, work starts pursuant to authority for work to be carried out up to a specified limit. Difficult issues may arise as to whether and, if so on what terms a contract has been created where the project proceeds without formal documentation being drawn up and a dispute arises mid-way through performance.

In 1974 I appeared before Lord Denning MR, Lord Diplock and Lord Justice Lawton in *Courtney and Fairbairn Ltd v Tolaini Bros (Hotels) Ltd*.[2]

Developers had approached my client, a contractor, seeking an introduction to a financier to fund a project in Hertfordshire. The contractor wrote to the developer stating it was prepared to make such an introduction but asked whether, if the introduction led to a financial arrangement, the developer would negotiate fair and reasonable sums with the contractor for the construction works based on agreed estimates of net cost and overheads with a margin for profit of 5 per cent. The developer wrote agreeing to the contractor's proposal, the contractor introduced the developer to the financier and

---

[2] *Courtney and Fairbairn Ltd v Tolaini Bros (Hotels) Ltd* [1975] 1 WLR 297 (CA).

the developer obtained the financial backing it needed for the development. However, after failing to agree on the cost of the construction works, the developer engaged other contractors. The contractor claimed its letter and the developer's response gave rise to a binding and enforceable contract.

Overturning the trial judge's conclusion that a contract had been formed by the letters, Lord Denning MR, who gave the lead judgment, pointed to a lack of agreement on the price or any method by which the price was to be calculated;[3] an agreement to 'negotiate' fair and reasonable contract sums based on estimates that were yet to be agreed could not be enforced by the court.

In a statement that is of universal application to the general law of contract, Lord Denning MR commented that the price:

> ... is so essential a term that there is no contract unless a price is agreed or there is an agreed method of ascertaining it, not dependent on the negotiations of the two parties themselves ...[4]

On a question of which there was scant authority at the time, Lord Denning MR dismissed the suggestion, and the tentative opinion by Lord Wright some 40 years earlier in *Hillas & Co Ltd v Arcos Ltd*,[5] that alternatively there was an enforceable contract to negotiate. He stated:

> If the law does not recognise a contract to enter into a contract ... it seems to me it cannot recognise a contract to negotiate. The reason is because it is too uncertain to have any binding force. No court could estimate the damages because no one can tell whether the negotiations would be successful or would fall through: or, if successful, what the result would be.

Lord Diplock said 'the dictum of Lord Wright ... for it is no more ... although an attractive theory, should in my view be regarded as bad law'. I recall this case well after 40 years. The combination of Lord Denning and Lord Diplock was fairly terrifying for a young barrister. They dispatched my appeal in a couple of hours by ex tempore judgments. Lord Diplock's was particularly withering. And I lost a case which Donald Keating had won at first instance.

The fact that this was a construction case was irrelevant. The important point is that it was undoubtedly a case of general

---

[3] At 300H.
[4] At 301B–C.
[5] *Hillas & Co Ltd v Arcos Ltd* (1932) 147 LT 503 at 515 (HL).

significance for the general law of contract. The holding that an agreement to negotiate cannot constitute a legally enforceable contract was applied in a number of first instance decisions.[6] It was ultimately approved by the House of Lords in *Walford v Miles*.[7] Whilst *Walford v Miles* is undoubtedly the better-known case on the topic, the issue and reasoning had arisen some time before in a construction dispute.

A question which often arises in commercial disputes where parties have started to perform before a formal contract has been executed is whether they have entered into contractual relations at all. Quite often A starts work pursuant to a letter of intent from B. It is by no means uncommon, for example, if things go awry for A to walk away. In that situation (where allegations of repudiation tend to abound) it is crucial to determine whether the parties made a contract and if so on what terms. This problem often occurs in the world of building and engineering disputes. The inherently complex nature of building and engineering projects is such that the problem is particularly likely occur in relation to them.

The applicable principles are now well known. They have been stated in a number of leading cases, many of which have been construction cases. A now fairly elderly authority is the construction case of *Atomic Power Construction v Trollope and Colls*.[8] Megaw J said that the defendant had to establish 'not only that the parties were ad idem on all terms which they then regarded as being requisite for a contract, but also that they had not omitted to agree any term which was, in law, essential to be agreed in order to make the contract commercially workable'. I think today's judges could strive a little harder to emulate this commendably succinct statement of the relevant principles. These were also helpfully summarised by Lloyd LJ in the Court of Appeal in *Pagnan SPA v Feed Products Ltd*,[9] which was cited with approval by the Supreme Court in the

---

[6] *Albion Sugar Co Ltd v Williams Tankers Ltd and Davies, The John S Darbyshire* [1977] 2 Lloyd's Rep 457 (QBD); *Scandinavian Trading Tanker Co AB v Flota Petrolera Ecuatoriana, The Scaptrade* [1981] 2 Lloyd's Rep 425 (QBD); *Trees Ltd v Cripps* (1983) 267 EG 596 (ChD); *Nile Co for the Export of Agricultural Crops v H & J M Bennett (Commodities) Ltd* [1986] 1 Lloyd's Rep 555 (QBD); *Voest Alpine Intertrading GmbH v Chevron International Oil Co Ltd* [1987] 2 Lloyd's Rep 547 (QBD); and *Star Steamship Society v Beogradska Plovidba, The Junior K* [1988] 2 Lloyd's Rep 583 (QBD).
[7] *Walford v Miles* [1992] 2 AC 128 (HL).
[8] *Atomic Power Construction v Trollope and Colls* [1963] 1 WLR 333 (QBD).
[9] *Pagnan SPA v Feed Products Ltd* [1987] 2 Lloyd's Rep 601 at 619 (CA).

construction case of *RTS Flexible Systems Ltd v Molkerei Alois Muller GmbH & Co KG*.[10]

RTS is a typical case of its kind. The claimant negotiated with the defendant, a dairy product supplier, to design and install two production lines in one of the defendant's factories. The defendant sent the claimant a letter of intent setting out a draft contract providing the price, completion date and standard terms. It was common ground that by the letter of intent the parties formed a limited contract to enable work to commence but agreement was subject to a formal contract being concluded and would come to an end after four weeks. The parties did not sign or execute the contract and yet proceeded with the project. During the project the parties renegotiated the proposed terms. Following completion of the work, after the claimant had received 70 per cent of the price set out in the letter of intent, a dispute arose as to whether the equipment supplied by the claimant complied with the agreed specification. The claimant sought the remaining sums from the defendant. In such circumstances the court considered, as a preliminary issue, on what basis a contract had arisen and on what terms.

As Lord Clarke expressly noted, the relevant principles for determining whether a contract has been formed in such circumstances apply to all contracts, including construction contracts.[11]

Inevitably, the application of those principles is highly fact specific. Here, like in *Courtney & Fairbairn*, whether the parties had reached agreement on the price was highly influential in determining whether a contract had been concluded at all. Lord Clarke adopted the price as a form of yardstick commenting:

> We agree with the judge that it is unrealistic to suppose that the parties did not intend to create legal relations. This can be tested by asking whether the price of £1,682,000 was agreed. Both parties accept that it was. If it was, as we see it, it must have formed part of a contract between the parties. Moreover, once it is accepted (as both parties now accept) that the LOI contract expired and was not revived, the contract containing the price must be contained in some agreement other than the LOI contract. If the price is to be a term binding on the parties, it cannot, at any rate on conventional principles, be a case of no contract …[12]

---

[10] *RTS Flexible Systems Ltd v Molkerei Alois Muller GmbH & Co KG* [2010] UKSC 14, [2010] 1 WLR 753.
[11] At [48].
[12] At [58].

I agree that, if the parties have not agreed the price (or a mechanism for determining the price), it is difficult to see how there can be a binding contract between them. But of course the corollary does not follow. There may be other essential terms without whose agreement there is no contract. The important point for present purposes, however, is that construction law cases have made a significant contribution to the development of this area of contract law.

IMPLIED TERMS

Construction cases have also made a considerable contribution to the law of implied terms. I wish to briefly mention two: *Young and Marten v McManus Childs Ltd*[13] and *Trollope & Colls Ltd v North West Metropolitan Regional Hospital Board.*[14]

The facts in *Young & Marten* were that a contractor required subcontractors to use specified roofing tiles that could only be obtained from one manufacturer. Owing to faulty manufacture, the tiles had a latent defect that made them liable to break in frosty weather. The owners of a number of houses successfully sued the builders for the cost of reroofing; and the builders (McManus Childs) claimed an indemnity by way of damages from the roofing subcontractors (Young & Marten). The claim was heard by an experienced Official Referee, HHJ Norman Richards QC. The case eventually went to the House of Lords.

Lord Reid said that there was not very much authority on the matter, so that it may be well first to consider it from first principles. He started by saying that no warranty ought to be implied in a contract unless it is in all the circumstances reasonable. Here we see straightaway at work the hand of one of the greatest masters of the common law of the twentieth century. He said that there were good reasons for implying a warranty against latent defects unless it was excluded by the terms of the contract. These were that, if the contractor's employer suffers loss by reason of the emergence of a latent defect, he will generally have no redress if he cannot recover damages from the contractor. But if he can recover damages, the

---

[13] *Young and Marten v McManus Childs Ltd* [1969] 1 AC 454 (HL).
[14] *Trollope & Colls Ltd v North West Metropolitan Regional Hospital Board* [1973] 1 WLR 601 (HL).

contractor will generally not have to bear the loss: he will have bought the defective material from a seller who will be liable under the law of sale of goods because the material was not of merchantable quality.

So far so good. But the particular problem in this case was that the tiles that had been specified were only made by one manufacturer. The contractor had to buy them from him or from someone who bought from him. Did that make any difference? The House held that, whist the sub-contractors did not warrant that the tiles were fit for purpose, the fact that the tiles had been specified by the contractor did not exclude the ordinary implied warranty of quality on the part of the sub-contractors. This was on the basis that the sub-contractor could claim against the manufacturer of the tiles creating a 'chain of liability from the employer who suffers the damage back to the author of the defect'.[15]

Of wider application, Lord Reid reasoned that where both the contractor and sub-contractor knew at the time when the contract was made that the sole manufacturer of the materials would only sell on terms excluding the warranty of quality, it would be unreasonable to make the sub-contractor liable for latent defects and such a term would not be implied.[16] One can see that this decision was driven by policy considerations based on their Lordships' assessment of what was reasonable.

The reasoning in *Young & Marten* has been applied further afield. For example, in *Rutherfield v Seymour Pierce Ltd*[17] Coulson J rejected an employer's contention that it was not obliged to pay a bonus to an employee for the quarter before it dismissed him on the basis that it was an implied term that he still had to be employed on the date of payment. In addition to the need for a term to be necessary or obvious before it would be implied, Coulson J held, relying on *Young & Marten*:

> Although these authorities and many others demonstrate that the emphasis must be on the necessity of the term, and not merely reasonableness, a term will not be implied unless it is equitable and reasonable.[18]

---

[15] Per Lord Reid at 466E.
[16] Per Lord Reid at 467B–C.
[17] *Rutherfield v Seymour Pierce Ltd* [2010] EWHC 375 (QB), [2010] IRLR 606.
[18] At [17].

On the facts, in addition to the term being neither necessary nor obvious, Coulson J held that such a term was 'manifestly unreasonable' and so ought not to be implied.[19]

Whilst the idea that the concept of reasonableness is relevant to whether a term will be implied was well established,[20] it is perhaps no surprise that Coulson J, a former member of Keating Chambers, drew on the reasoning in a construction case to support his conclusion.

The second case I wish to mention, *Trollope & Colls Ltd*, is one in which two other well-known former members of Keating Chambers appeared, Donald Keating and Sir Anthony May. This is another important case in the development of the law on implied terms. It concerned whether a term could be implied into a building contract that the completion date for a third phase of a project should be read as amended by the addition of a particular extension of time to the first phase. If the terms of the contract were to be construed literally and no such term were to be implied, the period in which the third phase had to be completed would have been reduced from 30 to 16 weeks. Unusually, the contractors wanted the period to be reduced as the employer was unable to nominate any sub-contractor that was prepared to assume an obligation to complete in 16 weeks, with the result that a new contract would have to be made at prevailing rates that were considerably higher than at the time of the original contract.

Having set out what he found to be a conflict of judicial opinion, Lord Pearson said this:

> ... the court does not make a contract for the parties. The court will not even improve the contract which the parties have made for themselves, however desirable the improvement might be. The court's function is to interpret and apply the contract which the parties have made for themselves. If the express terms are perfectly clear and free from ambiguity, there is no choice to be made between different possible meanings: the clear terms must be applied even if the court thinks some other terms would have been more suitable. An unexpressed term can be implied if and only if the court finds that the parties must have intended the term to form part of their contract: it is not enough for the court to find that such a term would have been adopted by the parties as reasonable men if it

---

[19] At [22].
[20] See the authorities summarised in *Exxonmobil Sales and Supply Corp v Texaco Ltd, The Helene Knutsen* [2003] EWHC 1964 (Comm), [2004] 1 All ER (Comm) 435.

had been suggested to them: it must have been a term that went without stating, a term necessary to give business efficacy to the contract, a term which, though tacit, formed part of the contract which the parties made for themselves.[21]

It was this reasoning that was drawn on by Lord Hoffmann in the later case of *A-G of Belize v Belize Telecom Ltd.*[22] After citing *Trollope & Colls*, Lord Hoffmann said this:

The proposition that the implication of a term is an exercise in the construction of the instrument as a whole is not only a matter of logic (since a court has no power to alter what the instrument means) but also well supported by authority ...[23]

Drawing on *Trollope & Colls*, Lord Hoffmann concluded (in a passage that is commonly relied on by counsel):

It follows that in every case in which it is said that some provision ought to be implied in an instrument, the question for the court is whether such a provision would spell out in express words what the instrument, read against the relevant background would reasonably be understood to mean.[24]

I do not wish to suggest that *Trollope & Colls* caused a marked shift in the law of implied terms. But it did resolve a conflict of judicial opinion that had emerged on the question of whether, in deciding whether a term should be implied, the court decides according to what is fair and reasonable or according to what the parties must be taken to have agreed. It resolved it in favour of the latter approach. This is the approach that Lord Hoffmann supported emphatically. It is not surprising that he drew on *Trollope & Colls* in reaching his conclusion in the later case.

CONTRACTUAL INTERPRETATION

In this whistle-stop tour, I move to the hugely important topic of contractual interpretation. Contracts are the cornerstone of commercial life. In principle, construction contracts are no different from any other commercial contracts. It is extraordinary how many cases

---

[21] At 609.
[22] *A-G of Belize v Belize Telecom Ltd* [2009] UKPC 10, [2009] 1 WLR 1988 at para [19].
[23] At [19].
[24] At [20].

are still being reported in the law reports in the twenty-first century on how to interpret a contract. I cannot help thinking that the great Lord Mansfield, who was perhaps the founding father of modern commercial law, would have been disappointed and probably astounded too.

I shall single out for mention two important decisions of the House of Lords and the Supreme Court, both of which involved construction contracts. They are both well known, although not for the fact that they were construction cases. *Chartbrook Ltd v Persimmon Homes Ltd*[25] concerned a dispute about the proper interpretation of a pricing formula in a contract for the development of a mixed commercial and residential development. After a comprehensive review of the law Lord Hoffmann said:

> What is clear from these cases is that there is not, so to speak, a limit to the amount of red ink or verbal rearrangement or correction which the court is allowed. All that is required is that it should be clear that something has gone wrong with the language and it should be clear what a reasonable person would have understood the parties to have meant.[26]

This decision reflects the important trend that rectification and interpretation are simply different aspects of the single task of interpreting a contract in its context,[27] rather than discrete tests. The House of Lords was also invited to overrule the long-standing rule that pre-contract negotiations are inadmissible as an aid to the proper interpretation of the contract. The House held that there was no clearly established case for departing from this exclusionary rule despite the superficially attractive argument in favour of doing so. This is an important decision, because a head of steam had been building to get rid of the rule.

The second case is *Rainy Sky SA v Kookmin Bank*.[28] It may be said that this was not a construction case at all. In fact it was a shipbuilding contract case which was heard at first instance in the Commercial Court. In essence a shipbuilding contract is a construction contract. It is a contract for the supply of materials and carrying out of construction work. Construction disputes do not always relate to the physical construction of a building, bridge, railway,

---

[25] *Chartbrook Ltd v Persimmon Homes Ltd* [2009] UKHL 38, [2009] 1 AC 1101.
[26] At [25].
[27] See Lord Hoffmann at [23].
[28] *Rainy Sky SA v Kookmin Bank* [2011] UKSC 50, [2011] 1 WLR 2900.

ship or oil rig. They often arise from the financial and insurance arrangements that make the projects possible.

Rainy Sky was one such case. It concerned the interpretation of six bonds issued by the defendant bank under six shipbuilding contracts. Each contract required the builder to refund the buyer with the full amount of all advance payments made in the event of the builder's insolvency. The Supreme Court was asked to consider whether this obligation was covered by the bonds, and in particular to decide the proper interpretation of the obligation to pay 'all such sums due to you under the contract'. The buyers contended 'such sums' referred back to 'pre-delivery instalments' mentioned in the first line of the paragraph, meaning the builder's insolvency was covered. In contrast, the bank claimed 'such sums' referred back to the sums mentioned in the previous paragraph, which did not include sums paid prior to insolvency of the builder. The issue for the Supreme Court was the role to be played by business common sense in determining what the parties meant.

Lord Clarke stated:

> If there are two possible constructions, the court is entitled to prefer the construction which is consistent with business common sense and reject the other.[29]

He held that, since both constructions were arguable,[30] and although the buyers did not advance a good reason for the inclusion of the previous paragraph of the bonds,[31] the buyers' construction was to be preferred because it was consistent with the commercial purpose of the bonds.[32]

This provided confirmation of the general shift away from 'black letter law' to a more purposive approach to interpretation of contracts. It also provides a helpful steer for the court in circumstances where the arguments for both sides are very finely balanced.

DAMAGES

Finally on contract law, I shall mention briefly two decisions in construction cases which contain important statements about damages.

---

[29] At [21] and [23].
[30] See [31].
[31] See [34].
[32] At [45].

Many of you will be familiar with the case of *Sempra Metals Ltd v Inland Revenue Commissioners*,[33] which established, amongst other things, that interest can be awarded at common law as damages for losses caused by late payment of a debt and that such losses were subject to the principles governing all claims for damages for breach of contract. This was not a construction case. But perhaps you might be surprised to learn that the same principles had been considered and distilled some time before in the construction case of *Minter (FG) Ltd v Welsh Health Technical Services Organisation*.[34] Here a dispute arose as to the amount of direct loss and expense to which a contractor was entitled under a term of a construction contract due to delays for which the employer was responsible.

The Court of Appeal considered whether interest and finance charges fell within the proper interpretation of 'direct loss and expense'. In doing so it was necessary to grapple with the long-standing hostility of the common law to awards of interest.

Both Lord Justice Stephenson and Lord Justice Ackner concluded that, in the context of building contracts, interest and finance charges were properly characterised as falling within the first limb of *Hadley v Baxendale*[35] and therefore were 'direct'.[36] Lord Justice Ackner said:

> Building Contractors in the ordinary course of things, when they require capital to finance an operation, either have to pay charges for borrowing their capital, or if they use their own capital, lose the interest which it otherwise would have earned. Accordingly, where a variation requires the expenditure of capital, not only is the primary expense—the money actually expended by reason of the variation—the direct loss or expense but so also is the secondary expenditure, the amount paid for or lost by the obtaining or the use of such capital.
>
> …
>
> what the appellants here are seeking to claim, is not interest on a debt, but a debt which has as one of its constituent parts interest charges …[37]

---

[33] *Sempra Metals Ltd (formerly Metallgesellschaft Ltd) v Inland Revenue Commissioners* [2007] UKHL 34, [2008] 1 AC 561.

[34] *Minter (FG) Ltd v Welsh Health Technical Services Organisation* (1980) 13 BLR 1 (CA).

[35] *Hadley v Baxendale* (1854) 9 Ex 341 (Exch Ct).

[36] At 15–16 per Stephenson LJ; at 23 per Ackner LJ.

[37] At 23.

In *Sempra Metals*, Lord Hope drew on the case of *FG Minter*, concluding that the House of Lords:

> ... should hold that at common law, subject to the ordinary rules of remoteness which apply to all claims of damages, the loss suffered as a result of the late payment of money is recoverable. This is already the law where the claim is for a debt incurred by a building contractor to raise the necessary capital which has interest charges as one of its constituents: see *FG Minter Ltd v Welsh Health Technical Services Organisation* (1980) 13 BLR 1, 23, per Ackner LJ ...[38]

I would not, however, wish to overstate the importance of the *Minter* case. The House of Lords were in a mood to sweep away the old common law rule anyway. As Lord Nicholls put it, 'legal rules which are not soundly based resemble proverbial bad pennies: they turn up again and again'. The unsound rule for consideration concerned the negative attitude of English law to awards of compound interest on claims for debts paid late. Nevertheless, the *Minter* case did point the way.

The second damages case is *Ruxley Electronics and Construction Ltd v Forsyth*,[39] known to many as 'the swimming pool case'. The plaintiffs contracted to build a swimming pool for the defendant. The contract specified that there should be a diving area 7 feet 6 inches deep. On completion the pool was suitable for diving, but the diving area was only 6 feet deep. The estimated cost of rebuilding the pool to the specified depth was £21,500. The Court of Appeal held that the measure of damages for the breach of the contract was the cost of rebuilding the pool. The House of Lords held that, where the expenditure was out of all proportion to the benefit to be obtained, the appropriate measure of damages was not the cost of rebuilding, but the diminution in value of the work occasioned by the breach. Rebuilding would have been unreasonable as it was out of all proportion to the benefit that would result. The House therefore concluded that the appropriate measure of damages was the difference between the value of the pool as built and the value of the pool as it ought to have been built. Lord Jauncey said:

> Damages are designed to compensate for an established loss and not to provide a gratuitous benefit to the aggrieved party from which it follows that the reasonableness of an award of damages is to be linked directly

---

[38] [2007] UKHL 34 at [16].
[39] *Ruxley Electronics and Construction Ltd v Forsyth* [1996] AC 344 (HL).

to the loss sustained. If it is unreasonable in a particular case to award the cost of reinstatement it must be because the loss sustained does not extend to the need to reinstate.[40]

This decision may now seem to be not only reasonable, but obviously right. But that is not how it appeared to everyone at the time. At all events, the principle that a claimant is not entitled to the cost of doing whatever is necessary to place him in the position he would have been in if the contract had not been broken where it would be unreasonable to do so has since been applied in many decisions spanning all areas of commercial law. For example, in the shipping cases of *The Maersk Colombo*[41] and *The Baltic Surveyor and the Timbuktu*[42] and in the solicitor's negligence case of *Fulham Leisure Holdings Ltd v Nicholson Graham & Jones*.[43] *Ruxley* therefore made a considerable contribution to the general law.

DUTIES OF CARE

The last topic to which I wish to refer is the issue of when a common law duty of care will arise. This is an area of the common law which has been the subject of much development in the last few decades and in which there has been a significant number of important construction cases. Cases such as *Anns v Merton London Borough Council*[44] and *Junior Books v Veitchi*[45] come to mind, but there are several others. I want to focus on *Governors of the Peabody Donation Fund v Sir Lindsay Parkinson & Co Ltd*,[46] partly because I was in this case. I am afraid that it was another of my failures.

The case concerned the construction of drainage for a housing development owned by my client. Plans had been submitted by the owners' architects to the local authority and approved.

---

[40] At 357E.

[41] *Southampton Container Terminals Ltd v Schiffahrts-Gesellschaft Hansa Australia MBH & Co, The Maersk Colombo* [2001] EWCA Civ 717, [2001] 2 Lloyd's Rep 275.

[42] *Voaden v Champion, The Baltic Surveyor and the Timbuktu* [2002] EWCA Civ 89, [2002] 1 Lloyd's Rep 623.

[43] *Fulham Leisure Holdings Ltd v Nicholson Graham & Jones (a firm)* [2006] EWHC 2017 (Ch), [2006] 4 All ER 1397 (Note). This decision was reversed in part by the Court of Appeal [2008] EWCA Civ 84 but on other grounds.

[44] *Anns v Merton London Borough Council* [1978] AC 728 (HL).

[45] *Junior Books Ltd v Veitchi Co Ltd* [1983] 1 AC 520 (HL).

[46] *Peabody Donation Fund (Governors) v Sir Lindsay Parkinson & Co Ltd* [1985] AC 210 (HL).

Subsequently, the architects instructed the contractors to depart from the approved design. The local authority drainage inspector became aware of this departure from the approved plans during installation but he took no action. It later became apparent that the drains were unsatisfactory and had to be re-constructed, causing the development to be delayed and the owner to incur losses. The House of Lords considered whether the owner could recover its losses from the local authority on the basis that it breached a duty of care owed to it.

We had succeeded at first instance before Judge Oddie, sitting as an official referee. He had held that the local authority owed a duty of care to the owner because there was proximity and it was reasonably foreseeable that, if the drainage inspector permitted the contractors to depart from the approved plans, the drainage would be defective and the owner would suffer damage as a result. This all seemed pretty straightforward to me. The Court of Appeal did not like the decision and allowed the appeal. The lack of merit in our case did not appeal to them. Nor did it appeal to the House of Lords. I battled away valiantly, but to no avail. Lord Keith gave the only substantive speech. He referred to a passage in the speech of Lord Morris in *Dorset Yacht v Home Office*,[47] a passage to which no reference had been made during the argument. Lord Morris said:

> ... it would not only be fair and reasonable that a duty of care should exist but that it would be contrary to the fitness of things were it not so ... the court is called upon to make a decision as to policy. Policy need not be invoked where reason and good sense will at once point the way. If the test as to whether in some particular situation a duty of care arises may in some cases have to be whether it is fair and reasonable that it should so arise, the court must not shrink from being the arbiter.

So it was that Lord Keith said:

> in determining whether or not a duty of care of particular scope was incumbent upon a defendant it is material to take into consideration whether it is just and reasonable that it should be so.[48]

I am not sure that the significance of this passage was appreciated at the time. I do, however, recall thinking when I read the speech with

---

[47] *Dorset Yacht Co Ltd v Home Office* [1970] AC 1004 at 1039 (HL).
[48] *Peabody Donation Fund (Governors) v Sir Lindsay Parkinson & Co Ltd* [1985] AC 210 at 241C.

that awful sinking feeling that this was a really important turning point. Recourse to what is fair and reasonable was not commonplace in those days, perhaps because it was uncertain and difficult to control. This approach to the question of whether a duty of care arises in a particular situation is now orthodox. It has been firmly cemented into our law since the House of Lords decision in *Caparo v Dickman*.[49]

On the facts Lord Keith concluded that it would not be just or reasonable to impose a duty on the council given that my client, the owner, had a statutory duty to ensure the drainage scheme conformed to the design approved by the local authority; the owner's loss resulted from reliance on the advice of its own architects, engineers and contractors.[50]

Lord Keith expanded on his expression of when a duty of care arises in the later construction case of *Murphy v Brentwood District Council*,[51] a case with which you are all no doubt familiar and the last one on which I wish to comment.

In this case the House of Lords considered whether a local authority exercising building control powers conferred on it by statute for the purpose of securing compliance with building regulations owed a duty of care to purchasers of houses to safeguard them against purely economic loss in remedying a dangerous defect in the building.

In holding that *Anns v Merton* was wrongly decided, a decision which Lord Keith described as 'a remarkable example of judicial legislation',[52] the House of Lords held that in such a situation the loss suffered was economic and the council were not liable for the negligent application of the building regulations where the resulting defects had not caused physical injury.

At one level, the case may be considered to be only about the duty local councils owe to building owners. But at a higher level, the case is an authority of importance for the law more generally not only for the law of negligence, but also as indicating the court's views as to the proper limits of its powers.

[49] *Caparo Industries plc v Dickman* [1990] 2 AC 605 (HL).
[50] *Peabody Donation Fund (Governors) v Sir Lindsay Parkinson & Co Ltd* [1985] AC 210 at 241E–F.
[51] *Murphy v Brentwood District Council* [1991] 1 AC 398 (HL).
[52] At 471G.

CONCLUSION

I am delighted to have been asked to give this lecture. As I have said, I was led by Donald Keating many times and occasionally appeared against him. He was a formidably good lawyer. He would have been so proud to have his chambers named after him and this lecture too. I am also delighted that members of his family are here tonight. I have no doubt that they are proud too.

He was a perfectionist. He demanded much of his juniors and himself. The book that he wrote (now in its ninth edition) is testament to that. The early editions contained a masterly analysis of the basic principles of law as they affect construction disputes. As good an introduction to the general law of contract as you could wish to find. Succinct and not a word wasted. If only we could say that about the judgments that many of us write today. He would have been thrilled to see how those who practise construction law have come down the rickety lift from the Official Referees' Corridor to occupy a central position in our justice system in the modern, well equipped Rolls Building and to see how construction law too has come to assume an important position, contributing significantly to the development of our general law.

Part II

Human Rights

12

*What is Wrong with Human Rights?**

T HE RECENT OUTBURSTS by the Prime Minister and the Home Secretary in the so-called 'catgate' saga are but the latest of many expressions of hostility to human rights, the Human Rights Act 1998, the European Court of Human Rights as well as our own courts. Some politicians and some of the media seem to think that human rights bashing is easy meat. There is nothing new in this. The Human Rights Act is still very young, but it has had a difficult and embattled life.

18 December 2008 marked its anniversary. In an anniversary encomium, Jack Straw described the Act as a 'defining piece of legislation, a landmark which set the liberties we have long enjoyed in the United Kingdom on to a constitutional footing.' He added, 'I believe that the 1998 Act will be seen as one of the great legal, constitutional and social reforms of this government.'

However it was not a cause for celebration for all. The then Shadow Justice Secretary, Nick Herbert marked the occasion by reflecting that the 'legislation has been a gift to lawyers, an encouragement for undeserving litigants and a burden on frontline public servants who struggle to decide what the law is in practice.'[1] This is not an uncommon view, perhaps most frequently expressed by the popular media.

It was not long before the attitude of the Labour government towards the HRA became, to say the least, ambivalent, especially as the practical constraints that the legislation imposed on its fight against crime, the treatment of asylum seekers and the so-called 'war on terrorism' became apparent. Labour government ministers,

* University of Hertfordshire, 3 November 2011.
[1] Nick Herbert, 'Human Rights Act: The law that has devalued your human rights' *The Daily Telegraph* (18 December 2008).

in particular successive Home Secretaries and Lord Chancellors made disparaging remarks about the Act. These were usually in reaction to the decisions of judges in individual cases. As one *Daily Mail* report proudly put it

> Blunkett, Reid and Clarke have all rallied against the Act and judges, and tried various measures to limit its effect. Tony Blair ordered a review of it and the former Lord Chancellor Lord Falconer issued briefings to judges to try and curb their one-sided interpretations.[2]

As early as 2003 and following a decision requiring state support to be provided to genuinely destitute asylum seekers,[3] David Blunkett stated he was 'personally fed up with having to deal with a situation where Parliament debates issues and judges overturn them.' The events of 9/11 soon after the Act came into force and the concern that the UK was facing unprecedented dangers brought into sharp focus the balance between national security and liberty. Following the London bombings in July 2005, Tony Blair declared 'let no-one be in doubt, the rules of game are changing.' Speaking about the issue of deportation and diplomatic assurances he indicated that 'should legal obstacles arise, we will legislate further including, if necessary, amending the Human Rights Act in respect of the interpretation of the European Convention on Human Rights.'

The HRA faced a barrage of criticism in 2006 following a number of high-profile incidents including the murder of Naomi Bryant by Anthony Rice following his release from prison on licence, and the High Court's decision that nine Afghani hijackers could not be deported to Afghanistan because they faced a real risk of torture or death there. John Reid described this decision, which caused widespread public disquiet, as 'inexplicable or bizarre' and Tony Blair considered that it was 'an abuse of common sense' to be in a position where the government were unable to deport people who hijack a plane. He immediately called for a review of the legislation in particular 'whether primary legislation is needed to address the issue of court rulings which overrule the government in a way that is inconsistent with other EU countries' interpretation of the European Convention on Human Rights.' One option under consideration was to amend the HRA, to require a 'balance between the rights of the individual and the rights of the community to basic security.'[4]

---

[2] 'What about OUR rights?' *Daily Mail* (5 October 2007).
[3] *R (Q, D, J, M, F & B) v Secretary of State for the Home Department* [2003] EWHC 195 (Admin).
[4] 'Revealed: Blair attack on Human Rights Law' *Observer* (14 May 2006).

A report by the Joint Committee on Human Rights published in November 2006 was highly critical of Ministers' statements in respect of events in the course of 2006. It concluded that

> in each case, very senior ministers, from the Prime Minister down, made assertions that the Human Rights Act, or judges or officials interpreting it, were responsible for certain unpopular events when ... in each case these assertions were unfounded. Moreover, when those assertions were demonstrated to be unfounded, there was no acknowledgement of the error, or any other attempt to inform the public of the mistake. We very much welcome the Lord Chancellor's assurance that there is now an unequivocal commitment to human rights right across the Government.

In response to a letter from the Chairman of the Joint Committee on Human Rights asking him to clarify the remarks he made in the interview, Jack Straw wrote:

> As I made clear in the interview I remain firmly supportive of the Human Rights Act 1998 and the way in which it has improved protection for human rights in the UK. Indeed, I regard it as one of the landmark achievements of the Government ... the Mail noted that I was 'quick to defend the Act' ... I acknowledged in the interview the fact that the Act is unfortunately perceived by sections of the public and media as a 'villain's charter.' I have drawn attention to that problem on many occasions ... I believe such a negative perception arises in part because of the public unease about the limits placed by the ECHR on the Government's ability to return terrorist suspects to their country of origin. In addition, I have often said that although rights are clearly identifiable in the HRA, the responsibilities which go with them are less visible. The rights enshrined in the HRA already encompass responsibilities—but implicitly. I believe that now we should seek to articulate them explicitly. Hence we want to build on the benefits of the HRA.[5]

In March 2009, the Labour government published a green paper entitled the *Rights and Responsibilities*, which emphasised that there was no intention to resile from or weaken the HRA.[6] It proposed a new 'Bill of Rights and Responsibilities' which would give prominence to responsibilities in addition to rights. The paper was somewhat difficult to pin down. On the one hand it made clear that rights would not be contingent on the exercise of responsibilities (para 2.22). On the other it stated that 'it would be possible in a future Bill of Rights and Responsibilities to highlight the importance

---

[5] Third Report of Session 2008–09, *A Bill of Rights for the UK? Government Response to the Committee's Twenty-ninth Report of Session 2007–08*, 32.

[6] *Rights and Responsibilities: Developing our Constitutional Framework* (March 2009).

of factors such as the applicant's own behaviour and the importance of public safety and security' (para 2.25).

The Conservative party was initially opposed to the HRA. But its position shifted somewhat under David Cameron's leadership. In June 2006 he delivered a speech to the Centre for Policy Studies announcing that the party proposed to replace the HRA with a British Bill of Rights whilst remaining a party to the European Convention on Human Rights.[7]

In thinking about the way forward, he distanced himself from the old Conservative policy of simply repealing the HRA, recognising that this would not solve the problem since 'we would still be left with a situation in which terrorist suspects could go to the European Court' and it had the 'strong disadvantage of taking a step backwards on rights and liberties.'

He also rejected the option of pulling out of the Convention. He proposed a new approach which

> protects liberties in this country that is home-grown and sensitive to Britain's legal inheritance that enables people to feel they have ownership of their rights and one which at the same time enables a British Home Secretary to strike a common-sense balance between civil liberties and the protection of public security ... I believe that the right way to do that is through a modern British Bill of Rights that also balances rights with responsibilities.

His vision was as follows:

> A modern British Bill of Rights needs to define the core values which give us our identity as a free nation. It should spell out the fundamental duties and responsibilities of people living in this country both as citizens and foreign nationals. And it should guide the judiciary and the Government in applying human rights law when the lack of responsibility of some individuals threatens the rights of others. It should enshrine and protect fundamental liberties such as jury trial, equality under the law and civil rights. And it should protect the fundamental rights set out in the European Convention on Human Rights in clearer and more precise terms. Greater clarity and precision would allow those rights to be enforced more easily and effectively in circumstances where they ought to be protected but it would become harder to extend them inappropriately as under the present law.

---

[7] D Cameron, 'Balancing Freedom and Security—A Modern British Bill of Rights' (26 June 2006).

No-one could surely quarrel with these noble aspirations or this heart-warming espousal of British values. But what would it all mean in practice and where would it leave the UK as a signatory to the Convention? So far as I am aware, there has never been a satisfactory answer to these questions.

On 18 March 2011, the Coalition government announced the establishment of an independent Commission to investigate the case for a Bill of Rights. It has undertaken to produce its final report by the end of 2012. It will explore a range of issues surrounding human rights law in the UK and will also play an advisory role in the government's continuing work to press for reform of the European Court of Human Rights in Strasbourg. On 28 July, it produced its Interim Advice to the government on reform of the European Court of Human Rights. It noted with concern that the backlog of cases now stood at more than 150,000 and suggested that a new and effective screening mechanism should be established that allows the court to decline to deal with cases that do not raise a serious violation of the Convention. The core of its interim advice was that the court should focus on its essential purpose as the judicial guardian of human rights across Europe. It should only address a limited number of cases that raise serious questions affecting the interpretation or application of the Convention and serious issues of general importance where the Court's intervention is justified. It should be a court of last resort and not a port of first call for all human rights issues. I shall return to the question of the European Court of Human Rights later. The Commission published a Discussion paper on 5 August to canvas views from the public on whether we need a UK Bill of Rights and if so what it might look like. It is no secret that the Conservatives are more enthusiastic about this than their Liberal Democrat coalition partners.

It will be seen from what I have said so far that one of the main reasons for the unpopularity of the HRA is the perception that it undermines public safety by making the fight against crime and terrorism harder. Another theme has been that it makes it more difficult for the government to control immigration. It is time to consider in a little more detail the areas that have excited such controversy and indignation and have provoked calls for changes.

One of the most controversial decisions of the Strasbourg court has been *Chahal v UK*,[8] where it decided that there is an absolute

---

[8] *Chahal v UK* (1996) 23 EHRR 413.

prohibition (not derogable in any circumstances) on torture, inhuman and degrading treatment, so that a state may not deport persons to a country where they face a real risk of torture etc regardless of how high a security risk they pose to the UK. This principle operates as a serious restriction on the ability of the state to deport convicted criminals as well as suspected terrorists. It means that even foreign nationals who have an appalling criminal record cannot be deported after they have served their sentences if there is a real risk that they will be tortured or killed in their country of origin. This decision has been frequently criticised by the press and politicians alike. It led former Home Secretary John Reid to regret that his government had ever introduced the HRA.[9]

But according to the Joint Committee on Human Rights, the *Chahal* judgment only prevents the government from taking into account the threat posed by a particular individual in a 'relatively small number of cases,' something which the Lord Chancellor acknowledged in his evidence to the Committee (he recognised that 'Article 3 affects an extremely small number of people').[10]

The UK government recognised that the '*Chahal* problem' was not attributable directly to the HRA: 'the HRA makes no difference ... not only because the *Chahal* decision pre-dates it, but also because it is an example of the Strasbourg Court directly interpreting Article 3 of the ECHR.' Together with other states, it therefore sought to persuade the European Court of Human Rights to re-consider *Chahal* in view of the 'threat posed by international terrorism,' intervening as a third party in cases involving deportations by the Netherlands and Italy (*Ramzy v The Netherlands, A v The Netherlands and Saadi v Italy*).

The Grand Chamber of the European Court unanimously rejected the UK's submissions and reaffirmed the decision in *Chahal*. They said:

> The Court cannot accept the argument of the United Kingdom Government, supported by the respondent Government, that a distinction must be drawn under Article 3 between treatment inflicted directly by a signatory State and treatment that might be inflicted by the authorities of another State, and that protection against this latter form of ill-treatment should be weighed against the interests of the community as a whole ... Since protection against the treatment prohibited by Article 3 is absolute,

---

[9] Interview in the *News of the World* (16 September 2007).
[10] Thirty-second Report of Session 2005–06, *The Human Rights Act: the DCA and Home Office Reviews*, para 118.

that provision imposes an obligation not to extradite or expel any person who, in the receiving country, would run the real risk of being subjected to such treatment. As the Court has repeatedly held, there can be no derogation from that rule ... It must therefore reaffirm the principle stated in the *Chahal* judgment ...

The Court observed that similar arguments were put forward and rejected in *Chahal*:

even if, as the Italian and United Kingdom Governments asserted, the terrorist threat has increased since that time, that circumstance would not call into question the conclusions of the *Chahal* judgment concerning the consequences of the absolute nature of Article 3.

Judge Myjer and Judge Zagrebelsky, in their concurring opinion, stated that 'they would not be surprised' if some readers of the judgment at first sight

find it difficult to understand that the Court by emphasising the absolute nature of Article 3 seems to afford more protection to the non-national applicant who has been found guilty of terrorist related crimes than to the protection of the community as a whole from terrorist violence.

However they emphasised that

states are not allowed to combat international terrorism at all costs. They must not resort to methods which undermine the very values they seek to protect. And this applies the more to those 'absolute' rights from which no derogation may be made even in times of emergency.

This is reminiscent of the oft-quoted judgment given in 1994 by President Barak in the Israel Supreme Court when he declared that violent interrogation of a suspected terrorist is not lawful, even if doing so may save human life by preventing impending terrorist acts:

This is the fate of democracy, as not all means are acceptable to it and not all methods employed by its enemies are open to it. Sometimes a democracy must fight with one hand tied behind its back. Nonetheless, it has the upper hand. Preserving the rule of law and the recognition of individual liberties constitute an important component of its understanding of security. At the end of the day, they strengthen its spirit and strength and allow it to overcome its difficulties.

But the Strasbourg decision has not been welcomed by all. Rosalind English argues:

By refusing to take account of the scale of the international terrorist threat and of the objective difficulties of combating it effectively, the Strasbourg

Court may be seen to be sticking its head in the sand, a position which though ideologically sound is probably not in the long run very realistic. Signatory states may in the end seek to avoid the consequences of these rulings by clamping down further on immigration—they may not be able to derogate from their obligations under Article 3, but derogation notices may be served under Article 8 to reduce the risk of allowing potential terrorist threats to penetrate—with the obvious hardship this entails for innocent applicants and genuine refugees. As ever, Strasbourg's generosity may have unintended consequences.[11]

In the result, the government was constrained to fall back on the policy of seeking diplomatic assurances or concluding memoranda of understanding if it wished to deport foreigners to their countries of origin. The UK has concluded agreements which embody assurances with countries such as Jordan, Libya, Lebanon, and Algeria, and has relied on them before the courts with mixed success. An important test of this policy was the case of *Abu Qatada*. When the Court of Appeal allowed his appeal in 2008, the *Daily Mail* headline read 'Bewigged madness: How our judges have just issued an open invitation for terrorists to flock to Britain.'[12] But the House of Lords allowed the Secretary of State's appeal in 2009.[13]

Another case which attracted a good deal of public interest and criticism was that of *Learco Chindamo*. Mr Chindamo was an Italian citizen who was serving a life sentence for the murder Philip Lawrence in 1995. The Home Office wished to deport Chindamo to Italy upon release, on the grounds that 'he posed a continuing risk to the public and that his offences were so serious that he represents a genuine and present and sufficiently serious threat to the public in principle as to justify his deportation.' The Asylum and Immigration Tribunal ruled that he could not be expelled, citing *among other things* his right to private and family life under Article 8 of the Convention. The *Daily Mail* called it a 'profoundly stupid and amoral ruling'. They wrote:

> We have of course seen many lunacies perpetrated in the name of human rights: compensation for IRA terrorist families, prisoners allowed porn, preachers of hatred freed to continue abusing our hospitality. But this ruling stands in a grotesque league of its own.[14]

---

[11] Case note, February 2008, available at www.1cor.com/1315/?form_1155.replyids= 1138.

[12] 10 April 2008.

[13] *Othman v Secretary of State for the Home Department* [2009] UKHL 10, [2010] 2 AC 110.

[14] 'When "human rights" are an insult to us all' *Daily Mail* (21 August 2007).

Mrs Lawrence was quoted as having said that she had always been a 'staunch advocate of the Human Rights Act' and could not understand how it has now 'allowed someone who destroyed a life to pick and choose how he wants to live his.' David Cameron (then leader of the Conservative Opposition) responded by saying that the HRA should be replaced:

> This does seem to be complete madness ... And I'm not surprised that Mrs Lawrence has said there is something rotten at the heart of the Human Rights Act. We agree with that we think the Human Rights Act should be scrapped and should be replaced with a British Bill of Rights.

In reaching its decision the AIT had relied principally on EU law. What they said on the issue of human rights was unnecessary for their decision. Nevertheless, they said that, if the human rights issue had been determinative, they would have found that the removal of Chindamo would have violated his rights under Article 8 of the Convention.

In my view, even if Article 8 had been the principal basis on which the AIT had made their decision, it is difficult to see how the decision could be described as 'complete madness' or 'lunacy.' Chindamo had been living in the UK since he was six years old, spoke no Italian and appeared to have no connections with Italy other than citizenship. All his connections were with the UK. It seems to me that, far from being mad, the decision of the AIT on the Article 8 issue was plainly right.

There have been many cases where the issue has been whether Article 8 is an obstacle to the deportation of foreigners on the grounds of their criminal offending or the fact that they are not lawfully present in the UK. In these cases, the court is called upon to carry out a difficult balancing exercise taking into account inter alia the alien's family situation, whether there are children of a relationship and, if so, their age and their best interests and well-being, and the seriousness of the difficulties which a spouse and any children are likely to encounter in the country to which the alien would be expelled. Those who are hostile to the Convention find this difficult to accept. Their attitude is that the UK should be able to rid itself of foreign criminals and those who have no right to be here in the first place; and that the fact that they and their families have put down strong roots here provides no justification for allowing them to stay.

But the concerns about the HRA are not confined to decisions in relation to crime, terrorism and immigration. A more general concern has been expressed that the Act has caused authorities to act in a risk-averse and sometimes ridiculous manner. In a speech to the Centre for Policy Studies, David Cameron noted that 'even without actual litigation, some public bodies are now so frightened of being sued under the Human Rights Act that they try to protect themselves by making decisions that are often absurd and occasionally dangerous.' A *Daily Telegraph* article criticises the HRA for engendering 'a set of attitudes in the public sector, especially in the Criminal Justice System, that have erred too much on the side of caution for fear of litigation'.

According to a *Daily Mail* report, the most 'worrying and insidious' thing about the HRA

> is that it has made authorities frightened to act in the public interest. For example, when Derbyshire Police refused to release pictures of two escaped murderers in case it infringed their right to privacy, they might have been over-interpreting the law but they were acting in line with the new legal culture.[15]

There is a concern that the HRA has unleashed a 'culture of grievance,' encouraging people to make frivolous claims which overburden the taxpayer and line the pockets of self-interested 'fat cat' lawyers. The fear of litigation causes officials to adopt a defensive attitude to the detriment of the interests of the wider community. Moreover there is a sense that the human rights provisions are being applied to trivial cases in a way which was not intended by the drafters of the Convention. It is argued that all this serves to 'devalue' human rights.

I have no doubt that many claims brought under the HRA *are* spurious and based on questionable interpretations of the Convention. Most, however, will not make it past the permission stage. There nonetheless remains a perception that such 'ludicrous claims' are permitted under the HRA, which is then criticised for 'bad decisions.'

If authorities make stupid decisions under the banner of the HRA or the Convention, it is almost certain that they are based on a misinterpretation of them. That is hardly a sensible reason for getting rid of the HRA or introducing a Bill of Rights, still less for abandoning the Convention. To the extent that there is a problem, it is a good reason for educating authorities to act wisely and with a proper understanding of the law.

[15] Above.

A yet further concern is that it is said that the HRA marks a shift in power from Parliament to the unelected and unaccountable judiciary. The *Daily Mail* expressed this concern in the following terms:

> The Act encourages judges to think of themselves as legislators, giving them power to strike down laws passed by Parliament. This is not just profoundly undemocratic—who elected the judges?—but can lead, in the word of Downing Street to 'barmy' decisions. While ministers frame legislation to strike a balance between conflicting interests—such as the rights of terrorists and the rights of the public—judges tend to take a very narrow, legalistic view.

Or as Nick Herbert wrote in the *Daily Telegraph* on 18 December 2008:

> It is claimed that the Act has helped to challenge unjust decisions by public bodies, such as the case of the elderly siblings who successfully overturned a council decision to house them apart in separate care homes. Yet it would surely be better to rely on democracy, rather than the courts, to make elected authorities behave properly. Leaving such decisions to judges places them in the political arena and undermines their independence. When the courts insist that the Ministry of Defence equips our soldiers properly, the temptation is to cheer. But governments are elected to shoulder such responsibility. Extending the ambit of human rights law to the theatre of military conflict is deeply problematic. The next decision of the courts might not be so palatable.

But I would respond that the HRA reflects a careful balance between Parliament, the executive and judiciary. It is not entrenched and it denies the courts the capacity to 'strike down' legislation for incompatibility. As Connor Gearty puts it, declarations of incompatibility 'are courteous requests for a conversation, not pronouncements of truth from on high.'[16] In this way the Act specifically preserves parliamentary sovereignty. If Parliament or the executive disagree with a decision it remains open to them to change the law.

Nonetheless, I would accept that there is some force in the point that the incorporation of the Convention has called on today's judges to determine issues which judges in earlier eras would have been horrified to be asked to decide. They would have refused to do so on the grounds that such issues belonged to the political dimension and were not justiciable. But this enlargement of the role of the judge is no more than the development of a trend that was in progress before

---

[16] C Gearty, 'Can Human Rights Survive?' (The Hamlyn Lectures, 2005).

1998 with the growth of judicial review. One only has to recall Lord Irvine of Lairg's memorable injunction to the judges: 'get your tanks off my lawn'. That warning, uttered with all the weight of one of Cardinal Wolsey' successors, was made well before the incorporation of the Convention.

Indeed, in their 2006 review the Department of Constitutional Affairs concluded that the HRA had not significantly altered the constitutional balance between Parliament, the executive and judiciary. This assessment was based on a review of court judgments which concerned either the relationship between the judiciary and executive or the relationship between the judiciary and Parliament.

Polemical attacks on the HRA coupled with complaints about the exorbitant power of the judiciary are sometimes made in order to advance a particular cause. For example, in his speech to the Society of Editors in November 2008, Paul Dacre discussed how the newspaper industry was facing a number of very serious threats to its freedoms. In his view by far the most 'dangerous' was the development of a 'privacy law' under the HRA:

> This law is not coming from Parliament—no, that would smack of democracy—but from the arrogant and immoral judgments—words I use very deliberately—of one man. I am referring of course to Justice David Eady who has, again and again, under the privacy clause of the Human Rights Act, found against newspapers and their age old freedom to expose moral shortcoming of those in high places … If Gordon Brown wanted to force a privacy law, he would have set out a bill, arguing his case in both Houses of Parliament, withstand public scrutiny and win a series of votes. Now, thanks to the wretched Human Rights Act, one Judge with a subjective and highly relativist moral sense can do the same with a stroke of his pen.[17]

It is difficult to discern whether he was expressing a concern about the implications for the media's role in acting as 'watchdog' or the financial consequences for mass circulation newspapers if they are unable to write about scandal. He began by saying that it undermines the ability of 'mass circulation papers to sell newspapers in an ever more difficult market' but later purported to link the two:

> All this has huge implications for newspapers and, I would argue, for society. Since time immemorial public shaming has been a vital element in defending the parameters of what are considered acceptable standards

---

[17] See his speech to the Society of Editors (10 November 2008), available at www.journalism.co.uk/2/articles/532774.php.

of social behaviour, helping ensure that citizens—rich and poor—adhere to them for the good of the greater community. For hundreds of years, the press has played a role in that process. It has the freedom to identify those who have offended public standards of decency—the very standards its readers believe in—and hold the transgressors up to public condemnation. If their readers don't agree with the defence of such values, they would not buy those papers in such huge numbers.

Put another way, if mass-circulation newspapers, which, of course, also devote considerable space to reporting and analysis of public affairs, don't have the freedom to write about scandal, I doubt whether they will retain their mass circulations with the obvious worrying implications for the democratic process.

It can be seen from this short survey that from time to time human rights attract a good deal of hostility in the Press and from some politicians. It seems to me that there is no simple explanation for this. It is easy enough to see why Paul Dacre is hostile to the promotion of Article 8 and the right to privacy at the expense of Article 10 and freedom of expression. The exposure of the seamy side of the lives of celebrities sells newspapers. It is also not difficult to see why a politician who suffers a reverse in the courts in a human rights case may blame the human rights law rather than himself or his department for his defeat. I can also understand why the *Chahal* decision is unpopular, although I think that the Strasbourg court has been right on this issue.

And yet the results in the overwhelming majority of cases in which a human rights point arises are the same post-HRA as they would have been pre-HRA. My impression is that the decisions in such cases are rarely criticised. So why the generalised and somewhat unfocused attack by some sections of the Press and some politicians on the HRA and the Convention? After all, none of the criticisms touches the text of the Convention, which to a great extent was intended to, and does, reflect common law understandings of human rights.

I think that if the complaints are properly articulated, they will be seen to be not so much about the substance of the Convention, but more about the approach by the European Court of Human Rights in Strasbourg to the interpretation and application of the Convention. This was the main thrust of what Lord Hoffmann said in his Judicial Studies Board lecture 'The Universality of Human Rights' (2009). His main thesis was that Convention issues should be decided at national level and not by a supra-national court manned by judges from 47 countries. He came close to suggesting that the

European Court of Human Rights should be disbanded or, if not disbanded, have its powers severely curtailed. Why, for example, he asked, should an Eastern European judge (appointed to the court by an opaque process) be empowered to decide questions of English national law? I wonder whether he would have similarly strong objections to a UK judge deciding a question of Turkish national law in which a human rights issue arises.

Lord Hoffmann said that human rights are universal in abstraction, but national in application. So why should an international court decide individual cases? For example, there is a human right to have a fair trial, but it does not follow that all the countries of the Council of Europe must have the same criminal procedure. What a fair trial requires is a matter for national courts to determine in the light of their own local circumstances and legal traditions. Lord Hoffmann acknowledges that the Strasbourg court has to a limited extent recognised the fact that human rights are national at the level of application. This it has done by the doctrine of the 'margin of appreciation'. But he criticises the court on the grounds that there is no consistency in the application of the doctrine and the court has not taken the doctrine nearly far enough.

These criticisms are reflected in the interim recommendations of the Commission on a Bill of Human Rights to which I have already referred. The European Court of Human Rights recognises the importance of the margin of appreciation and the need to take account of the special factors that apply at national level. The charge of inconsistency in the application of the doctrine of the margin of appreciation is easy to make. Anyway, which court has an unblemished record for consistency?

The Strasbourg court is aware of the concerns that the margin of appreciation is not being applied with sufficient rigour and it is only too keenly aware of the inexorable rise in the backlog of cases waiting to be dealt with. The margin of appreciation took centre stage in its controversial decision in the case of *Hirst v United Kingdom*,[18] where it decided that the blanket ban imposed by the UK on the right to vote of all prisoners serving a sentence of imprisonment breached Article 3 of the first protocol. It said in terms that the rights bestowed by Article 3 of the first protocol were not absolute and that the margin of appreciation in this area was wide. It accepted that the ban pursued a legitimate aim, but concluded that 'such a

---

[18]   *Hirst v United Kingdom* (2006) 42 EHRR 41.

general, automatic and indiscriminate restriction on a vitally important Convention right must be seen as falling outside any acceptable margin of appreciation, however wide that margin might be'.
The decision caused a furore here. The government proposed a ban
on all prisoners serving a sentence of four years' imprisonment or
more. This proved unacceptable to their own back-benchers. But a
compromise proposal of one year or more is also proving unacceptable. Those who object to allowing any serving prisoner the right
to vote say that anyone who commits an offence sufficiently serious
to warrant a custodial sentence not only forfeits his right to liberty,
but also his right to vote. The issue has raised passions to a level of
surprising intensity. David Cameron said that he was 'exasperated
and furious' at having to accept that there was no way to keep the
140 year-old blanket ban on prisoners voting.

It is to be noted that the European Court of Human Rights simply held that a blanket ban was contrary to Article 3 of the first
protocol and left it to the member state to devise a proportionate
scheme which complied. It was not for the court to draft a legislative scheme to remedy the problem any more than it would be for
our domestic courts to do so either.

Another example of a case where Strasbourg has arguably nar-
rowed the margin of appreciation too much is *S and Marper
v United Kingdom*.[19] This decision left the United Kingdom in the
uncomfortable position of being told that a 'blanket and indiscriminate' power to hold fingerprints, cellular samples and DNA profiles,
as applied to the applicants in that case, overstepped the margin of
appreciation. Yet beyond saying that it went too far in those cases,
the decision gave little guidance on what rules would be proportionate to the admittedly legitimate and important aim of detecting
and deterring crime.

In any event, our national courts are not always bound to follow where Strasbourg leads. First, the obligation of our courts when
interpreting the Convention is to do no more than 'take account'
of any relevant Strasbourg jurisprudence. As is well known, that
obligation has been interpreted to mean that our courts should, in
the absence of special circumstances, follow any clear and constant jurisprudence of the Strasbourg court.[20] It is true that this is
of no relevance in cases where Strasbourg has pronounced on the

---

[19] *S and Marper v United Kingdom* (2009) 48 EHRR 50.
[20] *R (Ullah) v Special Adjudicator* [2004] UKHL 26, [2004] 2 AC 323, para 20.

very question at issue, such as in *Hirst* and *S and Marper*. Once Strasbourg has spoken on the very question at issue, there can be no further debate. But in most cases, Strasbourg has not yet spoken and section 3 of the HRA does afford a modest degree of flexibility to our courts.

Secondly, although the domestic court is required to take account of the Strasbourg jurisprudence, in a case which involves the application of principles which are clearly established and where the court is concerned that the European Court of Human Rights has not sufficiently appreciated or accommodated particular aspects of the domestic process, it might decline to follow a decision of the European Court of Human Rights. *R v Horncastle*[21] is an example of this. This was a case about whether our procedural rules for admitting hearsay evidence in criminal trials is compatible with the right to a fair hearing given by Article 6 of the Convention. But it is clear that the flexibility afforded by section 3 of the HRA and the *Horncastle* principle is very limited. I regret that I cannot agree with the view recently expressed by the Lord Chief Justice that national courts can refuse to follow clearly established Strasbourg authority. Such a course can be justified only in exceptional circumstances. In my view, a refusal to follow clear jurisprudence of the European Court of Human Rights is likely to result in the case being taken to Strasbourg, with all the delay and additional cost that this will inevitably entail. The whole point of the enactment of the HRA was to avoid the need for that.

It is time to draw some of the threads together. I do not believe that there is anything wrong with the Convention itself. So far as I am aware, there is no pressure to amend its text. For the most part, the problem is seen as stemming from the role of the court in Strasbourg. There is a feeling in many quarters that Strasbourg takes too many cases and that it does not sufficiently leave the national courts to decide individual complaints of violations of human rights. The result is that there is thought to be too much interference in our processes. It should, however, be pointed out that only relatively few cases adverse to the UK have been criticised.

I accept that there have undoubtedly been cases which Strasbourg has decided in a different way from our own courts. I have already referred to *Hirst* (the prisoners voting rights case). That was one. We should not make the mistake of thinking that our courts are

---

[21] *R v Horncastle* [2009] UKSC 14, [2010] 2 AC 373.

always better than Strasbourg. They are not. A good example of a case where Strasbourg corrected our view of the law was the case of *Smith* which concerned the lawfulness of the policy of excluding gays from our Armed Forces.

At all events, in my view the criticisms of the court have been overstated, perhaps as a reaction to a small number of controversial decisions. Let me give an example of an explosive reaction to one of our domestic court human rights decisions, which was plainly exaggerated and unwarranted. The Sexual Offences Act 2003 provides that any person who is convicted of a specified sexual offence and is sentenced to a custodial term of 30 months or more is automatically subject for an indefinite period to certain requirements to notify the police of their whereabouts. In the case of *R (F (A child)) v Secretary of State for the Home Department,*[22] the claimants sought a declaration of incompatibility with the Convention on the grounds that the absence of any mechanism for review of the notification requirements was a disproportionate interference with the right to respect for private and family life guaranteed by Article 8 of the Convention. A declaration was granted by the Supreme Court in April 2010. Surprisingly, this did not cause an outcry at that time. But when the government proposed legislation which provided for a right of review in specified circumstances, its proposal attracted some very adverse comment from some of the Press. The usual cry of promoting the interests of sexual perverts over those of their potential victims was heard. It was only at this stage that the government protested that it had been obliged to take this regrettable course by the courts, who were making it impossible to govern the country.

But to revert to Strasbourg, I do not subscribe to Lord Hoffmann's root and branch criticisms of the court. I believe that, for the most part, the European Court of Human Rights has been a force for good. Most of its decisions have not been the subject of adverse criticism. It is true that some of its decisions have been criticised with justification. But (dare I say it) the same can be and is said of some of the decisions of any court, including our Supreme Court. On the whole, the case-law of the European Court of Human Rights has strengthened and enriched our own human rights law. Take, for example, the development of our law on the investigation into deaths consequent on the interpretation by Strasbourg of Article 2 of the Convention. The access that its jurisprudence gives us to the

[22] *R (F (A child)) v Secretary of State for the Home Department* [2010] UKSC 17.

experience of how human rights issues are resolved throughout the 47 member states of the Council of Europe is one which we should not lightly abandon. There is also no doubt that the European Court of Human Rights has had a beneficial effect on human rights in some member states which do not enjoy the democratic traditions which we so much take for granted. That is surely a very good thing. For example, there has been a substantial reduction in the number of cases against Turkey that have been taken to Strasbourg in recent years. There has been a noticeable improvement in Turkey's human rights record and there can be little doubt that the European Court of Human Rights has played a significant role in this. We would be taking a myopic view of what is in our national interest if we were to disregard this as of no consequence for us.

Nevertheless, the court faces serious problems and this seems now to be recognised by most, if not all, of the members of the Council of Europe. I think that it is clear that the margin of appreciation is sometimes applied too narrowly. This has brought about two important consequences. First, the court takes too many cases and this has caused the alarmingly accelerating backlog to which I have already referred. This is unsustainable and cannot be allowed to continue. Secondly, there is a real danger that what is considered to be undue interference in the decisions of domestic courts will destabilise the carefully-calibrated relationships between member states and the court in Strasbourg. I have already referred to the Commission established by the Coalition government of the UK. In April 2011, a high level conference was held in Izmir on the future of the European Court of Human Rights organised within the framework of the Turkish Chairmanship of the Committee of Ministers of the Council of Europe. It produced a fairly elaborate declaration recalling that the subsidiary character of the Convention mechanism constitutes 'a fundamental and universal principle which both the ECtHR and the States Parties must take into account'; recalling the 'shared responsibility of both the Court and the States Parties in guaranteeing the viability of the Convention mechanism'; and noting 'with concern the continuing increase in the number of applications brought before the Court'. The Conference made a number of proposals to streamline the process in order to reduce the backlog. One interesting proposal was to invite the court, when examining cases related to asylum and immigration, 'to assess and take full account of the effectiveness of domestic procedures and, where these procedures are seen to operate fairly and with respect for human rights, to avoid intervening except in the most exceptional circumstances.'

The fact that such a proposal is expressed in these terms is an acknowledgement that at the present time the court applies the margin of appreciation too narrowly. There are reflections here of the thinking which underpins the proposal that is contained in the interim advice of the Commission established by the Coalition government in the UK to which I referred earlier.

But great care needs to be taken. As the Izmir declaration stated, it is necessary to recognise 'the extraordinary contribution of the ECtHR to the protection of human rights in Europe'. We must never forget that the Convention came into being in order to reduce the risk of a repetition of appalling human rights abuses of the kind that were committed in Europe in the twentieth century. I am far from sure that the extraordinary contribution that the European Court of Human Rights has made to the protection of human rights would have been achieved if the court had done no more than decide cases of general importance and scrutinise domestic procedures to ensure that they were effective. It seems to me that much of the achievement of the court is attributable to the fact that it has been willing to decide individual cases and intervene where an individual applicant has shown that he has been a victim of a violation of his Convention rights. Some of these cases have raised important points of principle and/or have involved violations of the utmost seriousness. Others have not. In assessing the role of the court, we should not forget that some member states do not share the strongly entrenched democratic values of countries such as the UK.

So as in most things, there is a need for balance. There will have to be change, if only because the court is being overwhelmed by the number of applications that are made to it. The member states recognise this. The easier part of the solution to the problem is to streamline the court's processes, for example, by introducing a filter procedure. The more difficult part is to decide whether to introduce criteria to restrict the type of cases that the court will entertain and, if so, what these criteria should be. I suspect that, in time, this will lead to the formulation of a test which will limit the court's caseload to cases which raise points of general importance and/or which really involve allegations of serious violations of Convention rights. This will mean that, in effect, it will be an appellate court whose function is tightly circumscribed. A move in this direction will be driven by the twin pressures of the current overloading of the court and a growing demand from member states for a widening of the margin of appreciation. The proposal of the Izmir conference in relation to asylum and immigration is highly significant.

As we have seen, asylum and immigration is one of the areas where the relationship between human rights and the need of a state to maintain a firm and effective immigration policy is most sensitive. Although the European Court of Human Rights asserts that it accords a margin of appreciation in this area, that view is by no means universally accepted. The Izmir proposal seems to me to be a sensitive attempt to find a solution which would restrict the type of case which comes before the court in this area. The interim advice of the Commission is another attempt, more broadly expressed.

One thing is clear. In its short life, the HRA has changed the legal landscape. Many said that it would not make much of a difference. They said that the principles would be established in the first five years and then things would settle down. Well, they were wrong. The flood of human rights cases in our jurisdiction continues unabated. The fact that, in the eyes of many, it has caused many changes to our law (some of them thought to be unwelcome) shows that they were wrong. My own view is that the criticisms of the Strasbourg case-law are largely unjustified. As I have said, for the most part it has been successful in raising standards. The court is not a wild maverick organisation. Its decisions are often criticised by human rights lawyers for being too conservative and not sufficiently protective of human rights. As we have seen, there are also those who think that the court goes too far the other way. Some complaints of the court and its decisions are based on reason and are expressed and with moderation. Lord Hoffmann's paper is a persuasive example. Others, I suspect, are fuelled by xenophobia and Euro-scepticism. I know from conversations with judges from other jurisdictions that the concern that Strasbourg is interfering too much is shared by other members of the Council of Europe. At all events, the Commission will report. Its interim recommendations give a strong hint as to what its final report will say. For the time being, all we can say is that Convention law has not yet settled down. It continues to arouse strong sentiments on both sides, some primitive and instinctive and others sophisticated and based on reason. It is almost certain that the landscape will change again before too long.

There is clearly nothing wrong with human rights or with the text of the Convention. It is, of course, possible to criticise courts (whether Strasbourg or domestic) for the way in which they interpret the Convention and to complain about individual decisions made on the facts of particular cases. To the extent that there is a reasonable basis for criticism, it seems to me that it lies in the fact that Strasbourg has applied the margin of appreciation too narrowly and without a sufficient understanding of reasonable domestic ideas. But great caution should be exercised in taking this criticism too far. Some of us may consider that we have no need at all for an international court, in effect, to oversee the way in which our domestic courts interpret the Convention. I do not accept this. It is a view born of the arrogant belief that we know best and have nothing to learn from foreigners. In any event, Strasbourg cannot apply one set of criteria for the UK and other states which it considers to have strong democratic traditions including a strong independent judiciary and a different set of criteria for other states. And one of the great achievements of Strasbourg has been to raise standards in some of these other states.

13

*Human Rights in an Age of Terrorism**

S
IR NIGEL RODLEY should have been standing here tonight
to speak about the work of the United Nations Human Rights
Committee. Tragically, he succumbed to a particularly aggressive form of lung cancer and died a few days ago. He was a great
human rights academic lawyer. He also had many achievements in
the field of international human rights. I would single out for particular mention the fact that he served as Special Rapporteur on
Torture of the UN Commission on Human Rights from 1993 until
2001 and from 2001 he was the UK Member of the UN Human
Rights Committee. Nigel was a dear friend. I had known him since
about 1950. We were at school together in Leeds. I am giving this
lecture in his memory.

I imagine that most people have a *general* idea of what terrorism is.
It is not new. The anarchists who were active especially in Russia in
the nineteenth century and who sought to provoke social upheaval
by violent means were regarded as terrorists. Anarchists seeking to
cause terror in London to secure their political objectives form the
background to Joseph Conrad's 1907 novel *The Secret Agent*. They
would have been understood to be terrorists. Britain has experienced spasmodic outbursts of terrorist violence (or attempted violence) since at least the time of Guy Fawkes in 1605. More recently,
it was subjected to three decades of terrorist violence at the hands
of republicans and loyalists in Northern Ireland and mainland
Britain. This terrorism was treated as a civil emergency, not a war;
and the terrorists were treated as criminals and not combatants.
It is worth noting that the British authorities, having resorted to
internment of those suspected of involvement in terrorism and to

* Middle Temple lecture, 13 February 2017. Based on a lecture given at Hebrew
University, Jerusalem, November 2016. First appeared in *Israel Law Review* 50(2) 2017
pp 251–264 © Cambridge University Press and the Faculty of Law, The Hebrew University of Jerusalem, 2017. Reprinted with Permission.

methods of interrogation that were condemned by the European Court of Human Rights as inhuman and degrading treatment (contrary to Article 3 of the European Convention on Human Rights 'the Convention'), abandoned these methods as ineffective and counterproductive, alienating the very people on whose support the stability of the state depended. It is easy for those of us who lived through the Northern Ireland troubles to forget how serious they were. But serious though they were, they were insignificant when compared with what was to come.

The events of 9/11 and what has happened in many parts of the world since then have shocked the world. These types of acts of terrorism have been fundamentally different from what preceded them both as to the ends that they pursue and the means employed to pursue them. Take the Troubles in Northern Ireland as an example. The means adopted by the terrorists were on a relatively limited scale. They were carried out through an identifiable paramilitary organisation with a clear hierarchy and leadership. There was little doubt as to the political ends that they sought to achieve. On the other hand, the act of terrorism perpetrated on 9/11 and the many acts that have been perpetrated worldwide since then were on a massive scale and committed by various shadowy organisations with a diverse range of supporters in many parts of the world. Moreover, their ideology is spread at the press of a button through social media, with the result that attacks can be made by individuals anywhere in the world; and the means employed are becoming increasingly unpredictable.

These developments have caused authorities in democratic societies to re-appraise the orthodox approach to dealing with terrorism which was described in these terms on 17 April 2000 by Madeleine Albright, the US Secretary of State, in a speech to the University of World Economy and Diplomacy at Tashkent in Uzbekistan:

> One of the most dangerous temptations for a government facing violent threats is to respond in heavy-handed ways that violate the rights of innocent citizens. Terrorism is a criminal act and should be treated accordingly—and that means applying the law fairly and consistently. We have found through experience round the world that the best way to defeat terrorist threats is to increase law enforcement capabilities while at the same time promoting democracy and human rights.

So what exactly is terrorism? There is an elaborate definition in our Terrorism Act 2000 the essence of which is (i) the use or threat of action which (ii) endangers a person's life, other than that of the person committing the action where (iii) the use or threat is designed to influence the government or an international governmental organisation or to intimidate the public or a section of the public and (iv) the use or threat is made for the purpose of advancing a political, religious, racial or ideological cause. This is a very broad definition.

As David Anderson QC (the UK Independent Reviewer of Terrorism Legislation) observed in one of his annual reports, it is wide enough to include a campaigner or blogger who voices a religious objection to vaccination against diseases. If the blogger's purpose is to influence the government and if his words are judged capable of creating a serious risk to public health, he could be treated as a terrorist; detained for long periods of time; prosecuted; have his assets frozen and so on. Voicing support for him could also be a terrorist crime.

A terrorist is defined in the 2000 Act as a person who is or has been concerned in the commission, preparation or instigation of acts of terrorism. Thus ideologies are a pre-condition for terrorist acts which must seek to advance (in the words of section 1 of the 2000 Act) 'a political, religious, racial or ideological cause'. As Mr Anderson says in his report dated September 2015 (paras 9.5–9.6), the evils of violent extremism are self-evident. No democracy that takes seriously the idea of individual liberty and self-determination (and I would add the duty to protect life) should tolerate those who threaten or incite violence irrespective of any claimed justification in politics, religion or social custom. While it is ultimately only social pressure that can cause such views to disappear, the state is entitled to use all legitimate means at its disposal to counter them, including prosecuting the various offences under the Terrorism Acts.

Non-violent extremism requires much greater caution. Most of us have little sympathy for those who campaign for a law against blasphemy or adultery; consider homosexuality to be an abomination; seek to deny the right to choose a religion; or maintain that sharia law is preferable to the law of the land. But the response of a vigorous democracy is to take them on, rather than to criminalise them, although the government may need to protect the vulnerable from indoctrination and intimidation, whether in schools, prisons or even the family.

The 2000 Act gives the authorities extensive powers. The powers conferred by Schedule 7 have been the subject of considerable scrutiny by our courts. They authorise an 'examining officer' to stop and detain a person and question him at a port or border area for the purpose of determining whether he appears to be a person who is or has been concerned in the commission, preparation or instigation of acts of terrorism. Strikingly, the powers may be exercised whether or not the officer has grounds for suspecting that a person is or has been concerned in the commission, preparation or instigation of acts of terrorism. A person who is questioned must give the officer any information in his possession which the officer requests and give the officer on request any document which he has with him and which is of a kind specified by the officer. Failure to comply is a criminal offence.

Any government that takes seriously its obligation to protect those who live in its country will want to do everything in its power to discharge that obligation. Hence legislation like the 2000 Act. In such a climate, the human rights of individuals are likely to come under pressure. Should some or all of the human rights which we would normally seek to protect in normal circumstances be somehow limited or given less importance when it comes to taking on the terrorists? There are many in the UK who would give a resounding affirmative answer to that question. Hostility to our Human Rights Act 1998 and the Convention has been common currency in the UK for some time now. This has been fuelled by some of the media. For example, last year the *Daily Telegraph* ran a headline 'the Human Rights Act has helped 28 terrorists remain in the UK'. There have been many more headlines to similar effect. There was widespread criticism in the media of the decision of our courts that Abu Qatada (a suspected terrorist) could not be deported to Jordan because he would be likely to face a trial there in which key prosecution evidence had been obtained by torture.

As a means of accommodating such court decisions, the UK government has concluded agreements with some states in the Middle East and North Africa that deportees will not be ill-treated if returned to them. Such an agreement was made with Jordan which, somewhat surprisingly, Abu Qatada found acceptable. Deportations to Algeria have been permitted on the strength of formal assurances, despite the absence of an agreement. But deportation to Libya was denied despite the existence of an agreement. This is a difficult area, not least because assessing assurances given by states that are guilty of routine torture can be a tricky business. Our courts do their best to assess the effectiveness of such assurances. But they are often not well placed to do so.

Human rights lawyers and responsible commentators know that the protection of human rights when national security is at stake is far more complicated than the popular media suggest.

Human rights law acknowledges that there are some rights whose full realisation must be balanced against competing considerations (such as national security) and that they may have to yield to those considerations. However, there are other rights which are unqualified and which are not required to be balanced against security considerations. Article 4 of the International Covenant on Civil and Political Rights allows states to derogate from some rights (subject to strict conditions) in times of public emergency: see too the similar provision in Article 15 of the Convention. Thus derogation is one way in which human rights law deals with the challenges posed by terrorism. The other and more common way is to operate what is essentially a hierarchy of rights, with absolute non-derogable rights (such as the right to protection from torture or degrading treatment) at one end of the spectrum, and limited or qualified rights (such as the right to respect for family and private life, the rights to religious expression, freedom of expression and freedom of assembly and association) at the other end of the spectrum.

The non-derogable nature of the right not to be tortured under Article 3 of the Convention was asserted emphatically by the Strasbourg court in *Chahal v UK*.[1] Mr Chahal was to be deported from the UK to India on the grounds that he posed a threat to national security in the UK. He opposed deportation on the grounds that there was a real risk that he would be tortured in India. The court rejected the argument advanced by the UK that Article 3 rights had to be balanced against threats to national security. Dr John Reid (then Home Secretary) described the judgment as 'outrageously disproportionate' and later suggested that those in the House of Commons who defended the decision 'just don't get it'. Rather measured language when compared with some of the recent utterances of President Trump. In the subsequent case of *Saadi v Italy*,[2] the Strasbourg court strongly reaffirmed its approach in *Chahal*. The court insisted that it did not underestimate the scale of the danger of terrorism and the threat it presents to the community, but that could not call into question the absolute nature of Article 3.

I wish to refer to three recent English cases in which our courts have had to grapple with issues arising from the exercise of the wide-ranging powers given by the 2000 Act to examining officers at ports and airports and the interplay between those powers and

---

[1] *Chahal v UK* [1996] ECHR 54.
[2] *Saadi v Italy* [2007] 44 EHRR 50.

the human rights of the individuals who were subjected to their exercise.

In *Beghal v DPP*,[3] the defendant went to visit her husband who was in custody in France in relation to terrorist offences. On her return, she was stopped at an airport and detained for almost two hours by police officers exercising their powers under the 2000 Act. She refused to answer most of the questions that she was asked. She was charged with wilfully failing to comply with a duty contrary to Schedule 7. At her trial, she submitted that the proceedings should be stayed as an abuse of the process of the court on the grounds that the powers given to the officers under Schedule 7 infringed her right to liberty, the privilege against self-incrimination and her right to privacy and family life under Articles 5, 6 and 8 of the Convention. The Supreme Court rejected all of these submissions.

It was not in dispute that the questioning and search under compulsion pursuant to Schedule 7 was an interference with the defendant's right to respect for his or her private life under Article 8 which required to be justified under Article 8.2 as meeting the requirement of legality ('in accordance with the law') and as being a proportionate means of achieving a legitimate end. By a majority, the Supreme Court held that the legislation is 'in accordance with the law', ie that it has some basis in domestic law and that the law is adequately accessible to the public and that its operation is sufficiently foreseeable to enable people affected by it to regulate their conduct with a degree of certainty of outcome.

Of greater importance for present purposes is the fact that the requirement of legality calls for the law to contain sufficient safeguards to avoid the risk that the power will be arbitrarily exercised and the risk that unjustified interference with a fundamental right will occur. On this point, the main focus was on whether the fact that questioning was not dependent on the existence of objectively established grounds for suspicion meant that there were no adequate safeguards against the arbitrary exercise of the power. Lord Hughes (in the first majority judgment) said that the safeguards were sufficient. These included that the powers were restricted to those passing in and out of the country; the powers had to be exercised for the specified statutory purpose; they were exercised by specially trained and accredited police officers; the questioning was restricted to a period of six hours; there were restrictions on the

---

[3] *Beghal v DPP* [2015] UKHL 49, [2016] AC 88.

type of search authorised by the statute; there was a requirement to give explanatory notice to those questioned, to permit consultation with a solicitor and notification of a third party; a requirement for records to be kept; the availability of judicial review; and there was continuous supervision by the Independent Reviewer. I was party to a second majority judgment which gave slightly different reasons. In his dissenting judgment, Lord Kerr asked the pertinent question: if the examining officer does not have to form a suspicion that the person is or has been concerned in the commission, preparation or instigation of acts of terrorism, how is the exercise of the powers to be reviewed by the courts?

I did not find this an easy case to decide. In the end, I was influenced by the reasoning of the important Strasbourg decision of *Gillan v UK*[4] that, in considering whether the legality principle is satisfied in relation to a particular system, one must not only look at the provisions of the statute or other relevant instrument in question, but also at how the system actually works in practice. To a lawyer schooled in the crucible of the common law, this may well seem unprincipled and unsatisfactory. But Strasbourg often adopts a pragmatic approach and that is what it did here. It was significant that in *Beghal,* the evidence showed that a relatively small number of people were interviewed under Schedule 7 and that number had decreased each year from 2009–10 to 2013–14. Unlike in the *Gillan* case, the exercise of the Schedule 7 powers had led to convictions for terrorist offences. Most significantly of all was the fact that the Independent Reviewer was very positive about the way in which the Schedule 7 powers were being exercised. Indeed, he described the system as an essential ingredient in the fight against terrorism.

I have spent a little time on this case because it shows how difficult it can be to apply the important 'in accordance with the law' safeguard. As in so many areas (including proportionality, to which I shall come a little later), the courts are required to make sensitive value judgments as to which it is not surprising that there is scope for more than one view.

I shall come back to *Beghal* when I consider the question of proportionality. But I would like to mention a recent decision of our Court of Appeal which illustrates our approach to the legality principle. I do so because this principle has been in the spotlight in cases where the court has been asked to decide how to resolve

---

[4]   *Gillan v UK* [2010] ECHR 28.

the tension between the state's wish to take measures to safeguard national security and the interference with human rights that such measures may engender. In *R (Miranda) v Secretary of State for the Home Department*[5] the facts in brief were these. Mr Miranda, the husband of a Guardian newspaper journalist (Mr Greenwald), was carrying data provided by Edward Snowden through Heathrow airport. He was stopped, questioned and detained for nine hours under Schedule 7 of the 2000 Act and the hard drives that he was carrying were retained by the examining officers. Mr Miranda sought judicial review of the action taken against him on a number of grounds including: (i) that the Schedule 7 powers, being exercisable without prior judicial scrutiny, were for that reason incompatible with the right to freedom of expression guaranteed by Article 10 of the Convention; and (ii) that the use of the powers was a disproportionate interference with his right to protection of journalistic expression.

The court noted at the outset that this was a case about Article 10, whereas *Beghal* was a case about Articles 5, 6 and 8 of the Convention. The Strasbourg court has always considered there to be a vital public interest in the protection of journalistic sources. The protection of a journalist's sources is one of the cornerstones of freedom of the press. Without such protection, sources may be deterred from assisting the press in informing the public on matters of public interest. Press freedom is one of the anchors of a democratic system. It is clear enough that the Strasbourg jurisprudence requires prior or (in an urgent case) immediate *post factum* judicial oversight of interferences with Article 10 rights where journalists are required to reveal their sources. In such cases, lack of judicial oversight means that there are no safeguards sufficient to make the interference with the right 'in accordance with the law', ie so as to avoid arbitrary interferences with the right. But the *Miranda* case was not about the protection of a journalist's source. The source was known. The court said that protection of a journalist's sources was no more than one aspect of a journalist's freedom of expression. There was no reason in principle for drawing a distinction between disclosure of journalistic material *simpliciter* and disclosure of journalistic material which may identify a confidential source.

Basing itself on the decision in *Beghal*, the court below had held that the constraints on the exercise of the power were an adequate

---

[5] *R (Miranda) v Secretary of State for the Home Department* [2016] EWCA Civ 6, [2016] 1 WLR 1505.

safeguard against its arbitrary exercise. The particular features relied on were the requirements of the general law that the power be exercised on a reasoned basis, proportionately and in good faith; the limitation on the meaning of terrorism given by reference to the mental or purposive elements prescribed by section 1(1)(b) and (c); the fact that the power could only be exercised at a port or border area; and the fact that the period of detention allowed was limited to nine hours. In giving the main judgment in the Court of Appeal, I said that these constraints did not afford effective protection of journalists' Article 10 rights. The central concern was that disclosure of journalistic material (whether or not it involved the disclosure of a journalist's source) undermines the confidentiality that is inherent in such material and which is necessary to avoid the chilling effect of disclosure and to protect Article 10 rights. If journalists can have no expectation of confidentiality, they may decide against providing information on sensitive matters of public interest. The only real safeguard against the powers not being exercised rationally, proportionately and in good faith is the possibility of judicial review. But that possibility provides little protection against the damage that is done if journalistic material is disclosed when it should not be disclosed. The court therefore declared that the stop power was incompatible with Article 10 of the Convention in relation to journalistic material in that it was not subject to adequate safeguards against its arbitrary exercise. It was for Parliament to enact a provision which would provide such protection. The most obvious safeguard would be some form of judicial or other independent and impartial scrutiny conducted in such a way as to protect the confidentiality in the material.

Beghal and *Miranda* illustrate well the difficulties which face the courts in deciding whether a legal system provides effective safeguards against the arbitrary exercise of a statutory power which interferes with the enjoyment of a qualified Convention right. The Supreme Court was split in *Beghal.* The Court of Appeal disagreed with the Divisional Court in *Miranda.* Whether a constraint provides an adequate safeguard is not a hard-edged question. As I have said, it calls for an exercise of judgement on which opinions may reasonably differ. In this respect, it bears some resemblance to proportionality, an issue that was also raised in both cases. It is to that topic that I now wish to turn.

In *Beghal,* it was submitted on behalf of the defendant that the questioning and search powers contained in Schedule 7 are incompatible with Article 8 of the Convention because they are disproportionate. In cases which concern human rights protected by the Convention, our courts apply the proportionality test as the standard of review. In other cases, we have moved away from the austere irrationality standard of review to something more nuanced. In the recent case of *Keyu v Secretary of State for Foreign and Commonwealth Affairs*,[6] the Supreme Court considered whether there should be a general move away from the traditional judicial review tests to one of proportionality. The court decided that, if this were to be done, it should require consideration by an enlarged court. So far this has not happened, but we are creeping forward in that direction As long ago as 2003, I said in *R (ABCIFER) v Secretary of State for Defence*[7] that the case for the recognition of proportionality as part of English domestic law in cases which do not involve Community law or the Convention was a strong one, not least because proportionality is a more precise and sophisticated standard of review than the *Wednesbury* test, although the latter has been relaxed in recent years, even in areas which have nothing to do with fundamental rights. Indeed, the *Wednesbury* test is moving closer to proportionality. Although the court said that it had difficulty in seeing what justification there now was for retaining the *Wednesbury* test, it was not for the Court of Appeal to perform its burial rites.

So the *Wednesbury* test is still just about alive. But as I have said, there is no doubt that we apply the proportionality standard of review in cases involving alleged violations of Convention rights. In *Bank Mellat v HM Treasury (No 2)*,[8] Lord Sumption conveniently stated that four questions were inherent in the concept of proportionality. These were: (i) is the objective of the measure under consideration sufficiently important to justify limitation on a fundamental right? (ii) Is the measure rationally connected to the objective? (iii) Could a less intrusive measure have been adopted? (iv) Has a fair balance been struck between the individual rights and the interests of the community? The second of these questions does not usually admit of more than one answer. It can be resolved by the application of objective criteria. But the first, third and especially the fourth questions raise issues of value judgement on which opinions may well differ. The first involves an assessment of the relative importance

---

[6] *Keyu v Secretary of State for Foreign and Commonwealth Affairs* [2015] UKSC 69, [2016] AC 1355.

[7] *R (ABCIFER) v Secretary of State for Defence* [2003] EWCA Civ 473, [2003] QB 1397.

[8] *Bank Mellat v HM Treasury (No 2)* [2013] UKSC 38, [2014] AC 700.

of the objective of the measure and the right that is affected by it. The third involves a judgement of whether the objective could be achieved by less intrusive means. The fourth involves an assessment of whether a fair balance has been struck between the right of the individual that is affected by the measure and the interests of the community which the measure is intended to serve. In varying degrees, the judicial responses to these questions depend on subjective considerations. Some judges give more weight than others to the protection of individual human rights in balancing these rights against the need to safeguard the security interests of the community at large. Some judges are more cautions and conservative than others. That is a fact of life. Differences of approach of this kind tend to be exposed particularly acutely when the court is asked to decide whether security measures interfere with human rights too much.

Issues of proportionality arose in both the cases of *Beghal* and *Miranda.* In *Beghal,* it was not in dispute that the objective of Schedule 7 was the prevention and detection of terrorism and that this was sufficiently important to justify *some* intrusion on Article 8 rights. The power of questioning and search was rationally connected to that objective: it was designed to serve it and the evidence was that it was useful in achieving that end. The real complaint was that *any* questioning and searching was disproportionate unless it was based on an objectively established reasonable ground for suspecting the person concerned of being engaged in terrorist acts. The defendant's case was that a less intrusive measure, namely a power based on objective grounds for suspicion, could and should have been adopted, and that by reason of its failure to do so, the legislation did not strike a fair balance.

The majority of the court held that the measure was not disproportionate. They reasoned as follows. It was common ground that the state was entitled to a generous margin of judgment in striking the balance. The importance for the public of the prevention and detection of acts of terrorism could hardly be overstated and the level of risk of such acts was at least as high as it had been at any time since the powers were introduced. The unanimous view of all independent observers was that the power to question and search which was not grounded on objectively demonstrable reasonable suspicion of involvement in terrorism was of undoubted value in the struggle against terrorism. The power would not have the same utility if it were restricted to those individuals in respect of whom a reasonable suspicion could be demonstrated to the satisfaction of the court. The level of intrusion into the privacy of an individual was comparatively light and not beyond the reasonable expectation of those who travel across the UK's international borders. Taking all the circumstances into account, the majority concluded that the port questioning and associated search powers represented a fair balance between the rights of the individual and the interests of the community at large.

Lord Kerr took a different view. He agreed with the majority that they had identified the four relevant questions. He agreed that the objective of the Schedule 7 powers of counteracting terrorism was a legitimate aim and that obtaining information about whether a person appears to be a terrorist is rationally connected to that aim. But he said that, while the state enjoys an area of discretionary judgment as to what measures are needed to pursue a particular aim, this does not relieve it of the obligation to produce some evidence that the specific means chosen were no more than is required. There was no evidence that a suspicion-less power to stop, detain, search and question was the only way to achieve the goal of combating terrorism. And the absence of any evidence of a need for such a power led Lord Kerr to conclude that the measure did not strike a fair balance between the Article 8 rights of the persons affected by the powers and the security interests of the community at large. It is noteworthy that, despite it being common ground that the state was entitled to a generous margin of judgment, Lord Kerr held that Schedule 7 did not strike a fair balance.

A similar issue arose in the *Bank Mellat* case to which I have referred. The Treasury made an order pursuant to Schedule 7 to the 2000 Act prohibiting all persons operating in the financial sector in the UK from entering into or continuing to participate in any transaction or business relationship with Bank Mellat, an Iranian bank, on the grounds that the Treasury reasonably believed that the development or production of nuclear weapons in Iran posed a significant risk to the national interests of the UK. The bank applied to the court to set aside the order on a number of grounds. These included that the requirements were disproportionate to the risk posed to the national interests of the UK. The majority acknowledged that the subject matter of the application lay in the areas of foreign policy and national security, areas in which the Treasury was to be accorded a large margin of judgment; that the consequences of nuclear proliferation justified a precautionary approach and called for experienced executive judgement; but that although the Order had a rational connection with the objective of frustrating the Iranian weapons programme, the distinction made between the claimant bank and other Iranian banks was irrational and disproportionate. The majority acknowledged that a large margin of judgement was required because of the importance of the public interest in nuclear non-proliferation; and the question of whether some measure is apt to limit the risk posed for the national interest by nuclear proliferation in a foreign country depends on an experienced judgement of the international implications of a wide range of information, some of which may be secret. This is something that is pre-eminently a matter for the executive. For the majority, however, the margin of judgement was not large enough to overcome the irrationality of the singling out of the claimant bank and the fact that it was disproportionate to any contribution that the measure could be expected to making it more difficult for Iran to finance its weapons programmes.

The minority analysed the evidence and concluded that an order directed against the claimant bank was not pointless or arbitrary. The court was in a poor position to weigh the effectiveness of a measure whose object was to reduce (if not eliminate) Iran's ability to fund its weapons programmes. This was not an area in which the court had any expertise. It should only hold that such a measure was irrational or disproportionate if it was confident that this had been clearly demonstrated. On the facts of the case, the court was not confident that it had been.

Before leaving this topic, I wish to return to *Miranda.* It was submitted on behalf of Mr Miranda that the exercise of the Schedule 7 power against him was an unjustified and disproportionate interference with his right to freedom of expression. The issue turned on the fourth question: had the exercise of the power struck a fair balance between Mr Miranda's Article 10 rights and the security interests of the wider community?

The examining officers (and those who were directing their operations) knew that the material in the possession of Mr Miranda contained personal information that would allow individuals involved in security operations to be identified and that it was highly likely to describe techniques that had been crucial in counter-terrorism operations. Mr Miranda sought to challenge the defendants' evidence as to the actual or potential damaging effects of the dissemination of the material seized from him. Mr Miranda placed much weight on the need to have regard to the importance of 'responsible journalism' as a factor when weighing the competing interests in the case. It was submitted on his behalf that the evidence of the defendants' witnesses indicated no more than a theoretical risk that would arise only if key parts of the data were released into the public domain. There was no evidence that there was a real risk that such disclosure would occur. There was nothing to suggest that Mr Miranda, Mr Greenwald or the *Guardian* newspaper would not approach the question of publication with the appropriate degree of responsibility.

The Court of Appeal started its consideration of the issue of fair balance by saying that, when determining the proportionality of a decision taken by the police in the interests of national security, the court should accord a substantial degree of deference to their expertise in assessing the risk to national security and in weighing it against countervailing interests. This is because the police have the institutional competence and the constitutional responsibility to make such assessments and decisions. Our approach differs somewhat from that taken by the courts, for example, in Israel whose judges are fiercely independent of the executive. This is well illustrated in the Israeli cases dealing with judicial review challenges to the route of the security fence or wall. The courts in Israel accept that the military commander is the expert in relation to the security considerations of one route as against another route. The courts do not normally second guess the military when it comes to the security assessments of particular decisions of this kind. They do not have the expertise to do so and may well not have access to secret material which is highly relevant to the decision that has been taken. I say 'normally' because one of the earliest lessons I learnt as a judge was never to say 'never'. There may be circumstances in which it can be shown without fear of contradiction that a decision taken by the military or the police ostensibly on grounds of national security cannot be justified even on the basis of military or police considerations alone. In a case of this kind, the court is unlikely to give special weight to the expertise of the decision-maker. But such cases are likely to be rare.

The courts in Israel have, however, said that, whereas the military commander is the expert as to where, from a security point of view, the fence should be erected, the court has the expertise to determine whether harm caused to local residents by the proposed route is proportionate. This is the fair balance question to which I referred earlier.

As the decisions to which I have referred show, our courts would accord a substantial margin of judgement to the military. In *Miranda*, we took into account the fact that the police were ultimately accountable to Parliament and that the constitutional responsibility for the protection of national security lies with the elected government. The greater the risk to national security, the greater the weight that should be accorded to it when balancing it against a countervailing factor. The assessment of the police and the Security Service was that the risk in that case was substantial. They had the expertise and access to secret intelligence material which made it very difficult to challenge such an assessment in a court. The greater the potential harm, the greater the weight that should be accorded to the community interests. The potential for harm in that case was very substantial. The court concluded that the compelling national security interests clearly outweighed Mr Miranda's Article 10 rights on the facts of that case.

At this point, it is also worth mentioning that it is well established in the US jurisprudence that the courts will pay substantial deference to the judgement of the executive in relation to decisions on national security. But that does not mean that national security always carries the day. The court has to weigh the rights afforded by the Constitution to individuals against the risk to national security. As I have said, it is usually very difficult for a court to assess the gravity of the risk. This weighing exercise lies at the heart of the current challenge to Donald Trump's Executive Order banning visitors from seven countries from entering the US for 90 days. So far, the litigation has only been about the order granted by the district court temporarily restraining the implementation of the Executive Order and whether it should be stayed pending the hearing of the substantive claim. In other words, despite the hype, it is something of a preliminary skirmish.

To end this lecture, I wish to return to the question of the protection of unqualified rights in an age of terrorism. I have already spoken about the unqualified Article 3 Convention right not to be subjected to torture or degrading treatment. I should say something about the Article 6 right to a fair trial. This too is an unqualified right, although issues can arise as to the content of the right. The right to a fair trial is a cardinal requirement of the rule of law. It includes the right in a party to know the case he has to meet and the evidence on which it is based, particularly in criminal cases. This is trite and elementary. But terrorist cases pose particular challenges here too. Under the Prevention of Terrorism Act 2005, the Home Secretary had the power to make a control order against a person if he had reasonable grounds for suspecting the person to be or to have been involved in terrorism-related activity and he considered that it was necessary, in order to protect the public against the risk of terrorism, to make such an order. The order could not lawfully deprive the controlee of his liberty, but could contain obligations not far short of house arrest whose cumulative effect could render any normal life impossible.

Following the making of such an order, there had to be a hearing before a judge at which the question whether the Home Secretary's decision to make the order was flawed would be considered. It would be flawed if there was no evidence reasonably capable of supporting the order. But under the Act and the rules made under it, no information was to be made available to the controlee or his lawyers if disclosure would be contrary to the public interest. A special advocate could be appointed to represent the interests of the controlee, but on condition that the advocate did not share with the controlee or his lawyers information judged to be contrary to the public interest. This could be very prejudicial to the interests of the controlee who, if the information were disclosed to him, might be able to provide a 'knock-out blow' which would completely destroy its effect. Here we find the tension between an unqualified right (the right to a fair hearing) and the community interest in national security exposed in a particularly acute form. It is not surprising that the lawfulness of the special advocate procedure was tested in our courts and in Strasbourg in a number of cases. The limitations of the special advocates system have been the subject of much criticism. Those who have acted as special advocates have spoken eloquently of the difficulties they face in representing their clients effectively when operating in what has been described as a 'Kafkaesque' setting. But in the end, the courts decided that the special advocates system did not violate Article 6. A compromise solution was devised. They said that Article 6 required that in such cases the 'gist' of the evidence relied on against the party had to be disclosed.

I am conscious that I have only touched on a few aspects of the vexed, difficult and important subject of my lecture. Terrorists present a real and continuing threat. In a nuclear age, the potential to wreak havoc is alarming. It is the duty of all responsible governments and security forces to do everything in their power to minimise the threat. But not at any price. Striking the balance in the right place between doing everything possible to reduce, if not eliminate, the threat on the one hand and protecting the human rights of individuals potentially affected by those steps on the other hand is one of the biggest challenges of our time.

14

Religion and the Law: Some Current Problems[*]

IT TOOK ENGLISH law some time to accept that different religious philosophies should be tolerated without arbitrary discrimination. In 1739, Elias de Pas made a will by which he left £1,200 for the purpose of teaching Jewish children about their religion. Lord Hardwicke, the Lord Chancellor, held in 1754 that because the purpose of Mr de Pas' bequest was to promote a religion other than Christianity, the Attorney-General should identify a different purpose for which Mr de Pas' money should best be used. The Attorney-General decided that the most appropriate use of the funds was to support a preacher to instruct children about Christianity.[1] Applying that authority, and others like it, Lord Eldon, the Lord Chancellor, stated in 1819 that it was

> the duty of every judge presiding in an English Court of Justice, when he is told that there is no difference between worshipping the Supreme Being in chapel, church or synagogue, to recollect that Christianity is part of the law of England.[2]

It is a long journey from Mr de Pas and Lord Eldon to the Human Rights Act 1998, which incorporated into our law Article 9 of the European Convention on Human Rights, which guarantees the right to freedom of thought, conscience and religion.[3]

---

[*] Lecture given in November 2016 at Centre for Islamic Studies, Oxford.
[1] *Da Costa v De Pas* (1754) Amb 228, 27 ER 150.
[2] *In Re Bedford Charity* (1819) 2 Swans 471, 527, 36 ER 696, 712.
[3] See *McFarlane v Relate Avon Ltd* [2010] EWCA Civ 880, (2010) 29 BHRC 249. Laws LJ (in the Court of Appeal) refused the applicant leave to appeal against the decision of the Employment Appeal Tribunal that he was not the victim of unfair dismissal or religious discrimination. His employer dismissed him as a relationship counsellor by reason of his refusal, in accordance with his Christian beliefs, to counsel same-sex couples on sexual matters. Laws LJ stated, at 257, para 22, that 'The precepts of any one religion, and belief system, cannot, by force of their religious origins, sound any louder in the general law than the precepts of any other'.

The European Court of Human Rights has emphasised that freedom of religion under Article 9 is 'one of the foundations of a "democratic society" ... [and] one of the most vital elements that go to make up the identity of believers and of their conception of life'.[4] Such a general statement, however welcome, cannot disguise the fact that the scope of, and the limits to, the right to religion pose some of the most sensitive questions facing the courts, and society, in the twenty-first century. How should the law address, for example, the wish of schoolchildren, employees and others to wear clothes and symbols which express their religious beliefs; the dispute about the right to build a mosque near Ground Zero in New York; and the plan by a pastor in Florida to institute 'International Burn a Koran Day'? When I started in practice more than 40 years ago, in England and Wales (and I suspect in most if not all other democratic societies) legal disputes involving issues of religion were collectors' items. In the last few years, they have become increasingly common. There is now a considerable body of Strasbourg and domestic jurisprudence on the subject. There is no sign that legal issues involving religion are abating.

The legal historian who is interested in the subject of religious freedom will be aware of the magnificent letter written in August 1790 by President George Washington to the Hebrew Congregation at Newport, Rhode Island, explaining that the government 'gives to bigotry no sanction, to persecution no assistance' and expressing the hope, with the use of biblical quotation:

> May the children of the stock of Abraham who dwell in this land continue to merit and enjoy the good will of the other inhabitants—while every one shall sit in safety under his own vine and fig tree and there shall be none to make him afraid.[5]

If only I had the skill to couch my judgments in such inspiring language. But these days we are rightly expected to identify legal principles and analyse the facts and the law raised by a dispute with the precision of a surgeon rather than the colour and imagination of a poet. So what are the principles by which we should decide disputes between, on the one hand, what individuals regard as religious matters of fundamental importance to the way they conduct their lives and, on the other hand, the rights of others and important state interests.

---

[4] *Kokkinakis v Greece* [1993] ECHR 20 at para 31.
[5] Mark A Mastromarino (ed), *The Papers of George Washington*, Presidential Series, vol 6 (University of Virginia, 1996) 284–286.

The law draws a distinction between freedom of belief and freedom to take action in furtherance of your beliefs. It has been said that a court is not equipped to weigh the cogency, seriousness and coherence of theological doctrine. On the whole, a person can believe what he or she likes. Religious belief is none of the state's business. But freedom to practise your religious beliefs in ways that may conflict with the rights of others or with the interests of society is a different matter. Article 9 does not protect every act inspired or motivated by religious belief. The freedom to manifest belief is qualified. In a pluralist society, a balance has to be struck between freedom to practise one's own beliefs and the interests of others affected by those practices.

The easiest cases are those where the manifestation of religious rights causes physical harm to others. We cannot, and do not, allow people to abuse a child believed to be possessed by the devil, to set fire to an abortion clinic, to carry out genital mutilation of young girls,[6] or to massacre infidels, however sincere the religious beliefs which motivate such action, and however important this may be to the faith of the believer.

In the *Williamson* case, the House of Lords held that Parliament was entitled to take the view that the protection of children required a prohibition on corporal punishment in schools, even in schools established to provide a Christian education in accordance with biblical doctrine, which the parents believed required corporal punishment. As Baroness Hale of Richmond concluded, the right of the child 'to be brought up without institutional violence' must be respected 'whether or not his parents and teachers believe otherwise' by reason of Proverbs 13:24: 'A father who spares the rod hates his son'.[7]

Less easy are cases where the manifestation of religious belief does not physically harm others but nonetheless conflicts with others' rights and their inclusion in society. In December 2010, our Court of Appeal decided that a local authority was entitled to require its employee, a registrar of births, marriages and deaths, to conduct civil partnership ceremonies between persons of the same sex even though such unions were contrary to her religious beliefs. A registrar could not claim any right not to perform part of her

---

[6] See the Female Genital Mutilation Act 2003.

[7] *R (Williamson) v Secretary of State for Education and Employment* [2005] UKHL 15, [2005] 2 AC 246 at para 86.

job, and thereby discriminate against members of the homosexual community.[8] If you are employed by a public authority to perform specific duties, you cannot claim an entitlement not to perform any of those duties, as defined by Parliament, because you disagree on religious grounds. Either you perform your duties or you find another job. This may seem to have been a harsh decision, because so strong were the religious beliefs of the registrar that she lost her job as a result. But the decision of the Court of Appeal was upheld by the European Court of Human Rights. Just as the registrar cannot demand special treatment if she objects on religious grounds to a black man marrying a white woman (not an unrealistic example if your religious opinions were formed in parts of South Africa or the deep South of the United States), so the registrar cannot demand special treatment if she objects on religious grounds to the civil partnership of a gay couple.

Similarly, a Catholic adoption agency cannot refuse to consider placing a child with a gay couple if that is in the best interests of the child, however much this may offend against its religious beliefs. In two other cases, our courts had to decide whether a couple could refuse to offer a double-bedded room in their bed and breakfast accommodation to a male homosexual couple. Their motivation was that, on religious grounds, they believed that monogamous heterosexual marriage is the form of partnership uniquely intended for full sexual relations and that homosexual relations are sinful. The Court of Appeal held in both cases that this was discriminatory of homosexuals and unlawful. An appeal in one of them was dismissed by the Supreme Court. The couple had no difficulty in manifesting their religious beliefs generally in society, but they could not do so in the commercial context that they had chosen. The fact that the bed and breakfast was also their home made no difference.

Most recently, in the case of *Lee v Ashers Baking Co Ltd*,[9] the county court in Northern Ireland had to consider whether a baking company, who had refused to make a cake for the plaintiff carrying a pro-gay marriage message, had directly discriminated against him on the grounds of sexual orientation or political opinion or religious belief. The defendants, the bakery, argued that the domestic provisions of the Equality Act prohibiting discrimination on the grounds

---

[8] *Ladele v London Borough of Islington* [2009] EWCA Civ 1357, [2010] 1 WLR 955 at paras 51–52 and 55.

[9] *Lee v Ashers Baking Co Ltd* [2015] NICty 2 (19 May 2015).

of sexual orientation should be read down to take account of their right to manifest their religious belief under Article 9 of the ECHR or their right to freedom of expression under Article 10. The judge found that there had been discrimination against the plaintiff on both grounds—sexual orientation (because he was gay) and political belief (because he supported same sex marriage). The judge found the restriction placed on the defendants' right to manifest their religion was legitimate and should not be read down. His appeal has been recently dismissed by the Northern Ireland Court of Appeal.

What we see from these cases is that the equality laws do not prevent people from *believing* that homosexual acts offend against the laws of God. But if you offer a service to the public, it must be on terms that do not discriminate against persons on grounds which society generally finds unacceptable. The Pope's contention, on his visit in 2010 to England, that religious bodies must be 'free to act in accordance with their own principles and specific convictions'[10] is unsustainable if those religious bodies are involved in the provision of secular services such as adoption or the provision of goods and services in the public domain.

Even where the manifestation of religious beliefs does not conflict with the fundamental rights of others, but with other interests which society considers of importance, the courts have given limited weight to religious interests. Applying such principles, the European Commission of Human Rights held in 1997 that there was no interference with Article 9 rights when an employee was required to work on Sundays, as she was free to resign.[11]

There are many examples of such cases. In 2001, the Court of Appeal in England and Wales rejected the contention that Rastafarians should be exempt for religious reasons from the criminal laws which prohibit the sale and use of cannabis.[12] In 2010, the Supreme Court of Canada decided that it was not a breach of religious rights to require those who want a driving licence to provide a photograph, despite religious objections by the Hutterian Brethren to having a picture taken. They relied on Exodus 20:4: 'You shall not make for yourself an idol, or any likeness ...'. The majority judgment concluded that, if you want the benefit of a driving licence, you must provide a photograph, which serves a useful purpose in

[10] *The Times* (18 September 2010).

[11] *Stedman v United Kingdom* [1997] ECHR 178.

[12] See, for example, *R v Paul Simon Taylor* [2001] EWCA Crim 2263, [2002] 1 Cr App Rep 519.

preventing licences being used by those to whom they have not been issued.[13] In early 2016, the Fourth Section of the European Court of Human Rights had to consider whether the Article 9 rights of a person who was under house arrest were breached by the decision to deny him leave to attend catholic mass once a week. The Court found that there had been interference but that this was justified. The claimant's house arrest pursued the legitimate aim of protecting public order and ensuring his presence throughout the criminal proceedings.[14] There is also a distinction to be made between manifestation of religious beliefs and choices an individual may make consistent with their religious beliefs but which are not a requirement of their religion. Last year, the Employment Tribunal found the London Underground was not required to provide to an employee five weeks' annual leave to attend a religious festival when that was more than the three weeks' leave to which all other employees were entitled. The Tribunal found that attending the festival was not a requirement of his religion.[15]

So you are entitled to believe almost anything you like. But society is entitled to impose the general laws which it considers necessary to restrict the manifestation of your religious beliefs, so long as society takes note of the conflict with religious rights and reasonably decides that the interests of society nevertheless require the application of those general laws. No doubt, as Justice Sachs suggested in the Constitutional Court of South Africa, 'the State should, wherever reasonably possible, seek to avoid putting believers to extremely painful and intensely burdensome choices of either being true to their faith or else respectful of the law'.[16] The importance of the principle 'live and let live' should not be underestimated. But if the state does conclude that important state interests or the rights of others are advanced by interfering with religious freedom, then religious freedom must give way.

The wish to wear clothes or other items of religious significance has generated a good deal of litigation in recent years and will, I am sure, continue to do so. There may well be good reasons for imposing a dress code at a school, in a university or at the workplace.

---

[13] *R in the Right of the Province of Alberta v Hutterian Brethren of Wilson Colony, A-G of Canada intervening* (2009) 28 BHRC 147 (Can SC).

[14] *Suveges v Hungary* [2016] ECHR 22 (5 January 2016).

[15] *Gareddu v London Underground Ltd* (2016) UKEAT/0086/16, [2017] IRLR 404.

[16] *Christian Education South Africa v Minister of Education* (2000) 9 BHRC 53 at para 35 (SA Const Ct).

The Grand Chamber of the European Court of Human Rights decided in 2005 that it was not a breach of the right to religious freedom for a female university student in Turkey to be refused admission to lectures if she insisted on wearing an Islamic headscarf.[17] It may also be appropriate to require people to remove the covering from their face when entering a public building or dealing with an official from whom they are claiming a benefit. In reaching its conclusion, the court had regard to the Turkish state's principle of secularism.

In 2006, the House of Lords rejected the complaint of a schoolgirl who wanted to manifest her Muslim religious beliefs by wearing the jilbab, at school.[18] In 2010 in another case, the Court of Appeal had to deal with the British Airways policy whereby employees who wore a uniform were only permitted to wear a religious item, such as a cross, if it was concealed by the uniform, unless it was a mandatory requirement of their religion to wear such an item and it could not be concealed (eg a turban for Sikhs). The claimant, a devout Christian, wore a cross at work visible over her uniform as a personal expression of faith, although it was not a requirement of her religion. She was suspended and claimed that she had been discriminated against on the ground of her religious beliefs. Her claim was dismissed. But the court in Strasbourg allowed her appeal on the grounds that the ban was a disproportionate interference with her right to manifest her religious belief. The cross was small; it did not interfere with her ability to perform her duties and did not have any negative impact on BA's brand or image. In another case, a nurse refused to remove a rather large visible cross and chain when instructed to do so by her employers and was moved to a non-nursing position. The reason for the restriction on jewellery, including religious symbols, was to protect the health and safety of patients and nurses. Her complaint of discrimination was rejected by the Employment Appeal Tribunal. The European Court of Human Rights held that there was no violation of the right to manifest religious beliefs, since the ban on the cross was proportionate.

In February 2010, the Strasbourg Court held that it was a breach of Article 9 for members of a religious group to be convicted of criminal offences in Turkey for wearing religious dress in public. The court emphasised that there is a distinction between wearing religious

---

[17]   *Sahin v Turkey* [2005] ECHR 819 at paras 104–123. See also *Dogru v France* [2009] ECHR 1579.
[18]   *R (SB) v Governors of Denbigh High School* [2006] UKHL 15, [2007] 1 AC 100.

dress in public and wearing it in schools or other institutions such as government offices where there may be good reason to insist on religious neutrality.[19] There is no public interest to weigh against the manifestation of religious beliefs, only the unease of the non-believer that women should wish so to conceal themselves from the public. As against this, some might say that there is a public interest in being able to identify people who commit crimes in public places and that clothing that makes this impossible is contrary to that interest.

France, with its strong secular tradition, has generated some important cases in this area. In 2004, it passed a law prohibiting the wearing in public schools of symbols or clothing by which students conspicuously indicate their religious beliefs. In 2010, it passed a second law which effectively banned the wearing of the burka and the niqab in public. The lawfulness of both laws has been the subject of legal challenge. I should say that there seems to be little appetite for such measures in the UK or in most other European countries.

In 2009, the Strasbourg court considered the compatibility of the earlier law with Article 9 of the Convention in six conjoined cases. The court held that, although the ban constituted a restriction on the applicants' freedom to manifest their religion, it pursued the legitimate aim of protecting the rights and freedoms of others and public order and was not disproportionate. It said that 'a spirit of compromise on the part of individuals was necessary in order to maintain the values of a democratic society' and 'expulsion was not disproportionate as a sanction because the pupils still had the possibility of continuing their schooling by correspondence courses'. The ban did not in any event apply to private schools. The court dismissed the claims as 'manifestly unfounded'. This may seem rather surprising. The possibility of being educated by correspondence course is not an obviously satisfactory alternative to education by face-to-face teaching and some might not have the means to pay for private education.

The compatibility of the later law with various articles of the Convention (including Article 9) was considered by the Strasbourg court in the case of *S.A.S. v France* in a decision given on 1 July 2014.[20] The legality of the law had been the subject of much debate in France. The official position taken by the state was that the practice of wearing clothing which concealed the face was at odds with the values of the Republic as expressed in the maxim 'liberty, equality,

---

[19] *Arslan v Turkey* App no 41135/98 (ECtHR, 23 February 2010).
[20] *S.A.S. v France* App no 43835/11 (ECtHR, 1 July 2014).

fraternity'. A report of a parliamentary commission had concluded that the practice was a symbol of subservience and negated the principle of gender equality and of the equal dignity of human beings. The full face veil 'represented a denial of fraternity, constituting the negation of contact with others and a flagrant infringement of the French principle of living together ('le vivre ensemble')'. On the other hand, the National Advisory Commission on Human Rights had said that it was not in favour of a general and absolute ban. It took the view that the principle of secularism alone could not serve as a basis for such a general measure. It was not for the state to determine whether a matter fell within the realm of religion; and public order could justify a prohibition only if it were limited in time and space. This report emphasised the risk of stigmatising Muslims and pointed out that a general prohibition could be detrimental to women, in particular because those who were made to wear the full-face veil would additionally be denied access to public areas. The *Conseil d'Etat* had questioned the lawfulness and the practicability of prohibiting the wearing of the full veil in public places, having regard to the rights and freedoms guaranteed by the Constitution, the Convention and European Union law. Instead of a blanket ban, it had recommended a more nuanced approach which included prohibition of the full veil only where identification was necessary in the interests of public safety and in certain other specified circumstances.

Despite the advice of the *Conseil d'Etat,* the uncompromising law of 2010 was passed. A challenge was inevitable and was duly made in the Strasbourg court. The court did not dismiss the claim as being inadmissible this time. It had little difficulty in finding that the law interfered with the applicant's rights guaranteed by Article 9 and that the interference was prescribed by law. The more controversial question was whether the interference was in pursuance of a legitimate aim and was proportionate to that aim. The French government contended that the Law pursued two legitimate aims: public safety and 'respect for the minimum set of values of an open and democratic society'. The court accepted that the Law was passed in pursuance of the aim of securing public safety. It also accepted the second aim. It understood the view that individuals who are present in open places may not wish to see the development of practices or attitudes which 'could fundamentally call into question the possibility of open interpersonal relationships, which, by virtue of an established consensus, forms an indispensable element of community life within the society in question'.

Finally, the court had to decide whether the interference with the applicant's Convention rights was necessary in a democratic society. As regards the question of public safety, it said that, in view of the impact on the rights of women who wish to wear the full-face veil for religious reasons, a blanket ban could be regarded as proportionate only in the context of a general threat to public safety. The aim of promoting public safety could be achieved by a mere obligation on the part of the women to show their faces and identify themselves where a risk to the safety of person or property is established or where particular circumstances entail a suspicion of identity fraud. This aim did not, therefore, justify a blanket ban.

The court then turned its attention to the other legitimate aim, namely the observance of the minimum requirements of life in society as part of the 'protection of the rights and freedoms of others'. It held that the ban could be regarded as justified in principle in so far as it seeks to guarantee the conditions of 'living together'. The question remained, however, whether the ban was proportionate to that aim. The court noted that, although the scope of the ban was broad, it did not affect the freedom to wear in public any garment or item of clothing (with or without a religious connotation) which did not have the effect of concealing the face. It was also relevant that the ban was not expressly based on the religious significance of the clothing, but only on the fact that it concealed the face. But the most important feature was that, in enacting the Law, the French government was responding to a practice which the state considered to be incompatible with the ground rules of social communication and the requirements of 'living together'. The French State was seeking to protect a principle of interaction between individuals which in its view was 'essential for the expression not only of pluralism, but also of tolerance and broadmindedness without which there is no democratic society'. In other words, for the Republic of France the question whether or not the full-face veil should be permitted in public places constituted a choice of society. For this reason, the court said that it had a duty to exercise a degree of restraint in its review of Convention compliance 'since such review will lead it to assess a balance that has been struck by means of a democratic process with the society in question'. It followed that France had a wide margin of appreciation in this case. The court also took into account that there was little common ground amongst the member states of the Council of Europe on the issue of wearing the full-face veil in public. In the result, the court decided that, having regard to the breadth of the margin of appreciation to be afforded in this case, the ban could be regarded as proportionate to the aim of the preservation of the conditions of living together as an element of the 'protection of the rights and freedoms of others'.

I have spent some time on these two decisions of the Strasbourg court because they are recent cases and they deal with difficult and sensitive issues which I think are likely to come before the courts of different countries for some time to come. In my view, it is revealing of the attitude of the European Court of Human Rights to these issues that it felt able to dismiss the challenges to the first Law as manifestly unfounded. The challenge to the second Law was dealt with in considerable detail and with much care. But despite the length of the judgment, it seems to me that the challenge failed simply and essentially because: (i) the Law was the product of the French democratic process and reflected the values of French society; and (ii) it should therefore be accorded a wide margin of appreciation. Absent these factors, I would have been very surprised if any court would have concluded that the ban was necessary in a democratic society. The Strasbourg court has been criticised both by the UK and by other member states for being insensitive to their views and to local considerations. In my view, some of these criticisms are unwarranted. However, the judges of the Strasbourg court are well aware of them and of the need to accord the member states an appropriate margin of appreciation. The decision in the second case would appear to be a striking example of a positive and perhaps surprising response to the criticisms.

There is currently pending before the European Court of Human Rights an application complaining about a ban in Belgian law against the wearing of a full-face veil in public spaces.[21] Earlier this year, the court dealt with an application by a lawyer in Spain who had been asked by the President of the Spanish court to move to the area reserved for members of the public, as she was wearing a hijab and lawyers appearing before the Court were only permitted to cover their heads with the official cap (a biretta).[22] The European Court of Human Rights declared the application inadmissible on the grounds that the way the applicant had conducted the domestic proceedings prevented the domestic court from being able to make a finding on the merits.

[21] *Belkacemi and Oussar v Belgium* (App no 377789/13) (a similar application *Dikir v Belgium* (App no 4619/12) is also pending).
[22] *Barik Edidi v Spain* [2016] ECHR 164.

The wearing of religious clothing is perhaps the manifestation of religious belief that has given rise to the most litigation, certainly in recent years. Generally, the manifestation of religious beliefs is given very limited weight by the courts. Other rights and interests often outweigh them. This is surprising in view of the Strasbourg court's statement that freedom of religion is one of the foundations of a democratic society. But there is an important exception in European human rights law. It gives very limited protection to freedom of speech which insults religious beliefs. Exercising freedom of expression can be very dangerous when it offends religious sensibilities. After Ayatollah Khomeini issued a fatwa in Iran in 1989, the novelist Salman Rushdie faced death threats from Muslims because of his novel, *The Satanic Verses*. His Japanese translator was murdered, and others associated with the book severely injured. Rushdie himself had to live in secret destinations, with police protection.[23] All of this for writing a book.

In 2004, violent protests by Sikhs led to the closure of a play, *Behzti* (dishonour), being staged at the Birmingham Repertory Theatre.[24] The publication in Denmark in 2005 and 2006 of cartoons of the Prophet Mohammed led to riots around the word, in which nearly 250 people died.[25]

The United States Supreme Court adopted a very clear principle in 1952 when overturning the ban on Roberto Rossellini's film 'The Miracle' issued by the New York Board of Regents authorities after Cardinal Spellman condemned its contents. The Board of Regents had decided that the 'mockery or profaning of these beliefs that are sacred to any portion of our citizenship is abhorrent to the laws of this great State'. Allowing an appeal by the film's distributors, Mr Justice Clark announced for the Court that

> it is not the business of government in our nation to suppress real or imagined attacks upon a particular religious doctrine, whether they appear in publications, speeches or motion pictures.[26]

That principle protects even those who use freedom of speech to provoke the faithful in an insulting and puerile manner which endangers the lives of others, such as Pastor Terry Jones, the leader

---

[23] Christopher Hitchens, *God is not Great* (Hachette, 2007) at paras 28–30.

[24] See *R (Singh) v Chief Constable of West Midlands Police* [2006] EWCA Civ 1118, [2007] 2 All ER 297.

[25] Jytte Klausen, *The Cartoons that Shook the World* (Yale University Press, 2009) at paras 106–107.

[26] *Joseph Burstyn Inc v Wilson* 343 US 495 (1952).

of a small sect in Gainesville, Florida, who instituted 'International Burn a Koran Day' in 2010 to reflect his opposition to Islam.

The European Court of Human Rights has, however, on at least three occasions refused to protect freedom of expression against strong religious feelings. In 1985, the Austrian courts ordered the seizure and forfeiture of a film because its contents would offend Christian religious feelings. God, Jesus Christ and the Virgin Mary were portrayed in a very unflattering light. The European Court of Human Rights held, by six votes to three, that there had been no breach of Article 10 of the European Convention on Human Rights, the right to freedom of expression, because of the need to protect people against insults to their religious feelings.[27]

Similarly in 1996, by a majority of 7 to 2, the court dismissed a complaint about the refusal of the Video Appeals Committee of the British Board of Film Classification to grant a certificate for a video work because it was considered blasphemous in that it portrayed a nun imagining sexual activity with Christ on the cross.[28]

In 2005, the court upheld by 4-3 the decision of the Turkish courts to impose a fine on a publisher for a novel critical of the Prophet Muhammad. The book was, said the court, an 'abusive' and an 'offensive attack on matters regarded as sacred by Moslems'. The three dissenting judges accepted that the novel could well cause deep offence to devout Muslims. But, they emphasised, 'a democratic society is not a theocratic society' and they argued that the majority judgments 'place too much emphasis on conformism or uniformity of thought'.[29]

The religious and political tensions which are now arising in many European communities over issues such as immigration and refugees are likely to give rise to more questions in this area. It is likely that it will be necessary to explore further and define more precisely the boundary between offensive free expression (which is and should be tolerated in a democratic society) and expression which incites hatred (which is not and should not be tolerated).

Francoise Tulkens, a judge and Vice President of the European Court of Human Rights, has suggested that Article 17 of the Convention

---

[27]   *Otto-Preminger Institut v Austria* [1994] ECHR 26.

[28]   *Wingrove v United Kingdom* [1996] ECHR 60.

[29]   *IA v Turkey* (Application no 42571/98, 13 September 2005). See also *Gunduz v Turkey* [2003] ECHR 652, para 37, where the European Court of Human Rights said that in the context of religious opinions and beliefs there is 'an obligation to avoid as far as possible expressions that are gratuitously offensive to others and thus an infringement of their rights, and which therefore do not contribute to any form of public debate capable of furthering progress in human affairs'.

may be increasingly invoked in the context of 'the current resurgence of certain forms of extremism across Europe.' Article 17 provides that nothing in the Convention is to be interpreted 'as implying for any State, group or person any right to engage in any activity or perform any act aimed at the destruction of any of the rights and freedoms set forth herein'. In practice, what this means is that a person cannot rely on the provisions of the Convention to assert that he may act in a way that destroys the rights of others.

In 2015, the Court invoked Article 17 in the case of *M'Bala M'Bala v France*.[30] M'Bala, a well-known comedian, invited Robert Faurisson, an academic who had been convicted several times in France of Holocaust denial, to join him on stage. M'Bala then invited an actor, who was wearing a striped prison uniform with a yellow star sewn on it, to present M. Faurisson with a 'prize' of a three-branched candlestick which had an apple on each branch. M'Bala was charged and found guilty of insulting a person or group of persons on the ground that they belonged to an ethnic community, nation, race or religion. M'Bala complained to the European Court of Human Rights that his conviction was in breach inter alia of his Article 10 right of freedom of expression. The Court found that, by reason of Article 17, M'Bala's show was not protected by Article 10. His pursuit of an Article 10 claim would be against the letter and spirit of the Convention.

In an earlier case in 2001, the British National Party's attempted reliance on Article 10 was also rejected by virtue of Article 17.[31] A regional organiser of the BNP had displayed in the window of his flat a sign which read 'Islam out of Britain—Protect the British People'. He was charged with, and convicted of, the offence of displaying a sign with hostility towards a religious or racial group. His application to the European Court of Human Rights was rejected as inadmissible. The Court said that 'the words and images on the poster amounted to a public expression of attack on all Muslims in the United Kingdom' and 'Such a general, vehement attack against a religious group, linking the group as a whole with a grave act of terrorism, is incompatible with the values proclaimed and guaranteed by the Convention, notably tolerance, social peace and non-discrimination'. The claim was therefore ruled inadmissible.

It seems to me that there is a danger that the use of Article 17 could get out of hand. It is potentially wide-ranging in scope. I agree

---

[30] *M'Bala M'Bala v France* [2015] ECHR 354.
[31] *Norwood v United Kingdom* App no 23131/03 (ECtHR 16 November 2004).

with the assessment of Francoise Tulkens that it should be deployed carefully and with moderation. Otherwise, there is a real risk that it will lead to the suppression of the right of freedom of expression.

When considering freedom of expression in the context of religion, we should not lose sight of the fact that, to use the language of the minority in *IA v Turkey*, 'a democratic society is not a theocratic society' and a democracy does not insist on 'conformism or uniformity of thought'. Indeed, quite the opposite. When it comes to criticism of religious doctrine or belief, it is worth remembering that the law governing this issue in this country has its origins in the law of blasphemy. Blasphemy was an offence in English criminal law, protecting only the doctrines of the Church of England, until it was abolished by section 79 of the Criminal Justice and Immigration Act 2008. The last blasphemy case was an unsuccessful attempt to prosecute the Director-General of the BBC, Mark Thompson, for broadcasting *Jerry Springer—The Opera*.[32] Extreme cases of hostility to religion can now be addressed under the Public Order Act 1986. As amended in 2006,[33] it makes it a criminal offence for a person to use threatening words or behaviour, or display any written material which is threatening if he intends thereby to stir up religious hatred. But section 29J of the Public Order Act contains a strong protection for freedom of expression:

> Nothing in this Part shall be read or given effect in a way which prohibits or restricts discussion, criticism or expressions of antipathy, dislike, ridicule, insult or abuse of particular religions or the beliefs or practices of their adherents ....

Public order offences may be an appropriate basis for dealing with people like Pastor Terry Jones if they commit inflammatory acts with copies of the Koran in public, but it is very important to protect freedom of expression in relation to religion. Those who want to express religious beliefs (including Christian beliefs) which offend others are, of course, equally entitled to freedom of speech.[34]

Thomas Jefferson's statement of principle 'It does me no injury for my neighbour to say there are twenty gods, or no god. It neither picks my pocket nor breaks my leg'[35] recognises that my neighbour

---

[32] *R (Green) v City of Westminster Magistrates' Court, Thoday and Thompson* [2007] EWHC 2785 (Admin).

[33] See Part 3A of the Public Order Act 1986 as inserted by the Racial and Religious Hatred Act 2006.

[34] *Redmond-Bate v DPP* (1999) 7 BHRC 375 (DC).

[35] Thomas Jefferson, 'Notes on the State of Virginia' (1782), Query XVII, in Paul L Ford (ed), *Works of Thomas Jefferson* (GP Putnam's Sons, 1904) 4:78.

may praise the god of his choice. But equally I have the right to criticise his god, or his religious beliefs. Neither of us, however, has a right to manifest his or her religious beliefs in a manner which breaches the rights or interests of others. This balance of interests will not satisfy the devout who may wish to place religious law above civil law. But they need to have in mind the warning given by Mr Justice Jackson in the United States Supreme Court in 1952: 'the day that this country ceases to be free for irreligion, it will cease to be free for religion ...'.[36]

It is time to draw this lecture to a close. The courts both here and abroad have been struggling in recent years to strike a satisfactory balance between freedom of religion and freedom of expression. The issues are legally difficult. They raise strong passions on both sides of the argument. You do not need to be a lawyer to have a view. I have no doubt that the issues will be the subject of litigation for many years to come. I am grateful to Lord Pannick QC for his permission to draw on parts of his FA Mann Lecture 2010.

---

[36] *Zorach v Clauson* 343 US 306, 325 (1952) (Jackson J, dissenting).

15

*The Extraterritorial Application of the European Convention on Human Rights: Now on a Firmer Footing, But is it a Sound One?**

T HIS ANNUAL LECTURE series is one of the most prestigious in what is becoming a fairly crowded field. I am acutely conscious of the high quality of the lectures that have preceded mine and the standard that they have set. This has presented me with a daunting task. I am, however, delighted to have been asked to give the lecture, particularly because Essex University generously bestowed an honorary LLD on me last year in a splendid ceremony on its beautiful campus at Wivenhoe.

Article 1 of the European Convention on Human Rights ('the Convention') provides:

> The High Contracting Parties shall secure to everyone within their jurisdiction the rights and freedoms defined in Section I of this Convention.

This small number of apparently simple words has proved to be remarkably troublesome for the European Court of Human Rights ('ECtHR') and other courts faced with the threshold jurisdictional question which arises from time to time in cases involving the Convention. This is a fundamental and important question. It is true that it is less controversial than the question of the relationship between the Contracting States and the ECtHR which is currently exciting such febrile political interest in our polity. But the scope of the Convention is not free from controversy. There are those who believe that the ECtHR is exercising exorbitant jurisdiction and is guilty of human rights imperialism.

---

* University of Essex/Clifford Chance Lecture, 30 January 2014.

We should perhaps be grateful to Turkey and the United Kingdom for pushing the jurisprudence forward. These two states were the respondents in many of the most important Strasbourg cases where applicants argued that their human rights were violated in foreign territories.

The decision of the ECtHR in *Al-Skeini v United Kingdom*[1] in 2011 resolved one of the most contentious and difficult issues, namely whether and in what circumstances the Convention applies to acts done in a foreign State, outside the Council of Europe, during armed conflict. The Court held the Convention applies to areas subject to the authority and control of an occupying Contracting State, but for reasons that Judge Bonello forcefully argued lacked coherence.

Dutifully lagging behind Strasbourg, as it has bound itself to do by the dual maxims 'no more but certainly no less' and 'no less but certainly no more', the UK courts caught up in the recent decision of *Smith v Ministry of Defence*.[2] In that case, the Supreme Court held that the Convention applies to British soldiers serving in Iraq since they are under the effective authority and control of the United Kingdom.

The history of the case law in this area gives us a fascinating insight into the workings of the Strasbourg court and the relationship between it and our own courts. We shall see how Strasbourg has struggled to find a clear and coherent interpretation of Article 1 of the Convention and how these shortcomings have perplexed and made life difficult, at least for the UK courts.

THE LAW

The initial text of Article 1, prepared by the Committee of the Consultative Assembly of the Council of Europe on legal and administrative questions, provided that Member States shall undertake to secure the rights and freedoms for all persons 'residing within their territories'. The words 'residing within their territories' were subsequently changed to 'within their jurisdiction'. The reasons were noted in the *travaux préparatoires*:

> It seemed to the Committee that the term 'residing' might be considered too restrictive. It was felt that there were good grounds for extending the

---

[1] *Al-Skeini v United Kingdom* (2011) EHRR 18.
[2] *Smith v Ministry of Defence* [2013] UKSC 41, [2014] AC 52.

benefits of the Convention to all persons in the territories of the signatory States, even those who could not be considered as residing there in the legal sense of the word.[3]

It was, therefore, recognised from the start that the phrase 'everyone within their jurisdiction' is broader than 'everyone who enjoys a legal right to reside in a Contracting State'. As can be seen by the comments in the *travaux préparatoires*, however, the focus of the amendment was not on the shift from 'their *territories*' to 'their *jurisdiction*'. Indeed, as we shall see the Court has always analysed the term 'jurisdiction' primarily from a territorial perspective. In *Banković*, the Court held that:

> Article 1 of the Convention must be considered to reflect this ordinary and essentially territorial notion of jurisdiction, other bases of jurisdiction being exceptional and requiring special justification.[4]

This analysis is consistent with the approach taken in accordance with the general principles of public international law. Under international law, 'jurisdiction is an aspect of sovereignty and refers to judicial, legislative and administrative competence.'[5] In his 1964 Hague lectures, Frederick A Mann described the foundation of modern jurisdictional law in the following terms:

> Jurisdiction is an aspect of sovereignty, it is coextensive with and, indeed, incidental to, but also limited by, the State's sovereignty. As Lord Macmillan said, 'it is an essential attribute of the sovereignty of this realm, as of all sovereign independent States, that it should possess jurisdiction over all persons and things within its territorial limits and in all cases, civil and criminal, arising within these limits'. If a State assumed jurisdiction outside the limits of its sovereignty, it would come into conflict with other States which need not suffer any encroachment upon their own sovereignty ... Such a system seems to establish a satisfactory regime for the whole world. It divides the world into compartments within each of which a sovereign State has jurisdiction. Moreover, the connection between jurisdiction and sovereignty is, up to a point, obvious, inevitable, and almost platitudinous, for to the extent of its sovereignty a State necessarily has jurisdiction.[6]

---

[3] *Collected Edition of the Travaux Préparatoires of the European Convention on Human Rights* vol III (Brill, 1976) 260.

[4] *Banković v Belgium* [2001] ECHR 890, para 61.

[5] I Brownlie, *Principles of Public International Law*, 7th edn (Oxford University Press, 2008) 299.

[6] Frederick A Mann, 'The Doctrine of Jurisdiction in International Law' (1964-I) 111 *Recueil des cours* 1, 30.

A state's sovereignty is understood by reference to a geographical territory and jurisdiction is understood by reference to a state's authority over persons within that territory. The primarily territorial perspective of jurisdiction must also be understood against the background of the historical period in which many international treaties, including the Convention, were written. In the post-World War II era, jurisdiction was a tool to allocate competency among fiercely independent and volatile nation states. In the minds of the drafters of such conventions, if one state assumed extraterritorial jurisdiction then it would, necessarily, encroach upon another state's jurisdiction.

THE CASES

Despite the primarily territorial nature of jurisdiction, from its early jurisprudence to date, the Court recognised what it refers to as 'exceptional' circumstances justifying and, indeed, compelling a finding of extraterritorial jurisdiction. It established various 'categories' of exceptional circumstances, but until recently it has not clearly articulated any overarching principle which bound the categories together of which they could be said to be manifestations. Seemingly, they were an ad hoc group of categories to which additions were made from time to time.

For example, the Court has held that detaining an individual in a foreign State and coercing that individual to return to a Contracting State so as to face legal proceedings there engages Article 1.[7] Likewise, negotiating on behalf of an individual who is on the premises of a foreign embassy or who has sought assistance from a consular official (and where that official has assumed responsibility in relation to the individual), engages Article 1.[8] By contrast, the mere presence of an individual on an embassy premises (without any assumption of responsibility)[9] does not.

---

[7] *Freda v Italy* (1980) 21 DR 250; *Ilich Sanchez Ramirez v France* (1996) 86-A DR 155; *Öcalan v Turkey* (2003) 37 EHRR 10; *Al-Saadoon and Mufdi v United Kingdom* (2009) 49 EHRR SE11; *Medevedyev v France* (2010) 51 EHRR 899; *Jamaa v Italy* (2012) 55 EHRR 627.

[8] *WM v Denmark* (1992) 73 DR 193.

[9] *R (B) v Secretary of State for Foreign and Commonwealth Affairs* [2004] EWCA Civ 1344, [2005] QB 643.

But recently, an underlying thread between all of the cases on extraterritoriality has clearly emerged: it is the degree to which a Contracting State is able to exert effective and purportedly legitimate authority over an individual. The reason jurisdiction has been established is because there is a relationship between the state and an individual that can and should entail a responsibility on the part of the state to observe that individual's human rights.[10] The categories of exceptional circumstances are *manifestations* of jurisdiction but they are not the *reason for* finding jurisdiction. Likewise, territory provides a convenient shorthand for determining whether there is a relationship between the state and the individual when the relevant act occurs within a State's borders, but even in those cases, the justification for engaging the Convention remains the same, namely the exercise of effective and legitimate control.

The cases that have proved the most difficult and contentious for the Strasbourg Court have been those relating to military intervention in a foreign territory outside the Council of Europe. To analyse this case law, one must start with the cases arising from the Turkish occupation of northern Cyprus and then go on to deal with *Banković*, which, until *Al-Skeini*, was regarded as a 'watershed' and now is regarded as an 'aberration'.

The Northern Cyprus Cases

The invasion and occupation by Turkey of northern Cyprus from 1974 to 1983 gave rise to a number of important judgments by the Court on the issue of extraterritoriality. In some ways, this case law is uncontroversial since it concerns the allocation of jurisdictional competence between different Contracting States. Moreover, the incentive to find a justification for extraterritorial jurisdiction in these cases was particularly pressing, since if none were identified, the citizens of northern Cyprus would have been deprived of the human rights they once were guaranteed.[11] The importance of

---

[10] Samantha Besson, 'The extraterritoriality of the European Convention on Human Rights: why human rights depend on jurisdiction and what jurisdiction amounts to' (2012) 25(4) *Leiden Journal of International Law* 857–84.

[11] The Court expressly recognised this risk in *Cyprus v Turkey (Inter-State application)*: 'any other finding would result in a regrettable vacuum in the system of human rights protection in the territory in question by removing from individuals there the benefit of the Convention's fundamental safeguards and their right to call a High Contracting Party to account for violation of their rights in proceedings before the Court' (para 78).

the case law has, however, arisen as a result of its application by analogy to more controversial areas: territories outside the Council of Europe.

In *Cyprus v Turkey*,[12] the government of Cyprus complained of systematic violations of human rights in northern Cyprus by Turkish State organs and other persons acting with the support and knowledge of Turkey. The government of Turkey maintained that the Commission had no jurisdiction to examine the application as Cyprus did not fall under Turkish jurisdiction. Turkey had not extended her jurisdiction to the island of Cyprus since she had neither annexed a part of the island nor established a military or civil government there.

The European Commission on Human Rights (the precursor to the Court) held that the words 'within their jurisdiction' in Article 1 were not equivalent or limited to the national territory of the Contracting States. It stated that:

> ... the High Contracting Parties are bound to secure the said rights and freedoms to all persons under their actual authority and responsibility, whether that authority is exercised within their own territory or abroad ... [a]uthorised agents of a State, including diplomatic or consular agents and armed forces, not only remain under its jurisdiction when abroad but bring any other person or property 'within the jurisdiction' of that State, to the extent that they exercise authority over such persons or property. In so far as, by their acts or omissions, they affect such persons or property, the responsibility of the state is engaged.[13]

In *Loizidou v Turkey (Preliminary Objections)*,[14] the Court again analysed the issue of whether the applicant's inability to access her property, located in northern Cyprus, came within Turkish jurisdiction. The Court reiterated that the concept of 'jurisdiction' in Article 1 was 'not restricted to the national territory' of the Contracting States. In addition, the Court stated:

> ... the responsibility of Contracting Parties can be involved because of acts of their authorities, whether performed within or outside national boundaries, which produce effects outside their own territory.

> Bearing in mind the object and purpose of the Convention, the responsibility of a Contracting party may also arise when as a consequence

---

[12] *Cyprus v Turkey* (1975) 2 DR 125.
[13] Para 8.
[14] *Loizidou v Turkey (Preliminary Objections)* (1995) 20 EHRR 99.

of military action—whether lawful or unlawful—it exercises effective control of an area outside its national territory.'[15]

So in these northern Cyprus cases we find reference to the concept of the exercise of extraterritorial control as the foundation for jurisdiction.

Banković

This broad notion of jurisdiction as encompassing acts of the Contracting States that affect persons or property located outside their geographical territory was abruptly curtailed in the case of *Banković v Belgium and 16 Other Contracting States*.[16] The applicants were the relatives of journalists killed during the NATO bombing of a radio and television station during the Kosovo war. Their application was brought against all the Contracting Parties to the Convention who were also members of NATO. The applicants argued that their relatives had been brought within the jurisdiction of the respondent states by the bombing of the station. They proposed adapting the 'effective control' test outlined by the Court in *Loizidou* such that the extent of the positive obligations imposed by Article 1 would be proportionate to the level of control in fact exercised by the state or states in question.

The Court found that the real connection between the applicants and the respondent states was the bombing, an extraterritorial act. Therefore:

the essential question was whether the applicants and their deceased relatives were, as a result of that extraterritorial act, capable of falling within the jurisdiction of the respondent States.[17]

It went on to state that Article 1 must be considered to reflect the ordinary and essentially territorial notion of jurisdiction in public international law; other bases of jurisdiction were exceptions that required special justification.[18] The Court analysed the case law on extraterritoriality and found that the facts in *Banković* did not fall into any of the existing 'categories' of exceptions to territorial jurisdiction.

---

[15] Para 62.
[16] *Banković v Belgium and 16 Other Contracting States* [2001] ECHR 890.
[17] Para 54.
[18] Para 61.

The Court elaborated on what was meant by the term 'effective control', outlined in *Loizidou*. To find jurisdiction on this basis, it was necessary to show that the state, 'as a consequence of military occupation or through consent, invitation or acquiescence of the Government of that territory exercises *all or some of the public powers normally to be exercised by that Government*' (emphasis added).[19] Applying this test, the Court decided that it lacked jurisdiction and declared the application inadmissible.

Further, the Court did not find that the wording in Article 1 provided any support for the applicants' suggestion that the positive obligation could be 'divided and tailored in accordance with the particular circumstances of the extraterritorial act in question'.[20] This Grand Chamber decision was intended to be authoritative and definitive on the Article 1 issue. At the time, it was thought that this would the last word on the subject. It is of some significance that the court said that (exceptionally) Article 1 was not to be interpreted as a 'living instrument' in accordance with changing conditions. This was a departure from the court's usual approach to the interpretation of the Convention. It rejected any expansive reading of its northern Cyprus case law and emphasised the fundamentally regional nature of the Convention:

> the Convention is a multi-lateral treaty operating … in an essentially regional context and notably in the legal space (*espace juridique*) of the Contracting States. The FRY [former Republic of Yugoslavia] clearly does not fall within this legal space. The Convention was not designed to be applied throughout the world, even in respect of the conduct of Contracting States. Accordingly, the desirability of avoiding a gap or vacuum in human rights' protection has so far been relied on by the Court in favour of establishing jurisdiction only when the territory in question was one that, but for the specific circumstances, would normally be covered by the Convention.[21]

Issa

The next significant case on this issue was *Issa v Turkey*,[22] which has experienced the converse fate of *Banković*: going from obscurity

---

[19] Para 71.
[20] Para 75.
[21] Para 80.
[22] *Issa v Turkey* (2004) 41 EHRR 567.

to pre-eminence in the jurisprudence on extraterritoriality. Six Iraqi women who lived near the Turkish border complained that Turkey had infringed their relatives' human rights under the Convention. They alleged that during the Turkish army's invasion of northern Iraq in 1995, the occupying soldiers had unlawfully arrested, detained, ill-treated and subsequently killed their sons and husbands. Turkey denied that its soldiers had been in the area and argued that, in any case, the presence of its troops would not have meant that the applicants' relatives were under Turkish jurisdiction.

The Court distinguished the case from *Loizidou* by finding that, notwithstanding the large number of troops involved in the military operation, it did not appear that Turkey exercised effective overall control of the entire area of northern Iraq. Further, Turkey denied that there had been any military operations in the area where the applicants claimed their relatives had been killed. After analysing the available evidence, the Court concluded that:

> it has not been established to the required standard of proof that the Turkish armed forces conducted operations in the area in question, and, more precisely, in the hills above the village of Azadi where, according to the applicants' statements, the victims were at that time.[23]

However, the Court did not exclude the possibility that, as a consequence of extraterritorial military action, a state could be considered to have exercised, temporarily, effective overall control of a particular portion of the territory of northern Iraq:

> a state may also be held accountable for violation of the Convention rights and freedoms of persons who are in the territory of another state but who are found to be under the former state's authority and control through its agents operating—whether lawfully or unlawfully in the latter state.[24]

Were that established on the facts, which was not done to the satisfaction of the Court in that case, those within that area would be within the jurisdiction of the state, even if that area were normally outside the legal space of the Contracting States. The Court concluded that a state's accountability in such situations:

> stems from the fact that art 1 of the Convention cannot be interpreted so as to allow a State party to perpetrate violations of the Convention on

---

[23] Para 81.
[24] Para 71.

the territory of another State, which it could not perpetrate on its own territory.[25]

This represented a fundamentally different perspective of jurisdiction from that expressed in *Banković*. In *Banković*, the Court saw jurisdiction simply as the allocation of competence among the Contracting States, where a failure to find extraterritorial jurisdiction, would lead to a vacuum in human rights protection. By contrast, in *Issa*, the Court saw jurisdiction as a means of ensuring state responsibility for human rights protection whenever that state exerts authority and control over an individual, regardless of whether they are located in a foreign territory.

Al-Skeini—The House of Lords' Decision

Given the apparent conflict between *Banković* and *Issa*, the House of Lords had to make a choice in *R (on the application of Al-Skeini) v Secretary of State for Defence*.[26] This was one of a series of UK cases arising out of the Iraq war. The case concerned the deaths of six Iraqi civilians as a result of actions by a member or members of the British armed forces in the British controlled area of Basrah. It was argued for the civilians that, because of the special circumstances in which British troops were operating in Basrah, the conduct complained of fell within the exception to the territoriality principle recognised by Strasbourg.

Lord Brown, with whom the majority agreed, gave the fullest examination of the Article 1 issue. He took as his starting point the decision in *Banković,* which he described as 'a watershed authority'. That was hardly a surprising description. As I have said, *Banković* was a decision of the Grand Chamber which was clearly intended to be authoritative and definitive. He considered that the following propositions could be derived from *Banković*:

(1) Article 1 reflects an 'essentially territorial notion of jurisdiction' ... other bases of jurisdiction being exceptional and requiring special justification in the particular circumstances of each case ...

---

[25] Para 71.
[26] *R (on the application of Al-Skeini) v Secretary of State for Defence* [2007] UKHL 26, [2008] 1 AC 153.

(2) The Court recognises article 1 jurisdiction to avoid a 'vacuum in human rights' protection' when the territory 'would normally be covered by the Convention' ....

(3) The rights and freedoms defined in the Convention cannot be 'divided and tailored'.

(4) The circumstances in which the court has exceptionally recognised the extra-territorial exercise of a state include [he then set out a number of the examples to be found in the case law of the court].

He then examined some of the post-*Banković* case law and concluded that it reinforced the principles established in *Banković*. In so far as *Issa* was said to support any wider notions of Article 1, Lord Brown could not accept it. Any such wider view of jurisdiction would be inconsistent with the reasoning in *Banković*. In characteristically blunt language, he said that either it would extend the effective control principle beyond the Council of Europe area (where alone it had previously been applied) or 'it would stretch to breaking point the concept of jurisdiction extending extraterritorially to those subject to a state's "authority and control"'. Lord Brown did not consider that the cases of five of the applicants fell into any of the exceptions to the territorial principle so far recognised by the Court. Moreover, he expressly supported the conclusions reached by the Court in *Banković*:

> It is one thing to recognise as exceptional the specific narrow categories of cases I have sought to summarise above; it would be quite another to accept that whenever a contracting state acts (militarily or otherwise) through its agents abroad, those affected by such activities fall within its article 1 jurisdiction. Such a contention would prove altogether too much. It would make a nonsense of much that was said in *Banković*.

> ... *Banković* (and later *Assanidze*) stands, as stated, for the indivisible nature of article 1 jurisdiction: it cannot be 'divided and tailored'. As *Banković* had earlier pointed out (at para 40) 'the applicant's interpretation of jurisdiction would invert and divide the positive obligation on contracting states to secure the substantive rights in a manner never contemplated by article 1 of the Convention.'

The position of the sixth applicant, Mr Mousa, was, however, different. He had been detained in a military detention facility in Basrah. Lord Brown recognised the UK's jurisdiction over Mr Mousa only on a 'narrow basis' 'essentially by analogy with the extra-territorial exception made for embassies and foreign prisons'.

Lord Rodger agreed with Lord Brown but added some comments of his own. He recognised that 'the problem which the House has to face, quite squarely, is that the judgments and decisions of the European Court do not speak with one voice.'[27] In an obvious sign of frustration with the guidance emanating from Strasbourg, Lord Rodger ultimately concluded that he was 'unable to reconcile [the Court's approach in *Issa*] with the reasoning in *Banković*.'[28] In light of the conflicting elements in the case law, he considered that national courts should give pre-eminence to the Court's unanimous and authoritative ruling in *Banković*.

Both Lord Brown and Lord Rodger recognised both the practical and political difficulties of giving an expansive interpretation to European jurisdiction to territories outside the Council of Europe.[29] In particular, Lord Rodger found the idea that the United Kingdom was obliged to secure the observance of all the rights and freedoms as interpreted by the European Court in the utterly different society of southern Iraq 'manifestly absurd' and said it would amount to a form of 'human rights imperialism'.[30]

So the basis for jurisdiction was unequivocally stated to be territorial, subject to exceptions in narrowly defined situations.

Gentle

But the application of Article 1 to the Iraq war continued to cast a dark shadow over our courts. Two further cases followed before long. Both involved human rights claims by British soldiers (as opposed to claims by Iraqi civilians). This gave greater strength to the submission that jurisdiction should be engaged, given the degree of authority and control the United Kingdom was able to exert over them.

In *R (Gentle) v Prime Minister*,[31] the appellants appealed against the refusal of their application for judicial review of the government's decision not to hold an independent inquiry into the circumstances that led to the invasion of Iraq. The appellants were the mothers of two soldiers killed whilst serving in the British army in Iraq.

---

[27] Para 67.
[28] Para 75.
[29] Paras 127–129.
[30] Para 78.
[31] *R (Gentle) v Prime Minister* [2008] UKHL 20, [2008] 1 AC 1356.

Lord Bingham dismissed the issue of jurisdiction out of hand:

> the deaths of Fusilier Gentle and Trooper Clarke occurred in Iraq and although they were subject to the authority of the defendants they were clearly not within the jurisdiction of the UK as that expression in the Convention has been interpreted: *R (Al-Skeini) v Secretary of State for Defence* [2008] AC 153, paras 79, 129.[32]

By contrast, Baroness Hale said that if Baha Mousa (the sixth applicant in *Al-Skeini*), detained in a military detention facility in Basrah, was within the jurisdiction of the United Kingdom for the purposes of Article 1, then a soldier serving under the command and control of his superiors must also be within the jurisdiction. Moreover, she felt compelled to reach this conclusion since the United Kingdom was in a better position to secure to its soldiers all their Convention rights, modified as their content is by the exigencies of military service, than it was to secure those rights to its detainees.[33]

The case was ultimately decided against the appellants on the basis that they were unable to establish the duty, which they asserted: the Court held that Article 2 of the Convention does not include any implied obligation on the government to take reasonable steps to satisfy itself of the legality of an invasion of another country under international law.

Catherine Smith

The second case was brought by the mother of Private Jason Smith who had been mobilised for service in Iraq and was stationed at Camp Abu Naji.[34] He collapsed while working off base and was rushed by ambulance to the Camp's medical centre but died there almost immediately of heat stroke. Crucially, Private Smith actually died after he had reached a UK military base. As a result of the House of Lords' reasoning in *Al-Skeini,* that fact alone was enough to bring Private Smith within the UK's jurisdiction. However, the question was raised in the lower courts whether he would have been within the jurisdiction even had he died outside the base but essentially under the same circumstances.

---

[32] Para 8.
[33] Para 60.
[34] *R (Smith) v Assistant Deputy Coroner for Oxfordshire* [2008] EWHC 694 (Admin).

In the High Court, Collins J said:

> members of the armed forces remain at all times subject to the jurisdiction of the UK. It would obviously be wholly artificial to regard a soldier sent to fight in the territory of another state as subject to the jurisdiction of that state.[35]

The Court of Appeal agreed. It adopted a personal conception of jurisdiction, based on the victim's status as a member of the armed forces. It said that it would defy common sense to say that a UK soldier was protected by the Convention while on a UK base, but would lose all protection once he stepped outside it.

A majority of the Supreme Court held that the Contracting States did not intend the Convention to apply to their armed forces when operating outside their territories. Lord Phillips said that the exceptions to the primarily territorial type of jurisdiction, as identified in *Banković*, were confined to circumstances where a state exercised effective control over part of the territory of another state, in contexts analogous to consular jurisdiction or where a state delegated particular government functions to another state authority. *Banković* had not recognised an extraterritorial jurisdiction based solely on a principle of 'state agent authority' and it was not for the Supreme Court to rush ahead of Strasbourg.

Lord Collins, with whose reasons Lords Hope, Walker and Rodger agreed, said that the case came within none of the exceptions recognised by the European Court, and that there was no basis in its case law, or in principle, for the proposition that the authority and control which States undoubtedly have over their armed forces abroad should mean that they are 'within their jurisdiction' for the purposes of Article 1.

The leading judgment for the minority was delivered by Lord Mance, with whom Lady Hale and Lord Kerr agreed. Lord Mance said that, to the extent that jurisdiction under the Convention exists over an occupied territory, it does so only because of the occupying state's pre-existing authority and control over its own armed forces.[36] An occupying state cannot have any jurisdiction over local inhabitants without already having jurisdiction over its own armed forces, in both cases in the sense of Article 1 of the Convention. He said that the United Kingdom's jurisdiction over its armed forces

---

[35] Para 12.
[36] *R (Smith) v Secretary of State for Defence* [2010] UKSC 29, [2011] 1 AC 1, para 188.

was essentially personal.[37] It could not be expected to take steps to provide in Iraq the full social and protective framework and facilities which it would be expected to provide domestically. But it could be expected to take steps to provide proper facilities and proper protection against risks falling within its responsibility or its ability to control or influence.

Al-Skeini—The Court's Decision

The issue of extraterritorial jurisdiction beyond the Council of Europe came to a head when, after the House of Lords dismissed the appeal, the applicants in *Al-Skeini* took their case to Strasbourg. The Court unanimously held that there was a sufficient jurisdictional link for the purposes of Article 1 in all six cases. On any view, this was a very important decision. But how did the court explain it? It did not say in terms that it was extending the reach of the Convention further than it had explained, in particular, in *Banković*. It started by reasserting the territoriality principle subject to exceptions in particular cases. It mentioned the familiar exceptions such as the acts of diplomatic and consular agents on foreign territory and cases where an individual is taken into custody of state agents abroad.

The Court said: '[w]hat is decisive in such cases is the exercise of physical power and control over the person in question.'[38] And then this at para 137:

> It is clear that, whenever the state through its agents exercises control and authority over an individual, and thus jurisdiction, the state is under an obligation under art. 1 to secure to that individual the rights and freedoms under s.1 of the Convention that are relevant to the situation of that individual. In this sense, therefore, the Convention can be 'divided and tailored'.[39]

A further exception to the territoriality principle would occur where, as a consequence of military action, a contracting state exercises effective control over an *area* outside that national territory. The obligation to secure, in such an area, the rights and freedoms set out

---

[37] Para 194.
[38] (2011) EHRR 18, para 136.
[39] Para 137.

in the Convention derived from the fact of such control. The Court found that it will be a question of fact whether a Contracting State exercises effective control over an area outside its own territory.

The Court clarified that the *Issa* interpretation of jurisdiction is the right one: extraterritorial jurisdiction is not simply used as a mechanism to fill a vacuum in the protection of rights of individuals who reside in a Contracting State when it is under the occupation of another Contracting State. Whilst extraterritorial jurisdiction has been recognised on that basis in the past, that 'does not imply, *a contrario*, that jurisdiction under Article 1 of the Convention can never exist outside the territory covered by the Council of Europe Member States.'[40]

Applying these principles to the present case, the Court concluded that the United Kingdom assumed in Iraq the exercise of some of the public powers normally to be exercised by a sovereign government. Accordingly, the Court held that, the British soldiers exercised authority and control over the individuals killed in the course of security operations in Basrah, 'so as to establish a jurisdictional link between the deceased and the United Kingdom for the purposes of Article 1 of the Convention'.[41]

There can be no doubt that the Strasbourg decision in *Al-Skeini* extended the scope of Article 1 well beyond *Banković*. The effect of para 137 of the judgment is that the statement in *Banković* that the rights and freedoms of the Convention cannot be divided and tailored in accordance with the particular circumstances of the extraterritorial act in question was reversed. This is important because that statement had informed much of the thinking of the House of Lords in *Al-Skeini* and of the majority in *Catherine Smith*.

All courts make mistakes from time to time. Moreover, the Strasbourg court is as entitled to change its mind as our Supreme Court or even our Court of Appeal. Conditions change. New ideas emerge over time. The ECtHR has repeatedly said that the Convention is a 'living instrument'. It evolves under the interpretative hand of the court. It is sometimes criticised for this. It is ironic that, having stated in *Banković* that Article 1 was not to be interpreted as a 'living instrument', in *Al-Skeini* it did just that.

---

[40] Para 142.
[41] Para 149.

Smith

Following the Court's decision in *Al-Skeini*, the Supreme Court was asked in a different *Smith* case to determine whether claims brought against the Ministry of Defence by British service personnel injured, and by the families of personnel killed, while serving in Iraq should be struck out.[42] Since the Court had decided that Iraqi civilians were capable of coming within the scope of the Convention by virtue of the acts of British soldiers, the applicability of the Convention to the soldiers themselves was practically a foregone conclusion.

Lord Hope delivered the leading judgment of the Court and the unanimous decision on the issue of extraterritorial jurisdiction. He drew the following two points from the Court's case law on extraterritoriality. First, the exceptionality of extraterritoriality is not an especially high threshold; it is there to make clear that the normal presumption of jurisdiction that applies throughout a state's territory does not apply. Secondly, the list of circumstances which may require and justify a finding that the state was exercising jurisdiction extraterritorially is not closed.[43]

Further, Lord Hope found that the view expressed in *Issa* that jurisdiction can be determined by looking at the authority and control exerted by a Contracting State is not an aberration; the decision in *Al-Skeini* puts *Issa* firmly in the mainstream of the Strasbourg jurisprudence on this topic. It is *Banković* which can no longer be regarded as authoritative on the issue of jurisdiction.[44]

He found the logic behind the statement in *Cyprus v Turkey*, articulated in 1975, that authorised agents of the state not only remain under its jurisdiction when abroad 'but bring any other person or property within the jurisdiction of that state, to the extent that they exercise authority over such persons' 'compelling' and said:

> It is plain, especially when one thinks of the way the armed forces operate, that authority and control is exercised by the state throughout the chain of command from the very top all the way down to men and women operating in the front line. Servicemen and women relinquish almost total control over their lives to the state. It does not seem possible to separate them, in their capacity as state agents, from those whom

---

[42] *Smith v Ministry of Defence* [2013] UKSC 41.
[43] Para 30.
[44] Para 47.

they affect when they are exercising authority and control on the state's behalf. They are all brought within the state's article 1 jurisdiction by the application of the same general principle.[45]

WHERE ARE WE NOW?

This review of the key cases on the extraterritorial application of the Convention outside the Council of Europe demonstrates that *Banković* put the jurisprudence off course for around ten years; but since *Al-Skeini*, it has now returned to a position that many would regard as more principled and more acceptable. It is likely that, if it were faced with the facts of *Banković* today, the Court would reach the same conclusion as it did in 2001, but its analysis would now depend on the degree of authority and control the respondent State exercised over the applicants, not where they were located or whether their cases could be squeezed into one of the exceptional categories to territorial jurisdiction.

Even in the judgment in *Al-Skeini* vestiges of the *Banković* approach remain visible. Under the heading 'the territorial principle' (which is identified as one of the general principles relevant to jurisdiction) the Court said at paragraph 131 that a state's jurisdictional competence under Article 1 is 'primarily territorial' subject only to 'exceptional cases'. But once it is appreciated that the fundamental principle is that of the exercise of control and authority, then the territoriality principle loses its special significance. It goes without saying that a state exercises authority and control over all persons and things within its territorial limits. Surely, it is clearer simply to say that, whenever the state exercises control and authority over an individual, it is under an obligation under Article 1 to secure the rights and freedoms of the Convention to that individual wherever he or she happens to be.

It is clear from the case law that the exercise of control and authority must be effective, such as: detaining an individual; assuming responsibility for an individual, exercising public functions in relation to an individual; militarily, financially or politically supporting a regime that exercises authority over an individual; or occupying a territory in which the individual resides. However, in the case

---

[45] Para 52.

of military occupation, it will not matter that the situation on the ground may be close to anarchy. If a Contracting State has taken over control of the civil administration of the foreign territory then its inability to control the situation is not a ticket out of the Convention.

It is also clear that the authority must, at least, purport to be legitimate. That is, the state agent must be acting under the ostensible authority of the state (whether lawfully or unlawfully). The Convention is concerned with the responsibility of states, not individuals; as a result, it needs to be shown that the state agent is purporting to act *on behalf* of the state to justify a finding of jurisdiction under Article 1.

Finally, it is clear that, contrary to the statement in *Banković*, the Convention can be divided and tailored according to the extent of authority exercised by the Contracting State. So in Iraq, the United Kingdom comes under an obligation to protect the Article 2 and Article 3 rights of those individuals residing in Basrah, including a positive obligation to conduct investigations of potential breaches of those rights. The United Kingdom is not, however, obliged to secure the whole package of rights contained in the Convention, such as Article 8 (privacy), Article 10 (expression), or Article 11 (association), which would clearly be unsustainable and inappropriate given the situation on the ground in Basrah and its vastly different legal traditions.

Bringing soldiers and those killed and injured by them during armed conflict 'within the jurisdiction' of a Contracting State, when military personnel are under the strictest authority and control of their supervisors, appears to me an obviously correct conclusion.

In *Al-Skeini*, Judge Bonello wrote a rousing concurring opinion in which he condemns some of the jurisprudence to which I have earlier referred. It is a wonderful read. He describes the jurisprudence as 'patchwork case law at best'. Principles settled in one judgment may appear more or less justifiable in themselves, but they then 'betray an awkward fit when measured against principles established in another'. He complains that Strasbourg has 'squandered more energy in attempting to reconcile the barely reconcilable than in trying to erect intellectual constructs of more universal application'. The cornerstone of the Convention is the aim of securing the *universal* recognition and observance of fundamental human rights. He says: universal 'hardly suggests an observance parcelled off by territory on the checkboard of geography'.

To overcome this lamentable state of affairs, Judge Bonello proposed what he called a 'functional jurisdiction test'. He identified what he called the 'functions' of the Convention:

> States ensure the observance of human rights in five primordial ways: firstly, by not violating (through their agents) human rights; secondly, by having in place systems which prevent breaches of human rights; thirdly, by investigating complaints of human rights abuses; fourthly, by scourging those of their agents who infringe human rights; and, finally, by compensating the victims of breaches of human rights. These constitute the basic minimum functions assumed by every State by virtue of its having contracted into the Convention.[46]

The 'functional jurisdiction test' would see a state effectively exercising jurisdiction whenever it falls within its power to perform, or not to perform, any of these five functions:

> Very simply put, a state has jurisdiction for the purposes of art.1 whenever the observance or the breach of any of these functions is within its authority and control.[47]

Moreover, where a State is acknowledged by international law to be 'an occupying power' pursuant to the Geneva and The Hague instruments, a rebuttable presumption ought to arise that the occupying power has 'authority and control' over the occupied territory.[48]

Applying this test to the facts in *Al-Skeini*, he concluded in these forthright terms:

> 'I find it bizarre, not to say offensive, that an occupying power can plead that it had no authority and control over acts committed by its own armed forces well under its own chain of command, claiming with one voice its authority and control over the perpetrators of those atrocities, but with the other, disowning any authority and control over atrocities committed by them and over their victims.

> It is my view that jurisdiction is established when authority and control over others are established. For me, in the present cases, it is well beyond surreal to claim that a military colossus which waltzed into Iraq when it chose, settled there for as long as it cared to and only left when it no longer suited its interests to remain, can persuasively claim not to have exercised authority and control over an area specifically assigned to it in the geography of the war games played by the victorious.'[49]

---

[46] *Al-Skeini v United Kingdom* (2011) EHRR 18, para O-II10.
[47] Para O-II11.
[48] Para O-II24.
[49] Paras O-II26–27.

I am not sure that, in their essentials, there is a fundamental difference between the approach of Judge Bonello and that of the majority of the court. The critical point is that, as a result of their commitment to observe and protect the rights and freedoms contained in the Convention, whenever Contracting States exert effective and purportedly legitimate authority over an individual, they must do so in a way that conforms to the requirements of the Convention. The Convention constrains a state's freedom to act, regardless of where that individual is located because the rights and freedoms are those of individuals, not those of territories. The question that the Court should ask is whether it is in a relationship of effective and purportedly legitimate authority over the individual (which is a threshold question). If it is, jurisdiction is engaged *because* the state has constrained its freedom to act in the context of such relationships. The extent to which the state's freedom is constrained by the Convention is *then* determined by the degree to which the state can perform the functions identified by Judge Bonello.

This is an important topic. I suspect that we have not heard the last word from Strasbourg on it. I should conclude by expressing my gratitude to Sophie Matthiesson, a former judicial assistant of mine, for her invaluable assistance in preparing this lecture.

Part III

Magna Carta and the Rule of Law

16

*Magna Carta—Liberties, Customs and the Free Flow of Trade**

IT IS A real pleasure to have been asked to give the keynote address at this 4th annual British Irish Commercial Law Forum. Given its theme—Magna Carta—I am particularly delighted to have been invited to do so this year. I am, as you may know, chairman of the Magna Carta Trust; a position held by all Masters of the Rolls since the Trust was established in 1956. You can imagine that my term of office as chairman has been rather busier than that of my illustrious predecessors.

One of the aims of the Trust is to 'perpetuate the principles of Magna Carta'[1] Magna Carta is a curious hotch-potch of a document. Many of its provisions cannot by any stretch of the imagination be described as principles. They include detailed measures of an intensely practical nature which reflect the economic and social conditions of the early thirteenth century. Some of them were aimed at resolving grievances that King John's barons had at the time; grievances that were not only directed at him but were a reaction to Angevin rule.

For example, the Charter required him to remove a number of his more troublesome supporters from office. Chapter 50 provided: 'We will entirely remove from our bailiwicks the relations of Gerard de Atheyes, so that for the future they will have no bailiwick in England; we will also remove Engelard de Cygony, Andrew, Peters and Gyon, from the Chan-cery; Gyon de Cygony, Geoffrey de Martyn and his brothers; Philip Mark and his brothers and his nephew, Geoffrey, and their whole retinue'. Quite a putsch.

---

* 4th Annual British Irish Commercial Law Forum, 800 Years of Magna Carta—the Commercial Rule of Law in the 21st Century, Dublin Dispute Resolution Centre, Ireland, 23 April 2015.

[1] See magnacarta800th.com/magna-carta-today/the-magna-carta-trust/.

But it is undeniable that Magna Carta does contain a number of chapters which we would recognise as setting out important principles which have real relevance today. They are the reason why it has grandiloquently been claimed that Magna Carta is the inspiration for democracy; and why thousands of people from all over the World are planning to congregate in a field at Runnymede on 15 June to commemorate the 800th anniversary of the sealing of the Charter. I have in mind in particular the famous Chapter 40 'To none will we sell, to none will we deny, or delay, the right of justice'. Words of captivating brevity. And Chapter 20: 'A freeman shall not be amerced for a small fault but after the manner of the fault; and for a great crime according to the heinousmess of it' (an early assertion of the principle of proportionality). I also have in mind other provisions concerning access to justice and due process of law and the right to a fair trial as well as the requirement that justice should be dispensed from a fixed place,[2] that it should be local;[3] and that judges should know the law, which often meant local law[4]—an early instance of subsidiarity, perhaps. And that only judges should sit in judgment.[5] The Charter was not, however, the source of trial by jury or the great writ of habeas corpus.

Its opening provision guaranteed the rights and liberties of the English Church,[6] although it did not specify what they were. Plenty of room for manoeuvre there, and work for lawyers. And it provided a series of significant guarantees concerning trade and commerce. While it was neither the first nor the last instrument to do so, it established uniform weights and measures.[7] England at the time was developing economically. Successful trade depends, to a large extent, on traders understanding and being in agreement as to what they are selling and buying. It would be a recipe for chaos if a seller took a length to mean 45 inches when the purchaser understood it to mean 37 inches.[8] A thriving mercantile economy, much of which involved trading in a variety of types of cloth, needed a uniform approach.

So Magna Carta standardised the basis of trade. It sought to secure the free flow of trade. It required the removal of all fishweirs from

---

[2] Magna Carta 1215, Ch 17.
[3] Magna Carta 1215, Ch 19.
[4] JC Holt, *Magna Carta* 2nd edn (Cambridge University Press, 1992) 63.
[5] Magna Carta 1215, Chs 24 and 45.
[6] Magna Carta 1215, Ch 1.
[7] Magna Carta 1215, Ch 35.
[8] I Judge and A Arlidge, *Magna Carta Uncovered* (Hart Publishing, 2014) 88.

rivers across England.[9] Bad for fisherman, but good for traders. Fishweirs led to rivers silting up. Consequently they became less and less navigable. Fishweirs clogged up important trade arteries. Their removal was needed to increase free trade.

Free movement of goods is not, however, sufficient for a thriving economy. There has also to be free movement of merchants. Thus Chapter 41 provided.

> All merchants shall have safe and secure conduct, to go out of, and to come into England, and to stay there, and to pass as well by land as by water, for buying and selling by the ancient and allowed customs without any evil tolls; except in time of war, or when they are of any nation at war with us.

What better evocation of the idea of free trade? An early embodiment of the ideals which informed what is now known as the European Union.

Encouraging the free movement of goods and tradesmen is one thing. But trade and investment do not simply depend on an ability to trade. If they are to flourish, it is imperative that property rights of traders and investors are protected by the law. The parties to the Charter well understood this. A trader or investor has little incentive to engage in trade or to invest if they are at risk of arbitrary dispossession of their property interests. Such dispossession was not uncommon. King John routinely stripped his subjects of their property in order to fund his military adventures.[10] An object of the Charter was to put a stop to this. It provided at Chapter 39 that 'no freeman shall be taken or imprisoned, or disseised, or outlawed, or banished, or any ways destroyed, nor will we pass upon him, nor will we send upon him, unless by the lawful judgment of his peers, or by the laws of the land'.[11] This was an early foreshadowing of Locke's theory of government and the 14th amendment of the US Constitution.

So the Charter made provisions to ease trade and secure property rights. It also affirmed that the City of London and all other 'cities, boroughs, towns and ports shall have their liberties and free customs.'[12] Commercial centres needed to be supported. The exact nature and extent of the liberties and free customs was not defined.

---

[9] Magna Carta 1215, Ch 33.
[10] Holt, *Magna Carta*, 192.
[11] Magna Carta 1215, Ch 39, and also see Ch 9 on debtor-creditor relations.
[12] Magna Carta 1215, Ch 13. And see Chs 33, 35 and 41–42.

It is right to note, however, that more than 70 charters had been issued to individual towns and cities. Magna Carta was declaratory of their continuing effect, as well as of the right of the City of London to be both self-governing and to continue to appoint its Lord Mayor.

THE IMPORTANCE OF MAGNA CARTA TODAY

So much for the Charter itself. What is its relevance for commerce and the rule of law today? Here I pause to note a warning that was given in a stimulating recent analysis of Magna Carta by Lord Sumption.

In a recent lecture in which he stripped away a number of what might be called the myths in which the Charter has become enveloped, Lord Sumption concluded with this warning:

> We are frighteningly ignorant of the past, in large measure because we no longer look to it as a source of inspiration. We are all revolutionaries now, controlling our own fate. So when we commemorate Magna Carta, perhaps the first question that we should ask ourselves is this: do we really need the force of myth to sustain our belief in democracy? Do we need to derive our belief in democracy and the rule of law from a group of muscular conservative millionaires from the north of England, who thought in French, knew no Latin or English, and died more than three quarters of a millennium ago? I rather hope not.[13]

Not for him Sir Anthony Eden's view that the road to 1215 'marked the road to individual freedom, to Parliamentary democracy and to the supremacy of the law.'[14]

It may be that nobody directly bases their belief in democracy or the rule of law on the document that was sealed at Runnymede 800 years ago. But it cannot be denied that the Charter does set out a number of principles which, however rudimentary the form in which they were expressed, are now taken for granted as being central to a modern liberal democracy. It is right that, from a historical point of view, we should locate the Charter in the social and economic conditions of the thirteenth century and acknowledge that it

---

[13] J Sumption, 'Magna Carta—Then and Now' (British Library lecture, 9 March 2015) at 18, available at www.supremecourt.uk/docs/speech-150309.pdf.

[14] The Rt Hon Sir Anthony Eden MP, Prime Minister, letter to the Magna Carta Trust (October 1956), available at magnacarta800th.com/magna-carta-today/the-magna-carta-trust/.

reflects the values and mores of that time. But it is an inescapable fact that the Charter principles to which I have referred have been influential in the development of modern democratic systems. This is not the place to trace the checkered history of these principles. Suffice it to say that the Charter endured for no more than ten weeks, before the Pope annulled it at John's request. It was brought back to life by William Marshall on John's death. Thereafter, it languished until, as Lord Sumption explains in a little detail, it was resurrected with enthusiasm by Edward Coke in the seventeenth century.

John Adams, the second President of the United States, said that 'Democracy never lasts long. It soon wastes, exhausts and murders itself.'[15] He believed that in democracies, as in other forms of government, individuals were prey to the same flaws of, as he put it, 'fraud, violence and cruelty.' The strength of any democracy lies in the robustness of its institutions of governance and in public confidence in them. Weaken either and democracy is weakened.

One of the great strengths of the UK and states which enjoy similar democratic systems has been their commitment to systems of justice. It is no good having wonderful laws if the state does not provide a fair and effective system of justice to enable individuals to vindicate their rights by reference to those laws. Everyone should have equal access to justice. And I do not simply mean formal equality of access in the sense that 'The doors of the Ritz are open to all.' I mean, of course, practical and effective equality. This includes that the courts, legal advice and representation are available to all those who require it. This is an essential aspect of democratic participation in society. It is because it is the means by which the law (these days largely the creation of elected Parliaments) is given life. It is also the means by which aggrieved citizens can hold public authorities to account by judicial review in the courts.

Free and fair elections are, rightly, understood to be the central mechanism by which democracy is nurtured and sustained. Equal and effective access to the justice system is another, and equally important, mechanism. At the present time the justice systems in many democratic societies are under strain. Budgetary constraints are having a serious effect. Governments are strapped for cash and have to make hard political choices. These tend to be driven by their assessment of what the electorate regards as important. Sadly

---

[15] J Adams, 'Letter to John Taylor of Carolina' in GW Covey (ed), *The Political Writings of John Adams* (Washington, 2000) 406.

for those to whom the maintaining of high standards of justice is of paramount importance, expenditure on justice systems is not seen as a high priority by those in power. In a number of jurisdictions there has been a marked shift away from state-funded legal aid for civil and family justice. This has been particularly controversial in England and Wales. This shift has, to a certain degree, been mirrored by a liberalisation in other funding methods, such as the introduction of various forms of contingency fee funding and the growth of third party funding.

The merits of the public and private funding of civil justice are issues for another day. However, if we are to continue to maintain access to the courts, our funding methods must be effective and affordable. If they are not, and individuals and small and medium-sized enterprises are unable to gain access to our courts, we will surrender our commitment to equality before the law and we will diminish our democracies, and their ability to develop their economies. A small or medium-sized business that is unable to enforce its debts, or to keep its trading partners to their bargains through litigation or the threat of litigation is one that will not long thrive or even survive. Diminution of funding is a modern analogue to the barriers to trade that Magna Carta sought to blow away.

Necessarily linked to litigation funding is the cost of litigation. By this I mean to refer to both court fees and lawyers' costs. If either is too high, they inhibit access to the justice system. The individual litigant who wishes to have recourse to the courts in order to vindicate his private law rights or to hold a public authority to account by judicial review proceedings may not be able to do so. This is potentially very serious. Judicial review is a valuable means of holding public authorities to account. To curtail the ability of a citizen to seek judicial review of a decision is no doubt good for the decision-maker. For public authorities, judicial review is at best an irritant and at worst a road block to the journey it wishes to make. But the denial of judicial review is bad for the rule of law. If citizens cannot afford to have their disputes resolved by the courts, that too is bad for the rule of law. The spectre of self-help and disorder is not fanciful.

From a commercial perspective, if litigation costs are high and a dispute cannot be settled consensually, businesses must divert resources from commercially beneficial activity, such as investing in new products and developing new markets, to litigation. This may be welcome to the legal profession; but it is of little benefit to the overall economy. Excessive litigation costs silt up the arteries of trade and access to justice as effectively as the fishweirs that were removed by Magna Carta were a barrier to river traffic in the thirteenth century.

The guarantee of due process vouchsafed by Magna Carta was predicated on the barons' complaint about John's resort to arbitrary justice. They wanted justice before the court of barons—their peers—which had been enjoyed before John decided to use the law as a means of increasing his finances. The barons have been portrayed as heroes. But that has not always the case. As Jeremy Bentham noted in his discussion about the laws which prohibited champerty and maintenance:

> a man [could] buy a weak claim, in hopes that power might convert it into a strong one, and that the sword of a baron, stalking into court with a rabble of retainers at his heels, might strike terror into the eyes of a judge upon the bench.[16]

The days of barons or anybody else stalking into court, sword in hand, are long gone. But Bentham's colourful image illustrates brilliantly what we now call 'inequality of arms'. These days, inequality is usually demonstrated by a lack of availability of equal resources to opposing parties. It is often manifested by an imbalance between defendants and prosecuting authorities in the criminal law context; and between claimants and public authorities in the public law context. In the case of private law disputes, there can be a serious imbalance between the resources available to an individual of modest means and those available to a wealthy individual or a large corporation. The rule of law requires that a justice system is open to all; and that all who come before the courts are treated equally. Justice should not be at the beck and call of the highest bidder, contrary to King John's view.

I recognise that the provision of an effective justice system is expensive. In England and Wales, as in many liberal democratic systems, the courts are under huge pressure to cut costs and improve efficiency. I accept that, in our system at least, there is scope for improvement without sacrificing access to justice. Lawyers are said to be conservative and resistant to change. There may be some force in that assessment. But in my country at least, the judges are co-operating in the reforms that are in train. There have been major changes in the processes of criminal, civil and family justice. These

---

[16] J Bentham, 'A Defence of Usury' in Bowring (ed), *The Works of Jeremy Bentham*, vol 3 (Edinburgh, William Tait, 1843) Letter XII at 19.

are reforms which would have been unthinkable when I entered the legal profession in the late 1960s. And there is much more to come. Perhaps the most fundamental change that now needs to be made is to modernise our IT systems. We have not yet realised the benefits that the IT revolution can bring to our system of justice, a revolution, which if carried through effectively, will increase the speed and efficiency of litigation and reduce costs. I hope, for example, that before long all documents will be filed and managed electronically; and that the majority of procedural applications will be dealt with electronically. The days when court buildings are bursting with paper files on the floor or stored on long shelves or in large cupboards are, I hope, numbered.

We are also exploring the possibility of a scheme for online dispute resolution. This is an exciting project which I am confident will get off the ground before long. We shall have to work out the details of how it will operate and, in particular, to what kinds of case it will apply. I can also see no practical reason why, assuming the court has jurisdiction, it should not be possible for hearings to take place across continents via the internet, bringing litigants from one continent into the same court as litigants from another continent. Changes are taking place at great speed. The main impetus is the need to improve efficiency and reduce cost. In principle, that is a good thing. We need, however, to be vigilant to ensure that this rush to change, increased efficiency and saving of cost does not undermine access to justice. There is no reason in principle why it should have that effect. But we need to take care to protect an ideal that owes not a little to Magna Carta and which is fundamental to the rule of law. It hardly needs to be said that the rule of law is one of the hallmarks of our cherished democratic societies.

It took hundreds of years to move from Runnymede to liberal democracy and to secure firmly the commitment to the rule of law. If we are to maintain that commitment, we need to recognise that it cannot be taken for granted. We must be vigilant to ensure that we maintain an effective, accessible system of justice. It is essential to the promotion of confident economic activity that parties are able to make bargains in the knowledge that their disputes will be resolved in a court of law by independent judges in accordance with the law of the land and that the judgments that they obtain from the courts will be enforced by the state. Without such a system, there is chaos and trade becomes difficult, if not impossible. Our system is not perfect. Indeed, the recent cuts in resources which have been introduced in England and Wales (and other jurisdictions too) as a result of the economic downturn have put our system under enormous strain. The political reality, however, is that there are fewer votes in Justice than, for example, in Health and Housing. But we still enjoy a system which is the envy of most countries in the world. It is precious and we should value it. We should certainly do all we can to protect it.

17

*Delay Too Often Defeats Justice**

IT IS A real pleasure to have been invited to celebrate the 800th anniversary of the sealing of Magna Carta with you this evening. It is a particular pleasure to have been asked to do so, as I am the chairman of the Magna Carta Trust; a position held by all Masters of the Rolls since the Trust was established in 1956. As you can imagine my term of office has been a little busier than that of my illustrious predecessors.

One of the aims of the Trust is to 'perpetuate the principles of Magna Carta'.[1] It is true that the majority of its clauses or chapters concerned what might be described as 'local difficulties'. Local in the sense that they were concerned with a number of grievances that King John's barons had at the time. These grievances were a particular symptom of Angevin rule, but they had been exacerbated by John. How had he done this? As one historian has put it, by demonstrating a marked inability to be an effective tyrant. Perhaps there would have been no Magna Carta if John had been as ruthlessly efficient in the pursuit of tyranny as, for instance, his father had been. I leave that to the historians.

I want to focus this evening on the principles of justice that are contained in Magna Carta. Foremost among these principles are the prohibition on the sale of justice; and the requirement that justice must be neither delayed nor denied[2] and that punishments must fit the crime[3] (an early example of proportionality in criminal procedure). There are also provisions concerning access to justice and due process of law (although that exact phrase did not appear in the Charter until its 1354 reissue[4]); provisions that led the US Supreme

---

* The Law Society, Magna Carta Event, 22 April 2015.
[1] See magnacarta800th.com/magna-carta-today/the-magna-carta-trust/.
[2] Magna Carta 1215, Chs 39 and 40.
[3] Magna Carta 1215, Chs 20 and 21.
[4] 28 Edw 3, c 3; and see Observance of Due Process of Law Act (1368) 42 Edw 3, c 3.

Court to develop its constitutional doctrine of substantive due process; the idea that legislative acts can be scrutinised by the courts to ascertain whether they are consistent with what we would perhaps describe as fundamental rights; and a provision guaranteeing what, in essence, is the right to a fair trial.[5]

As Lord Sumption reminded us recently, we should not lose ourselves in unthinking reverence for Magna Carta: what he described as 'the force of myth'.[6] We should not, as some do, praise the Charter for creating trial by jury. It did not. Trial by jury predated the Charter. And it was in any event very different in nature to jury trial today. Jurors were akin to witnesses. Their decisions were informed by their own knowledge of the parties and the facts of the case that formed the basis of the trial as by anything else.[7] They were not a passive tribunal. Nor should we think of Magna Carta as the basis of the great writ of habeas corpus. It was not.[8] The Assize of Clarendon 1166 has that honour, and as with jury trial, the writ at that time differed from what it was later to become.[9]

Being careful should not, however, stop us from noting a number of demands that Magna Carta did make. It required justice to be local; that judges should know the law, which often meant local law—an early instance of what perhaps came to be known as subsidiarity; and that judges be appointed on merit. And the Charter demanded that only the judges sit in judgment.[10] It was no use requiring judges to know the law if anybody could sit in judgment.

MAGNA CARTA—TO NO ONE WILL WE DENY OR DELAY RIGHT OR JUSTICE

In this evening's address I want to focus on one specific principle of justice articulated by Magna Carta: the demand for timely justice. The principle is articulated in two places in the Charter. It underpins the provision in chapter 17 that 'Common pleas shall not follow our

---

[5] See, for instance, E Chemerinsky, 'Substantive Due Process' (1999) *Touro Law Review* 1501.

[6] J Sumption, 'Magna Carta—Then and Now' (British Library Lecture, 9 March 2015) at 18 www.supremecourt.uk/docs/speech-150309.pdf.

[7] J Zane, 'The Attaint' (1916–1917) 15 *Michigan Law Review* 1 and 127.

[8] JC Holt, *Magna Carta*, 2nd edn (Cambridge University Press, 2003) at 13.

[9] A Gregory, *The Power of Habeas Corpus in America* (Cambridge University Press, 2013) at 14ff.

[10] Magna Carta 1215, Chs, 17, 19, 24 and 45.

court, but shall be holden in some place certain.'[11] The consequence of this was the re-establishment of the court sessions at Westminster.

Prior to 1209 an informal arrangement had existed. The court which dealt with common pleas sat in two divisions. One followed the King. The other held its sessions in Westminster Hall. In 1209 John put a stop to the Westminster sessions, although from 1212 a limited number of sessions was held there.[12] The elimination in practice of the fixed court in Westminster placed an increased cost burden on litigants, as they had to travel round the country with the King's court in order to prosecute their claims. It also caused delay. Westminster sessions were typically longer than those before the King. And they sat more frequently than the King's court, which for obvious reasons had other matters to deal with. The aim of chapter 17 was to reduce delay and cost, by requiring John to turn the clock back to the start of his reign and provide for common pleas to sit once more in Westminster on a permanent basis.

Chapter 17 simply called for the court to sit in a 'place certain'. It is easy to assume that the Charter was referring to what was to become the Court of Common Pleas. But its meaning in 1215 was not so clear. The reference to 'our court' was a reference to the King's court, ie 'the whole body of counsellors, ministers, knights, clerks and domestic servants who (accompanied the King).'[13] That is a far cry from a court as we know it today. Nor did the chapter specify where the 'fixed place' should be. It did not suggest that it had to be in Westminster Hall. Nor did it suggest, as Sir Orland Bridgman, Chief Justice of the Court of Common Pleas in the seventeenth century is said to have believed, that the court was to be held in a specific part of Westminster Hall. Bridgman is said to have refused to move the court a few metres away from where it habitually sat in the Hall—in front of a door that let in a nasty draught of air. The reason? To move the court in that way was prohibited by Magna Carta. Of course, it did no such thing. Clarification of the meaning of chapter 17 was to come in the 1217 re-issue of the Charter. This made it clear that common pleas were to be heard by 'justices of the Bench'. What was implicit in 1215 was now made explicit: the court meant the judges, and particularly the judges who sat in Westminster Hall.

---

[11] Magna Carta 1215, Ch 17.
[12] Holt, *Magna Carta* at 323–324.
[13] D Carpenter, *Magna Carta* (Penguin, 2015) at 157.

Securing a fixed place for the court to sit and hear claims is not, however, the most famous of the chapters that deal with administrative inefficiency. That honour goes to chapter 40 which proclaims in ringing terms:

'To no one will we sell, to no one will we deny or delay right or justice.'[14]

What mischief did this provision seek to address? McKechnie in his magisterial account of Magna Carta gives a flavour of the answer. As he described it, in the years running up to Runnymede, John used the machinery of justice as 'ministers to his lust and greed'.[15] What for others would be instruments of government and justice were, for John, 'instruments of extortion and outrage.'[16] To fill the coffers of the exchequer, litigants were expected to pay sums of money to ease their path to a favourable decision. Judgments went to the highest bidder.

For example, Gilbert de Gant paid 100 marks for judgment. William de Mowbray paid 2,000 marks in respect of an action brought against him. His opponent had already paid a similar amount. And William de Briouze offered to pay 100 marks in the event he lost the claim or 700 marks for success.[17] And what could be sold could also be bought. Payments were not only made to secure a favourable decision. Speculative investment in claims was also commonplace. Barons provided the funds for others to pursue claims in the expectation of profiting from a favourable decision. Champerty and maintenance was thus a thriving business. Money was not only paid to secure favourable decisions. It was also paid to halt justice in its tracks. Gerard de Furnivall paid 1,000 marks to ensure that an action brought against him was simply stopped. And, in order to secure support for his war efforts, in 1206 John offered an incentive to his knights. If they joined, the army claims against them would be stayed.[18]

It is, therefore, readily apparent what chapter 40 was intended to achieve. The King was not to use the justice system as an instrument of financial policy. To a large degree it succeeded. While some future kings did sell and delay justice for their own ends, none did so in the manner that had been adopted by John.[19] That it did achieve its aim did not bring an end to delays in the administration of justice generally. Looked at in context it was not intended do so.

[14] Magna Carta 1215, Ch 40.
[15] Cited in Holt, *Magna Carta* at 179.
[16] Cited in Holt, *Magna Carta* at 179.
[17] Carpenter, *Magna Carta* at 219–220.
[18] Holt, *Magna Carta* at 84.
[19] Holt, *Magna Carta* at 327.

DELAY—A MEANS TO DEFEAT JUSTICE

Confined to its immediate historic context, the focus of chapter 40 was to put a stop to abuse of the justice system by the monarch. It was aimed at ensuring that improper interference with due process of law came to an end. This is a resounding principle of the rule of law which we take for granted as being fundamental to a democratic society. It underpins a commitment to judicial independence, which John could undermine through requiring the court to attend on him rather than sit at a distance from him in Westminster Hall. It underpins the rules against bias. Most fundamentally it, underpins the court's constitutional role as the means by which rights are determined, vindicated and—importantly in our common law jurisdiction—the law developed. The latter role is, of course, subject to Parliament's legislative sovereignty. These ideas may not have been apparent to the barons or to John at the time. The former no doubt were firmly focused on ensuring that John did not use the justice system to exploit them anymore. But it is still possible to see these wider principles of justice underpinning their immediate concerns.

The main focus on chapter 40 has tended to be on the prohibition of the sale of justice. That is understandable. The idea that a judge will decide a case in favour of the highest bidder is deeply shocking to us, although corruption of this kind is still endemic in many parts of the world. Confidence in the independence of the judiciary is essential to the maintaining of the rule of law. Less attention has been paid to the prohibition on delayed justice. That may be because delayed justice is rarely as clear-cut, stark and shocking as the sale of justice. Cases of delayed justice as extreme as *Jarndyce v Jarndyce* in Dickens' *Bleak House* were unusual even in nineteenth century England. But delay can unquestionably frustrate the achievement of justice. Sir Edward Coke CJ's commentaries on Magna Carta (or should I say reinterpretation of Magna Carta for his own political ends) drew this out. In a passage where he described justice, he said that it has three qualities:

> Justice ... must be Libera, Free; for nothing is more odious than justice let for sale; Plena, Full, for justice ought not to limp, or be granted piece-meal; and Celeris, Speedy ... Because delay is a kind of denial.[20]

---

[20] Cited in W Martin, 'Because delay is a kind of denial' (Australian Centre for Justice Innovation, 17 May 2014) at 3 www.civiljustice.info/cgi/viewcontent.cgi?article=1015& context=timeliness.

Coke CJ was not the first to equate delay with the denial of justice, nor would he be the last. Complaints about the delays of justice would echo through the centuries, culminating in the great complaints in the nineteenth century about the delays inherent in the courts. Those problems no doubt spurred Gladstone to utter the now famous phrase that 'justice delayed is justice denied.'[21] They clearly inspired Bentham in his detailed attacks upon the justice system and his claim that unnecessary delay and unnecessary expense were inimical to the achievement of justice.

He said that the justice system should secure the achievement of correct decisions with minimal delay, as well as minimal expense. For Bentham 'every moment beyond what was necessary (to achieve a correct decision) was detrimental (to its achievement).'[22] The reason for this was that delay may mean justice is delivered too late to benefit the claimant. An example given by Bentham is that the claimant might die before judgment is given. But a claimant does not have to die to be denied the fruits of successful litigation by delay. The effect of a delayed judgment may be that effective execution or enforcement becomes impossible. The defendant may have become insolvent or have spirited away his assets so that they are beyond the reach of the successful claimant. Even a freezing injunction is of no use if it is granted after the defendant has removed his money from the jurisdiction. Bentham's other examples are less stark. Delay led to the destruction of evidence and the fading of memories. It not only tended to eliminate the practical value of a judgment, but it also reduced the prospect that the judge would reach the right decision.[23]

Since the nineteenth century we have made a significant number of attempts to reduce delays in litigation. Systemic delay has been as big a barrier to the effective operation of the justice system as excessive costs and the complexity of procedures. The three inter-related problems are, as Professor Andrews has said, the unholy trinity of civil procedure.[24] Complexity breeds both unnecessary expense and delay. Delay leads to complexity, as applications for relief from

---

[21] See in *Gohman v City of St Bernard* 111 Ohio St. 726 (1924) at 737.

[22] J Bentham, 'Rationale of Judicial Evidence' in Bowring (ed), *The Works of Jeremy Bentham*, vol 6 (Edinburgh, William Tait, 1843) 212–213.

[23] J Bentham, 'Principles of Judicial Procedure, with the outlines of a Procedure Code' in Bowring (ed), *The Works of Jeremy Bentham*, vol 2 (Edinburgh, William Tait, 1843) at 17ff.

[24] N Andrews, 'A new civil procedural code for England: party-control "going, going, gone"' (2000) 19 (Jan) *Civil Justice Quarterly* 19 at 20.

sanctions are for instance made and case authorities accrete, which in turn leads to the expense of such applications. And as the case-law expands and becomes more complex, so too does the length and expense of hearings increase. And around we go.

The problems I have highlighted so far have a direct impact on individual litigants. They undermine the individual litigant's private interest in securing effective access to justice. They also have an adverse effect on the wider public interest. This arises in two ways. First, they undermine the rule of law. If cost, delay and complexity are too great, litigants are not able to use the justice system effectively and in some cases are not able to do so at all. If this happens, they are denied justice altogether. That is a serious erosion of the rule of law. Citizens should be able to vindicate their rights. If they cannot do so, there is a real danger that, in some cases, they will resort to self-help. This may pose a real threat to law and order. So here we can see the private interests of litigants marching hand in hand with the wider public interest in reducing the unholy trinity to the bare minimum. Reducing delay promotes both interests.

Secondly, however, the two interests do not always run together. In any system where there are limited resources and demand outstrips supply, a degree of rationing is necessary. As I have said before, that is the case with our justice system[25] which must be managed for the benefit of all litigants. The system cannot operate by looking solely at the needs of each individual claimant. A litigant's private interest in securing effective access must be looked at in the wider context of the public interest in securing the effective and affordable administration of justice in the interests of all litigants.

Resources are used in tackling delay that could properly have been spent elsewhere in the system and spent to better purpose. Time is taken up by Her Majesty's Courts and Tribunals Service and by the judiciary in dealing with matters that they would not otherwise have to deal with. Again that diverts precious time and resources away from where they could more usefully be employed. The same is true where unnecessary procedural complexity causes delay, as time is taken up in dealing with such process properly, which a simpler approach would not have created. And, of course, there is also the systemic delay caused by administrative processes

---

[25] J Dyson, '18th Jackson Implementation Lecture' (22 March 2013) at [18], available at www.judiciary.gov.uk/wp-content/uploads/2014/10/mr-speech-judicial-college-lecture-2013-1.pdf.

that stand in need of updating. In the nineteenth century the complaint was focused on the Chancery's court's interminable paper processes, which manufactured delays by the dozen. I wonder how far we have really come in this, the IT-age.

These points seem to leave me with a question: what steps should we be taking to promote the private and the public interest in reducing delay. Unlike King John, we may not use delay deliberately to deny litigants access to justice. We may not sell delay in order to deny justice. But how do we ensure, as far as possible, that delay does not defeat justice?

DEALING WITH DELAY TODAY

If we are to deal with delay effectively we must ensure that we bear two things in mind. The first rests on fundamental principle. The second is financial.

The issue of principle was recently examined in a paper given by Wayne Martin AC, the Chief Justice of Western Australia. He discusses the issue of delay in litigation and the denial of justice that it produces. His paper shows that the problems are common to most if not all common law jurisdictions. I believe that they are also shared by civil law jurisdictions as well. Discussing the aim of reducing justice's delays he makes the following point,

> ... reforms undertaken in order to improve timeliness should not view expedition as an end in itself, but must view timeliness in the context of the broader objectives of the civil justice system including most particularly of all, the provision of qualitatively just outcomes ... The challenge ... is improving timeliness without detracting from the achievement of the fundamental objectives of the civil justice system ...[26]

Those objectives are, as I have already mentioned, the private and public interests in rights-vindication and enforcement in order to secure the rule of law.

The point Chief Justice Martin makes is in my view of fundamental importance. First, it requires us to acknowledge something that may tend to be forgotten in the pursuit of efficiency: some delay is inevitable. Just as excessive delay can undermine the quality or availability of evidence and the quality of a judicial adjudication,

---

[26] Martin, 'Because delay is a kind of denial' at 20.

so too can excessive speed. If litigants are not given reasonable time to obtain evidence or prepare for trial, the court will not be able to determine their claim effectively. A rush to justice can be just as pernicious as the opposite. Reforms that promote administrative efficiency must therefore only do so in so far as they are consistent with and promote the achievement of both the private and public interest in the procurement of high quality justice. Efficiency for efficiency's sake should be rejected. And efficiency that undermines the public interest in the rule of law should also be rejected. Again as he put it:

> ... when one is endeavouring to construct a system for the administration of justice which strikes the right balance between the fairness and justice of the process and the time which it takes, it must always be remembered that the interests served by the courts extend beyond the interests of the parties to any particular dispute and includes the broader public interest which includes the affirmation of the rule of law and the delivery of outcomes which can be qualitatively assessed as just, as compared to dispositions quantitatively assessed as timely.[27]

I agree.

The second issue that must be considered is financial. Efficiency can and should be pursued in order to reduce the financial cost of litigation to individuals. Cost reduction is a sure way to increase access to justice, and thereby ensure that the courts are better able to perform their constitutional role. Efficiency can also ensure that the state does not waste financial resources. Unnecessarily used resources are lost resources.

It should be apparent, therefore, that the pursuit of efficiency serves the valuable purpose of enabling the justice system to act as an effective branch of the State. What can we do to further this end? I want to focus on three things: proper use of technology; effective procedural reform; and effective case management.

The Proper Use of Technology

A constant feature of procedural reform from at least Woolf until today has been the call for proper investment in and use of technology. I expect that many of you are aware of the Civil Justice

---

[27] ibid.

Council's recent working party report on the development of an Online Court.[28] I believe that it convincingly demonstrates one of the ways in which we should develop the justice system to make it more accessible. And here greater accessibility does not simply mean make it available to individuals who would not otherwise be able to seek to vindicate their rights before the courts. It also means that justice can be delivered more efficiently than in the past.

The courts in a number of other jurisdictions (including France) are some way ahead of us in the use of IT. Processes can, to a greater extent than here, be carried out online. I await the day when all claims can be filed online, when paper bundles and authorities are past history; and when the court file is an online file. I can see no reason, in principle, why case and costs management should not be facilitated through the proper use of technology. The potential savings in terms of costs and time to all involved are patent.

The system in France, however, allows for something more than simply greater efficiency. It has embraced innovation. One innovation has been the creation of a website that provides an e-filing service for litigants-in-person.[29] Individuals are able to attempt to resolve their dispute through an ODR mechanism. If that does not succeed, the website enables the electronic creation and filing of the court documents necessary to commence a claim. It is primarily aimed at small—as the website puts it 'everyday' claims. As a private body it does so for a fee.

Such services open up justice. That the starting point for the French website is an informal means of ADR cannot but be a good thing. It is right that it is backed-up with access to the court if ADR does not lead to a resolution of the dispute. We should be looking at similar innovations, to secure more efficient and cost-effective ADR and formal adjudication. That is what we are seeking to do by means of the ODR project that we intend to pilot later this year.

In developing such ideas, however, we need to keep in mind the public interest. It is one thing to develop virtual, internet-based, systems and processes that enhance efficiency and cost-savings. We cannot, however, lose sight of the fact that justice is an aspect of governance. It cannot therefore be developed in a way that is inconsistent with open justice. We cannot afford as a society to allow ourselves to be blinded by modern technology and thereby

---

[28] Civil Justice Council, *Online Dispute Resolution*, (February 2015) www.judiciary. gov.uk/wp-content/uploads/2015/02/Online-Dispute-Resolution-Final-Web-Version.pdf.
[29] See www.demanderjustice.com.

lose sight of the need to ensure that justice is seen to be done. Technology must be the servant of justice, not its master.

Effective Procedural Reform and Case Management

Finally, I want to turn to effective procedural reform and case management. If we are to achieve fair and efficient justice we are going to have to ensure that the pre-trial and trial processes are carried out properly. There are two aspects to this: first, the rules must not be so complex that complying with them causes unnecessary delay and expense; and secondly, they must be applied in a fair and efficient manner.

The search for simple rules has been present for as long as there have been complaints about delays to justice. It is undoubtedly right to say that each set of procedural reforms has, as one of its aims, procedural simplification. And it has been a common complaint that the CPR has grown like topsy, with its collation of rules, practice directions, protocols, guides and practice statements. There must be room for rationalisation. To give one example, there is a considerable amount of overlap between CPR rules, 76, 79 and 80, which deal with three types of terrorism-related procedures. There is a good case for consolidating these rules. Other examples undoubtedly exist. And there is equally undoubtedly scope for wider rationalisation. In Scotland such a process has begun. The Scottish Civil Justice Council, which performs the role of both our Civil Justice Council and Rule Committee, has embarked on a project aimed at rule simplification. With proper resources there seems to me no reason why a joint sub-committee of our CJC and Rule Committee could not embark on a similar exercise. If we are genuinely concerned with curing delay in the system, this seems to me to be an investment that could pay dividends for both litigants and HMCTS.

Procedural reform should go further than striving to ensure that the rules are as simple as possible. We should innovate. We can learn from other jurisdictions. I want to give you one example. It is drawn from Brazil. Last December a new civil procedure code was approved. It comes into force in December this year.[30] Article 191 of that Code introduces a new provision. It allows parties to agree to modify the procedure as it applies to their claim. This idea may be

---

[30] See www.loc.gov/lawweb/servlet/lloc_news?disp3_l205404244_text; www.planalto. gov.br/ccivil_03/Leis/L5869compilada.htm.

one that could be adopted here. For example, parties might want to agree, with the court's consent, to opt out of certain aspects of procedure in order to ensure that their claim is dealt with more speedily. Might there be something in this?

That is for the future. One current issue now appears to be the present approach to costs management. The present complaint is that costs management hearings are taking up a considerable amount of court time. They have introduced a new form of delay into the system. Any new procedure carries with it the potential to cause delay while it is bedding-in. Novelty brings its own costs, but soon becomes familiar. When we learn to drive a car it takes time to get used to the process of changing gears. But with time and practice we can change gears without thinking. Now I am not suggesting that the litigation process is something that can be carried out on automatic pilot and that, like changing gears, it can or should become an unconscious process. Litigation requires thought. What I am saying is that, with greater familiarity, cost management and cost management hearings will take up less time. In the same way that case management hearings initially took greater time than they do now, the same will be true of cost management.

There is, however, a wider point. Let us assume for the sake of argument that cost management hearings have an irreducible additional cost, both in terms of time and money. The benefit of the additional time should outweigh its cost. By planning and budgeting a claim and fixing a proportionate process, unnecessary work and, therefore, unnecessary cost and delay will be avoided. The value of cost management and budgeting (just as the value of the proper application of the menu-option approach to disclosure) accrues to the parties to the index litigation. It is also a benefit to other court users, as it helps to ensure that claims only use a proportionate amount of the courts' resources—thus facilitating the wider public interest in promoting access to justice for all court users. Looked at in terms of the private and public interest in efficiency, costs management promotes both overall.

The final point I want to make in terms of efficient case management relates to *Mitchell*[31] and *Denton*.[32] These two authorities seek to promote greater procedural efficiency. They seek to eliminate, as far as possible, a laissez-faire approach by the courts and litigants to rule-compliance. The aim of this is not to punish litigants

[31] *Mitchell v News Group Newspapers Ltd* [2013] EWCA Civ 1537.
[32] *Denton v TH White Ltd* [2014] EWCA Civ 906.

who do not comply with rules or court orders. Nor is it to render rules tripwires. Its aim is simple: to ensure that claims are properly prosecuted at proportionate time and cost to the parties, and to the court system. Its aim focuses both on the private and public interest I identified earlier.

This tough approach may appear unfair in some individual cases. For example, if a claim is struck out for non-compliance, it might be said that permanent denial of access to a court for determination of the claim in that case is the very antithesis of access to justice. Justice, however, goes beyond the individual case. Justice requires the court to be able to secure the public interest in the rule of law. The courts can only do that if they are able to ensure that no more than a proportionate amount of court time and resources are expended on a single claim. The courts must look beyond the individual case in managing litigation and look to the effect of case management decisions on the system as a whole. Only through proportionate management can the courts maximise the prospect that all claims that need to be determined by adjudication can be determined efficiently and proportionately. As Carr J put it recently in *Su-Ling v Goldman Sachs International* when setting out the principles to be derived from, amongst others, *Mitchell*:

> The achievement of justice means something different now. Parties can no longer expect indulgence if they fail to comply with their procedural obligations because those obligations not only serve the purpose of ensuring that they conduct the litigation proportionately in order to ensure their own costs are kept within proportionate bounds but also the wider public interest of ensuring that other litigants can obtain justice efficiently and proportionately, and that the courts enable them to do so.[33]

CONCLUSION

I started this address by noting that one of the aims of the Magna Carta Trust is to perpetuate the principles of Magna Carta. Eight hundred years ago the barons were concerned at the King's deliberate abuse of the justice system. John pursued delay as a matter of policy. Magna Carta was intended to put a stop to that and ensure that the courts were able to fulfil their role effectively.

Our concern today is different. Delay is not now a product that can be sold. It is an avoidable consequence of systemic problems.

---

[33] *Su-Ling v Goldman Sachs International* [2015] EWHC 759 (Comm) at [38].

But the principle underpinning the barons' action remains equally applicable today. We too must do our best to ensure that the justice system delivers timely justice, not just for a small number of litigants but for all who need to call upon the state to fulfil its duty and secure the rule of law. This is not to resort to the myth of Magna Carta. It is to remind ourselves that justice is not a commodity. It is to remind ourselves that the justice system must be allowed to operate in the public interest and that reforms, whether they are aimed at reducing delay or litigation cost, must be carried out consistently with that public interest. Delay may defeat justice. But equally we—just as the barons did—can defeat delay and its causes.

18

Magna Carta and Religion

I T GIVES ME great pleasure to make a few observations to bring this remarkable day's events to a close. As Master of the Rolls, I am Chairman of the Magna Carta Trust, a body which, with the support of the then Prime Minister, Sir Anthony Eden, was established in 1956 by a number of institutions as successor to the Magna Carta Society. Its objects were and are the perpetuation of the principles of Magna Carta; the preservation for reverent public use of sites associated with Magna Carta; and the commemoration triennially, and on such special occasions as shall be determined by the Trust, of the grant of Magna Carta as the source of the constitutional liberties of all English-speaking peoples, and a common bond of peace between them.

As a nation, we love commemorations and we are rather good at them. We celebrate them with efficiency and, where appropriate, panache and even pomp. We love commemorating historical events, whether they are momentous or of a rather more specialist and limited interest.

On any view, the sealing of the Magna Carta in 1215 was a momentous historical event which changed the history of this country and has affected the lives of millions of people across the world. You have heard a good deal about this from our speakers during the course of this splendid day. It was inevitable that the Magna Carta Trust would wish to commemorate the 800th anniversary of the sealing of the Magna Carta. And many others are joining in both here and abroad. There will, for example, be major celebrations next year in the US. Today's event has been a tasty hors d'oeuvre for the feast that is to come next year.

Why has Magna Carta generated such excitement? Many of its 63 clauses are rather technical and of no relevance to us today and have had little, if any, impact on succeeding generations, although they are no doubt of great interest to the medieval historian.

But a few of the clauses are gems whose influence has been incalculable. As you all know, it enshrined the rule of law in English society. It limited the power of authoritarian rule. The king was to be subject to the law. It defined limits on taxation. For centuries, it has influenced constitutional thinking worldwide. The US included many of its ideas in the 1791 Bill of Rights. In 1870, Bishop William Stubbs asserted 'the whole of the constitutional history of England is a commentary on this Charter'. In 1965, Lord Denning, then Master of the Rolls, described Magna Carta as 'the greatest constitutional document of all times—the foundation of the freedom of the individual against the arbitrary authority of the despot'. In 1948, Mrs Eleanor Roosevelt when speaking to the UN General Assembly about the UN Declaration of Human Rights, said: 'we stand today at the threshold of a great event both in the life of the United Nations and in the life of mankind. This declaration may well become the international Magna Carta for all men everywhere'.

The focus of today's event has been on Magna Carta and religion. King John sealed Magna Carta 'from reverence for God and for the salvation of our soul and those of our ancestors and heirs, for the honour of God and the exaltation of Holy Church and the reform of our realm'. His advisers included two archbishops and seven bishops (and the Master of the Temple).

Stephen Langton, Archbishop of Canterbury, had returned to England in 1213 after eight years of exile. He had spent his time in Paris lecturing on theology, and in particular on the Old Testament. He had developed four principles for the constitution of a nation governed justly under God: (i) for protection against wicked kings in Israel, God has ordered the written codification of laws; (ii) in honour of God, the people have the right to resist a wicked king if he commands a mortal sin; (iii) the people have a particular right to resist a king who renders a decision without the judgment of his court; and (iv) the Archbishop, because of his particular dignity, has the duty to act in the name of all the faithful, both clergy and laity.

Within weeks of his return, Langton made John swear at Winchester to abolish evil laws, establish good laws and judge all his subjects by the just sentences of his courts. Days later, he warned the king that to act against anyone without judgment of his court would violate the Winchester oath.

Langton was relentless in the promotion of the interests of the Church. The most conspicuous fruits of this endeavour are to be found in clause 1 of Magna Carta itself. It is worth reminding ourselves of what it says:

> We have first of all granted to God, and by this our present charter confirmed, for ourselves and our heirs in perpetuity, that the English

Church is to be free, and to have its full rights and its liberties intact, and we wish this to be observed accordingly, as may appear from our having of our true and unconstrained volition, before discord arose between us and our barons, granted, and by our charter confirmed, the freedom of elections which is deemed to be the English Church's very greatest want, and obtained its confirmation by the Lord Pope Innocent III; which we will ourselves observe and wish to be observed by our heirs in good faith in perpetuity. And we have also granted to all the free men of our kingdom, for ourselves and our heirs in perpetuity, all the following liberties, for them and their heirs to have and to hold of us and our heirs.

Like so much else in the document, the principles that it establishes are imprecise. What exactly were the 'rights' and 'liberties' of the English Church guaranteed by this clause? A similar point can be made about clause 39, which is one of the most famous clauses: 'no free man will be taken or imprisoned or disseised or outlawed or exiled or in any way ruined, nor shall we go or send against him, save by the lawful judgment of his peers and by the law of the land'. Who were the 'peers' whose judgment alone could lead to the outlawry of free men? What constituted 'lawful judgment'. Above all, given that there was no written code of laws that applied throughout England or that was officially recognised as royal law, how was anyone to determine whether a judgment had been delivered in accordance with 'the law of the land'? Lawyers would have a field day with these vague clauses.

But to return to clause 1, it is not clear what freedoms of the English Church were intended to be guaranteed, but they seem to have included: (i) episcopal elections being free from royal interference; (ii) respect for special privileges for the clergy; and (iii) leaving certain areas of life to the judgment of the Church.

The relationship between religion and the law has been the subject of discussion earlier today. It is now recognised to be a complex subject, involving balancing the interests of different religious faiths and the rights of those who have no faith at all. I am not sure that today's human rights-based respect for equality of religions derives much from Magna Carta. The Jews did not fare too well under Magna Carta. To a modern audience, clauses 10 and 11 might be read as evidence of medieval anti-semitism.

It seems to me that the equality of all religions under the state's secular law is the best guarantee in a secular society of equal freedom for each religion and its adherents. Faith leaders no longer have the power that they once had. But they continue to have a very important role in promoting such equality of freedom as a fundamental and indispensable social good.

The convenors of this conference hope that the conference and the book will help all UK's faith communities to become the conciliatory peace-making heirs of Stephen Langton, although they do not enjoy the pervasive power of religion which he could take for granted.

19

*Runnymede**

WE LOVE ANNIVERSARIES in this country. Of battles, the start and end of wars, the birth and death of famous people and significant events which have helped to shape our history. Any excuse for a commemoration, and we take it. When it comes to really important anniversaries, new stamps are printed and coins minted; new music is written; and the media pull out all the stops.

The anniversary that we are celebrating today is worthy of the royal treatment that it is receiving. We are commemorating the making of a treaty, an event which has turned out to be of huge significance for the development of this country and other democratic systems throughout the world. King John and the barons would have been bemused that thousands of people from all over the world were willing to set off at the crack of dawn to come here today, in order to stand for several hours in a field without shelter and uncertain of the elements. All this to mark what they did in 1215.

They would surely have been astonished to learn that over time Magna Carta came to be regarded as one of the most important constitutional documents in our history and that it continues to be so regarded 800 years after it was sealed on this very spot. They would not have believed that the barons' list of demands would become a symbol of democracy, justice, human rights and perhaps above all the rule of law for the whole world. But that is exactly what has happened.

Magna Carta has had its ups and downs. But it was a hugely significant step on a journey which led to the building of a society where everyone has equal rights and nobody is above the law. A few clauses of Magna Carta are still part of our law, including famously the provision that no free man shall be taken or imprisoned except

---

* Speech at the 800th Anniversary of the signing of Magna Carta, 15 June 2015.

by the lawful judgment of his peers or by the law of the land; and to no one will we sell, to no one will we deny or delay right or justice. These words still have a thrilling majesty even today.

Magna Carta was one of the English documents that inspired the US Bill of Rights. Other governments around the world have been greatly influenced by Magna Carta. The fact that visitors from far and wide are here today is eloquent testament to its continuing significance.

Lord Denning went so far as to describe Magna Carta as the greatest constitutional document of all time, the foundation of the freedom of the individual against the arbitrary authority of the despot.

With those ringing words in our minds, it now gives me great pleasure to invite the Prime Minister to speak.

20

*Advocates as Protectors of the Rule of Law**

I**T IS A** great honour to have been asked to address you today, to talk about the rule of law, current challenges to it and the role of advocates in protecting it. The phase 'the rule of law' can mean many things. It can, as Gordon and Tamanaha have put it, mean no more than that there are clear general rules whose application is, or ought to be, universal and predictable.[1] On that basis, the rule of law is no more than rule by law. A more expansive view is that the law must have a certain substantive content and must provide certain minimum rights.[2] There is much scope for argument as to what those rights should be, but this is not the place to develop this enormous subject. It is not, therefore, my intention to enter into a deep discussion of what is meant by the rule of law. I would need longer than a keynote address to do so.

More than 100 years ago, in the case of *Chambers v Baltimore & Ohio Railroad Co* US Supreme Court Justice Moody noted that:

> The right to sue and defend in the courts ... is the right conservative of all other rights, and lies at the foundation of orderly government. It is one of the highest and most essential privileges of citizenship ....[3]

The effective vouchsafing of that right to all members of society, without discrimination, is a *sine qua non* for the rule of law whichever meaning of the phrase is chosen. To render the right effective, the state must satisfy a number of conditions. It must ensure the

---

* Keynote Address, World Bar Conference, Queenstown, New Zealand, 9 September 2014.
  [1] R Gordon, 'The Role of Lawyers in Producing the Rule of Law: Some Critical Reflections (2010) 11 *Theoretical Inquiries in Law* 441, Faculty Scholarship Series Paper 1397, available at digitalcommons.law.yale.edu/fss_papers/1397 at 441; B Tamanaha, *On the Rule of Law: History, Politics, Theory* (Cambridge University Press, 2004) at 26ff cited in Gordon at 1.
  [2] Gordon at 442ff.
  [3] 207 US 142, 148 (1907).

existence of an independent and impartial judiciary which is free from improper pressure or influence and which has the 'moral courage'[4] to decide cases without fear or favour, affection or ill-will according to right fact and law. It must also provide a properly resourced and effective court system through which the judiciary can administer the law and thereby secure effective access to the courts. Absent these features, the right to sue and defend in the courts is scarcely worthy of the description of a 'right' at all: it is no more than a bare right, empty of content and meaning.

In 2009, Lord Judge, the former Lord Chief Justice of England and Wales, said the following with reference to judges:

> Judges must ... have moral courage—it is a very important judicial attribute—to make decisions that will be unpopular whether with politicians or the media, or indeed the public, and perhaps most important of all, to defend the right to equality and fair treatment before the law of those who are unpopular at any given time, indeed particularly those who for any reason are unpopular.[5]

But an effective, accessible court system and an independent and impartial judiciary are only part of the story. Another crucial requirement of the rule of law is that there should be a vigorous and independent legal profession, and particularly a profession of advocates. They too must have moral courage.

It was as a result of his moral courage that Thomas (later Lord) Erskine refused to buckle under pressure from the establishment, to bow to threats, including the risk of loss of status and potentially ruinous loss of future prospects. He insisted on representing Thomas Paine, the revolutionary writer, in his trial for seditious libel. He said this:

> I will for ever, at all hazards, assert the dignity, independence and integrity of the English Bar, without which impartial justice, the most valuable part of the English Constitution, can have no existence. From the moment that any advocate can be permitted to say that he will, or will not, stand between the Crown and the subject arraigned in the court where he daily sits to practise, from that moment the liberties of England

---

[4] A Clarke, 'Selecting Judges: Merit, Moral Courage, Judgment and Diversity' (2009) 5 *High Ct Q Rev* 49.
[5] I Judge, 'Diversity Conference Speech' (London, March 2009), available at webarchive. nationalarchives.gov.uk/20131202164909/http://judiciary.gov.uk/Resources/JCO/ Documents/Speeches/lcj-speech-diversity-conf.pdf at 2.

are at an end. If the advocate refuses to defend, from what he may think of the charge or of the defence, he assumes the character of the Judge ...[6]

Erskine believed passionately that it was the duty of advocates to promote effective access to justice by acting on behalf of their clients even in circumstances where this might result in personal disadvantage to themselves. He also believed that an advocate should not refuse to act for a client simply because he considered the client or his case to be repugnant or distasteful or lacking in merit. Moral courage required counsel to abide by what we call 'the cab rank rule' and not flinch from doing justice.

Serjeant Sullivan KC showed moral courage in *Hobbs v Tinling*[7]—a libel action—when he walked out of court in the face of what he considered to be the improper conduct of the then Lord Chief Justice, Lord Hewart. Such conduct was as unusual then as it would be considered to be today. It was also risky: it might have redounded to the disadvantage of his client. He walked out for two reasons. First, his client had, in his view, just been subjected to an unfair trial at the hands of Lord Hewart. Secondly, Lord Hewart had refused an application to adjourn a second trial, involving the same parties as the first trial. Sullivan KC concluded that the second trial would go the same way as the first, and that he could not participate in a second trial which would be as unfair as the first. His decision was vindicated by the Court of Appeal, which set aside the verdict in the first trial. Scrutton LJ in delivering his judgment said,

> I cannot see it was the duty of the plaintiff's counsel to incur the expense of a second hearing, in order to obtain the same rulings (as in the first trial), and have the same appeal ... in convincing the Court that the first case was not satisfactorily tried, they succeed in showing that the second and similar case should not have been tried before the same judge, with the same opposing counsel ...

If you read the Court of Appeal's judgment you might think that the Court of Appeal also displayed a degree of moral courage in expressing its conclusion about the conduct of the Lord Chief Justice in such forthright terms.

History is full of examples of brave advocates fearlessly standing up for the rights of their clients in the face of a hostile court. Perhaps even more striking and worthy of admiration are those advocates who take on an oppressive executive. For example, most if not all of

[6] J Ridgway (ed), *The Speeches of the Hon. Thomas Erskine*, vol 1 (Eastburn & Co, 1813) at 276.
[7] *Hobbs v Tinling* [1929] 2 KB 1 (CA).

you will be aware of the remarkable moral, and often physical, courage the Zimbabwean advocate Beatrice Mtetwa regularly exhibits in defending journalists and press freedom and generally seeking to uphold the rule of law in her country, at great personal peril. But, important though it is, I do not wish to explore the ambit of the duty of an advocate to stand up to the might of the state. Instead, I intend to discuss whether recent developments in England and Wales concerning legal representation may be tending to undermine the rule of law by adversely affecting access to justice. I shall consider first whether these developments present a threat to the adherence by advocates to the ethical standards and the concomitant professional rules which have long been the hallmark of the advocate in our country. I shall then examine the effect on access to justice of the growth of litigants in person.

In England and Wales, and other common law jurisdictions, the legal profession is undergoing substantial reform. Of particular importance is the Legal Services Act 2007, which modernised the regulatory structure of the profession and liberalised the manner in which lawyers can practice. It did not go as far as to fuse the various branches of the profession. In some ways it has done the opposite, entrenching the different branches of the profession whilst also creating other niche forms of lawyer, such as costs lawyers. To a certain extent it has turned the clock back to before the 1870s, when there were various specific and different types of lawyer: attorneys, proctors, solicitors, barristers, serjeants, notaries. This development, and the attendant growth in regulators and potentially differing regulatory standards and practices, raises questions about adherence to common ethical standards. I certainly do not wish to suggest or imply that some types of lawyer are more ethical or have more moral courage than others. The point is rather that different institutional arrangements may promote different approaches, which in turn will entrench different standards. Care is needed.

What the 2007 Act has done is enable new business arrangements to emerge. Barristers, for instance, can now be self-employed and employed at the same time. They can thus be both in independent practice in chambers and employed by a solicitors' firm. Equally, solicitors and barristers can enter into business together; they can form partnerships. Lawyers can enter into business, into partnership, with non-lawyers. And, as in Australia, non-lawyers can invest in legal practices. It has, as I mentioned, also reformed the regulatory structure of the profession. The traditional regulators, the Law Society and Bar Council, have separated out their regulatory and representative functions. They are now subject to overarching regulation by the Legal Services Board.

In themselves none of these reforms poses a risk for the continued adherence to professional ethics. None should reduce the likelihood of advocates continuing to act with moral courage. New arrangements always, however, carry with them some degree of risk. There is the risk that new regulatory and business arrangements may subtly undermine advocates' professional ethos. External investment may be a benign development. It may not. It may, for instance—as William T Robinson III, a past president of the American Bar Association put it—bring with it 'inherent conflict of interest' between investor and lawyer and their client. As he put it 'he or she who has the gold makes the golden rule'.[8] Such a golden rule might create a cultural pressure for a modern day Sullivan KC to remain in court for the second trial and secure his full fee, or a modern day Erskine to refuse Paine's case. And if the high ethical professional standards observed by the advocates of our country were to be eroded, it would be very difficult to restore them.

That is one issue. Another is raised by legal aid. A consequence of the Legal Aid, Sentencing and Punishment of Offenders Act 2012 has been substantially to reduce the availability of legal aid in criminal cases. It had already been withdrawn for most civil and family cases. Roger Smith, the former director of Justice, has criticised our government for providing no more than the minimum level of service sufficient to meet our commitments under the European Convention on Human Rights.[9] Opposition to the Act in relation to legal aid has given rise to discussions between the Ministry of Justice, the Bar Council and The Law Society. The latter's response to the situation resulted, at the end of last year, in the first successful vote of no confidence in its President and senior management.[10] Earlier this year the criminal bar, in two one-day protests, withdrew its labour in protest at cuts to criminal legal aid. To all intents and purposes it went on strike.[11]

---

[8] Reported in *The Law Society Gazette* (4 October 2012), available at www.lawgazette. co.uk/news/iba-2012-formerpresident-american-bar-dismisses-abss.

[9] R Smith, 'After the Act: what future for legal aid?' (Justice Tom Sargant Annual Lecture 2012, London, 16 October 2012), available at www.justice.org.uk/data/files/ resources/332/After-the-Act-what-future-for-legal-aid.pdf at [2].

[10] See at www.lawgazette.co.uk/practice/no-confidence-motion-passed-at-sgm/ 5039204.article.

[11] See www.independent.co.uk/news/uk/home-news/courts-hit-as-lawyers-stage-unprecedented-national-walkout-over-legal-aid-cuts-9040222.html; www.bbc.co.uk/news/ uk-26472809.

As a serving judge I cannot express a view about these responses. Nor is it appropriate for me to comment on the nature of the legal aid reforms themselves. In my view, it is proper for a serving judge to comment on government *proposals* for legislation affecting the justice system. This I frequently do (but not through the media). But once proposals are enacted, I regard it as my duty to apply the law conscientiously and to the best of my ability. If experience shows that the legislation is not working effectively or fairly, I consider that a serving judge may, and indeed should, draw attention to the problems. The position of barristers and solicitors is, of course, very different. In protesting against the government's changes to legal aid, they were acting in order to promote access to justice and to protect the rule of law. So too were the Bar Council and the Law Society in the constructive dialogue in which they engaged with the government.

What these various actions show is that advocates do not simply see their role as protecting the rule of law within the court room in individual cases. They, rightly, see protecting the rule of law as something that goes beyond acting in particular proceedings. They do this in different ways. Thus in the 1940s they helped devise the legal aid scheme in our country.[12] In 2013 and 2014 they have taken controversial steps to defend it. In the 1940s a legal aid scheme was one option for the provision of effective representation. Another was a national legal service. Promoting the rule of law seems to me to require advocates to consider all possible means to secure effective representation in our courts. In 1940 legal aid was thought to be the best way of doing this. In today's climate of economic austerity, legal aid is under threat as never before. Our government says that the country cannot afford legal aid at the level to which we had become accustomed in the second half of the twentieth century. Alternatives are being considered. It seems to me that advocates have the skills, experience, understanding and moral courage to participate in the debate about these alternatives. Both as individuals and under the aegis of the Bar Council and the Law Society, they have shown a great aptitude for participating in such discussions. I have no doubt that they will continue to do so.

One of the consequences of the withdrawal of legal aid in civil and family cases has been the huge rise in the number of litigants-in-person. I want to say something about this development and the

---

[12] M Cook, *Cook on Costs 2012* (Lexis Nexis, 2012) 693–694.

challenges that it poses to our justice system generally and to professional advocates in particular.

The growth in the number of litigants-in-person is not, of course, unique to England and Wales. It is an increasingly common feature of very many common law systems. Litigants-in-person are not skilled in the law and are not familiar with the way in which we traditionally conduct cases in court. Traditional court processes were not developed with them in mind. That is not surprising. From the earliest days of the common law, litigants were represented by advocates. Court processes and court rules have always been drafted with lawyers in mind. They are expressed in terms which are commonly understood by advocates, but which are obscure to lay people. Lawyers, for instance, talk about 'filing' and 'serving'. What is meant by 'filing' a document in court is 'giving' it to the court; and what is meant by 'serving' a document on the opposing party is 'giving' or 'sending' it to that party. Even where the rules do not use language that might persuade George Bernard Shaw that the legal profession is party to a conspiracy against the laity, they are rarely clear and simple; they tend not to be user-friendly unless the user is a lawyer.

This makes it incumbent on those who draft court rules to try harder to ensure that procedures are as simple as possible. As someone who has chaired our civil procedure rule committee both as deputy head of civil justice and now as Master of the Rolls, I know as well as anyone that this is easier said than done. One way in which we might consider changing our approach to drafting is not just to engage lawyers in the drafting process, but to involve individuals from the advice sector who have expertise in drafting documents which are easily understood by the layperson. We should perhaps change the focus of our approach and, as has been done recently in our family procedure, draft new rules on the basis that they are primarily for use by litigants-in-person and not lawyers. Advocates have a key part to play here, in helping rule-makers change the drafting process and then working with the courts to create a new culture where plain English and accessible processes are the order of the day. This is easier said than done. Civil litigation is an inherently complicated business. The traditional approach to rule-drafting in England and Wales has been to try to anticipate every eventuality and deal with it expressly in the rules. In other words, to try to cover the entire ground in all its detail. No doubt, the rules could be made much shorter. But if that were done, there would inevitably be gaps which would have to be filled by court decisions. Would that not be even worse than what we currently have? In that event, the court processes would be found both in the rules and the decisions of the court. How would that help the litigant-in-person?

To move away from simplifying procedural law, an important question that arises is what are the implications of the growth in litigants-in-person for advocates and the role they play in protecting the rule of law? It seems to me that advocates can do a number of things which would be of benefit to litigants-in-person.

Knowing that you have a right or duty is essential for the maintaining of the rule of law. Assisting lay people to acquire legal knowledge and understanding is, therefore, self-evidently important. Governments and Parliaments must make laws that can be easily understood by the average intelligent lay person. These should be drafted in clear and simple terms. Charles Dickens famously created the Circumlocution Office to parody the complexity, as well as the inefficiency and delay, of the early Victorian civil service. A good degree of legislation appears to take the ethos of that fictional office as its guiding spirit; a point most recently noted in the Australian Productivity Commission's draft report on access to justice. It noted that:

> The law itself is a source of complexity in the justice system … making it more difficult for people to self represent. Participants noted that the average lawyer, let alone the average person, is struggling with increasing complexity in areas such as social security law and taxation law.[13]

If the average lawyer is struggling after undergoing university and professional training, there is little hope for the average layperson. Noting this problem, the UK government has recently taken steps to ensure that simplicity is the order of the day. It has acknowledged that complex legislation undermines the rule of law and is seeking to ensure that complexity becomes the exception rather than the rule.[14] This is a noble aspiration. We shall see whether anything comes of it.

Advocates have a key role to play here. Through everyday contact with legislation, they are well placed to identify statutory provisions which are opaque, unduly complex and difficult to understand. They can point out the difficulties they encounter when working their way through difficult legislation. Take, for example, the Equality Act 2010 which has been described by one commentator as

---

[13] ibid at 439.
[14] www.gov.uk/government/publications/when-laws-become-too-complex/when-laws-become-too-complex.

'a dense and complex statutory framework, despite its aim of simplifying and harmonising [a] labyrinth of domestic discrimination law'.[15]

Advocates can engage constructively with the legislative process to point out where *proposed* legislative provisions create unnecessary complexity, and suggest simpler forms of drafting. They can draw the attention of Law Commissions and government to those aspects of *existing* law which are unnecessarily complex. Governments are increasingly concerned with what is often described as the regulatory burden of too much law. Advocates promoting the rule of law ought to take a role in highlighting the burden—regulatory or otherwise—of badly-drafted law.

Advocates can (and do) also contribute to public legal education and provide free legal advice in advice centres as well as outside or inside the courtroom. There seems to me to be no reason why advocates cannot work with court administrations to set up such free advice centres in court buildings. The internet has a clear role to play here. Working with advice centres, advocates could provide straightforward introductions to frequently encountered areas of the law, such as consumer contracts, personal injury, employment, debt, social security disputes and, perhaps most importantly, civil procedure and give advice as to how to present cases in court. They could also provide worked through practical examples to put the law in context, again in as straightforward a way as possible.

There is a need to engage the advice sector who have the expertise to ensure that what is produced is readily accessible to all and not just to lawyers. Such material could then be placed on the internet. Advocates could provide web tutorials on YouTube showing how to make an effective submission, how to cross-examine, how to address the court. Practical, realistic examples could go a long way towards taking some of the mystique out of the court process, helping to familiarise lay people with it and remove some of the stress and anxiety they may have regarding appearing in court. Perhaps some advocates already do this.

By providing such services to litigants-in-person, advocates can promote access to justice and the rule of law in two ways. First, increasing accessibility to the law helps individuals understand their legal position before disputes arise, thereby avoiding disputes altogether. Secondly, where a dispute does arise, advocates can

---

[15] M Malika, 'Book Review' (2011) 40(4) *Industrial Law Journal* 466.

help individuals to make a realistic assessment of the merits of their claim or defence. In this way, they can help promote settlement; and where settlement is impossible, they can assist the litigant prepare for and participate more effectively in the court process. Studies have shown that the ability of litigants to participate effectively in proceedings is an important element in securing their confidence in the trial process. The importance of advocates helping laypersons to achieve proper participation in this way cannot be underestimated.

So far I have talked about what advocates can do before a dispute reaches court. What can they do when matters go that far? Let us imagine that our litigant-in-person has taken advantage of as much pre-court assistance as is available and has watched whatever tutorials are available on YouTube. Many will still need support at the court hearing.

One thing that can be done—and is currently being done in both the Queen's Bench and Chancery Divisions of our High Court—is to provide a pro bono litigant support scheme. Let me take the Chancery Bar Litigant in Person Scheme as an example.[16] It operates as a partnership between the Bar Pro Bono Unit, the High Court citizens' advice bureau and the Chancery Bar Association. The judges of the Chancery Division and the Chancellor of the High Court support it. It is also given support by two further assistance and advice services: the Personal Support Unit and Law Works. In addition to providing pro bono advice to litigants-in-person before they go into court, it also provides on the spot representation for litigants who have an interim application before the court. Volunteer barristers make themselves available at court from 10.00 until 16.30 and provide such advice and representation as in necessary, and is professionally appropriate in the circumstances, on a first-come, first-served basis.

As I have said, a similar scheme is available in the Queen's Bench Division, specifically in respect of interim applications. With a degree of co-operation between the Bar, Specialist Bar Associations, Law Societies and pro bono advisory and advice bodies, there is—I think—a strong argument for extending such court-based assistance more generally throughout our courts and tribunals.

So far, I have been considering what qualified advocates are doing and what they can and should do to assist litigants-in-person in England and Wales. The serious implications of the growth in the

---

[16] See   www.chba.org.uk/about-us/the-association/clips-chancery-bar-litigant-in-person-support-scheme.

numbers of litigants-in-person have only recently been appreciated in my country. They are entitled to have access to the courts and a fair trial just as much as represented parties. Judges are having to learn to adapt to a new landscape. How inquisitorial should they be? It may not be difficult to act inquisitorially where both parties are litigants-in-person, although the judge may lack the necessary experience to do it well. But it is more difficult for the judge to know what to do when one party is represented and the other is not. We have not begun to work out how to manage these problems. And if the litigant-in-person may make life difficult for the judge, what about the advocates who appear against a litigant-in-person? They may have to adapt their techniques to accommodate the fact that their opponent is not a lawyer and has little or no experience of court processes. And yet they must always continue to act in the best interests of their client.

In addition to advocacy training for litigants by volunteer barristers (and qualified solicitor advocates), the question arises whether *trainee* advocates should be permitted to advise and represent litigants-in-person. It has long been the case that litigants in our tribunals can be represented by whomsoever they choose. There are no restrictions on rights of audience in that court. As a consequence, through such bodies as the Free Representation Unit, trainee advocates routinely act as advocates on a pro bono basis for litigants-in-person in tribunal cases. In this way, young trainee advocates undoubtedly gain valuable experience, as they put their academic and vocational training into practice, and the litigants are represented.

Should such a system be extended to all courts and to all categories of case? It is difficult to see what is so special about tribunal cases that rights of audience should be granted more liberally in these courts than in any other. An issue which is being currently debated in England and Wales is whether to accord so-called McKenzie friends the right to represent litigants and, if so, whether to extend the right of representation even to professionally paid McKenzie friends. Opinion is divided on the issue. There are those who say that litigants-in-person should be given all the assistance that they want; and if they want a McKenzie friend to represent them, that is what they should be permitted to have; and if they are willing to pay for such representation, they should be permitted to do so. The opposing school of thought is that a representative must owe a duty of candour to the court like any legal representative. Since McKenzie friends are not regulated by any professional body and are not subject to any professional standards and obligations, they should not be allowed to represent litigants-in-person in court. I cannot predict how this issue will be resolved. To put it at its lowest, there is a real possibility that, subject to certain safeguards, McKenzie friends will be permitted to represent litigants-in-person. Whether professional McKenzie friends will be permitted to do so must be much more open to doubt.

Trainee advocates are not McKenzie friends. They will necessarily have obtained a university degree and a professional vocational qualification in law. But unless they are subject to professional regulation and discipline, the litigant-in-person is not as well protected as he would be if he were represented by a qualified advocate. In my view, there is much to be said for permitting trainee advocates to represent litigants-in-person. Careful consideration should be given as to what safeguards, if any, to introduce as a condition of permitting McKenzie friends to represent them.

I started this address by referring to Justice Moody's dictum that the right to sue and defend in the courts is the right that underpins and gives life to all other rights and that it lies at the foundation of orderly government. In other words it lies at the heart of the rule of law. Without the ability to assert or defend your rights before the courts, the rule of law is a hollow promise. The common law system, which places great weight on the ability of advocates to prepare and present cases to the courts—to give life to our adversarial systems—depends on independently minded advocates. Without them it could not properly function, and the rule of law would become that false promise.

I have only been able to touch upon some of the issues that are facing advocates in England and Wales, and which may have an impact on their fundamentally important role in our system. I have referred to the pressures that have arisen as a consequence of reductions in legal aid spending. There are many ways in which the legal profession can ensure that advocates continue to thrive and to exhibit those fine qualities for which they have been renowned throughout the centuries. I am confident that all those who practise in courts and tribunals throughout the world will meet today's challenges, that they will adapt and—most importantly—do so whilst maintaining a commitment to their professional values, ethos and integrity. That they do so is not just important for our commitment to the rule of law today. In all jurisdictions—like England and Wales—where tomorrow's judge is today's advocate—that they are able to adapt and thrive whilst maintaining their moral courage and integrity is all the more important.

An advocate's commitment to the rule of law is not simply a matter for today's case, or tomorrow's case. It is a commitment that stretches from today to the possibility that they may become a member of the judiciary, and bring to that role their character and experience gained and honed in arguing cases, representing and assisting their clients and litigants-in-person. William Wordsworth once said that the child is father to the man. The advocate is father—or mother—to the judge. The greatest challenge for today's advocates is to ensure that, whatever changes are presently occurring and may occur in the years to come, they are fit and proper fathers and mothers to the judges of the future. As such they will help secure the rule of law both today and tomorrow.

Part IV

Access to Justice and Civil Procedure

21

*Litigators—Survive and Thrive**

INTRODUCTION

O VER 100 YEARS ago, in the case of *Chambers v Baltimore &
Ohio Railroad Co* US Supreme Court Justice Moody had this
to say,

> The right to sue and defend in the courts ... is the right conservative of all
> other rights, and lies at the foundation of orderly government. It is one of
> the highest and most essential privileges of citizenship ....[1]

Without the ability of citizens—through cost-effective, efficient and
proportionate litigation—to vindicate and enforce rights and hold
government to account, no democratic society can long remain committed to the rule of law. Access to justice, that right conservative of
all other rights, is under pressure today.

In the present age of austerity, governments are taking difficult
decisions and reducing public spending in many areas. Justice systems are no exception. Reduced public spending is resulting in
court closures, the reduction in court staff, in some countries the
reduction in judicial salaries is part of wider schemes to reduce
public sector pay, and a reduction in legal aid. It is perhaps no
understatement to say that the present economic crisis is having,
and is likely to continue to have, a profound effect on the manner
in which we are able to secure that highest and most essential privilege of citizenship.

In the next 20 minutes I want to outline some of the steps we are
taking, and some we may need to consider taking, in order to ensure
that justice remains readily accessible. I want to particularly focus
on one consequence of austerity: the growth in litigants-in-person
and the need to ensure those individuals who have to act as their

---

* Rome, 4 July 2013. Australian Bar Conference.
[1] *Chambers v Baltimore & Ohio Railroad Co* 207 US 142, 148 (1907).

own lawyer do not just survive but can thrive; and that they can realise their right of access to justice without the assistance of a professional litigator.

LITIGANTS-IN-PERSON

My starting point is that justice systems exist for those who seek justice. Our systems and their procedures have however developed and been designed for use not by litigants but rather by lawyers acting on their behalf. Consequently, as Lord Woolf noted in his now rightly famous Access to Justice reports, this rendered 'the court system and its procedures ... (all) too often inaccessible and incomprehensible to ordinary people'.[2] This problem is not confined to the justice system. Substantive law is very often inaccessible to the layperson as well.

Where individuals can afford to pay for lawyers, either from private funds, litigation funding arrangements such as contingency fee arrangements, third party litigation funding—which is far more developed in Australia than it is yet in England—or (where it survives), state-funded legal aid, such complexity may be regarded as tolerable by some, but not by me. I say tolerable only because such individuals have the benefit of professional expertise to guide and advise them. In other ways it is intolerable, as legal complexity inevitably increases litigation cost and delay. This is wasteful of society's resources, as individuals are forced to expend unnecessary amounts of money on litigation, which could otherwise be used more productively. Austerity has, however, brought the effects of complexity into sharper focus. We expect to see a significant increase in litigants-in-person, for whom its adverse effects will be all the greater. This is likely to be the case specifically due to the reduction in state-funded legal aid.

In England and Wales, since the Legal Aid and Assistance Act 1949, legal aid been the primary means by which the impecunious have been able to afford legal representation. When it was introduced in 1950 legal aid was available to around 80 per cent of the population. Eligibility rested on a means-test. By 2008, following a number of reductions in scope over the intervening period, only

---

[2] H Woolf, *Interim Report to the Lord Chancellor on the Civil Justice System in England & Wales* (HMSO, 1995) 119.

29 per cent of the population were eligible.[3] The Legal Aid, Sentencing and Punishment of Offenders Act 2012, which came into force in April 2013, effected further reductions in scope. Legal aid is, consequently, no longer available for private family law matters, such as divorce proceedings, some clinical negligence claims, some employment claims, and some debt and housing claims. Eligibility changes mean that only the very poorest members of society can now obtain legal aid in those areas where it remains available in principle. It is said by the government that the reductions should reduce the £2.2 billion legal aid budget by approximately £350 million: a 16% reduction. Time will tell.

It is obvious that this stark reduction in legal aid will produce a sharp increase in litigants-in-person; a point which was made in advance of the reforms coming into force by the Civil Justice Council. As it put it in a report from 2011,

> Every informed prediction is that, by reason of the forthcoming reductions and changes in legal aid, the number of [litigants-in-person] will increase, and on a considerable scale. Such litigants will be the rule rather than the exception. Where there is not an increase the reason will be that the individual was resigned to accepting that the civil justice system was not open to them even if they had a problem it could solve or it could give access to the rights they were entitled to.[4]

(I should point out that since October 2012, as Master of the Rolls, I have been chairman of the Civil Justice Council, which is an advisory body created at the turn of the century. The report predated my appointment.)

Such an increase in litigants-in-person is unquestionably going to have an effect on access to justice. First, it will no doubt increase the already significant number of individuals who do not litigate in order to secure their rights. They just wring their hands in despair and anger and walk away. As important an issue as this is, it is one I cannot touch upon today. Secondly, it will have an effect on the three stages of litigation: pre-litigation, pre-trial and at trial. I want to say a little about each of these stages, and what we may have to consider to ensure that litigants-in-person can both survive, and thrive.

---

[3] Hynes & Robins, *The Justice Gap* (LAG, 2009) 21.

[4] Civil Justice Council, *Access to Justice for Litigants in Person (or self-represented litigants): A Report to the Lord Chancellor and Lord Chief Justice* (November 2011) at 8, available at www.judiciary.gov.uk/JCO%2fDocuments%2fCJC%2fPublications%2fCJC+papers%2fCivil+Justice+Council+-+Report+on+Access+to+Justice+for+Litigants+in+Person+(or+self-represented+lit.

PRE-LITIGATION

If access to justice is to be a genuinely practical right individuals must have real and effective access to the law. Having an abstract right is one thing. Knowing you have that right, understanding what it is, and how it is applicable in any given situation is another thing entirely. A genuine right is one that is understood or at least understandable. Knowing the law is, however, not enough. Effective access to justice requires an ability properly to assess the application of substantive law to your dispute. Identifying the relevant law, delving through statute and the authorities, and then applying them to the facts is meat and drink for lawyers. That is not the case for most litigants-in-person.

The first question raised by the growth in litigants-in-person is how we can best ensure that individuals know their rights and are able to assess whether they have a genuine, and meritorious claim. I doubt whether there is a straightforward answer to this question. There are, however, a number of things which could be done to mitigate the problem.

First, legislation should be made simpler and clearer and, therefore, more accessible. This is easier said than done. Much law in inherently complex and despite serious efforts by parliamentary draftsmen, a good deal of legislation is difficult to understand to put it no higher. To be fair to them, sometimes the fault lies with their clients, their political masters who are given to insisting on things which are just very difficult and convoluted or deliberately vague; and all of this often in a great rush with impossibly tight timescales. Secondly, we may have to take more steps to improve public legal education. We could take steps to improve legal education in schools. We could also provide targeted public legal education in respect of those areas of the law that a litigant-in-person is most likely to encounter. Contract disputes, particularly consumer contracts, personal injury matters, employment, debt and housing disputes, for instance, could form the basis of a public legal education campaign. Such a campaign could utilise the best elements of the internet. It could utilise open-source material, wikis and more formally, a legal version of NHS Direct, which could provide information both over the internet and via the telephone.

Increased public legal education could serve two purposes. First, in the same way that businesses conduct legal audits of their activities in order to minimise the chance that they will end up in litigation, it could help citizens avoid disputes. This may seem to lie outside the scope of access to justice. But access to justice is not simply synonymous with access to the courts and adjudication. That is one way to vindicate and enforce rights. If, however, we can increase the enforcement of rights through minimising the incidence of legal disputes in the first instance, then that seems to me to be as much an instance of justice as court-based adjudication and enforcement.

Secondly, it could help litigants-in-person consider their disputes sensibly and make a reasonably informed and balanced assessment of whether they have a claim with real merit and prospects of success. Assessing the merits of a claim is not always, if ever, straightforward, not least when it is your own claim. The old adage has some force: a lawyer who has himself for a client is a fool. Here I think that a legal version of NHS Direct or—as Roger Smith, the director of Justice, put it in last year's Tom Sargant lecture[5]—Legal Direct could play an important, cost-effective, role. At a time when we are having to reduce legal aid and reducing funding of free legal advice centres, could we not 'put on the net a diagnostic alternative that provides everyone with a basic service?'[6] Such a service could operate on a number of levels.

First, it could provide simple advice on the nature of a variety of substantive legal issues. It could provide clear, straightforward guides outlining court procedure and how to present cases in court. Secondly, it could provide interactive advice, either over the phone or over the internet. Such advice could help an individual consider his dispute in the relevant legal framework and it could help him consider the merits of his claim.

Thirdly, it could provide online access to all the relevant court forms and, where necessary, assistance in filling them out. Assistance could be in the form of embedded weblinks to simple guidance on each section of the forms. (In saying this I am sure that the properly web-savvy would be able to come up with far more innovative ways in which such assistance could be given.) Such an innovation could also prove a spur to a thorough redesign of our court forms, which I regret to say were described in a recent review, commissioned by the Civil Justice Council and carried out by *Advicenow*, by an expert asked to review them as 'the worst set of public documents I've ever seen.' The report went on to note that

---

[5] R Smith, 'After the Act—What future for Legal Aid' (Annual Tom Sargant Memorial Lecture 2012) at 13, available at www.justice.org.uk/data/files/resources/332/After-the-Act-what-future-for-legal-aid.pdf.

[6] ibid.

one particular form had, in the words of an advice worker 'become impossible to complete for the litigant in person—and for us'.[7] In a world where there will be more litigants-in-person such a situation cannot continue.

Fourthly, a Legal Direct could provide a basic means of asking specific questions, both on substantive law, procedure and regarding court forms that could be answered via email, via instant messaging or internet-based videolink. Access to this, and basic advice on a Legal Direct website, is going to be particularly important not just on account of the reduction in the availability of free legal advice centres, but also as a consequence of the reductions in court staff and the availability of counter services in court buildings across the country. This is because, in the words of Judith March, the Director of the Personal Support Union, a court-based charity that helps litigants-in-person, 'budget cuts being absorbed by the courts service [have] removed many court staff who previously provided basic information to litigants in person.'[8]

Finally, it could provide a gateway to issuing or filing the court form, paying the issue fee or applying for a fee exemption. A Legal Direct could be a cost-effective, to borrow the phrase, one-stop-shop for litigants. A small proportion of court fees could fund it.

LITIGATION

What can we do if a claim has to be issued and proceedings commence? The first thing, as I have said, is to make it easier to complete and file forms and pay court fees online. We should be able to do this for all claims and all stages of litigation. In many ways it is surprising that we have not done this already. In a world where we can all buy things via Amazon and Ebay, it is remarkable that we have not established an equally accessible, secure, web-based system for all claims in England and Wales. It should be obvious that the gains that such a system would bring would not just benefit litigants-in-person, but also those who instruct lawyers. The former would, of course, more keenly feel the benefit. It would be cost-effective and would undoubtedly increase efficiency and accessibility.

---

[7] See www.lawforlife.org.uk/ple-news/good-information-saves-stress-and-money,10262, FP.html.
[8] G Langdon-Down, 'Litigants in person could struggle to secure access to justice' *Law Society Gazette* (19 January 2012), available at www.lawgazette.co.uk/analysis/litigants-in-person-could-struggle-to-secure-access-to-justice/63815.article.

Secondly, we may need to revise the way in which we prepare court orders. Pre-trial, case management directions are designed with lawyers in mind. Where one or more litigants act in person, directions should be drafted in more readily accessible language. Lawyers will know what it means to file and serve. Can we reasonably expect a litigant in person to know what that means? Equally, should we not be doing more to ensure that court orders inform litigants-in-person of the steps that they can take to challenge directions and to ensure that relevant provisions and rules are drawn to their attention? The wider challenge will be to simplify our rules and procedures. Simplification is, of course, a goal that we have sought for a long time. It is all the more imperative now that we take steps to realise it. Simplification increases accessibility.

Thirdly, we will need to ensure that we give proper effect to our commitment to proportionality. Since the Woolf reforms, proportionality has underpinned the structure of our justice system and how its rules and procedures are supposed to operate. As regards the structure of our system, we introduced various case tracks, matching procedure to the value of the claim. As for rules and procedures, civil procedure is supposed to operate so that each claim is prosecuted at no more than proportionate cost. To achieve this, all parties are required to properly comply with their procedural obligations: this of course is also an aspect of securing equality of arms. We have just implemented reforms arising from a review of the justice system conducted by Sir Rupert Jackson. These reforms are intended to ensure that the system does in fact work this way.

One consequence of this is that fewer cases will now be given Rolls Royce treatment than before. Fewer expert witnesses will be allowed; disclosure or discovery will be less extensive than it was previously in the majority of cases; examination of witnesses can and will be limited and so on. This approach can be criticised for reducing the quality of justice. Justice, like everything else, must be affordable: perfect justice is simply unaffordable for all but a small minority. Proportionality is intended to secure practical justice for the many rather than perfect justice for the few. How does it do so? First, by ensuring that litigation is carried out at no more than proportionate cost, it should enable more people to be able to afford legal representation. It should thus play a role in enabling some of those who would otherwise have to act in-person to be able to afford legal representation. Secondly, it should help to ensure that civil procedure is more accessible to litigants-in-person. A proportionate process is one that is simpler and more certain in its structure and operation. It should be easier to use by individuals who have no legal training. In an age of austerity, as proportionality facilitates access to justice, it is of the utmost importance that it works.

TRIAL

If the litigation process pre-trial is daunting for the untrained, then presenting your case before a judge must be absolutely terrifying for all but a few hardy souls. The adversarial trial is, in many ways, predicated on both parties being represented by skilled advocates, by individuals who by training and practice are adept at knowing which questions to ask and which points to take. Litigants bringing their own case are unlikely to be able to do this. If the increase in the numbers of unrepresented individuals continues to grow unabated, we are going to have to ask searching questions about our continuing commitment to the traditional adversarial process.

Such questions have already been asked in respect of family proceedings. It may be that, as in family proceedings, real consideration will have to be given for the first time to the introduction of an inquisitorial form of procedure. We already have the basis for such a process in small claims, that is to say those that have a value of less than £10,000. The small claims track procedure was specifically designed with litigants-in-person in mind. It is a truncated process, proportionate to the value of the claim. It departs in a number of respects from elements of adversarial process applicable to higher value claims. There is, for instance, no requirement to disclose documents apart from those you intend to rely upon. Expert evidence is rarely adduced. The usual costs shifting rule does not apply. We are also on the verge of introducing a form of inquisitorial process in family proceedings.

We may have to consider whether a similar approach to that used in small claims and about to be introduced in family proceedings should be introduced more widely in the civil courts. It may be that adopting such a form of process will be needed to provide practical equality of arms where one party is represented and the other acts in person. It may be the most practical means of securing justice where both parties act in person, in that it may be necessary in such cases for the judge to direct the questioning of witnesses, to direct what evidence is adduced and so on.

Such a process is not without its drawbacks. It will inevitably raise questions about whether it is appropriate for the judge to descend into the arena, something our judiciary has traditionally considered to be out of bounds. But we may have to change our minds about this. It may be the only means by which we can secure an effective trial process. It may also raise practical questions. How will a judicial-led inquisitorial process affect the length of time trials take? It may result in proceedings taking longer than they do under a traditional adversarial process. Judges may not like this. Dealing with large numbers of litigants-in-person is not every judge's idea of fun and there is a risk that, especially at the lower judicial levels, this may make the job less attractive than it used to be, with possible knock-on effects on recruitment. We shall have to wait and see.

A more inquisitorial approach may necessitate the introduction of a staged-trial process, more akin to the ongoing trial process well known to some established inquisitorial systems. It may be the case that trials will have to take place over a number of hearing dates, in order to enable the judge to ensure that relevant evidence and witnesses are before the court. This has obvious potential adverse consequences: it may impose a heavier cost burden on the State. Supervising evidence-gathering and examining witnesses take time and cost money. In an inquisitorial process, that cost will fall on the court. It is not clear that resources are in place, or are likely to be in place, to meet these additional needs. It may be that any steps towards a more inquisitorial process will have to be limited in scope; they may be limited to simply ensuring that witnesses are examined effectively.

In addition to, or instead of, the development of an inquisitorial form of trial process, we may have to consider other reforms. It has long been the case in the Employment Tribunal that trainee barristers, particularly those who have yet to undergo their formal training during pupillage, have been able to act as advocates for otherwise unrepresented claimants. We may have to consider authorising trainee barristers and solicitors, who do not yet have rights of audience, to represent litigants-in-person just as they do in the Employment Tribunals.

This may seem like a radical departure so far as the courts are concerned. In one sense it clearly is, as historically only those with rights of audience could appear in courts. The position in the Employment Tribunal has never been so restricted. However, the courts have increasingly been willing to grant under the inherent jurisdiction, and on a case-by-case basis, rights of audience to unqualified individuals who offer their help to litigants-in-person. They have done so where such an approach is in the interests of justice. There is no reason in principle why this approach could not be applied to trainee lawyers who have not yet formally obtained rights of audience. As in the Employment Tribunal such an approach could improve the quality of submissions and cross-examination and help to move proceedings along more smoothly and efficiently. It could improve access to justice for those who would otherwise be without any legal representation. It is, of course, not ideal. We are, however, living in the real world where pragmatism has to be our guide. Who is to say that a bright and enthusiastic young lawyer at the start of his or her career may not do a better job than a tired third-rate old trooper who can't wait to retire?

CONCLUSION

When our government presents us with yet another cut in resources, they often tell us that every challenge presents an opportunity. It is almost as if we should rejoice at the deluge of opportunities. Many of us feel that this theme is wearing rather thin. It is easy for us to become rather gloomy about what is going on. But we need to remind ourselves that we lawyers, whether we are judges, barristers, solicitors or legal executives, are all performing different roles with the same overarching objective of helping to maintain the rule of law. Without that, there would be chaos. We should try to be a little more upbeat about the positive things that we do. The work is, for the most part, very interesting. It is certainly very important. Things are less good for us than they used to be; but for most of us, they are still pretty good. I think that it is occasionally worth reflecting on that.

But to return to my main theme, it is likely that we are going to have to think quite creatively in the coming years. We may have to reappraise some of our long-standing traditions. We may well have to arrive at conclusions that in other less financially straitened times we would not have reached. In doing so, though, our guide must be a commitment to ensuring that access to justice remains a practical right. Only that way will we maintain 'the fabric of justice (as) part of the fabric of society'.[9] Only then will we all, and our democratic societies, not merely survive but thrive.

---

[9] *Nield v Loveday* [2011] EWHC 2324 (Admin) at 202.

22

The Jackson Reforms and Civil Justice[*]

INTRODUCTION

IT IS A pleasure to have been asked to speak to you today. My subject is civil justice reform, and in particular, the recent Jackson reforms in England and Wales. It is now just over 18 months since these reforms were brought into force.

IMPLEMENTATION

The reform process itself began in November 2008, when my predecessor-but-one as Master of the Rolls, Sir Anthony Clarke (now Lord Clarke), commissioned Sir Rupert Jackson to carry out a fundamental review of litigation costs. Sir Rupert succeeded in doing this within the extraordinarily ambitious timescale of 12 months. He gathered a huge amount of evidence, consulted widely and examined and drew on the experience of other jurisdictions. He produced both a detailed Preliminary Report[1] and an equally detailed Final Report.[2] On any view, this was a magnificent achievement.

The principal reason why Lord Clarke asked Sir Rupert to conduct this review was his grave concern about the cost of civil litigation. Despite the Woolf reforms, which were introduced in the late 1990s, the cost of litigation remained disproportionally high. Sir Rupert's task was to make recommendations to reduce the cost

[*] University of New South Wales Lecture, Sydney, 9 September 2014 and AIJA Oration, Queensland, Australia, 22 September 2014.
[1] R Jackson, *Review of Civil Litigation Costs: Preliminary Report*, vols I and II (May 2009), available at www.judiciary.gov.uk/publications/review-of-civil-ligation-costs-preliminary-report/.
[2] R Jackson, *Review of Civil Litigation Costs: Final Report* (TSO, December 2009), available at www.judiciary.gov.uk/publications/review-of-civil-litigation-costs-final-report/.

of litigation and, in particular, to make it more proportionate. Most of Sir Rupert's recommendations were accepted and have been implemented through a combination of statute (the Legal Aid and Sentencing of Offenders Act 2012) and changes to rules of court.

Professor Judith Resnick of Yale University once very perspicaciously noted that 'The history of procedure is a series of attempts to solve the problems created by the preceding generation's procedural reforms.'[3] It would, however, be wrong to say that the aim of the Jackson reforms was to remedy problems created by the Woolf reforms. Sir Rupert's task was, as explained by Lord Clarke, to carry out 'a review ... entirely consistent with the approach Woolf advocated ...' He would do so by looking 'for answers to the problems of costs ... consistent with the new approach to litigation Woolf's reforms introduced'.[4]

The aim of Jackson was not, therefore, to turn the clock back. He was to identify any flaws in individual aspects of the Woolf reforms and to recommend remedies. He was also required to examine the various litigation funding mechanisms which were in place at that time. One of those mechanisms was a form of contingency fee agreement, known as a Conditional Fee Agreement or CFA. These types of agreement have been available for some time in England and Wales. They were the subject of statutory reform in 2000, ie at about the same time as the Woolf reforms were introduced. CFAs had nothing to do with Woolf. The reforms of CFAs were enacted in order to encourage their use as a means of funding litigation. This was thought to be necessary in view of the reduction in the availability of legal aid. Sir Rupert concluded that the post-2000 CFA regime was 'the largest single cause of disproportionate costs'.[5] Accordingly, in addition to making recommendations to improve the operation of the Woolf reforms, he suggested how the CFA regime could be reformed. As a result of his recommendations, a number of elaborate provisions have been enacted for the funding of civil litigation.

I hope that these reforms to CFAs will succeed, and eliminate *the* major source of excess litigation cost. Important though this aspect of the Jackson reforms may be, I do not intend to focus on it today.

---

[3] J Resnick, 'Precluding Appeals' (1985) 70 *Cornell Law Review* 603, 624. I am grateful to both Professor Resnick and Benjamin Woodring, of Yale University, for their kind assistance in tracking down this quotation.

[4] A Clarke, 'The Woolf Reforms: A Singular Event or an Ongoing Process?' in D Dwyer, *The Civil Procedure Rules Ten Years On* (Oxford University Press, 2010) 48.

[5] R Jackson, 'The Review of Civil Litigation Costs in England and Wales' in G Meggitt (ed), *Civil Justice Reform—What has it Achieved?* (Sweet & Maxwell, 2010) 137.

I want to look at other aspects of civil justice reform. I shall concentrate on two broad themes: first, internationalism as a source for reform and secondly, the Jackson reforms to case management.

INTERNATIONALISM

The common law has always been eclectic. It has always drawn upon a wide range of materials for inspiration. For example, equity procedure drew on the civil and canon law tradition from mainland Europe; in developing English commercial law, Lord Mansfield drew heavily on mercantile law; and more recently our common law had been considerably influenced by the European Convention on Human Rights and the jurisprudence of the European Court of Human Rights. This eclecticism is also, I believe, a feature of the legal landscape of other countries of the common law world. This is a point which Lord Parker CJ made in *Smith v Leech Brain & Co Ltd*,[6] when he said how 'it is important that the common law, and the development of the common law, should be homogeneous in the various sections of the Commonwealth.' To promote this homogeneity, Lord Denning, one of my predecessors as Master of the Rolls, noted that it was the duty of members of the Bar to refer judges to relevant Commonwealth decisions just as they would English and Welsh decisions.[7]

This international approach has never been limited to substantive common law. It extends to the development of civil procedure and more broadly civil justice systems. Both Lord Woolf and Sir Rupert Jackson studied and learnt a great deal from comparative approaches in Australia, New Zealand, Canada and the United States. More recently the Australian Productivity Commission returned the compliment and visited England and Wales to discuss procedural reform. The same applies to Canada, New Zealand and Hong Kong to name a few. We learn from each other.

A good example of this is 'hot tubbing', or the concurrent giving of evidence by opposing expert witnesses. Sir Anthony Clarke first mentioned this in our jurisdiction in a lecture he gave in July 2007.[8] He noted its origin here in Australia, and Justice Heerey's

---

[6] *Smith v Leech Brain & Co Ltd* [1962] 2 QB 405 at 415.
[7] Lord Denning MR, cited in *The Supreme Court Practice 1999*, vol 1 (Sweet & Maxwell, 1999) 1480.
[8] A Clarke, 'The Role of the Expert after Woolf' (Clinical Disputes Forum lecture, 12 July 2007), published in (2008) 14(3) *Clinical Risk* 85.

views about it and its advantages.[9] Sir Anthony understood that it reduced the cost of expert evidence, saved court time and, importantly, had the potential to promote impartiality in experts. He suggested that we should consider introducing it in England and Wales. Sir Rupert Jackson provided that consideration.[10] Having looked at how it worked in practice in Australia, he concluded that it could produce cost savings. Following a pilot study, our Civil Procedure Rules were amended to allow for 'hot tubbing' in respect of expert evidence. We had learnt from developments here in Australia.

Discovery or disclosure of documents is another example. Equity derived the idea of discovery from canon law. In 1999 we changed its name to disclosure. This was one of the Woolf reforms. In recommending the change of name, Lord Woolf was influenced by reforms previously introduced in Queensland.[11] There had also been substantial cross-fertilisation between the common law jurisdictions so far as the *substance* of disclosure was concerned. For more than a century, the scope of the duty of discovery (as it was then called) had been the wide-ranging test propounded by Brett MR in *Compagnie Financiere du Pacifique v Peruvian Guano Co*.[12] Many of us have already forgotten this classic test of relevancy. Parties were obliged to disclose any document which it was reasonable to suppose 'contains information which may enable the party (applying for discovery) either to advance his own case or to damage that of his adversary'. This even included 'a document which may fairly lead him to a train of inquiry which may have either of these two consequences'. The object of making discovery 'virtually unlimited'[13] in scope (to use the words of Lord Woolf) was to ensure that the courts were best placed to ascertain the truth and thereby 'base their decisions on a sure foundation of fact.'[14] It was one of the principal

---

[9] P Heerey, 'Recent Australian Developments' (2004) 23 *Civil Justice Quarterly* 386.

[10] Jackson, *Review of Civil Litigation Costs: Preliminary Report*, vol II at 593; Jackson, *Review of Civil Litigation Costs: Final Report* at 384; R Jackson, 'Focusing Expert Evidence and Controlling Costs—Fourth Lecture in the Implementation Programme' (Bond Solon Annual Expert Witness Conference, 11 November 2011) at [4.3], available at webarchive. nationalarchives.gov.uk/20131202164909/http://judiciary.gov.uk/Resources/JCO/Documents/Speeches/lj-jackson-lecture-focusing-expert-evidence-controlling-costs.pdf.

[11] H Woolf, *Access to Justice: Interim Report to the Lord Chancellor on the Civil Justice System in England and Wales* (HMSO, 1995) ch 21, para 10; P Matthews and HM Malek, *Disclosure*, 2nd edn (Sweet & Maxwell, 2001) 16.

[12] *Compagnie Financiere du Pacifique v Peruvian Guano Company* (1882) 11 QBD 55 at 62–63.

[13] Woolf, *Access to Justice* ch 21, paras 1 and 15–17.

[14] *Tweed v Parades Commission for Northern Ireland* [2006] UKHL 53, [2007] 1 AC 650 at [2].

means by which the courts could deliver justice on the merits. The *Peruvian Guano* test was adopted throughout the common law world. It was, however, an approach that took no account of cost or delay for the parties to the particular litigation or for other litigants and the courts generally. In his reports, Lord Woolf rejected the test as too costly. The Australian Law Reform Commission noted in 2000 in its report *Managing Justice* how nearly all studies showed that disclosure was too costly, too open to abuse and most in need of court control.[15] Similar conclusions were reached in Canada and New Zealand.[16]

Under the Woolf reforms, the *Peruvian Guano* test became the exception. The general rule (known as 'standard disclosure') simply required litigants to disclose those documents they intended to rely on, those adverse to their case and those that supported their opponent's case. Unfortunately changing rules does not necessarily bring about a change in practice. Disclosure remained a source of excess costs. This failure was first noted in a report prepared in 2007 by Sir Richard Aikens, at the time a High Court judge, now a judge of the Court of Appeal. It has also been noted here by Supreme Court of Queensland Justice Byrne, who concluded that the move away from the *Peruvian Guano* test appeared 'not to have had a major impact on the burdens of disclosure ...'.[17]

Sir Richard's report considered problems that arose from what were known as 'super-cases', ie very complex, extremely high value litigation. He noted how in those cases, and commercial cases more generally, disclosure remained a blunt instrument which led to the production in court of large numbers of documents that were generally irrelevant and useless.[18] A more targeted approach than that introduced by the Woolf reforms was needed. He recommended the introduction of what he called a 'shopping list' approach to disclosure. Parties were to prepare disclosure schedules by reference to a list of issues. This was an echo of the approach previously recommended in New Zealand in 2002: to limit disclosure to matters directly in issue.[19]

---

[15] *Managing Justice: a Review of the Federal Civil Justice System*, ALRC Report 89 (ALRC, 2000) at 6.67.

[16] See www.courtsofnz.govt.nz/about/system/rules_committee/consultation/Discovery-Consultation-Paper-Sep-2009.pdf.

[17] Cited in Australian Government Productivity Commission, *Access to Justice Draft Report* at 343, available at www.pc.gov.au/projects/inquiry/access-justice.

[18] R Aikens, *Report and Recommendations of the Commercial Court Long Trials Working Party* (Judiciary of England and Wales, 2007) 58ff.

[19] See www.courtsofnz.govt.nz/about/system/rules_committee/consultation/Discovery-Consultation-Paper-Sep-2009.pdf at 4.

The approach ultimately endorsed in the Jackson review was in many ways an extension of the Aikens and New Zealand approaches. Disclosure would be tailored to the individual needs of the case, whilst being kept within the bounds of proportionality. Rather than a shopping list, a new menu approach to disclosure was to be adopted. This would enable the court to either order no disclosure at all, or disclosure only of documents relied on by the parties, or only of specific documents, or disclosure by reference to issues, or standard disclosure (the Woolf approach) or the full *Peruvian Guano* approach (including train of inquiry disclosure). As Sir Rupert Jackson noted in a lecture gave in 2011, New Zealand had led the way having adopted a similar approach in 2011. Its 2011 reforms were developed with explicit reference to Jackson's recommendations.[20] This is another example of the countries of the common law world learning from each other.

The new tailored approach to disclosure requires far greater consideration to be given to the nature and extent of any disclosure than was previously the case. This should be started (if not completed) before the first case management conference. Decisions taken at that stage will shape the extent of disclosure throughout the life of the claim.

Disclosure will, therefore, in future match the claim to a far greater extent than in the past. It will be more proportionate. We are likely to be able to learn from the approach that is taken to discovery in the United States. I have in mind the effect that the introduction of proportionality had into the discovery process under rule 26 of the Federal Rules of Procedure. This reform was introduced as long ago as 1983.[21] The rule imposes an obligation on the court to limit discovery through the application of a cost-benefit analysis. This analysis involves the consideration of a number of factors that should be familiar to all jurisdictions that have introduced proportionality into their justice systems: 'the needs of the case, the amount in controversy, the parties' resources, the importance of the issues at stake …'.[22] These considerations are echoed in the 'overriding

---

[20] See   www.courtsofnz.govt.nz/about/system/rules_committee/consultation/Discovery-Consultation-Paper-Sep-2009.pdf; R Jackson, 'Controlling the Cost of Disclosure' (7th Implementation Lecture, 24 November 2011), available at webarchive.nationalarchives.gov.uk/20131202164909/http://judiciary.gov.uk/Resources/JCO/Documents/Speeches/controlling-costs-disclosure.pdf.
[21] See, for instance, J Carroll, 'Proportionality in Discovery: A Cautionary Tale' (2010) 32 *Campbell Law Review* 455.
[22] ibid at 458.

objective' which is enshrined in our Civil Procedure Rules, as well as the procedure rules of other common law jurisdictions.

The main benefit of the US reform is that it focuses the minds of the parties on the real issues and on cost.[23] The same considerations underpin our new disclosure rule and, I would suggest, similar disclosure rules in other jurisdictions. Parties should identify the real issues in the case at an early stage. In most cases, this should be done before the first case management conference. They should also attempt to agree what level of disclosure is reasonably necessary to deal with these issues and what is the most cost effective means of providing such disclosure. Can it be done by limited e-disclosure? Can it be done by party A providing specific documents or classes of document to party B, or can it be best achieved by party B simply being invited to search all of party A's documents? The right approach will vary from case to case.

In deciding on the right approach to adopt, the court and the parties will have to consider what budget should be allocated to the exercise. The budgeted cost should not outweigh the likely benefit of the chosen approach. An assessment of the cost benefit should be made at as early a stage as possible. One of the problems identified with the US approach was that proportionality in discovery was not considered early enough in the process. One of the complaints that was made about the Woolf reforms on disclosure was that they did not take account of the need for proportionality. In practice, little had changed. Both in the United States and England and Wales, the benefits of proportionality were lost.[24] Some US courts are now, I believe, moving towards early intervention. One of the real advantages of Sir Rupert's approach has been to bring discussions about the scope of disclosure right to the start of the pre-trial process. I hope that the new approach will reduce the scope and cost of disclosure and make it more proportionate. We can and should learn from developments in the US.

Hot tubbing and disclosure are two examples of similar approaches being adopted in various countries of the common law world. They are areas where reforms in one jurisdiction are being developed under the influence of developments in others. We are influencing and learning from each other. This is greatly to be welcomed.

A more general development in England and Wales has been the introduction of active case management by the court. We introduced

---

[23] ibid at 460.
[24] ibid at 462.

it in 1999. We were not the first to do so. Lord Woolf recommended it following the Australian lead. In his Interim Report, Lord Woolf noted how the introduction of case management in the 'Higher Courts of Australia' had led to a 'quiet but enormously significant revolution', one which produced a

> dramatic shift from the laissez faire approach in conducting court business to an acceptance by the courts of the philosophical principle that it is their responsibility to take an interest in cases from a much earlier stage in the process and to manage them ...[25]

I shall return to court management in a moment when I consider one specific development that has taken place in England and Wales pursuant to the Jackson reforms, a reform that is in some ways similar to a change in approach to case management made here by the High Court of Australia decision in *Aon v Australian National University*.[26]

But before doing so, I should conclude this part of my lecture with some general remarks. The common law world is constantly seeking to update its civil procedure processes. We share many problems and have much to learn from each other. Case management underpinned by a common commitment to proportionality provides the framework within which the individual aspects of our systems operate. Inevitably the nature of these changes will, to some extent, differ from system to system. The differences may be attributable to matters which lie outside procedure altogether, such as differences of substantive law, different approaches to litigation funding, different approaches to out-of-court settlement, the availability of ombudsmen and so on. In other cases the differences will be matters of differing judicial interpretation. But on the whole what unites us is far greater than what divides us.

It seems to me that there is plenty of scope for further cross-fertilisation. We should be constantly looking to see how problems of civil procedure are tackled in other jurisdictions. We are always facing new problems. In England and Wales, we are currently facing problems generated by the seemingly endless reduction in public funding for civil justice. In particular, the huge reduction in the availability of legal aid for civil and family litigation has resulted in a massive increase in the numbers of litigants-in-person who

---

[25] Professor Sallman, cited in Woolf, *Access to Justice* ch 5, para 19.
[26] *Aon v Australian National University* [2009] HCA 27, (2009) 239 CLR 175.

are now litigating in our courts. This presents difficult challenges for our judges as well as for the advocates who appear against the unrepresented parties. The complexities of our civil procedure rules are often totally impenetrable to litigants-in-person. This is by no means a problem uniquely faced by our country. Real efforts are now being made to accommodate the needs of these litigants. More needs to be done to help them. But what should we do about our rules? It is tempting to say that we should scrap the Civil Procedure Rules and produce something far shorter and simpler. But civil litigation is an inherently complicated business; and if there are great gaps in the rules, it is likely that the interstices will have to be filled by decisions of the court. That would lead to more litigation. Even worse for the litigant-in-person, it would lead to a state of affairs in which there were two sources of procedural law: the rules and the decisions of the court. We are feeling our way in this difficult area. I believe that the problem of how to meet the needs of the litigant-in-person is likely to occupy centre-stage in the next few years. This is a particular area in which common law countries may be able to help each other.

But it is time that I returned to the Jackson reforms and to case management and recent developments in our approach to it England and Wales.

CASE MANAGEMENT AND THE *MITCHELL* CASE

Over the last 20 years there has been a distinct shift in the approach to litigation across the common law world. The traditional approach that left the control of litigation in the hands of litigants has been replaced by court-controlled case management. This development has been accomplished by the introduction of a series of explicit overriding objectives that govern the operation of procedural rules and practices.

Those overriding objectives can be seen in rule 1 of our Civil Procedure Rules by which the court is required to deal with cases justly and at proportionate cost; it can also be seen in rule 1 of the Supreme Court Rules of South Australia; rule 5 of the Queensland Uniform Civil Procedure Rules; and rule 1.04 of the Ontario Rules of Civil Procedure. There are many other examples. It would appear that there is also some discussion in the United States, which pioneered the use of explicit overriding objectives in rule 1 of its Federal Rules of Procedure, and of introducing proportionality into a revised version of that rule.[27] Again we can see an international current of activity, and one that has come about through the study of reforms across the common law world.

It is one thing to introduce active case management and to specify its purpose by means of an overriding objective. It is another to ensure that it is carried out effectively and consistently with that purpose. An issue of central importance to the effectiveness of case management is what approach the court takes to the failure by a party to comply with rules and court orders; and how generous the court is to a party who seeks the indulgence of a variation of a court order where, for example, it fails to serve documents on time or where it seeks an adjournment in order to obtain further evidence or to amend its pleading.

Historically, the court's approach to such applications was heavily coloured by the idea that its sole function was to secure justice for the immediate parties to litigation. Applications of this kind would usually be granted unless the opposing party had suffered prejudice which could not be compensated by an order for costs. This approach was usually adopted in relation to applications for relief from sanctions as well as applications to amend pleadings. It was supported by a series of English and Welsh Court of Appeal decisions in the 1870s and 1880s.[28] The most famous of these decisions was *Cropper v Smith* in 1884, in which Bowen LJ said:

> Now, I think it is a well established principle that the object of Courts is to decide the rights of the parties, and not to punish them for mistakes they make in the conduct of their cases by deciding otherwise than in accordance with their rights ... I know of no kind of error or mistake which, if not fraudulent or intended to overreach, the Court ought not to correct, if it can be done without injustice to the other party. Courts do not exist for the sake of discipline, but for the sake of deciding matters in controversy, and I do not regard such amendment as a matter of favour or of grace.[29]

As the High Court of Australia noted in 2009 in *Aon v Australian National University* at [9]ff, this approach and the rationale that underpinned it was historically adopted in Australia as well.

---

[27] See, for instance, Institute for the Advancement of the American Legal System, *Pilot Rules Project*, (University of Denver) 2.

[28] *Tildesley v Harper* (1876) 10 ChD 393; *Collins v The Vestry of Paddington* (1879–1880) LR 5 QBD 368.

[29] *Cropper v Smith* (1884) 26 ChD 700 at 710–711.

The shift in philosophy in England and Wales meant that this approach was no longer valid. Rather than simply focus on individual litigants and on the need to secure justice as between the parties, court process was now to be managed to ensure that individual claims, the pursuit of individual justice, must be achieved economically, efficiently and at proportionate cost as between the parties. It was also to be managed so that the courts were able to secure a more distributive form of justice than in the past: in managing individual cases, they were to ensure that the needs and rights of other litigants to secure access to due process were preserved.

This shift also required a change in approach by our courts to how they dealt with applications for relief from the consequences of breaches of rules and court orders. The principle articulated in *Cropper* could no longer stand. A tougher approach to such applications was needed in order to ensure both that individual litigation costs remained proportionate and to ensure that no one claim utilised more than a proportionate share of the total resources the justice system could make available to all litigants. Lord Woolf articulated this idea in 1996, when he stated how case management was to be carried out, in order to

> ... preserve access to justice for all users of the system [so that] it [was] necessary to ensure that individual users [did] not use more of the system's resources than their case require[d]. This means that the court must consider the effect of their choice on other users of the system.[30]

The Court of Appeal articulated this idea in a number of cases following implementation of the Woolf reforms;[31] the point was also articulated here in the *Aon* decision, which emphasised the need to secure justice to all litigants and not simply to those in specific litigation.[32]

This change in approach did not, however, take hold in England and Wales in the post-Woolf era. The courts failed to adopt a stricter approach to non-compliance despite a number of reminders from the Court of Appeal. Sir Rupert Jackson decided that the time had come for more than reminders. A stricter approach had to be introduced. This was achieved by revising the definition of the

---

[30] Woolf, *Access to Justice* 24.

[31] Eg, *UCB Corporate Services Ltd (formerly UCB Bank plc) v Halifax (SW) Ltd* [1999] CPLR 69 (CA); *Worldwide Corpn Ltd v GPT Ltd* [1998] All ER (D) 667 (CA); *Arrow Nominees Inc v Blackledge* [2000] 2 BCLC 167, [2001] BCC 591 (CA); *Savings & Investment Bank Ltd v Fincken* [2003] EWCA Civ 1630.

[32] [2009] HCA 27, (2009) 239 CLR 175 at [23]–[24] and [92]–[95] for instance.

overriding objective to include an explicit reference to the need to deal with cases at 'proportionate cost' and to say that dealing with cases 'justly' includes 'enforcing compliance with court rules, practice directions and orders'. The rule governing relief from the consequences of procedural non-compliance was revised so as to provide that, on an application for relief, the court would consider all the circumstances of the case so as to enable it to deal justly with the application, including specifically the need for litigation to be conducted 'efficiently and at proportionate cost' and so as to 'enforce compliance with rules, practice directions and orders'.[33]

The new stricter approach was first considered by the Court of Appeal last November in *Mitchell v News Group Newspapers Ltd.*[34] I sat together with Richards LJ, the deputy Head of Civil Justice and Elias LJ. We attempted to explain how the courts should approach applications for relief from non-compliance under the new rule.

The facts of *Mitchell* were straightforward. Andrew Mitchell MP issued defamation proceedings against News Group Newspapers Ltd. The alleged defamation arose from an incident which became known as the 'Plebgate' scandal. *The Sun* newspaper had reported that Mr Mitchell MP, who was at the time the Conservative Party's Chief Whip, had 'raged against police officers at the entrance to Downing Street in a foul mouthed rant shouting "you're f...ing plebs".'[35] Mr Mitchell MP has always denied use of the word 'pleb' or 'plebs'.

As part of the Jackson reforms both the court and litigants are required to engage in costs management and, to this end, to prepare and exchange budgets of their litigation costs at the start of the proceedings and to file their budgets with the court seven days before the date fixed for a costs budget hearing. Mr Mitchell's solicitors failed to file their costs until the day before the date of the hearing. The rules provide that a party who does not file his costs budget in time is to be treated as having filed a costs budget comprising only the amount of the applicable court fees. Unsurprisingly, Mr Mitchell

---

[33] CPR 3.9(1) On an application for relief from any sanction imposed for a failure to comply with any rule, practice direction or court order, the court will consider all the circumstances of the case, so as to enable it to deal justly with the application, including the need:

    (a)   for litigation to be conducted efficiently and at proportionate cost; and
    (b)   to enforce compliance with rules, practice directions and orders.'

[34] *Mitchell v News Group Newspapers Ltd* [2013] EWCA Civ 1537.
[35] [2013] EWCA Civ 1537 at [2].

applied for relief from this sanction. The explanation given by the solicitors was pressure of work.

If the traditional *Cropper* approach had been adopted, the application for relief would inevitably have been successful. But this would have done nothing to discourage a lax attitude to compliance with rules and court orders and nothing to promote the need to ensure that parties expend no more than proportionate resources on their own case and use no more than a proportionate amount of the court's overall resources.

The Master who dealt with the application refused to grant relief from the consequences of non-compliance. She noted that the main object of the Jackson reforms was to eliminate the previously lax approach to rule-compliance. She also emphasised that the solicitor's failure to file the budget on time had had an adverse impact on other court users and on their right to receive justice: the hearing date had to be adjourned with the consequence that the date fixed for a hearing in a different case also had to be adjourned.

Mr Mitchell appealed. We endorsed and explained the Master's approach. The guidance that we gave did not, however, meet with universal approval. Some commentators described it as too harsh and as turning rule compliance into an end in itself. One described it as unconstitutional. We said that it would usually be appropriate to start by considering the nature of the non-compliance. If it could properly be regarded as trivial, the court would usually grant relief if the application was made promptly.[36] We gave as examples of trivial default cases where there was a failure of form rather than substance and where a deadline had only just been missed but the defaulting party was otherwise fully compliant. If the default could not be characterised as trivial, then the burden was on the defaulting party to persuade the court to grant relief. A good reason had to be shown why the default occurred. We provided some examples of good and bad reasons. As we put it,

> ... if the reason why a document was not filed with the court was that the party or his solicitor suffered from a debilitating illness or was involved in an accident, then, depending on the circumstances, that may constitute a good reason. Later developments in the course of the litigation process are likely to be a good reason if they show that the period for compliance originally imposed was unreasonable, although the period seemed to be reasonable at the time and could not realistically have been

---

[36] ibid at [40].

the subject of an appeal. But mere overlooking a deadline, whether on account of overwork or otherwise, is unlikely to be a good reason. We understand that solicitors may be under pressure and have too much work. It may be that this is what occurred in the present case. But that will rarely be a good reason. Solicitors cannot take on too much work and expect to be able to persuade a court that this is a good reason for their failure to meet deadlines. They should either delegate the work to others in their firm or, if they are unable to do this, they should not take on the work at all.[37]

The approach was followed by subsequent Court of Appeal decisions. These showed that the court was now insisting on a new strict approach to the grant of relief from sanctions for non-compliance.[38] This was not, however, the end of the story. The guidance proved difficult to apply in practice. It led some courts to apply it too strictly, taking the view that the triviality test meant that relief from non-compliance would only be granted in exceptional circumstances. It led some lawyers to adopt what was described by judges as an 'opportunistic' approach to litigation. The prize of successfully opposing an application for relief and potentially achieving a great windfall was worth taking the risk of having to pay the relatively modest costs of unsuccessfully opposing the application. Some went so far as to say that lawyers would be in breach of duty to their own clients if they did not advise them to oppose applications for relief from sanctions in almost any circumstances. This is a good example of the law of unintended consequences. In these circumstances, it was inevitable that the court would be asked to revisit the guidance it had given in *Mitchell*. And we did so in July in the three conjoined appeals of *Denton v TH White Ltd*.[39] Vos LJ and I gave the majority judgment. We endorsed the approach in *Mitchell* but amplified and explained our guidance in more detail. We propounded a three-stage approach.

The first stage is to assess the seriousness or significance of the default. The focus should no longer to be on the question of the triviality of the default, which had given rise to considerable problems. Rather, it should be on whether the default has been material, ie on whether it has imperilled a future hearing date or otherwise

---

[37] ibid at [41].
[38] *Durrant v Chief Constable of Avon and Somerset Constabulary* [2013] EWCA Civ 1624, [2014] 1 WLR 4313; *Thevarajah v Riordan* [2014] EWCA Civ 15.
[39] *Denton v TH White Ltd* [2014] EWCA Civ 906, [2014] 1 WLR 3926.

disrupted the conduct of the litigation in which the application is made or litigation generally. We also made clear that a serious breach might arise even where it was not material in this sense. If the court concludes that the default is not serious or significant, then relief from sanctions will usually be granted. If, however, it concludes that the default is serious or significant, then the second and third stages assume greater importance.

The second stage of the test requires the court to consider the question why the default occurred and whether there is a good reason capable of excusing the default.

Finally, the third stage. We said that the misunderstanding that had occurred was the belief that *Mitchell* was authority for the proposition that, if there is a non-trivial (now serious or significant) breach and there is no good reason for the breach, then the application for relief from sanctions will automatically fail. Rule 3.9(1) explicitly requires that the court will consider 'all the circumstances of the case so as to enable it to deal justly with the application'. I hope that we have laid this misunderstanding to rest. It was also said that the use of the phrase 'paramount importance' in *Mitchell* had encouraged the idea that the factors other than the need: (a) for the litigation to be conducted efficiently and at proportionate cost; and (b) to enforce compliance with rules, practice directions and orders were of little weight. In fact, we had said that these factors were to be given 'less weight' than the other factors. In *Denton,* the majority of the court maintained this view. The third member of the court who was no less than Jackson LJ (the master himself) dissented on the proper interpretation of the third stage. He preferred the view that the two factors to which I have referred were not to be given particular weight, but to be regarded as having no more weight than all the other factors.

In addition to this we emphasised that the overriding objective required parties to co-operate in the conduct of litigation. Taking the type of procedural points that had occurred following *Mitchell* was contrary to that duty. We stressed that, in order to secure the efficient and proportionate conduct of litigation, parties were not just require to comply with rules, but to co-operate with each other. Opportunistic behaviour by lawyers was to be deprecated and if it occurred would be penalised by the court.

What of the future? Some have suggested that *Denton* amounted to the Court of Appeal waving of the white flag; that the stricter approach had its moment in the sun but it was no more than a moment. I do not accept this and I do not believe it to be a widely held view. The better view is that given by Lord Justice Richards. At a recent symposium in Oxford he said this:

> The judgment in *Denton*, whilst recognising and responding to the concerns caused by *Mitchell*, is very far from a capitulation to pressure from the profession. On the contrary, I regard it as a fine example of judicial realism, skill and subtlety, effecting a brilliant adjustment of *Mitchell* with the aim of overcoming the problems without losing the emphasis on compliance and the need for a change of culture.[40]

He went on to note that it would appear that, taken together, the two decisions had had the desired effect. *Mitchell* had effected a change in culture, although there had been an over-reaction to it. *Denton* had maintained the culture-shift while having a calming effect.[41] From what I have seen that appears to be the case. Arguments to the effect that *Denton* in some way departs from rather than explains the principle articulated in *Mitchell* have not succeeded in the courts. For example, in *Lord Chancellor v Former Partnership of Taylor Willcocks Solicitors*, Globe J said:

> Denton has clarified and amplified Mitchell in certain respects so as to avoid any misunderstanding and misapplication of the guidance given in Mitchell. The guidance has not been overruled. It has been strengthened. Attention has been drawn to the importance of a careful examination of the text in CPR 3.9 itself.[42]

There might, however, be a lingering doubt. This stems from *Cropper v Smith*. In Australia, for instance, when Woolf-inspired reforms were introduced, Bowen LJ's dictum cast the same shadow as it has done here. Attempts at introducing an approach to case management that took proper account of the need to ensure that the court's resources were equitably distributed across all those who sought access to justice foundered on it. So too did a stricter approach to compliance. That was until the High Court of Australia repudiated it in *Aon v Australian National University*,[43] a decision concerning late amendment. The new stricter approach that it adopted, akin to our approach in *Mitchell* and *Denton*, has since been extended widely, not least to include relief from sanctions.[44]

---

[40] S Richards, 'The *Mitchell/Denton* line of cases: securing compliance with rules and court orders' (Oxford, 14 November 2014) at [25].

[41] ibid at [26].

[42] *Lord Chancellor v Former Partnership of Taylor Willcocks Solicitors* [2014] EWHC 3664 (QB) at [70].

[43] *Aon v Australian National University* [2009] HCA 27, (2009) 239 CLR 175.

[44] *Mijac Investments Pty Ltd v Graham* [2010] FCA 87.

Neither *Mitchell* nor *Denton* expressly set aside Bowen LJ's test. But in a single paragraph in *Prince Abdulaziz v Apex Global Management Ltd (Rev 2)*[45] our Supreme Court has done here what the *Aon* decision did in Australia. The case concerns a substantial dispute arising from a joint venture between two companies. One of the parties to the claim is a Prince of Saudia Arabia. Vos J gave case management directions in July 2013. These included an order requiring the parties to serve disclosure statements verified with a statement of truth signed by the parties personally.

The Prince did not comply with the order. An order was made that, unless he complied, his defence would be struck out and a default judgment would be entered against him. He continued to refuse to comply and his defence was struck out. The Prince applied for relief from sanction. If the Bowen LJ test had been applied, relief would probably have been granted. But relief was refused. An appeal to the Court of Appeal was dismissed. Surprisingly, the Supreme Court gave permission to appeal. Lord Neuberger PSC, with whom Lords Sumption, Hughes and Hodge agreed, gave the lead judgment. Lord Clarke dissented. All, however, agreed that their judgments were not intended to 'impinge on the decisions or reasoning of the Court of Appeal in *Mitchell* ... or *Denton* ...'.[46]

The Supreme Court rejected the appeal. In the course of argument for the Prince, reliance was placed on the Bowen LJ test as a basis for granting relief from sanction. Lord Neuberger PSC expressly rejected its continuing validity. He put it this way:

Mr Fenwick relied on *Cropper v Smith* (1884) 26 Ch D 700, 710, where Bowen LJ said that he knew of 'no kind of error or mistake which, if not fraudulent or intended to overreach, the Court ought not to correct, if it can be done without injustice to the other party'. There are three problems for the Prince in this connection. The first is that these observations were made in connection with a proposed amendment to a pleading, ie an attempt by a litigant to do something which he would be entitled to do, but to do it late; whereas here we are concerned with a party who does not even now intend to obey a court order. Secondly, as the points made in the last few sentences of the immediately preceding paragraph of this judgment illustrate, there would be prejudice to the other parties if the Prince's current proposal was adopted. Thirdly and even more importantly, the approach laid down in *Cropper* has been overtaken by the CPR.[47]

---

[45] *Prince Abdulaziz v Apex Global Management Ltd (Rev 2)* [2014] UKSC 64, [2014] WLR 4495.

[46] ibid at [40] per Lord Neuberger PSC, Lords Sumption, Hughes and Hodge, and at [79] per Lord Clarke.

[47] ibid at [27].

The first two reasons appear to assume that the Bowen LJ test was alive and well. The third reason, however, undercuts both of these points. The question did not turn on the application of Bowen LJ's test on the facts of the case. It turned on an issue of principle of whether the test still remained good law. The third reason is therefore, as Lord Neuberger rightly said, the most important reason to reject reliance on Bowen LJ's test. In short, following the introduction of the CPR, *Cropper v Smith* is no longer authoritative. The test for relief is now that laid down in the CPR, which in turn has now been explained and interpreted by *Mitchell* and *Denton*.

We shall have to see how the revised guidance works in practice. Early indications are that it has been received more favourably than the original formulation in *Mitchell*. Time will tell, not only regarding whether it is being applied correctly but more importantly whether the courts relapse into the pre-Woolf and pre-Jackson lax approach to case management. Changing litigation culture is not easy. That the Court of Appeal was unable to secure a stricter approach to default and non-compliance from 1999 until the Jackson reforms demonstrates that. The *Mitchell* experience again highlights the point.

The proper way to achieve this change is by setting realistic case and cost management timetables, by adopting a consistent approach to enforcement of procedural obligations so as to ensure that claims proceed consistently with the overriding objective, and by adopting a proper approach to relief from sanctions. And that approach has finally been given practical and just form by the court's decisions in *Mitchell* and *Denton*.

Looked at in the broader context, a wider lesson can perhaps be learnt from our experience. I outlined earlier how we might all learn not just from structural reforms to our justice systems, but also from case law developments. In *Mitchell* and *Denton* we embarked on a development similar to that adopted here in *Aon*. The tests we arrived at differ in point of detail, but their underlying rationale is the same. In this regard it is interesting that both the Woolf reforms are referred to in *Aon*, as is case law from our Court of Appeal that formed part of our post-Woolf attempt to take a stricter approach in order to manage cases so that justice could be done to all litigants. In the nineteenth century *Cropper v Smith* influenced the approach taken across the common law world. While any such decision is unlikely to be so influential today, there is no reason why our decisions should not have a wide influence. *Aon* has, I understand, been cited in over 1,000 reported cases.[48] Although it is a case about late amendments, it is now considered to be one of general application[49] to the issue of relief from the consequences of non-compliance. It seems to me that, as we develop our post-*Mitchell* and post-*Denton* practices, we should learn from how *Aon* and similar decisions have been applied in other jurisdictions. If we learn from each other, we stand a better chance of improving our civil justice system and reducing the risk of making the mistakes identified by Professor Resnick.

CONCLUSION

Having talked about developments in England and Wales and briefly discussed the extent to which common law jurisdictions can influence each other, I thought I would conclude by calling to mind something that the great US Supreme Court Justice Louis Brandeis once said. He noted that it was 'one of the happy incidents of the [US] federal system that a single courageous state may, if its citizens choose, serve as a laboratory; and try novel social and economic experiments without risk to the rest of the country'.[50] The sentiment is one that can equally be applied to the common law world and our civil justice systems. Each can serve as a laboratory of jurisprudential invention. All our reforms owe a debt to innovation and invention in other jurisdictions. As we seek to implement our latest set of reforms, we will I hope do so with an eye to further developments elsewhere, and will do so not least through events such as today's. And I hope that other common law jurisdictions will continue to act in the same way. We benefit from our inventiveness. We learn from each other. We are all the better for it and, most importantly of all, our ability to do justice for all litigants is enhanced as a consequence.

---

[48] P Spender, 'Wavering alternations of valour and caution: Commercial and regulatory litigation in the French CJ High Court' (2013) 2 *Journal of Civil Litigation and Practice* 111.

[49] A Lyons, 'Recasting the landscape of interlocutory applications: Aon Risk Services Australia Ltd v Australian National University' (2010) *Sydney Law Review* 549.

[50] *New State Ice Co v Liebmann* 285 US 262 (1932).

23

*Sharpening the Public Gaze: Advances in Open Justice in England and Wales**

INTRODUCTION

I
T IS A real pleasure for me to be back in Hong Kong after an interval of more than 20 years and to have been asked to address such a distinguished audience today. When I was a barrister, I came here several times to do construction cases. That was in the pre-1997 era. I always enjoyed my visits. This is such an exciting place. I imagine that most of the buildings that I saw have been replaced as being out of date. Nothing stands still here. There is no clinging to the past; no nostalgia for days gone by. Change is the name of the game, whether it is physical change to the environment or economic or constitutional change. But even in the UK, that most traditional of countries, changes have been taking place. Some of them have been forced on us by the economic crisis that has afflicted the world in recent years. Others have occurred as a response to the remarkable technological developments of our time. As I shall explain, these developments are relevant to the subject of this address.

My subject today is open justice and recent developments that have been introduced and are being considered in England and Wales to enhance it. At the end of my lecture, I shall also say a few words about the recent changes that have taken place to the way in which we handle defamation litigation.

Open justice is a principle that has long been a central feature of our justice system. When civil trials were conducted before a jury drawn from the local community, justice was done under the eyes of ordinary citizens. They performed a central role in the process.

---

* Hong Kong, 18 October 2013.

Ordinary citizens also had free access to the courts if they wished to see what was going on inside them.

As a general rule, the days of the civil jury trial are now long gone. As you know, when the Defamation Act 2013 comes into force, the presumption will be that civil jury trials will be confined to proceedings for civil fraud, malicious prosecution and false imprisonment.[1] The days when the general public would attend civil trials in large numbers are also long gone. Television may secure high ratings for legal and courtroom dramas, but an interest in compelling fiction does not translate into increased attendance to witness real proceedings. This may have something to do with a general impatience and unwillingness these days to sit through long and often rather dull hearings with no guarantee of excitement. The falling attendances at county cricket matches in England and Wales may be another example of this.

The decline in public attendance at court, as well as the decline in media reporting of civil proceedings in general, poses a problem. This is a problem identified by the great nineteenth century philosopher and advocate of law reform, Jeremy Bentham. Professor Andrews, of Cambridge University, succinctly described the problem nearly 20 years ago. He put it this way:

> Justice administered behind closed doors will soon reek to high heaven. This is the procedure of a despotic legal system, not an open and liberal one. Bentham supplied the theory. He insisted that justice should take place publicly in order that the judges be kept up to scratch: [He said this]
>
> 'Publicity is the very soul of justice. It is the keenest spur to exertion, and the surest of all guards against improbity. It keeps the judge himself, while trying, under trial'.[2]

Professor Andrews' solution to the problem was to suggest that 'The principle of publicity [ought to] be emblazoned on a banner and displayed aloft the Royal Courts of Justice.'[3]

Such a banner would have the virtue of making it plain to everyone passing by the courts that they know the courts are there and that they are open to the public. That was 20 years ago. It was a suggestion from an era when the internet was in its infancy; mobile phones

---

[1] See Senior Courts Act 1981, s 69 and Defamation Act 2013, s 11.
[2] N Andrews, *Principles of Civil Procedure* (Sweet & Maxwell, 1994) 23–24.
[3] ibid.

were a long way from being smart; and social media platforms like Twitter were unknown.

Today I want to discuss the steps we have taken and are considering taking, in the light of 20 years of advances in communication technology, to raise a metaphorical banner over all our courts; a banner which will give practical reality in the twenty-first century to what Lord Brown recently described as that highest of constitutional principles: open justice.[4] I shall focus on the following specific issues: televising courts; the use of social media; and the Judicial Communications Office and the Judicial Media Panel.

TELEVISING COURTS

It is nearly 100 years now since photography in courts was banned by section 41 of the Criminal Justice Act 1925. The first UK television broadcast was not made until 1929. With the advent of national television, the ban was extended to cover filming as well as photography. The reason why photography was banned was that there was a growing concern that newspaper coverage of trials, specifically criminal trials, was becoming increasingly sensationalist. The issue had first come to a head in 1912 following the murder trial of Frederick Seddon. After he had been convicted, photographs were taken of him in court whilst he was being sentenced to death. The question arose whether the photographs were taken with permission of the relevant authorities. It seemed that no permission had been sought or granted. Questions were then raised in Parliament, and the Prime Minister was asked to consider whether legislation should be brought in to render the publication of such photographs unlawful.[5] The issue was, we would say now, kicked into the long grass until 1925.

The rationale behind the ban was to stamp out sensationalism in reporting. Photographs of defendants being sentenced to death did little to inform the public of what occurred in the court that could not be communicated fairly and accurately in writing. They did, however, excite a degree of prurience, perhaps resembling a little that experienced by those who in earlier times used to go to Tyburn

---

[4] *Al-Rawi v Security Services* [2011] UKSC 34, [2012] 1 AC 531 at [84].
[5] HC Deb 21 March 1912, vol 35, col 2067, available at hansard.millbanksystems. com/commons/1912/mar/21/photographs-criminal-courts#S5CV0035P0_19120321_ HOC_216.

to witness hangings. At all events, the ban stood in England and Wales from 1925 until the creation of the UK Supreme Court. The ban did not apply to that court, since it is not by definition a court of England and Wales.

The Supreme Court was, therefore, able to come to an arrangement with Sky Television to provide live coverage on its News Channel of appeal hearings and the delivery of judgments.[6] It is now possible for the public and aspiring barristers to watch the best advocates in the country argue before its highest court from the comfort of their homes, their smart phones or their laptops. Apparently approximately 22,000 people do so each month.[7] As someone who sat in that court for more than two years, I can honestly say that I did not find the TV cameras (which were very unobtrusive) at all disconcerting. In fact, I rarely even thought about their presence. And my indifference to them was not always brought about because I was dazzled by the brilliance of the legal argument that I was hearing. Nor did I ever have any sense that the behaviour of any of my colleagues or the advocates was in any way influenced by an awareness that they were being televised. I believe that the President of the Supreme Court, Lord Neuberger, commented that he had been told off by his wife and daughter for slouching on camera and having an evidently smug smile.[8] I cannot of course comment on that other than to say that, if he was guilty as charged, it is good proof the presence of the camera is not causing any change in behaviour on the part of the judges.

Following the introduction of live televised broadcasts of proceedings in the Supreme Court, it was understandable that the question would be asked: why limit them to the Supreme Court? The ensuing discussions led to a government consultation paper in May 2012, which proposed introducing filming of both civil and criminal appeals, and at some future date sentencing remarks in the Crown Court. Filming would not extend to the High Court. The government said that it was 'aware of concerns that televising our courts may open the judicial process to sensationalism and trivialise serious

---

[6] See news.sky.com/info/supreme-court.

[7] Ministry of Justice, 'Proposals to allow the broadcasting, filming, and recording of selected court proceedings' (May 2012) at 10, available at www.gov.uk/government/uploads/system/uploads/attachment_data/file/217307/broadcasting-filming-recording-courts.pdf.

[8] As reported by Joshua Rozenberg at www.theguardian.com/law/2013/feb/13/judicial-review-judges-supreme-court.

processes to a level of media entertainment.'[9] Those concerns were, of course, as applicable to the Crown Court as the High Court, and the consultation paper noted the danger of criminal trials becoming show trials if they were to be televised.[10] Subsequent to the consultation, televising the courts was made lawful by section 32 of the Crime and Courts Act 2013. This provision gives the Lord Chancellor the power, with the concurrence of the Lord Chief Justice, to make an order disapplying section 41 of the 1925 Act.

We are proceeding cautiously. Plans are well under way to introduce a pilot scheme in the Court of Appeal in October 2013. The consequences of this reform are therefore yet to be seen. The government, in its consultation, took the view that opening up the courts to television cameras, so that the public can understand how courts work, and how in particular the sentencing process works, was 'critical to confidence in the system and to its effectiveness in ensuring that justice was done.'[11] Greater accessibility should help to blow away the mystery that surrounds the process. Public ignorance as to what goes on in courts is not surprising in view of the fact that so few individuals have the time or inclination to visit a court during the working day. The reform will certainly help to promote open justice.

There are those who fear that televising court proceedings will undermine the due administration of justice and that it will encourage the very kind of prurience that caused Parliament to ban photography almost a century ago. In these days when anyone can see almost anything on the internet, it seems to me that it is absurd to worry about prurience. But we do need to make sure that televising court proceedings does not harm justice itself.

I can see no objection to filming appeals at any level of our system. Why limit television to appeals to the Supreme Court? The experience of that court has shown that the televising of appeals has been an unqualified success. Different considerations arise in those few appeals in the lower courts where evidence is given during the course of the appeal. The general consensus in England and Wales, so far as one can tell, is that the camera should be excluded from trials at which witnesses give evidence and from all jury trials.

---

[9] Ministry of Justice, 'Proposals to allow the broadcasting, filming, and recording of selected court proceedings' (May 2012) at 8.

[10] ibid at 21.

[11] ibid at 23.

Some may say that this is rather pusillanimous. My personal view is that, as a general rule, we should not exclude the camera even from witness trials, but that the judge should have the power to direct that certain cases are not televised if he considers this to be necessary in the interests of justice. For example, it is difficult to conceive circumstances in which it would be in the interests of justice to televise proceedings involving children. But having expressed my personal view, I think it is wise that we are proceeding on a step-by-step basis and that each step of the way is the subject of a pilot study.

The reforms provide an important means of bringing court proceedings to a far wider public audience than in the past. It is true that reforms often carry certain risks and we should be cautious in how we proceed. But legal proceedings have evolved over time in response to changes in society and they will undoubtedly continue to do so. We live in an age of television and technology. Opening up courts to the cameras is a necessary reform of this age. It is one that we must make work in the public interest. Television has been with us for a long time. I need to turn to some of the other technological changes which are relevant to my theme. With that in mind I propose to consider the changes that social media has brought about.

SOCIAL MEDIA

Not so long ago, if court reporters wanted to report what was going on in particular proceedings, or to report the outcome of a trial or a judgment, they had to wait in court and then, when they had the information they needed, they would make a dash for the public phones within the court building. With the advent of the mobile phone there was no need to dash; the reporter could just walk out of the courtroom and make a call to the news desk. The dash to the public phone now seems to be a rather quaint piece of history; and even the use of the mobile is receding into the past. This is because of the arrival of smart phones and social media. As most of us know, it is now possible to report in 140 characters or less and to give a running commentary of whatever you want in real time through Twitter. Equally it is possible through the use of mobile email to file a report with the news desk from within the courtroom itself or to put a report onto a live blog.

But the opportunity for court reporting by means of the internet and the use of smart phones was frustrated by the prohibition on the use of mobile phones within the court. The ban was explained in the Lord Chief Justice's 2011 Consultation on the use of mobile technology in courts, because of the potential they have

> ... to interfere with the proceedings, and the fact they may be used with ease to make illegal sound or video recordings, or to take photographs. [In addition the] blanket prohibition against the use of mobile telephones in court is also easier for court staff and security officers to enforce than if there were some permitted uses and some prohibited uses.[12]

The blanket ban meant that whatever benefits might arise through smart phones and the internet could not be realised.

In December 2010, however, the Lord Chief Justice issued Interim Guidance to the courts that provided an initial framework for the use by the media of mobile phones in court, so that live text-based reporting could be carried out in court.[13] This was followed by a formal consultation on whether and if so how such reporting should be permitted.[14] In December 2011 formal Practice Guidance was issued.[15] It covered the use of mobile email, social media and internet-enabled laptops in and from courts in England and Wales to provide live text-based communications. It emphasised that the court has the overriding responsibility to ensure that proceedings are conducted consistently with the proper administration of justice, and that open justice is a fundamental aspect of that. It noted, however, that there are exceptions to open justice; that photography from court and making sound recordings of proceedings was prohibited.

It went on to say:

> 8) The normal, indeed almost invariable, rule has been that mobile phones must be turned off in court. There is however no statutory prohibition on the use of live text-based communications in open court.

> 9) Where a member of the public, who is in court, wishes to use live text-based communications during court proceedings an application for

---

[12] Judicial Communications Office, *A Consultation on the Use of Live, Text-Based Forms of Communications from Court for the Purposes of Fair and Accurate Reporting* at 9, available at www.judiciary.gov.uk/Resources/JCO/Documents/Consultations/cp-live-text-based-forms-of-comms.pdf.

[13] See www.judiciary.gov.uk/Resources/JCO/Documents/Guidance/lcj-guidance-live-text-based-communications-20122010.pdf.

[14] See www.judiciary.gov.uk/Resources/JCO/Documents/Consultations/cp-live-text-based-forms-of-comms.pdf.

[15] See www.judiciary.gov.uk/Resources/JCO/Documents/Guidance/lcj-guidance-live-text-based-communications-20122010.pdf.

permission to activate and use, in silent mode, a mobile phone, small laptop or similar piece of equipment, solely in order to make live, text-based communications of the proceedings will need to be made. The application may be made formally or informally (for instance by communicating a request to the judge through court staff).

10) It is presumed that a representative of the media or a legal commentator using live, text-based communications from court does not pose a danger of interference with the proper administration of justice in the individual case. This is because the most obvious purpose of permitting the use of live, text-based communications would be to enable the media to produce fair and accurate reports of the proceedings. As such, a representative of the media or a legal commentator who wishes to use live, text-based communications from court may do so without making an application to the court.

11) When considering, either generally on its own motion, or following a formal application or informal request by a member of the public, whether to permit live, text-based communications, and if so by whom, the paramount question for the judge will be whether the application may interfere with the proper administration of justice.

The Guidance noted that the issue of improper interference with the administration of justice was likely to be most acute in relation to criminal proceedings. Witnesses outside court would be able to read evidence given in court via Twitter or live blogs. Inadmissible evidence posted on Twitter might influence the jury. Live reporting in any proceedings might serve to create pressure on witnesses or litigants more generally, distracting them or worrying them so as to weaken the quality of their evidence.

It is perhaps not surprising that, following the publication of the Guidance, there were some teething problems. For example, shortly after it came into force, the criminal trial for tax evasion of Harry Redknapp, a famous football manager, was interrupted because a journalist had tweeted the name of a juror and some of the evidence given by a witness in the absence of the jury. A fresh jury had to be sworn in, the matter was referred to the Attorney-General and tweeting was barred for the rest of the proceedings.[16] But since then, as far as I am aware, court-based tweeting and blogging has taken place without any significant hitches. The recent High Court action concerning David Miranda, the partner of the US journalist Glenn

---

[16] See, for instance, www.legalweek.com/legal-week/news/2141015/judge-bans-court-tweeting-redknapp-tax-trial-reporting-breach.

Greenwald, was for instance live tweeted by *The Guardian* newspaper with no apparent difficulty.[17]

It is difficult for the judiciary to know to what extent live tweeting and blogging from court is finding an audience. No doubt the means exist to discover how many people follow such tweets and blogs, but I am not aware of any research yet which has collated such data as exists. It would, I think, be useful if someone were to undertake the research. In the absence of such evidence, and on the assumption that there is an audience for such court reporting whether through journalistic tweets tied to a newspaper or TV channel or by members of the public or legal bloggers, I think it can be said that the use of technology is enabling important advances to be made in opening up the courts to the public. As long as technology can continue to be used in a way that does not impede the proper administration of justice, its use should continue to be permitted.

THE JUDICIAL COMMUNICATION OFFICE AND MEDIA PANEL

I now want to say a few a words about the Judicial Communication Office ('the JCO') and the Judicial Media Panel. The traditional attitude of the judiciary to the media was one of deep suspicion. Generally speaking, reporters were not to be trusted. The judges behaved like Trappist monks. They spoke only through their judgments and, occasionally, through lectures. The media knew that this was the convention. Therefore, if they wanted a judicial view on an issue, they tended to seek out retired judges. There were one or two of these, usually people who had had fairly undistinguished judicial careers. They enjoyed the publicity which they had not previously enjoyed. The silence of the serving judges was imposed on them by the Kilmuir Rules.[18] So from 1955, when they were framed, until 1987 when Lord Mackay set them aside, they effectively barred public comment by members of the judiciary.[19] In this there was no conflict with the principle of open justice. The intention behind the prohibition was to help secure public confidence in the judiciary

---

[17] See, for instance, www.theguardian.com/world/2013/aug/22/david-miranda-high-court-tweets.

[18] Letter from Lord Kilmuir LC (12 December 1955), in Barnett, 'Judges and the media—the Kilmuir Rules' (1986) *Public Law* 383, 384–385.

[19] See Lord Mackay LC, *The Administration of Justice* (Stevens & Co, 1993) at 25–26.

by preventing them from being drawn into political and other controversies.

The relaxation of the Kilmuir Rules in 1987 did not lead to a rush of judges jostling to give interviews with the press, nor did it lead to pressure from the media for comment from the judiciary. Where such comment was called for in respect of the judiciary or judicial decisions, the Lord Chancellor would make it under his historic duty to defend the independence of the judiciary. Occasionally, the Lord Chief Justice would speak. But his public utterances were comparatively rare and not always an unqualified success. Lord Taylor's one and only appearance on the TV show 'Question Time' alongside politicians was generally regarded as a flop.

In 2005, however, our constitutional arrangements were changed by the Constitutional Reform Act. As I am sure you all know, the effect of this legislation was that the Lord Chancellor lost his tripartite role of being a member of the executive and legislative branches of our constitution as well as Head of the Judiciary; and the Lord Chief Justice became the Head of the Judiciary of England and Wales instead.

The 2005 Act imposed a duty on the Lord Chancellor to uphold the independence of the judiciary, thereby maintaining his historic duty to defend the judiciary from adverse public or media comment of the kind that is likely to reduce public confidence in the judicial system. But the wider role of representing the judiciary to the media and the public passed to the Lord Chief Justice and with it, as the House of Lords' Constitution Committee noted, the duty to 'increase public understanding of the judges and the justice system, ... [as well as to] help the judiciary to place constructive pressure on the executive over areas where there is disagreement or unease'.[20] Informing and educating both the public and the executive about what goes on in the courts is clearly an important aspect of open justice administered in an open society. Increasing an understanding of what is done and, most importantly, why it is done is an essential element of securing public confidence in an independent judiciary and thereby the rule of law.

To help the Lord Chief Justice to carry out this duty effectively the JCO and the Judicial Media Panel were created. Let me explain what they are and what they do. First, the JCO. It is, in a nutshell,

---

[20] See House of Lords' Select Committee on the Constitution, 6th Report at [156], available at www.publications.parliament.uk/pa/ld200607/ldselect/ldconst/151/15106.htm.

the judiciary's press office and carries out on its behalf the role that the Lord Chancellor's press office used to play prior to the 2005 reforms. It was created with the explicit aim of increasing 'the public's confidence in judges ... as part of an overall requirement to enhance public confidence in the justice system.'[21] It operates in a number of ways. It maintains the judicial website, which contains a wealth of information about the judiciary, its role and function, and about judicial independence and accountability. It publishes important judgments as well as summaries of judgments which outline the key factual and legal issues and the reasons for the decision (something the JCO shares with the UK Supreme Court, which routinely publishes such summaries at the same time as it hands down judgments[22]). It also publishes judicial lectures and speeches, judicial responses to government consultation papers, as well as reports and Practice Directions and Guidance.[23]

The JCO does not simply ensure that the judiciary has a web presence, as important as that might be today. It also ensures that, wherever possible, a member of its press team is available to talk to the press on issues of interest that arise, in particular contentious issues that arise from judgments. The Office cannot explain or interpret judgments or a judge's sentencing remarks. What the judge says in his or her judgment or sentencing remarks must speak for itself. But the Office can and does help to place the judgment or sentencing remarks in their proper context by, for instance, ensuring that the press is aware of the full picture. If an enquiry relates to the length of a sentence handed down for a certain criminal offence, it can, for instance, ensure that the enquirer is aware of the relevant sentencing guidelines. What might at first blush have appeared to be a very lenient sentence can then be seen in its proper context. The aim of the Office is to ensure that the sentence, or judgment, is reported fairly and accurately. In this way, if the sentence or judgment still appears to be unsatisfactory once the context has been fully explained and understood, the issue may be seen as one for political debate concerning whether the law itself should be changed rather than an occasion for criticising the judge.

One interesting issue that was raised by the respected legal journalist Joshua Rozenberg shortly after the JCO was created was

[21] Lord Woolf LCJ cited ibid.
[22] See www.supremecourt.gov.uk/news/latest-judgments.html.
[23] See www.judiciary.gov.uk.

whether it should 'act as the public spokesman for the judges'.[24] By this he meant: should it employ a trained lawyer, or perhaps as others suggested a panel of senior or retired judges, who could comment on judgments so as to 'correct inaccuracies, highlight significant sections in judgments or sentencing remarks, and possibly even explain complex points of law to facilitate more informed media coverage.?'[25] It seems to me that the idea that a senior judge could play such a role is a non-starter. First, such a judge would not be able to sit on an appeal from such a decision. But more importantly, it would risk undermining judicial comity and judicial independence. It is one thing for a judge's decision to be overturned on appeal. The risk of that happening is an incident of judicial life which every judge accepts. But I would regard as unacceptable the risk of being exposed to adverse criticism by another judge without the benefit of adversarial argument.

There is perhaps something to be said for a legally-trained spokesman or a retired judge explaining complex points of law or the background to sentencing remarks so as to facilitate accurate reporting. This is an idea that we might perhaps consider in the future, although given the existence of the judge's media panel, it is perhaps an unnecessary development or one that carries with it too great a danger of the spokesman drifting into the realm of defending judgments or explaining that when the judge said X he or she really meant to say Y.

Let me turn then to the media panel. It too was created following the 2005 reforms. It is the responsibility of the Judges' Council's communications sub-committee. I can best describe its role by setting out how my predecessor as Master of the Rolls, Lord Clarke, explained its role to Parliament in 2009. In evidence to the Culture, Media and Sport Select Committee he said this,

> The media panel was set up as a means by which the judiciary could clear up media confusion which can simply and easily be rectified and thereby improve public understanding and confidence in the justice system. It does not exist to enter into a debate with the media or to respond to adverse comment by the media ...

> The panel is selective in respect of the interviews it gives. Panel judges are not available 'on tap' on any and every topic. There are occasions when we feel that an objective opinion voiced by a judge will be helpful

---

[24] ibid at [166].
[25] ibid.

eg, where confusion has arisen about bail decisions, sentencing and housing repossession processes. There are also matters on which panel judges cannot comment. They never comment, for example, on individual judgments, sentencing or other judicial decisions. Equally, there are areas on which panel judges decline and will continue to decline giving interviews ie, on matters that are overtly political, raise social policy issues or concern party political argument. Media attention on bail is a good example of where an issue developed and became too political for it to be appropriate for judges to give interviews about it. Once it became political and an announcement was made to review the law on bail it was decided that any interview would draw the judge into a conversation about what changes should be made.[26]

In practical terms the panel works in this way. A small group of judges of wide experience was given media training. A system was then established that, if the media wanted to seek comment on a particular subject from the judiciary they could approach the JCO. They would then check with the Lord Chief Justice and the relevant Head of Division, say for instance the President of the Queen's Bench Division, if the matter on which the media sought comment related to defamation. If they felt comment was appropriate, the JCO would then arrange for a panel judge with relevant experience to be available to the media. Importantly, the panel judges could not comment on individual cases. They could only deal with issues such cases raised in general terms, explaining the role of the judge in the proceedings, the types of facts that have to be taken account of by the judge and the nature of any relevant guidelines or principles of law a judge would have to apply or follow in reaching a decision.

At the time when this evidence was given, the media panel was 'still in its infancy'.[27] Few requests for interview had been granted. In fact, only 12 interviews had been given. Since then, the panel has not been called upon to speak as often as might have been expected. This may reflect the care that has been taken to ensure that the members of the panel are not available to comment on issues which are perceived to be too controversial. There is, of course, an obvious tension between the need to ensure that the panel judges do not get drawn into political or otherwise sensitive issues and the desire to

---

[26] Lord Clarke, Written Submission to the House of Commons' Select Committee on Culture, Media and Sport, in *2nd Report of 2009–2010 Session on Press Standards, Privacy and Libel* at Ev 201–202, available at www.publications.parliament.uk/pa/cm200910/cmselect/cmcumeds/362/362ii.pdf.

[27] ibid.

provide, as the creation of the panel intended, a form of public legal education. The media are, inevitably, more interested in the former; an area where the judiciary cannot properly tread.

While there has only been a very cautious approach to using the media panel, the establishing of it and the JCO shows that since 2005 there has been an acceptance that the voice of the judiciary should not only be heard through their judgments. Like Parliament and the Executive, the judicial arm of the state needs to engage with the public and to explain its role. Engagement—a form of openness— as a means of furthering public legal education is essential if public confidence is to be maintained in the justice system. We are feeling our way and proceeding with care. I think this is the right thing to do. A careful balance has to be struck. On the one hand, people think that the majesty of the law should be preserved. One aspect of this is that judges should keep their distance. If judges become too famil- iar, there is a danger that respect for the law will be undermined. On the other hand, what judges do is of enormous importance to the maintenance of the stability and well-being of our society. Judges should act in the public interest. Ultimately, they are public serv- ants. That is why the public has a right to understand what they are doing. I can well imagine that what has been done since the 2005 Act came into force to inform the public about the work of the judi- ciary is only a start and that both the JCO and the media panel will develop their respective roles further in the years to come.

CASE MANAGEMENT IN DEFAMATION CASES

Before I conclude what I have to say on the main subject of this lecture, I want to say a few words about case management in defa- mation cases in England and Wales. I do so because I know that there are many here who are interested in defamation law and that you have already heard others speak on the subject. It is relevant to a consideration of open justice. As you will all know, and indeed may have been wondering when I would mention it, Lord Hewart famously articulated the principle by stating that it was 'of fundamen- tal importance that justice not only be done, but should manifestly and undoubtedly be seen to be done.'[28] Historically in defamation cases justice was done by judge and jury. As I mentioned earlier, the

---

[28] *R v Sussex Justices, ex p McCarthy* [1924] 1 KB 256 at 259 (KBD).

Defamation Act 2013 has changed that. The presumption now is that justice will be done in such cases by judge alone.

The rationale lying behind this reform is the need to ensure that justice is achieved more efficiently and at proportionate cost. Where trial is by jury and questions of the meaning of allegedly defamatory statements are a matter for it rather than a judge, it is not possible to utilise a number of case management procedures, the use of which can secure those aims. If I can quote from the parliamentary debates concerning the question of jury trial reform, the Justice Minister, Jonathan Djanogly MP put the point this way,

> ... the retention of the right to jury trial creates practical difficulties and adds significantly to the length and cost of proceedings. This is because of the role that juries, if used, have to play, such as deciding the meaning of allegedly defamatory material. It means issues that could otherwise have been decided by a judge at an early stage cannot be resolved until trial, whether or not a jury is ultimately used. That means that proceedings take longer and cost more than they should.[29]

It is important to note here that since the Woolf reforms and the more recent Jackson cost reforms, issues of efficiency and proportionality, especially in respect of cost, now form part of what it means to talk of doing justice. For justice to be done, and to be seen to be done, it must be carried out consistently with that change in approach. The removal of the presumption in favour of jury trial is thus a means to secure our new approach to justice. In practical terms how will it do so?

In the first instance it will enable much greater use of the court's case management powers. In a wider range of cases the court will, where the circumstances justify it, be able to promote the earlier use of pre-action and pre-trial ADR, whether that be through mediation, early neutral evaluation or other such means. It will be able to deal with issues of meaning, for instance, by way of preliminary issue. Determining such issues will both help to bring some claims to a close at an earlier stage than previously, while in others it will help to narrow the issues that will ultimately go to trial. In the same vein summary judgment and strike out applications can be more widely used. The absence of the restrictions imposed on case management

---

[29] HC Deb 26 June 2012, vol 547, col 166, available at www.publications.parliament. uk/pa/cm201213/cmpublic/defamation/120626/am/120626s01.htm.

by the fact of jury trial will, I am sure, enable it to be carried out much more actively and robustly.

The ability for the court to promote the greater use of case management techniques that have long been available in other civil cases will, it seems to me, go a long way to reducing the cost and length of defamation proceedings. It will help ensure that our post-Woolf and Jackson form of justice is done. It will, however, through its removal of the jury in the majority of such cases, reduce public involvement in justice. It will to a certain degree have an adverse effect on open justice—on it being seen to be done. A reform that both the Jackson Cost Review and ultimately Parliament concluded was necessary emphasises how important it is for us to ensure that we take positive steps to otherwise increase public scrutiny of the courts.

CONCLUSION

To return then to my main theme, it is perhaps fitting that I should conclude my presentation today by noting something that was said by another of my predecessors as Master of the Rolls, Lord Donaldson. He famously noted that,

> The judges administer justice in the Queen's name on behalf of the whole community. No one is more entitled than a member of the general public to see for himself that justice is done.[30]

It is true, as he went on to acknowledge in another case, that there are circumstances which justify limits being placed on public access to the courts[31]—where, for instance, such limits are strictly necessary to ensure that justice is done. But apart from these situations, all steps should be taken to secure public scrutiny of the courts. This is essential to maintain public confidence in the justice system, and by that means the rule of law itself.

In the past, the public could exercise their right to see justice done by going to court. They could also read press reports. But necessarily these could only be read hours, if not days, after the event; and a journalist's summary of court proceedings is highly selective and hardly a satisfactory substitute for witnessing the real thing.

---

[30] *R v Chief Registrar of Friendly Societies, ex p New Cross Building Society* [1984] QB 227 at 235 (CA).

[31] *A-G v Leveller Magazine Ltd* [1979] AC 440 at 450 (HL); and see *Scott v Scott* [1913] AC 417 at 437 (HL).

Anyway, the days when a journalist sat in court all day have gone. In the nineteenth century we reformed our courts and their procedures to make them fit for an industrial age. A system that had evolved to serve the needs of an agrarian society was no longer regarded as sufficient to deliver justice. We now live in a technological age. We have the means to enhance public access to the courts. If we want justice to be truly public, for the courts to be properly open, we will have to continue to build upon recent advances and utilise that technology as far as is consistent with our commitment to making sure that justice is done.

24

Threats to Justice in the Twenty-first Century *

INTRODUCTION

JOHN AND MARY Conkerton's contribution to the law as university lecturers in Liverpool was immense, as was their inspiration of generations of law students and young solicitors and their work with the Liverpool Law Society. That this memorial lecture has gone from strength to strength since its inception in 1982 is a fitting testament to all that they achieved. It is a great honour to have been invited to give the lecture this year.

There are many threats to justice in the twenty-first century both in this country and abroad. In this country, the growth of terrorism and the recent economic crisis which led to the so-called Age of Austerity have imposed strains on justice in different ways. I propose to focus on the threats to access to justice. Access to justice is a fundamental human right recognised alike by the common law and the European Convention on Human Rights. In this respect, as in so many others, the two systems are in harmony with each other. Lord Diplock said that in 'any civilised society' the provision of access to justice was 'a function of Government to maintain': *A-G v Times Newspapers Ltd.*[1] 68 years ago, Sir Hartley Shawcross informed Parliament that a Bill that he was introducing would 'open the Doors of the Courts freely to all persons who may wish to avail themselves of British justice without regard to the question of their wealth or ability to pay'.[2] This Bill became the Legal Aid and Assistance Act 1949. Like so many of the reforms introduced by the Attlee government, it was a progressive piece of legislation. By a combination of

---

* Conkerton Memorial Lecture 2016, Liverpool Law Society, 6 October 2016.
[1] *A-G v Times Newspapers Ltd* [1974] AC 273 at 307 (HL).
[2] H Shawcross KC, cited in H Brown and A Marriott, *ADR: Principles and Practice* (Sweet & Maxwell, 2011) at vii.

a means and a merits test, it opened the doors of justice to many in whose face it had previously been firmly shut.

Putting to one side for a moment questions of litigation funding, the most common threats to access to justice, at least in recent decades, have been excess cost, delay and complexity. As was said in 1997 by His Honour David Marshall Evans QC (former designated civil judge for Liverpool), these three factors worked in combination to 'deny justice to many.' Already expensive process became yet more expensive as a function of the complexity of our justice system. And as excessive cost deterred people from bringing and prosecuting claims, so too complexity led to valid claims and defences failing on technical grounds. As His Honour Marshall Evans QC went on to say, it:

> ... must be remembered that every legitimate claim not pursued is an example of injustice, and of an important economic loss to the claimant deterred by the system from claiming.[3]

He was absolutely right. There is injustice whether a legitimate claim is not pursued because an individual does not have the financial means to litigate, or because litigation costs are prohibitive, rendering pursuit of the claim uneconomic, or because delay or complexity makes its determination impracticable or impossible. His point can, however, be taken further in two ways.

First, injustice does not only occur where legitimate claims cannot be brought before the courts. It also occurs if judgments are not capable of being effectively enforced. It makes a mockery of the trial process for a successful litigant not to be able to enforce his judgment economically and expeditiously. And it undermines public confidence in the courts.

Secondly, society as a whole has an interest in the effective vindication of legitimate claims and enforcement of judgments. A failure to secure these objectives undermines the rule of law. It undermines the framework of rights and obligations which underpin our social and economic development. People who know or believe that they cannot vindicate their rights by due process of law are likely to pose a threat to the stability of society. The spectre of resort to self-help in such circumstances cannot be dismissed as mere fantasy. And neither of the alternatives of would-be claimants in desperation

---

[3] D Marshall Evans, 'Access to Justice' (1997) XIX(1) *The Liverpool Law Review* 37 at 37.

abandoning good claims or being forced to accept low settlements is a recipe for a good society.

It might be thought that, 68 years after the enactment of the Legal Aid and Assistance Act 1949, litigation funding would no longer be an issue of concern. Furthermore, after almost 30 years of procedural reforms, it might reasonably have been hoped that the complexity and cost of litigation would no longer pose a threat to access to justice. Yet the two biggest threats facing civil justice at the present time are, first, the huge reduction in the availability of legal aid, and secondly the fact that the cost of civil litigation remains too high. These two factors in combination are having a serious impact on the ability of many to have access to justice.

As you know, there has been a massive paring back in the provision of legal aid. There is no prospect that this trend will be reversed. Neither of the two main political parties is committed to doing that. There are no votes in justice. It is not like the Health Service. The Department of Justice is not a protected department. In a time of cutbacks, we have to learn to accept the harsh realities of political life. We are constantly being reminded by government that we still have the most generous legal aid system in the world. Most of the budget for the justice system goes to fund criminal cases. That is inevitable.

Acceptance of these facts of life does not, however, mean that we should simply do nothing. Whether the threat to access to justice stems from an absence of funding or from excessive costs, we can and should seek ways to ameliorate the situation. I want to consider tonight what steps can be taken to that end (some of them are already being taken). In particular, I want to look at two issues. First the question of funding; and secondly how we can reduce the cost of litigation.

LITIGATION FUNDING

As I have said, the prospects of reversing the reductions in civil and family legal aid appear to be slim to say the least. Roger Smith, former director of *Justice*, said earlier in 2016, '… the paradigm since World War II for public funding of legal aid is over: that system is bust'.[4] A number of other measures have been adopted or proposed

---

[4] R Smith, evidence to the Access to Justice Commission, dated 31 March 2016, available at sirhenrybrooke.me/2016/03/31/the-new-access-to-justice-commission-update-5-roger-smith/.

to compensate for the reduction in legal aid. You will all know about CFAs. They were once seen as providing the complete answer to the withdrawal of civil and family legal aid. Although in some respects they have become discredited, they still serve a purpose. And the possibility of having a Contingent Legal Aid Fund in this country—a CLAF—is now also being examined again. The previous Lord Chancellor expressed a real interest in this, not least because he was not very keen on CFAs.

A CLAF was first proposed here in the late 1970s by *Justice*.[5] CLAFs have been established throughout Australia.[6] Northern Ireland was, at one time, developing a CLAF, but it was not introduced for what have been unhelpfully described as 'technical reasons'.[7] Sir Rupert Jackson in his Costs Report recommended that work be done to assess the viability of a CLAF here.[8] He recently returned to the fray. At the Solicitors' Costs Conference earlier in 2016 he called on the Law Society and Bar Council to establish a joint working party to consider how to introduce such a scheme pursuant to powers available under existing legislation.[9] In July 2016, they and CILEx, heeded the call and established a joint working party.[10] Its report, which is due by the end of 2016, is awaited with interest.

The introduction of a CLAF has, historically, foundered on a number of rocks. The first of these was the fact that a CLAF was considered to be less attractive (ie, I fear, less profitable for the lawyers) than a CFA/ATE scheme. In 2007, when the Civil Justice Council looked into the possibility of introducing such a scheme, it identified as the fundamental weakness a CLAF's 'inherent inability to compete effectively with now well-established CFAs.' It went on to conclude however that if 'the current CFA/ATE mechanism were to deteriorate significantly the situation would be entirely different

[5] See R Jackson, 'The case for a CLAF' (Keynote Address, Solicitors' Costs Conference, 2 February 2016), available at www.judiciary.gov.uk/wp-content/uploads/2016/02/lj-jackson-speech-clf-160202.pdf.

[6] For a summary of the schemes, see, Civil Justice Council, *Improved Access to Justice—Funding Options & Proportionate Costs* (June 2007) at 20.

[7] J Peysner, *Access to Justice—A Critical Analysis of Recoverable Conditional Fees and No-win No-fee Funding* (Palgrave, 2014) at 118.

[8] R Jackson, *Review of Civil Litigation Costs: Final Report* (TSO, December 2009) ch 13, s 2.

[9] Jackson, 'The case for a CLAF'.

[10] M Fouzder, 'CLAF revived to support access to justice' (Law Gazette) (18 July 2016), available at www.lawgazette.co.uk/news/claf-revived-to-support-access-to-justice/5056628.article.

and a CLAF approach might need to be reconsidered ...'.[11] The Civil Justice Council could not have anticipated at that time that there would be a significant change in the CFA/ATE regime, such as that effected by the Legal Aid, Sentencing and Punishment of Offenders Act 2012. Competition with the pre-2013 CFA regime is thus no longer a problem.

The second rock on which a CLAF scheme foundered was the lack of money to provide the seed corn from which the funding crop would grow. I fear that it may not be possible to clamber over this rock even today. I hope I am wrong about this because, in principle, a CLAF is an excellent idea. So how may a CLAF be funded?

The government might be persuaded to provide initial funding. Alternatively, the legal profession or institutional bodies might be persuaded to make an initial contribution, perhaps as Sir Rupert Jackson has suggested in return for a fixed-rate bond. Another possibility is that some funding is provided through a small charitable increment incorporated into practising certificate fees. Further contributions could be drawn from crowdfunding.[12] There are various possible options. They need to be given due consideration, which the professional bodies are currently doing.[13]

A CLAF cannot, however, be seen as a complete answer to the problem of access to justice that we currently face. This point has already been made by the Bar Council. It noted in February 2016 that as good an idea as a CLAF is, it is an 'additional source of funding'.[14] It is not a complete answer. The legal aid scheme was not a complete answer either.

Even in its heyday, legal aid did not cover all members of society. A large proportion of them was outside its scope. The means test was pitched at such a level that, in practice, litigation was outside the reach of all but the seriously poor, the seriously wealthy, those who had the support of a trade union or who could afford after the event insurance and any associated premiums. As John Peysner has said, for a 'large and increasing number of citizens' there was 'a justice

---

[11] Civil Justice Council, *Improved Access to Justice—Funding Options & Proportionate Costs* at 24.

[12] See for instance, H Spendlove, 'Litigation: crowdfunding' *Law Society Gazette* (27 April 2015), available at www.lawgazette.co.uk/law/practice-points/litigation-crowdfunding/5048431.fullarticle.

[13] See Bar Council Press Release, 4 February 2016, available at www.barcouncil.org.uk/media-centre/news-and-press-releases/2016/february/bar-council-response-to-lord-justice-jackson-claf-proposal/.

[14] ibid.

gap'; and 'no access to justice'.[15] Most middle income would-be litigants who did not qualify for legal aid because their income was too
high could not afford to litigate. It was simply too expensive. But I
must resist the temptation of entering into the thickets of legal costs
prematurely. I should first complete what I want to say about the
funding of civil litigation.

There is another possibility. It is one that the Civil Justice Council is beginning to examine, namely legal expenses insurance. In
some jurisdictions, such as Germany, legal expenses insurance is a
significant if not the main form of litigation funding. In other jurisdictions, such as Ontario, where—as here—there has been a retreat
from civil legal aid, there is a push for the development of a public
legal expenses insurance scheme as a means of supplementing legal
aid.[16] Very many people in this country already have some form
of before the event insurance at the present time, whether through
household insurance, car insurance or insurance provided as part of
packaged bank accounts. I think I can safely say that many people
may not be aware of this. Might it be possible to build on this, so
that it forms a central plank of an access to justice strategy here?
A number of considerations arise.

First, should any expansion of legal expenses insurance be private
or public, or a combination of the two? In Germany, LEI provision
is mainly private. The German approach is, however, predicated on
one central difference between litigation there and litigation here:
fixed recoverable costs.[17] That is to say, the costs recoverable by
the winning party from the losing party are fixed and, therefore,
predictable. Where a fixed recoverable costs regime is in place, it
becomes practicable for insurers to underwrite legal costs.[18] I shall
return to fixed fees shortly. A LEI scheme could be made compulsory, thus providing a broad, diverse risk pool for insurers, which in
turn might make it both viable and cost-effective.[19]

---

[15] Peysner, *Access to Justice—A Critical Analysis of Recoverable Conditional Fees and No-win No-fee Funding* 5.

[16] See S Choudhry et al, 'Growing Legal Aid in Ontario into the Middle Class: A Pro-
posal for Public Legal Expenses Insurance' in M Trebilcock et al, *Middle Income Access to Justice* (University of Toronto Press, 2012) at 385ff.

[17] Peysner, *Access to Justice—A Critical Analysis of Recoverable Conditional Fees and No-win No-fee Funding* 13.

[18] Peysner, cited in J Robins, 'Legal insurance: will Britain buy it?' *The Guardian*
(28 May 2010), 'Professor John Peysner, head of law at Lincoln Law School, points out
there is a radically different litigation landscape in Germany, not least because transac-
tional legal costs are fixed. "The basic problem is you can't inject BTE insurance into
an environment where costs are so uncertain," he says', see www.theguardian.com/
law/2010/may/28/legal-insurance-uk-germany.

[19] Choudhry et al, 394ff.

It has been suggested that a compulsory scheme might meet resistance from consumer groups. But if there was a diverse market for LEI, it is difficult to understand why that would be the case. There is, as far as I am aware, no consumer-based objection to compulsory car insurance.[20] The Consumer Association, *Which*, was a powerful advocate of the introduction of consumer class actions as a means of promoting access to justice. It might be thought they—and other such bodies—would support such a proposal.

The proposed approach in Ontario is another model. Rather than mandatory private cover, it is based on the idea that 'all taxpayers are enrolled by default, although free to "opt out"'[21] and take up better private cover. Such an approach would, it is said, ensure that everyone has a basic level of cover administered by a public body and paid for out of general taxation, whilst maintaining freedom of choice for users and stimulating the private sector.

I hope that the CJC, and others, will consider the possibility of extending LEI and examine how it could fit into an overall funding strategy so as to ensure that a proper funding framework exists and is accessible to all members of society. Piecemeal development is something which we can no longer afford. A coherent, structured strategy—whether it is based on one approach to funding or the co-ordination of a number of different approaches—is now necessary.

FEES

This takes me naturally to the question of legal fees. The quality of the service provided by the Bar and solicitors in the delivery of civil justice is, for the most part, extremely high. But who can afford it? How many of you would start proceedings, instructing a solicitor and barrister in the traditional way in pursuit of a claim? I suspect very few of you. I say 'in the traditional way', because I recognise that CFAs, and even DBAs, do promote access to justice, although the latter are in need of improvement to make them a more robust funding mechanism. But you have to be pretty desperate or very rich to be willing to engage lawyers in the time-honoured way, being charged at an hourly rate. It is the open-endedness of the dreaded hourly rate which is so terrifying to the average would-be litigator.

---

[20] ibid at 397.
[21] ibid at 399.

That is why I have been convinced for some time that we have to extend the scope of fixed costs in litigation to include all fast-track cases and, at any rate, all cases in what I have referred to as the 'lower reaches of the multi-track'. I have been pressing for this for two or three years. I am not the first. Lord Woolf recommended fixed fees in his Access to Justice Reports. Fixed scale costs were, as far as I am aware, first proposed by the Lord Chancellor's Legal Procedure Committee as long ago as 1881.[22] This came after Lord Justice Bramwell's earlier condemnation of itemised billing. In 1869 he had this to say:

> There is something wrong somewhere. The thing has got into the wrong groove. The system is wrong ... The obvious tendency of this practice is to multiply items and augment costs.[23]

His answer was that solicitors should charge by way of a fixed lump sum. You do not have to agree with Bramwell LJ's view that itemised billing—hourly billing—tends to multiply items and artificially inflate costs, to take his point that a form of fixed-fee system would be better than the present system. I believe that it is a system to which solicitors can adapt. This is a point recently made by Kerry Underwood. Mr Underwood is a longstanding critic of the ways in which the civil justice system has been reformed over the last decade or so. However, he has stressed that fixed recoverable costs work and, as he put it, if fixed 'at the right level, [they] reward talented lawyers.'[24] It is in any event interesting to note that it appears from a recent Legal Services Consumer Panel survey that approximately 48 per cent of legal work is already conducted on a fixed rather than hourly fee basis.[25]

At long last, the government has decided in principle to extend the scope of fixed fees. The challenge will be to set them at the right level. Sir Rupert Jackson made some suggestions as to what the level might be in January 2016. They were illustrative only. Serious work will need to be carried out to ensure that sensible, reasonable and

---

[22] S Rosenbaum, *The Rule-making Authority in the English Supreme Court* (HardPress Publishing reprint, 1917) at 77.

[23] Cited in Rosenbaum, 69–70.

[24] K Underwood, *Making Fixed Fees Work* (15 February 2016), available at communities.lawsociety.org.uk/civil-litigation/news-and-features/civil-litigation-features-and-comment/kerry-underwood-making-fixed-fees-work/5053643.fullarticle.

[25] See J Hyde, 'Trust in Lawyers falling but client satisfaction remains high' *Law Society Gazette* (19 July 2016), available at www.lawgazette.co.uk/news/trust-in-lawyers-falling-but-client-satisfaction-high/5056661.article.

proportionate figures are arrived at. I fully understand the fears of some solicitors that the fees will be set at a level which makes it uneconomic for them to conduct litigation. In my view, that should most certainly not be the objective. If solicitors were deterred from conducting litigation in the fast track and the lower reaches of the multi-track, the result would either be that some litigants would be denied access to the courts or they would be compelled to conduct their cases as litigants-in-person. Determining the right figures for fixed costs will be difficult and can only be done after careful and wide consultation. It will require a proper evidence-based approach and analysis.

But I make no secret of the fact that in my view costs are too high. Although assessed costs should be reasonable and proportionate, they are still too high. I have seen bills when we summarily assess costs at the conclusion of a short appeal which make one's hair stand on end. Costs out of all proportion to what is at stake. That must stop. I think that a sensible regime of fixed costs should help. I say 'sensible', because I repeat that it is no part of my agenda to drive lawyers away from conducting litigation.

I have little doubt that an extended fixed costs regime will have an effect on solicitors' business models and working practices. Experience has shown that those who have already had to adapt to operating in the fixed costs world of road traffic accident litigation and in the Intellectual Property Enterprise Court have done so successfully.

I accept that an extension of fixed costs will represent a challenge to law firms. It may also encourage the courts to adopt a tighter and more Spartan approach to case management and the conduct of hearings than they currently do. A comparison with the German system might be salutary. That is the paradigm fixed-fee jurisdiction whose pre-trial process is very different from ours. For example, they do not have disclosure as we understand it.[26] Evidence-gathering is more of a cooperative exercise between the court and the parties. The scale of the exercise is constrained by the fixed-fee limit. I am not saying that we should necessarily adopt the German system. But there are other ways of conducting litigation than the ones to which we are all accustomed. We should be open to other influences. In principle, the level at which the fixed costs are set should reflect how much it is reasonable to spend on legal fees, having

---

[26] P Murray and R Sturner, *German Civil Justice* (Carolina Academic Press, 2004) 595.

regard to what is at stake in the litigation. The same thinking should influence the court's approach to case management. The procedural steps required by the court should reflect how much it is reasonable to do, having regard to what is at stake in the litigation. The level of costs and the procedural steps required should go hand in hand.

Two further benefits would accrue from an extension of fixed costs. First, it should obviate or at least reduce the need for cost budgeting in cases which are the subject of fixed costs. Cost budgeting adds to the cost of litigation. Cost budgeting conferences can be expensive for the parties and they absorb valuable court time and resources.

Secondly, the assessment of costs in cases which are subject to a fixed costs regime should be very straightforward, if it is necessary at all. These two benefits alone will reduce the cost of litigation. Costs incurred in arguing about costs assist nobody. I am horrified that cost litigation is now a recognised specialism. Costs law is so complicated that there is a Costs Bar, there are specialist costs lawyers and Costs Law Reports. What would Bramwell LJ have made of that? The rise and rise of costs litigation has occurred during my professional lifetime. It is a blot on the landscape of our system of civil justice. It is time we did something about it. The extension of fixed costs would be a start.

The cost of litigation is not, however, simply a matter of lawyers' fees. There is the question of court fees to consider: the price of admission to the justice system. Until recently, I think court fees were barely noticed. They were very low as compared with the cost of legal fees and proportionate to the proposed claim. They were not a significant element in the total cost of litigating. But that has now changed. The chorus of opposition to the recent massive increases in court fees has been very loud and, in my view, justifiably so. The senior judiciary have been among the most vociferous critics of the increases. But so too have been the professions. The hike in fees is a matter of the greatest concern. We warned the government that these increases were likely to make litigation unaffordable for many: not the very poorest in Society who do not have to pay; and plainly not the wealthy. But the average modestly comfortable-off. And many small and medium enterprises, who are said by the government to be the engine for economic recovery, would be unable to afford or unwilling to pay these fees upfront. As a result, the increased fees were likely to be a further barrier to access to justice. They were also likely to be counter-productive in the sense that if they resulted in a reduction in the number of claims being issued, the government's hoped-for rise in fee income would not materialise. And so it is proving to be.

It is argued by some that parties who have to litigate to enforce their rights should not have to pay anything for doing so, any more than they have to pay for a call to the police, the ambulance or fire service. I do not subscribe to this view. It has long been accepted by Parliament that it is reasonable to ask a would-be litigant to pay a court fee for using the courts. I can see nothing wrong with that in principle. But the fee must not be set at a level which is disproportionate and is likely to deter the litigant from exercising his right of access to the courts. As I said at the outset, access to justice is a fundamental human right. The vice in the recent increases in court fees is that they are tending to have precisely that deterrent effect. The Russian oligarchs will not be deterred from using our courts by the recent court fee increases, but many small and medium enterprises and individuals will be. That is unacceptable. Now that the evidence of the effect of the increases is to hand, I would urge the government to think again. It is one thing to ask a litigant to make a reasonable contribution to the cost of his litigation. The fact is that the fees collected in respect of civil litigation substantially exceed the aggregate cost of providing a civil justice system. Civil fees subsidise other parts of the justice system which have nothing whatsoever to do with civil justice. It is strongly arguable that it is wrong in principle that those who use the courts in order to vindicate their civil rights should be required to subsidise other parts of the system. Be that as it may, it is unquestionably wrong that the civil litigant should be asked (where the civil justice system was already in profit) to subsidise other parts of the system by having to pay additional court fees which are disproportionate and are set at a level that he is unable to afford. That, in my view, is outrageous.

ONLINE COURTS AND JUSTICE

Finally, let me turn to a more positive development; one that is truly exciting. I greatly welcome the decision by the government to invest in digitising the courts, to the point where litigation becomes paperless by 2020. It is long overdue. I can remember Lord Woolf calling for the introduction of effective IT systems in the mid-1990s. They were needed to ensure that his reforms would work optimally. I can also remember Sir Henry Brooke, Sir Rupert Jackson and others calling for the introduction of modern IT systems.

The investment is finally in place, and I hope that the days when rooms and corridors in court buildings groan under the weight of files of papers will soon become a distant memory. And in its place there will be a system that works more economically and efficiently. Gone will be the days of court files going missing when they are transferred between court buildings. Filing documents will be as simple as uploading a document to Dropbox. Tracking cases, and compliance with case management directions, will be as easy as tracking your latest Amazon delivery.

We are also close to seeing the creation of an Online Court. The proposal for such a court was made by the Civil Justice Council, in particular its Online Dispute Resolution working party under the inspiring guidance of Professor Richard Susskind. Richard has been a tireless campaigner for increased and better use of IT in the courts since the days of Lord Woolf. I am delighted that his ideas have, at long last, been accepted and are being translated into reality.

The CJC's proposal, now developed through Sir Michael Briggs' Civil Courts Structure Review and the HMCTS modernisation programme, will result in the development of a unique standalone Online Court. It is not entirely without precedent, as those familiar with the British Columbia Civil Resolution Tribunal will know.

Underpinning both the CJC's proposals and Sir Michael's detailed examination of the civil courts and online justice was a real concern, as Sir Michael put it, that:

> ... the single, most pervasive and indeed shocking weakness of our civil courts is that they fail to provide reasonable access to justice for ordinary individuals or small businesses with small or modest value claims ...[27]

This weakness—threat to justice—has been compounded by the reduction in legal aid, which has led to increasing numbers of individuals not being able to afford lawyers. The development of a court that is as accessible to individuals as Amazon is long overdue. Effective use of technology is the means by which it can be achieved, so that litigants will no longer have to navigate rules, practices and procedures that pose problems for the most experienced lawyers. It is the means by which those who cannot afford lawyers, or whose disputes do not justify the expense of hiring a lawyer on either a traditional hourly-rate or on a fixed-fee basis, can achieve effective access to our courts, and importantly, to a dispute resolution system that, in appropriate cases, facilitates consensual settlement.

---

[27] M Briggs, *Civil Courts Structure Review—Final Report* (July 2016) at 5.14.

This is not, as Sir Michael Briggs has properly stressed, to suggest that lawyers will have no role to play. It is intended that they have a role in the Online Court in providing unbundled advice and assistance and early advice on the merits.[28] The key here is to ensure that technology is—as I have said before—the servant of justice not its master.[29]

CONCLUSION

I want to give the last word this evening to Sir Jack Jacob; the greatest twentieth century master of procedure. In the late 1970s, he said this:

> The need for access to justice may be said to be two-fold; first, we must ensure that the rights of citizens should be recognised and made effective, for otherwise they would not be real but merely illusory; and secondly, we must enable legal disputes, conflicts and complaints which inevitably arise in society to be resolved in an orderly way according to the justice of the case, so as to promote harmony and peace in society, lest they fester and breed discontent and disturbance.[30]

I am sure that both John and Mary Conkerton would have agreed with these beautifully expressed sentiments, as surely we all do. To me, Sir Jack Jacob will always be Master Jacob, the towering senior Queen's Bench Master who presided in the Masters' Corridor when I started as a young barrister. His knowledge of civil justice was unrivalled, but he was also the embodiment of good sense and reasonableness. I am sure that he would have been astounded to see how the landscape has changed since his day.

In this lecture, I have identified the problem of litigation funding, the cost and complexity of litigation and excessive court fees as the most serious current threats to access to justice. Since the threats come from diverse sources, it follows that there can be no single over-arching solution. We have been struggling to find an effective solution to the problem of litigation funding ever since legal aid was reduced and, in some areas, withdrawn altogether. A CLAF may

---

[28] Briggs, 6.38–6.39.

[29] J Dyson, 'Delay too often defeats justice' (Law Society, 22 April 2015) at [30], available at www.judiciary.gov.uk/wp-content/uploads/2015/04/law-society-magna-carta-lecture.pdf.

[30] J Jacob, cited in Peysner, *Access to Justice—A Critical Analysis of Recoverable Conditional Fees and No-win No-fee Funding*, 24.

be the answer to this. We continue to grapple with the issue of the cost and complexity of litigation. I have suggested that a substantial extension of the fixed costs regime will both reduce the cost of litigation and go some way to eliminating the uncertainty which is inherent in the current rate-based system of assessing costs, an uncertainty which is bound to deter at least some from embarking on the hazardous business of litigation. Finally, I have suggested that the government should reconsider the level of court fees. We are living in fast moving times. I am sure that the landscape will look very different again in 10 years' time. I cannot predict what it will look like. The only thing that I can safely predict is that in 10 years' time I shall not be giving a lecture such as this.

25

Halsey *10 Years On— The Decision Revisited*[*]

INTRODUCTION

IT IS A pleasure to have been asked to deliver a keynote address today and to consider the way in which mediation has developed in England and Wales since the *Halsey*[1] decision in 2004. Given some of the press I have had since the judgment was handed down you would be forgiven for thinking that I am not the greatest mediation zealot. One of the more colourful accusations to be levelled at me is that I am an 'ADR non-believer' or, if not quite that, 'at least' an 'ADR sceptic'.[2] I am quite happy to admit that I am not evangelical about mediation. I would not recommend it for every case and, in my view, the answer to all of a litigant's woes does not lie in mediation. However, I do not consider that either of the epithets reflects accurately my views on mediation. Far from indulging in ADR-scepticism, I am a strong believer in its merits. In this I agree with Sir Alan Ward who, together with Sir John Laws and myself, was party to the *Halsey* decision, and described mediation as 'a perfectly proper adjunct to litigation'.[3]

I don't really think I need to point out that *Halsey* was a controversial judgment and that it has had a mixed press. But I think that suggestions that we were attempting to turn the tide or close the door on ADR, or worse, are wide of the mark. The main point we were addressing was how a refusal to mediate should be viewed by the courts when deciding the question of costs. It was certainly not

---

[*] Belfast Mediation Conference, 9 May 2014.
[1] *Halsey v Milton Keynes General NHS Trust, Steel v Joy & Halliday* [2004] EWCA Civ 573, [2004] 1 WLR 2434.
[2] H Genn, *Judging Civil Justice* (Cambridge University Press, 2010) 101.
[3] *Egan v Motor Services (Bath) Ltd* [2007] EWCA Civ 1002, [2008] 1 WLR 1589 at [53].

an attempt to thwart or sabotage the development of mediation as a supplement to the adjudicative process. Far from mediation being impeded by *Halsey*, since 2004 it has gone from strength to strength. Despite the fears of those who believed it marked the end of mediation, it is now such a well-established feature of the system that it has recently been described by Professor Andrews, of Cambridge University, as 'a pillar of civil justice'.[4]

In today's address I do not intend to revisit the facts and findings of *Halsey*. Today my focus will be threefold. First, I shall give some general reflections on *Halsey* itself. I shall then look at developments in mediation in England and Wales in the ten years since it was handed down. I will conclude by considering where mediation may be heading.

TEN YEARS ON—REFLECTIONS ON *HALSEY* ITSELF

Where do I stand ten years on? If anyone came here today expecting some act of wholesale recantation for any of the so-called 'ADR-scepticism' of *Halsey*, they will be disappointed. I remain of the view that it was, on the whole, correct and that the guidance it gave was sound. Whilst this may seem complacent, I do think it is right for a number of reasons, which I shall develop later. Three main propositions can be derived from *Halsey* which I continue to believe are sound: first, that mediation is important and should be used in many cases but it is not a universal panacea; secondly, parties should not be compelled to mediate; and thirdly, that adverse costs orders are an appropriate means of encouraging parties to use mediation.

On the first of these points, I share the general view that recourse to the informality of ADR can reduce cost, delay and emotional strain. However, this is not always the case; some mediators are very expensive. Couple that with the price of instructing solicitors and counsel to represent you during your mediation and your costs may well have soared. Then consider that your mediation may fail. In this situation not only have you lost your money, but also your time and, I think it would be fair to say, you would probably have been subjected to considerable and unnecessary stress. Moreover, I think that

---

[4] N Andrews, 'Mediation: a Pillar of Civil Justice in Modern English Practice' (2007) 12 *ZZP Int* 1, 2.

it must be accepted even by the most zealous supporters that there are some cases to which mediation is simply unsuited. Whilst cases in the family law courts undoubtedly are suitable, as are personal injury or clinical negligence claims and as are most fact-intensive cases, there remains a not unsubstantial number of cases where one or both parties positively want an adjudication by a court. Take, for example, the litigant whose case discloses a point of law that is disputed, ambiguous or unclear which should be settled by a court to provide precedent and legal certainty. And Dame Hazel Genn is surely right to say that there is a public interest in the courts developing and clarifying the law and, I think, most importantly, securing the rule of law.

Should parties ever be compelled to mediate, even if they really do not want to do so? On this point, I remain of the same view as in May 2004: truly unwilling parties should never be compelled to mediate. Cajole yes; encourage yes; but compel no. However, what I would now say is that ordering parties to mediate in and of itself does not infringe their Article 6 rights. *Halsey* suggested that to oblige truly unwilling parties to refer their disputes to mediation would be to impose an unacceptable obstruction on their right of access to the court in breach of Article 6 of the ECHR.[5] Ten years on, I think that these words require some tempering: only in certain circumstances might compulsory mediation impose an unacceptable obstruction on parties' right of access to the court.

Where EU rights are concerned, the Article 6 question was determined by the ECJ in March this year in *Rosalba Alassini*, a preliminary reference from Italy.[6] The question for the ECJ arose out of a dispute between two telephone companies and their customers who had brought proceedings seeking damages for breach of contract under the EU Directive on the provision of electronic communications networks.[7] The telephone companies contended that the actions were inadmissible as the applicants had not first attempted mediation in accordance with the Italian implementing law. The Italian law in question made such legal actions conditional on a prior attempt to achieve an out-of-court settlement. If the parties declined to submit to mediation, they would forfeit their legal right to bring proceedings before the courts.

---

[5] *Halsey* at [9].
[6] Joined Cases C-317/08, C-318/08, C-319/08 and C-320/08 *Rosalba Alassini v Telecom Italia* [2010] I-02213 (18 March 2010).
[7] Directive 2002/22/EC (The Universal Service Directive).

The ECJ held that there was no contravention of Article 6. In particular, it recognised that the right to effective judicial protection is not granted unconditionally and that every judicial procedure requires procedural rules and conditions governing admissibility. In order not to infringe Article 6, any such restrictions must correspond to objectives in the general interest and must not be disproportionate. The Court found that the Italian provisions did pursue legitimate objectives in the general interest, namely, the quicker and less expensive resolution of disputes.[8] The Court then held that the measure was proportionate as in its view no less restrictive alternative existed to the implementation of a mandatory procedure, since the introduction of an out-of-court settlement procedure which is merely optional is not as efficient a means of achieving those objectives.[9]

The ECJ also analysed the Italian rules from a perspective of the EU principle of effectiveness, finding that the rules did not make it impossible or excessively difficult to exercise the rights derived from the Directive. This was because the parties were coerced to mediate, not to settle. Accordingly, if the parties failed to settle the case, they could then bring the action before the courts. The delay to bringing proceedings was minimal as the time-limit for completion of the mediation procedure was 30 days. During this period time was stopped for limitation purposes and there were no fees involved in the mediation process.

Article 5 of the Mediation Directive[10] adopts a similar position to that taken by the ECJ. Whilst Article 5(1) does not require Member States to impose compulsory mediation, Article 5(2) permits Member States to use compulsory mediation, either before or after proceedings have commenced, provided that it does not prevent parties from exercising their right of access to justice.[11] It is clear then, that in and of itself compulsory mediation does not breach Article 6. The Directive has now been transposed into UK law

---

[8] *Rosalba Alassini*, [64].

[9] ibid [65].

[10] EU Directive on Mediation in Civil and Commercial Cases (Directive 2008/52 EC), requiring transposition before 21 May 2011, Art 12.

[11] Art 5(2): This Directive is without prejudice to national legislation making the use of mediation compulsory or subject to incentives or sanctions, whether before or after judicial proceedings have started, provided that such legislation does not prevent the parties from exercising their right of access to the judicial system.

by the Cross-Border Mediation (EU Directive) Regulations 2011[12] and through amendments to Part 78 of the Civil Procedure Rules. Neither the Regulations nor the CPR amendments have taken up the possibility afforded by the Directive to make pre or post-issue mediation compulsory.

Whilst I agree with the EU legislator and judiciary on the Article 6 point, I am less convinced that compulsory mediation is more efficient than when it is voluntary. I remain of the view I advanced in my judgment in *Halsey*[13] (which may perhaps be attributed to the UK legislator and Civil Procedure Rule Committee) that if the court were to compel parties to enter into a mediation to which they objected, that would achieve nothing except to add to the costs to be borne by the parties, possibly postpone the time when the court determines the dispute, and damage the perceived effectiveness of the ADR process.

DEVELOPMENTS IN ENGLAND AND WALES SINCE 2004

What has happened in England and Wales since 2004? I shall look at the general reception of *Halsey*, developments in the subsequent case law and the recent Jackson Costs Review.

The first thing to say is that *Halsey* remains good law. It has been followed in a number of cases.[14] This is not to say that it has not been called into question in the authorities. Sir Alan Ward, in what I believe was his final judgment in the Court of Appeal, has for instance suggested that what it said about compulsory mediation may be in need of review by the courts. In this he would no doubt have found support from, amongst others, Dr Ahmed of Leicester University, who in 2012 suggested that what *Halsey* had to say about compulsory mediation was obiter (which in my view it was) and as such had left intact the High Court's decisions in *Shirayama*

---

[12] SI 2011/1133.

[13] *Halsey* at [10].

[14] Eg *Carleton (Earl of Malmesbury) v Strutt & Parker* [2008] EWHC 424 (QB); *Hickman v Blake Lapthorn* [2006] EWHC 12 (QB); *Daniels v Commissioner of Police of the Metropolis* [2005] EWCA Civ 1312; *PGF II SA v OMFS Company 1 Ltd* [2013] EWCA Civ 1288, [2014] 1 WLR 1386.

Shokusan Co Ltd v Danovo Ltd[15] and *Guinle v Kirreh*,[16] where compulsory mediation had been ordered, as good law.[17]

Sir Alan's judgment was given in the case of *Wright v Wright*.[18] The case concerned a dispute between two former business associates. It featured something that the civil and family courts are becoming ever more familiar with: individuals who by reason of financial circumstance are unable to afford legal representation. Sir Alan, as I am sure you all know, is a keen supporter of mediation and since his retirement from the Bench continues his support as the Chairman of the Civil Mediation Council. You may also be aware that Sir Alan considers that mediation is a route that every reasonable litigant should pursue. As he put it in *Egan v Motor Services (Bath) Ltd* in 2007, a litigant who did not pursue mediation when they had the chance to do so would have to be 'completely cuckoo'.[19]

The problem Sir Alan identified in *Wright v Wright* was that where litigants act in person it is markedly more difficult for the court to encourage them to seek to mediate their dispute. They are too close to the dispute and unable to take the detached view that a lawyer can take in assessing whether to mediate. He raised the question whether it was time for the courts to revisit *Halsey*. He put it this way,

> My ... concern is that the case shows it is not possible to shift intransigent parties off the trial track onto the parallel track of mediation. Both tracks are intended to meet the modern day demands of civil justice. The raison d'être (or do I simply mean excuse?) of the Ministry of Justice for withdrawing legal aid from swathes of litigation is that mediation is a proper alternative which should be tried and exhausted before finally resorting to a trial of the issues. I heartily agree with the aspiration and there are many judgments of mine saying so. But the rationale remains a pious hope when parties are unwilling even to try mediation. Judge Thornton attempted valiantly and persistently, time after time, to persuade these parties to put themselves in the hands of a skilled mediator, but they refused. What, if anything, can be done about that? You may be able to drag the horse (a mule offers a better metaphor) to water, but you cannot force the wretched animal to drink if it stubbornly resists.

---

[15] *Shirayama Shokusan Co Ltd v Danovo Ltd* [2004] 1 WLR 2985 (ChD).

[16] *Guinle v Kirreh* (3 August 1999, unreported).

[17] M Ahmed, 'Implied Compulsory Mediation' (2012) *Civil Justice Quarterly* 151 at 161.

[18] *Wright v Wright* [2013] EWCA Civ 234.

[19] *Egan v Motor Services (Bath) Ltd* [2007] EWCA Civ 1002, [2008] 1 WLR 1589 at [53].

I suppose you can make it run around the litigation course so vigorously that in a muck sweat it will find the mediation trough more friendly and desirable. But none of that provides the real answer. Perhaps, therefore, it is time to review the rule in *Halsey v Milton Keynes General NMS Trust* [2004] EWCA Civ 576, [2004] 1 WLR 3002, for which I am partly responsible, where at [9] in the judgment of the Court (Laws and Dyson LJJ and myself), Dyson LJ said:

> 'It seems to us that to oblige truly unwilling parties to refer their disputes to mediation would be to impose an unacceptable obstruction on their right of access to the court.'

Was this observation obiter? Some have argued that it was. Was it wrong for us to have been persuaded by the silky eloquence of the *éminence grise* for the ECHR, Lord Lester of Herne Hill QC, to place reliance on *Deweer v Belgium* (1980) 2 EHRR 439?

See some extra-judicial observations of Sir Anthony Clarke, The Future of Civil Mediations, (2008) 74 *Arbitration* 4 which suggests that we were wrong. Does CPR 26.4(2)(b) allow the court of its own initiative at any time, not just at the time of allocation, to direct a stay for mediation to be attempted, with the warning of the costs consequences, which Halsey did spell out and which should be rigorously applied, for unreasonably refusing to agree to ADR? Is a stay really 'an unacceptable obstruction' to the parties right of access to the court if they have to wait a while before being allowed across the court's threshold? Perhaps some bold judge will accede to an invitation to rule on these questions so that the court can have another look at Halsey in the light of the past 10 years of developments in this field.

The view expressed in *Wright v Wright* is one that chimes to a certain degree with comment by other judges regarding *Halsey* since it was handed down. My predecessor as Master of the Rolls, Sir Anthony Clarke, in a speech to the Second Civil Mediation Council National Conference in Birmingham in May 2008[20] discussed the Article 6 part of the *Halsey* judgment. In his view, 'we can safely say' that 'there may well be grounds for suggesting that *Halsey* was wrong on the Article 6 point'.[21] He based this conclusion on two points. First, the fact that compulsory mediation existed in other Council of Europe Member States, such as Belgium and Greece; and secondly an understanding of mediation—unlike arbitration—as

---

[20] A Clarke, 'The Future of Civil Mediation' (2008) 74 *Arbitration* 419.
[21] ibid 422.

forming part of court proceedings.[22] Foreshadowing both Dr Ahmed and Sir Alan Ward, he went on to note that this aspect of *Halsey* was obiter and suggested how the question of compulsion could be revisited by the courts.[23]

I see the force of both Lord Clarke's points, which, as I have mentioned, have now been reinforced by recent developments in Europe. But whilst it is undoubtedly true that compulsory mediation exists in the legal order of Council of Europe Member States and in other common law jurisdictions (Spain,[24] France,[25] Italy,[26] the USA,[27] Canada,[28] and Australia[29] to name but a few) this, of itself, is not proof that ordering parties to mediate or forfeit their access to the court would not, *in certain circumstances*, breach Article 6 or equivalent US, Canadian or Australian constitutional rights of due process. As far as I am aware, apart from the recent ECJ judgment, the issue has not been litigated in other jurisdictions. Accordingly, the fact that compulsory mediation exists in some jurisdictions is not determinative of its legality.

As for the second point made by Lord Clarke, that mediation is different in quality from arbitration because it is an integral part of the civil procedure process, it does not necessarily follow that compulsory mediation is compatible with Article 6. It all depends on the nature of the court's order for mediation. In his view, at worst, an order to mediate delays trial if mediation is unsuccessful. I accept that the form of compulsory mediation that he appeared to be describing (namely, where courts order parties to mediate but do not penalise parties for not taking part in mediation so that at worst, trial is delayed)[30] would certainly not fall foul of Article 6. The position would be quite different if the mediation order expressly stated that, if the parties refused to mediate, they would be prevented from litigating their dispute; a point that Lord Phillips, then

---

[22] ibid 422.

[23] ibid 422.

[24] See ec.europa.eu/civiljustice/adr/adr_spa_en.htm.

[25] See ec.europa.eu/civiljustice/adr/adr_fra_en.htm.

[26] See ec.europa.eu/civiljustice/adr/adr_ita_en.htm.

[27] Alternative Dispute Resolution Act (28 USC) s 652, as noted in Clarke at 421.

[28] For the approach to compulsory mediation in New South Wales see S Prince, 'Mandatory Mediation: the Ontario Experience' (2007) *Civil Justice Quarterly* 79.

[29] For the approach to compulsory mediation in New South Wales see B Tronson, 'Mediation orders: do the arguments against them make sense?' (2006) *Civil Justice Quarterly* 412.

[30] Clarke, 422–423.

Lord Chief Justice, also advanced in a speech he gave in India in 2008 on mediation. As he put it:

> What if you say—unless you attempt mediation you cannot continue with your court action. In quite a lot of jurisdictions mediation is ordered by the court on this basis.

> I think that if a litigant in Europe was subjected to such an order, refused to comply with it and was consequently refused the right to continue with the litigation, the European Court of Human Rights at Strasbourg might well say that that he had been denied his right to a trial in contravention of Article 6.[31]

So, if Lord Clarke was suggesting that mediation does not breach Article 6 because it is an integral part of the civil procedure process, I would say that this does not necessarily mean that compulsory mediation is compatible with Article 6. It all depends on the terms of the court order for mediation. In considering how the court might approach the question whether to compel parties to mediate, Lord Phillips noted how this was a question that came within the scope of active case management.[32] As such it was subject to the CPR's overriding objective of dealing with cases justly.

On this basis, the central question is whether requiring parties to engage in mediation furthers the overriding objective. It should be noted that the overriding objective is consistent with and was drafted in the light of Article 6. In some cases compulsory mediation would not further the overriding objective; in others it would do so. Lord Clarke's approach is not as far from my own position as might immediately appear to be the case, as it implicitly accepts that there may well be cases where compulsory mediation would breach Article 6 notwithstanding his view that mediation is an integral part of the procedural process.

In any event, I remain of the view that I expressed *in Halsey* that, whatever the Article 6 position may be, the real question is not whether or not a power exists to order mediation. Rather, it is whether or not the court should exercise the power. I remain in the 'carrot' camp: it is one thing to compel parties to consider mediation, it is another to frog march them to the mediation table and deny access to the courtroom if they refuse. The judgment of the

---

[31] N Phillips, 'Alternative Dispute Resolution: An English Viewpoint' (India, 29 March 2008) 13, available at www.judiciary.gov.uk/Resources/JCO/Documents/Speeches/lcj_adr_india_290308.pdf.

[32] Clarke, 423.

ECJ in *Rosalba Alassini* does not rule that compulsory mediation will never breach Article 6. I remain of the view that in some circumstances, for example, where the costs of mediation would be very high (and it is noteworthy that in the *Rosalba Alassini* case the compulsory mediation was free), compelling a party to mediate could still perhaps be considered to be a denial of access to justice.

Perhaps the real reason why compulsory mediation troubles me is that forcing individuals who do not feel ready or able to do so raises an ethical issue. Can it be right that parties who have exercised their right to go to court can be *forced* to sit down with the individual they believe to have wronged them to try to find a compromise which might leave them worse off than had they had their day in court? It is not the role of the law to force compromise upon people who do not want compromise, either directly or indirectly, through forcing them to engage in a mediation process. Parties who have a strong case and who seek vindication rather than compromise should not be denied their day in court. With this in mind, it is my strong view that the courts should not order compulsory mediation. I am bolstered in that view by both a recent decision by the Court of Appeal—not this time by Sir Alan Ward—and by the outcome of the Jackson Costs Review.

First, the Court of Appeal. In October last year, in *PGF II SA v OMFS Company 1 Ltd* it considered an issue arising from the guidance *Halsey* gave that had not previously arisen for determination. The question was

> what should be the response of the court to a party which, when invited by its opponent to take part in a process of alternative dispute resolution ... simply declines to respond to the invitation in any way?[33]

Halsey had, of course, given guidance on how it should respond to an unreasonable refusal to participate in ADR. Did silence in the face of an offer the mediate amount to a refusal and if so was it, or could it amount to, an unreasonable refusal?

Briggs LJ gave the leading decision and in doing so summarised the *Halsey* principles, including its rejection of the idea that the court should compel parties to mediate, none of which were in dispute in the proceedings.[34] He then went on to answer the questions in the case by way of, as he put it, a 'modest extension to the principles and guidelines set out in the *Halsey* case'.[35] He did so by holding

---

[33] [2013] EWCA Civ 1288 at [1].
[34] ibid at [22]ff.
[35] ibid at [35].

that silence in the face of an invitation to participate in ADR is, as a general rule, of itself unreasonable, regardless whether an outright refusal to engage in the type of ADR requested, or to do so at the time requested, might have been justified by the identification of reasonable grounds.

He noted that there may be 'rare cases where ADR is so obviously inappropriate that to characterise silence as unreasonable would be pure formalism'.[36]

The decision in *PGF* is an important endorsement of the approach taken in *Halsey*. There was no suggestion in the Court's discussion that the time may be right to revisit the question of compulsion. Moreover the decision emphasised the voluntary nature of mediation and the court's role as being one to encourage it. It noted, for instance, that *Halsey* was a decision that sent out an important message to litigants, namely, that they had to engage with serious invitations to participate in ADR and that it was all the more important to do so in the present economic climate.[37] This was entirely consistent with the message sent out by *Halsey*: the court's approach should be one of robust encouragement. This was, by its very nature, another judgment embodying that approach.

Briggs LJ referred to, and endorsed, guidance given by the then recently published *Jackson ADR Handbook*,[38] chapter 36 of which is devoted to ADR. It recognised that mediation is a highly effective means of achieving a satisfactory resolution of many disputes, while noting that it was not a universal panacea and that the process can be expensive and, on occasions, result in failure.[39] It concluded that ADR had a 'vital role' in resolving civil disputes, but that—in line with *Halsey*—it should not be compulsory, although courts should, in appropriate cases, encourage mediation by pointing out its benefits, by directing parties to meet and/or discuss mediation and by using *Ungley* orders in the field of clinical negligence.[40] As I explained in my judgment in *Halsey*, this has been happening in the Admiralty and Commercial Court since 1993 where, in cases identified as suitable for mediation, judges may make an order directing the parties to attempt ADR.

The Jackson Review noted that, despite the promotion of ADR since the Woolf reforms came into force in 1999, its benefits were

---

[36] ibid at [34].
[37] ibid at [56].
[38] (Oxford, 2013).
[39] Jackson *Review on Costs*, para 3.2.
[40] ibid para 3.4.

still not properly appreciated or understood. While there had been an ongoing debate on the issue of compulsory mediation, there had been a failure to properly educate both the legal profession and litigants so as to enable them to appreciate the benefits of mediation. In order to tackle this problem it recommended that there should be a 'serious campaign' to educate lawyers, litigants and particularly the public and small businesses of those benefits. One way in which this was to be done was through the production of an authoritative handbook that would, in a straightforward and comprehensive manner, explain ADR and provide practical help to those resorting to it. As I have said, the *Jackson ADR Handbook* is an excellent guide to ADR which I hope in time will become the first port of call for any lawyer or litigant.

Where does this leave us? It seems to me that ten years on from *Halsey* not all that much has changed. The ECJ has settled the Article 6 issue for cross border cases, but its decision has not altogether settled the question of whether compulsory mediation breaches Article 6, still less the question whether mediation should be compulsory in our system. For the time being, English and Welsh courts will continue to follow the *Halsey* guidance on the impact of a refusal to mediate on orders for costs and lawyers and parties, under the guidance of the *Jackson ADR Handbook*, will continue to be taught the benefits of, and means to carry out, voluntary mediation. So what is next for mediation?

CONCLUSION—WHERE NEXT?

It is one thing to look back; it is another entirely to attempt to forecast the future. So what I have to say now should be viewed with a good degree of caution. There are, however, two areas where developments are likely, each of which seem to me to suggest that *Halsey* will have a continuing influence: the Briggs Review and the continuing growth in the number of litigants-in-person.

First, the Briggs Review, or to give it its proper title, *The Chancery Modernisation Review*.[41] This was a review of practice and procedure in the High Court's Chancery Division. As part of a fundamental review of the Division, it examined the approach that

---

[41] See www.judiciary.gov.uk/Resources/JCO/Documents/CMR/cmr-final-report-dec2013.pdf.

ought to be taken to ADR. In this regard it noted—and here we can see shades of both the *Ungly Order* that *Halsey* endorsed and Lord Clarke's idea that mediation orders could become a regular feature of the case management timetable—how the Chancery Division had played an important part in encouraging the use of ADR. It had done so through the development of a standard form of case management directions, which included 'an optional provision for a one month stay' to enable the parties to try to resolve their dispute through formal or informal ADR.[42] It recommended, however, that reforms could take this form of encouragement further. It did so through advocating a change in approach to case management. Rather than being a process which has as its predominant aim that of managing cases to trial, it recommended that a more holistic approach should be taken: that, no doubt consciously echoing the Woolf reforms, there should be a culture change. Case management should focus on 'the management of the dispute resolution process as a whole'[43] and not just managing cases to trial.

This change in approach was said to have five advantages.[44] It would enable the court to encourage a more widespread appreciation of the need to treat ADR as an integral part of the process. It was to enable the court and parties to build ADR into the process through enabling them to better identify when ADR may be most beneficial. In this sense it would help to combat one of the problems identified in the post-*Halsey* case law, ie, when is the right time for the court to encourage mediation and for the parties to engage in it. For instance, as HHJ Coulson had, noted in *Nigel Witham Ltd v Smith & Isaacs* in 2008:

> It is a common difficulty ... trying to work out when the best time might be to attempt ADR or mediation. Mediation is often suggested by the claiming party at an early stage. But the responding party, who is likely to be the party writing the cheque, will often want proper information relating to the claim in order to be able to assess the commercial risk that the claim represents before embarking on a sensible mediation. A premature mediation simply wastes time and can sometimes lead to a hardening of the positions on both sides which make any subsequent attempt of settlement doomed to fail. Conversely, a delay in any mediation until after

---

[42] Lord Justice Briggs, *The Chancery Modernisation Review: Final Report* (December 2013) 67.

[43] ibid 68.

[44] ibid at 68.

full particulars and documents have been exchanged can mean that the costs which have been incurred to get to that point themselves become the principal obstacle to a successful mediation. The trick in many cases is to identify the happy medium: the point when the detail of the claim and the response are known to both sides, but before the costs that have been incurred in reaching that stage are so great that a settlement is no longer possible.[45]

The culture change sought to be introduced by the Briggs Review would bring an end to this problem. This would lead to the third benefit, which was to enable the court to time its encouragement by giving directions to maximise the prospect that mediation would succeed, while minimising costs. Fourthly, it would enable the court to develop greater expertise in dealing with issues of timing and the choice of type of ADR. Finally, it was suggested that greater familiarity would enable the court to innovate and to develop new forms of ADR. To facilitate these goals the judiciary and ADR providers were to engage in regular and constructive discussions.

The culture change recommended was to be implemented through changes to the case management process. For instance, the parties were to be required to focus their minds on a number of questions, such as: whether ADR was suitable; which type of ADR was preferable; when would it be most cost-effective; whether private or court provided ADR was preferable; whether the court could take any steps to facilitate ADR, eg by assisting the parties to exchange information. All of this would, however, be facilitative, and would require the court to monitor the progress of any ADR process throughout the life of the proceedings at each case management conference. Compulsion was ruled out, as it was in the Jackson Review. Greater engagement by both the court and the parties was to become the norm.

Equally, it was to be implemented through changing a particular perception that stubbornly refuses to go away: that unless mediation produces a settlement it is viewed to have failed. The Review noted, however, that this view was misconceived. Mediation may not result in settlement, but it may well result in the narrowing of issues, in enabling parties to identify and focus on the real issues in dispute and thereby enable the litigation to be conducted more economically, efficiently, and proportionately.[46] In this way both the

---

[45] *Nigel Witham Ltd v Smith & Isaacs* [2008] EWHC 12 (TCC) at [32].
[46] ibid 72.

immediate parties and the justice system as a whole benefits. The latter because the court can ensure that those of its resources which are not required to be used as a consequence of the narrowing of the issues during the mediation can be expended on other litigants. In a time when court and party resources are under pressure as a consequence of our age of austerity, it is all the more important for both the parties and the court to take such steps as can reduce the cost of litigation.

The Briggs Review is in the process of being implemented. The manner in which its recommendations regarding ADR are implemented will, I am sure, be watched with interest. I have no doubt that they are recommendations that are not Chancery-specific. They are likely to be of equal utility throughout the civil justice system. If they succeed in Chancery, I would anticipate that they will be implemented more widely, to the benefit of all.

What then of litigants-in-person? I mentioned earlier the view expressed by Sir Alan Ward that it may be that the only way to ensure that mediation is seriously considered by litigants-in-person is to introduce compulsory mediation. This need not be an expensive process. There are court-based mediation schemes, which work well. As the *Jackson Handbook* notes, there has, for instance, been a Small Claims Mediation Scheme in place since 2007. It deals with 10,000 claims a year and has a 70 per cent success rate. A similar scheme operates in the Court of Appeal. It has a 40 per cent success rate.[47] Some might argue that there should be compulsory mediation for litigants-in-person. But I am not convinced that compulsory mediation (to which I am opposed for reasons already given) could properly be restricted to litigants-in-person. Such a restriction might suggest an inequality of treatment based on whether an individual had a lawyer or not. That would seem to me to be impermissible. In the words of the Heilbron-Hodge civil justice review:

'... it is fundamental to the basic precepts of any civilised society that no section of the community should be excluded from their just entitlement to equality before the law, whether or not circumstances necessitate their using the courts ... Public confidence in the administration of the law has to be maintained.'[48]

---

[47] *Jackson Handbook*, 7–8.
[48] H Heilbron and H Hodge, *Civil Justice on Trial—A Case for Change*, Joint Report of the Bar Council and Law Society (1993) 4–5.

Compulsory mediation for some, but not for others, would suggest we had abandoned a commitment to equality before the law.

I imagine that Sir Alan's response to this fear would be to suggest that what was sauce for the goose was sauce for the gander, and that everyone should be subject to the possibility of court-ordered compulsory mediation. It seems to me that the better view, one consistent with *Halsey* and the Briggs Review, is that the court should adopt a more active approach to encouraging ADR. In addition to the practical steps that Briggs Review recommended, there are other steps that should be taken. More information regarding ADR and its benefits should be provided to litigants-in-person and the court staff should be trained to provide it. We should consider introducing an ADR-focused case management conference into the procedural timetable. This would not be a mediation, but would rather be a forum in which the judge could take the parties through the various forms of ADR and consider with the litigants-in-person which, if any, was most suitable to their case and encourage them to take up any available opportunity to engage in such a process.

The courts will have to adapt so as to ensure that litigants-in-person are able to secure the benefits of mediation. The latter, at least, is an issue that is likely to become more pressing. If the court is to continue to secure equality of arms, it will have to take steps to ensure that ADR is as readily available an option for litigants-in-person as it is for legally represented litigants. How we do this is an open question at the present. It is, however, a question that is, in all likelihood, going to be answered against the background of the continuing influence of *Halsey*.

26

Arbitration versus Litigation[*]

THE RESPECTIVE ADVANTAGES of arbitration and litigation have been debated for many years. As a barrister, I arbitrated and litigated. As a judge, I was concerned with litigation. As Head of Civil Justice from 2012–2016, I was particularly keen to improve civil litigation in England and Wales. Despite the improvements to the efficiency of civil litigation brought about by the Woolf and Jackson reforms, the fact remains that litigation in this country is terrifyingly expensive for all but the seriously wealthy; and, in many cases, it is still far too slow.

My litigation days are now behind me. Although I hope that arbitration days lie ahead of me, I think I am well placed to express a reasonably balanced view of the respective advantages of arbitration and litigation at the present time.

The advantages of litigation in this country are not difficult to find. First, in our Commercial Court, Chancery Division and TCC, you have access to some of the finest judges in the world. Indeed, our government never tires of saying that our judges are the very best in the world. Of course, much of that is politician-speak uttered either in order to rubbish the judges of the European Court of Human Rights or the Court of Justice of the European Union; or to schmooze judges who are disgruntled about their pay, pensions and working conditions. Whatever the politicians may say, there undoubtedly are fine judges in other jurisdictions too. But our High Court judges (and those who sit in the appellate courts above them) are excellent judges whose integrity is unquestionable and unquestioned. They include specialist judges who have a real understanding of most of the areas of law in which parties might consider arbitrating. If you litigate, you are very likely to have your claim determined by an excellent judge.

[*] Lecture at Addleshaw Goddard, 4 May 2017.

Secondly, litigation is generally cheaper than arbitration. I regard the recent increase in court fees for lower value claims as deeply regrettable. But in the large cases, these are of little or no significance. The court fees are dwarfed by the fees paid to arbitrators (not to mention the lawyers). And judges come for free.

Thirdly, the consensual nature of arbitration usually means that an arbitral tribunal will usually lack the power to add or substitute a party to the proceeding without the consent of all the existing parties. For the same reason, absent agreement of the parties, an arbitral tribunal has no power to consolidate its arbitration with another in order to bring before one tribunal related claims for determination. This is an issue which some arbitral institutions have sought to address by including provisions within their rules which provide for consolidation of arbitrations in specified circumstances: for example, Article 10 of the ICC Rules.

Fourthly, judges have greater powers to enable them to press on with litigation robustly than, in the absence of consent, are available to arbitrators. The summary procedures provided by CPR Part 24 to judges are not available in arbitration. Judges have greater case management powers to impose their will on the way a case is conducted so as to ensure that this is done efficiently and proportionately. They also have powers to deal with default which, save with the consent of the parties, are not available to arbitral tribunals. These include the power to strike out a claim or defence for failure to comply with rules or orders. In the absence of agreement, the tribunal's powers to ensure the proper and expeditious conduct of the arbitration are more limited than those of a judge. But this limitation is more apparent than real. The tribunal has considerable powers to control the conduct of an arbitration. It can make an award dismissing the claim where there has been delay in pursuing it, admittedly only if there has been inordinate and inexcusable delay on the part of the claimant in pursuing the claim; and if the delay gives rise or is likely to give rise to a substantial risk that it is not possible to have a fair resolution of the issues in the claim, or the delay has caused or is likely to cause serious prejudice to the respondent. Furthermore, the arbitral tribunal can make peremptory orders where there has been default and direct that the party in default shall not be entitled to rely on any allegation or material which is the subject-matter of the order and/or draw adverse inferences from the act of non-compliance and/or make an award on the basis of the materials provided and/or make an order as to the payment of costs. These are considerable powers. It is true that if the tribunal wishes to make a more draconian order (such as striking out the claim or defence for non-compliance), it cannot do so. It must instead apply to the court for an order requiring a party to comply with a peremptory order made by the tribunal. To summarise, in the absence of the agreement of the parties, an arbitral tribunal has fewer powers than a judge to manage the conduct of proceedings in an efficient and proportionate manner. But as against that, the powers that are available to arbitrators are sufficient to enable them in most cases to conduct references effectively.

I have mentioned the excellence of most of our judiciary. But you may have to wait rather a long time before you get your first class judgment. That may be because an unacceptably long period of time elapses between the date of issue of proceedings and the date of the hearing. It may also be because some judges take too long over their judgments. If you are unlucky, you may have to wait many months and occasionally more than a year between the conclusion of the hearing and the delivery of the judgment. On the other hand, in an urgent case the courts system will give you an early hearing date; and most judges deliver their judgments with expedition.

You must be wondering when I intend to get round to identifying the advantages of arbitration. There obviously are substantial advantages. Otherwise, why do so many commercial entities opt for arbitration? Despite the additional cost, they generally consider the advantages of arbitration to outweigh the advantages of litigation. The advantages of arbitration are well known. First, privacy and confidentiality. Although the reasons for this preference are not always obvious, some parties prefer to know that their disputes will be determined out of the public gaze. This preference is not limited to cases in which sensitive business practices are disclosed. I doubt whether that is often the reason. Rather, it is simply that parties generally prefer to have their disputes resolved away from public gaze.

Secondly, they can often choose the tribunal which they consider, for whatever reason, is best suited to resolve their dispute. The reason may be that the dispute is highly technical and it is preferable to have an expert tribunal rather than a less expert judge who has to rely on expert evidence to resolve the dispute. This seems to me to be a powerful factor in favour of arbitration in certain types of case. Another reason may be that the parties do not have confidence in the courts. We believe (with justification) that our judges are good and of great integrity. But foreign parties may be unpersuaded of this. They may be accustomed to a system whose judges are not independent and who may even be, or are suspected of being, corrupt. Where parties are from different countries, arbitration may be preferable to litigation if neither party is willing to submit to the jurisdiction of the national court of the other. By agreeing to arbitration, the parties may be more confident that they will receive equal treatment. They may also want an arbitrator from their jurisdiction because he or she understands the commercial culture of that country. I am afraid to say that they may also want an arbitrator from their jurisdiction to look after their interests for a more ignoble reason. For them, this is an additional advantage, although it is not one that can be articulated, still less applauded.

Another advantage of arbitration is that it can be more flexible than other dispute resolution mechanisms. If the dispute requires urgent resolution, the parties can choose a tribunal who can act quickly, even within a matter of days. As arbitration is consensual, the parties can also choose what they consider to be the most suitable procedure. They are not tied to formal rules of court. They can be represented by anyone of their choice, because they are not limited by rules limiting representation to persons with particular legal qualifications.

A further important advantage of arbitrating in this country is the extensive enforceability of the award. As a result of various conventions, arbitral awards are recognised and enforceable in many more countries than English court judgments. Thus although there are certain treaties under which court judgments are enforceable, these are more limited than the New York Convention. For example, there is no treaty between the UK and the USA for the enforcement of judgments, but both countries have acceded to the New York Convention. This is a major advantage. Having incurred the cost of proceedings, the successful party wants to be in a position to enforce the award if that proves to be necessary.

Finally, there is the fact that in this country the Arbitration Act 1996 gives only a very limited opportunity for a party to challenge an award. The grounds are lack of substantive jurisdiction (section 67); serious irregularity (section 68); or an appeal on a question of law arising out of the award (section 69). As is well known, the ability to appeal is very limited indeed. This is not the place to enter into the fascinating debate about whether Parliament went too far in restricting the right of appeal. No doubt this has led to a striking reduction in the number of commercial cases coming to our courts. But all the evidence strongly suggests that most commercial parties want finality. Of course, they usually want an arbitral tribunal which they can be confident will conduct the arbitration efficiently and fairly. They want to have confidence in the process. But subject to these conditions, they want a final decision so that they can move on. They are rarely interested in contributing to the development of the corpus of English commercial law. There is less finality in the first instance decision of a judge in our courts. An appeal will lie if the losing party can show that it has a real prospect of success on an appeal. This is not a stringent requirement. The appeal process can take up to two years. It seems to me that this is a real advantage of arbitration. In enacting the 1996 Act, Parliament clearly recognised this.

When, as Master of the Rolls, I was Head of Civil Justice, I saw part of my role as being to encourage the use of our courts for the resolution of commercial disputes. Although I am now trying to build an arbitration practice, I remain of the view that there are some disputes which, viewed objectively, are better suited to resolution in our courts. The most obvious examples are disputes on points of law or fact whose public resolution may be used as a precedent for other cases. But there are many disputes whose resolution, even viewed objectively, is better suited to arbitration. And there are many disputes which, for understandable and perfectly rational reasons, parties prefer to have determined in private by an arbitral tribunal over which they have greater control than they have over a court. It is important that parties should have the choice.

27

Arbitration After Brussels I Reform[*]

INTRODUCTION

IT IS A real pleasure to have been asked to deliver this year's Lord Mustill Lecture. It is, however, a daunting pleasure. There can be few people whose knowledge of arbitration begins to approach that of Michael Mustill. I had the pleasure of appearing before him when I was at the Bar, but sadly only once. As a tribunal, he was both delightful and formidable. He wore his brilliance lightly. He has left a legacy of important principled judgments. You can find many of them in the law reports. They are expressed with great clarity. It was a great loss to the law that he retired as a judge when he was at the height of his powers and after sitting all too few years in the House of Lords. The pastures of academic life and the world of arbitration were too tempting for him to resist.

In addition to having been a great judge, he is also a great Yorkshireman. He is intensely proud of his Yorkshire roots (as I am of mine). He has a great love of the Dales, and Nidderdale in particular. We both started our education in an establishment in north Leeds, long-since disappeared, called Ingledew College. He once described it to me as a school for the sons of Yorkshire gentlemen. I think that our teachers would have been incredulous if they had been told that two of their little boys had scaled the heights of the judicial ladder. I could spend the next 45 minutes reminiscing about Leeds in the 1950s, but I think you would find the connection between that and arbitration somewhat tenuous. So I shall resist the temptation.

I thought that I would take as my subject this morning the recently concluded reforms to the EU legislation which started with the 1968 Brussels Convention on Jurisdiction. As many of you will know,

---

[*] Lord Mustill Lecture, Chartered Institute of Arbitrators, Leeds, 11 October 2013.

this convention was substantially replaced by the 2001 Brussels I Regulation 44/2001 which came into force on 1 March 2002; and this regulation has now been recast by Regulation 1215/2012 in a number of important respects, some of which are relevant to arbitrations within the EU. I want to concentrate on the impact of the recast regulation on arbitrations.

But before doing so, I want to remind you of something that was noted in a lecture given to your East Anglian branch in June 2012 by Professor Beresford Hartwell. In a detailed elaboration of the development of arbitration from John Locke to the present day, he noted something that was said in the *Law Quarterly Review* about the establishment in 1892 of the City of London Chamber of Arbitration—the precursor to the London Court of International Arbitration. The City of London Chamber was, it was said, 'to have all the virtues which the law lacks.' It was 'to be expeditious where the law is slow, cheap where the law is costly, simple where the law is technical, a peacemaker instead of a stirrer-up of strife.'[1]

Any form of alternative dispute resolution should aspire to achieve these goals so that those who wish to resolve their disputes practically and amicably are able to do so, both in their private interests and in the wider public interest. I shall be considering whether, by excluding arbitrations from the scope of the recast Regulation, the EU Member States have undermined the achievement of these goals, or at least whether they have lost the opportunity of further promoting them.

There may be those who think that arbitrations which have an international dimension are the preserve of the City of London and that an audience in this great city of people who are interested in arbitration would think that the Regulation has nothing to do with them. It would be idle to pretend that London is not the arbitration capital of England and Wales; it is one of the arbitration capitals of the world. But I know that there is a great deal of important commercial arbitration activity in the regions, and that much of it has an international dimension. So I hope that what I have to say will be considered by you to be relevant to what you do.

Let me first set the scene.

---

[1] *Law Quarterly Review*, cited in G Beresford Hartwell, '"Arbitration Reborn" or "Arbitration—the New Alternative to Adjudication"' (1 June 2012) 2, available at www.anglian-arbitrators.org.uk/pdf/2012/01-06-12-Geoffrey-Beresford-Hartwell-paper.pdf.

BACKGROUND TO REFORM

The 1968 Brussels Convention had a simple aim. It was to provide a single, uniform, regime governing the mutual recognition and enforcement of national judgments across what were then the six countries that formed the European Economic Community. The idea was not only to reduce the time and cost of enforcement across the nascent internal market, but also to increase legal certainty and mutual trust between the EEC Member States.[2] The Convention was not, however, intended to have anything to do with arbitral proceedings. That fact could not have been more clearly emphasised by Professor Jenard, the rapporteur for the committee that prepared the Convention and author of the explanatory report that accompanied it. In that report he described arbitration's exclusion from its scope in this way:

> There are already many international agreements on arbitration. Arbitration is ... referred to in Article 220 of the Treaty of Rome ... the Council of Europe has prepared a European Convention providing a uniform law on arbitration, and this will probably be accompanied by a Protocol which will facilitate the recognition and enforcement of arbitral awards to an even greater extent than the New York Convention. This is why it seemed preferable to exclude arbitration. The Brussels Convention does not apply to the recognition and enforcement of arbitral awards ...; it does not apply for the purpose of determining the jurisdiction of courts and tribunals in respect of litigation relating to arbitration for example, proceedings to set aside an arbitral award; and, finally, it does not apply to the recognition of judgments given in such proceedings.[3]

On the face of it, that seemed fairly clear: the Convention and arbitration had nothing to do with each other. Things are, however, not always as simple as they first appear. This became apparent when the United Kingdom acceded to the Convention in 1979. Prior to its accession, the UK government questioned whether arbitration was in or out. As the Schlosser Report put it at the time, the UK view was that it was out. The original signatories did not agree. In the words of the Report:

> The point of view expressed principally on behalf of the United Kingdom was that [the arbitration exclusion] covers all disputes which the parties

---

[2] *Jenard Report: Report on the 1968 Brussels Convention* (1968, published in [1979] OJ C 59/2) preliminary remarks; Chapter 4.2.

[3] *Jenard Report* (1968) at Chapter III, IVD, available at www.dutchcivillaw.com/legislation/jenard011.htm.

had effectively agreed should be settled by arbitration, including any secondary disputes connected with the agreed arbitration. The other point of view, defended by the original Member States of the EEC, only regards proceedings before national courts as part of 'arbitration' if they refer to arbitration proceedings, whether concluded, in progress or to be started.[4]

The question was left unresolved. Perhaps they should have referred the question itself to arbitration. That there was a difference of opinion would however have repercussions, particularly following the imaginative activities of a certain Mario Franzosi.

Franzosi was, and perhaps still is, an Italian advocate. In 1997 he made a suggestion that would ultimately bring the relationship between arbitration and the Convention into sharp focus, while at the same time serving to promote use of the Italian courts. He invented the so-called Italian torpedo.[5] The idea was simple, but devastating. Imagine, as Franzosi did, that you wish to engage in a little patent infringement. You want to get away with it for as long as possible. More than that, you want to put yourself in the best bargaining position with the patent holder. Rather than wait for the patent holder to bring proceedings against you in his home jurisdiction, you pay a visit to the Italian courts. You launch a pre-emptive strike and issue proceedings for a declaration of non-liability in Italy. In this way you entangle the patent holder in lengthy, costly litigation in a jurisdiction not renowned for the speed with which it resolves disputes. Moreover, the operation of the *lis pendens* rule in the Convention meant that, because you launched the proceedings first, if the patent holder issues proceedings in his home jurisdiction—which we assume is a Convention state—they are subject to a stay. The court first seised takes precedence. The cynicism of this approach was nicely summed up by Trevor Hartley recently, when he noted how, even if the patent infringer

> were bound to lose in the end, they could keep the Italian proceedings going for many years, thus buying themselves time to negotiate a settlement. According to Franzosi, it did not matter if the Italian courts had no jurisdiction, since it would take a long time for a definitive decision to this effect to be obtained.[6]

---

[4] *Schlosser Report: Report on the Convention* (1979, published in [1979] OJ C 59/71) at [62].

[5] M Franzosi, 'Worldwide Patent Litigation and the Italian Torpedo' (1997) 7 *European Intellectual Property Review* 382.

[6] T Hartley, 'Legislative Comment—Choice-of-court agreements and the new Brussels I Regulation' (2013) 129 *LQR* 309, 310.

As he went on to point out, Franzosi was not wrong on the delay point. The torpedo action in *Trasporti Castelletti v Hugo Trumpy*[7] took eight years to resolve.[8]

The application of Franzosi's idea was not limited to patent disputes. It was applied more generally. Nor could it be thwarted by the incorporation of an exclusive jurisdiction clause in a contract. This was made clear by the Court of Justice of the European Communities in *Erich Gasser GmbH v MISAT Srl.*[9] Gasser and MISAT had entered into a commercial contract which contained an exclusive jurisdiction clause providing for disputes arising under the contract to be brought in Austria. A dispute arose. Taking its lead from Signor Franzosi, MISAT launched its torpedo and issued proceedings in Italy. Gasser then issued proceedings in Austria. Would the torpedo work? The European Court decided that it did. By reason of the operation of the *lis pendens* rule, the Austrian court was obliged to stay the proceedings in that court pending the outcome of the Italian proceedings. The court first seised took precedence until it determined whether it had jurisdiction. The Convention could, as Franzosi had suggested, be used or misused to frustrate the vindication of rights. What value would an exclusive jurisdiction agreement have in these circumstances? What was readily evident about this approach to the question of jurisdiction was that the Convention (and later the Regulation) had created a situation whereby contracting parties could in reality abuse the justice system.

And what held good for exclusive jurisdiction clauses and patent disputes was also applied to arbitration clauses. If contracting parties could issue proceedings in one Regulation State in breach of an exclusive jurisdiction clause, they could do the same in breach of an arbitration clause. But before I come to arbitrations, I need to say something about the anti-suit injunction.

One way in which a litigant could historically protect legal proceedings properly brought in one court from abusive proceedings brought before another court was through the use of an anti-suit injunction. For a long time, the English courts have been willing in appropriate cases to grant such injunctions. The old Court of Chancery was, for instance, often called upon to issue what in the pre-1870 era was known as a common injunction. This injunction

---

[7] C-159/97 *Trasporti Castelletti v Hugo Trumpy* [1999] ECR I-1597.

[8] Hartley, 'Legislative Comment—Choice-of-court agreements and the new Brussels I Regulation'.

[9] *Erich Gasser GmbH v MISAT Srl* [2005] QB 1.

would enjoin litigants from taking steps in litigation before the old common law courts. It could thus be used to stop parties taking points, or even re-litigating issues, already decided in other proceedings. The injunction was an order directed to the litigant and not the court. The modern anti-suit injunction is, in a sense, the successor to this old equitable jurisdiction. It is of particular value in cases where a litigant issues proceedings in one jurisdiction where proceedings are properly on foot in another. In principle, it could be deployed to stop litigants attempting to bring proceedings whose aim was to frustrate the proper conduct of litigation before English courts. It could be invoked to uphold choice of jurisdiction clauses, which designated England as the proper forum for resolving disputes. Unfortunately, the European Court of Justice in the case of *Turner v Grovit*[10] held that the use of such injunctions by the English courts was incompatible with the aim of promoting the mutual trust that underpinned the Convention. This was the case even where it was plain that the proceedings were brought in another Member State in bad faith and for the purpose of obstructing and delaying the English proceedings. It was held that a prohibition by a court of the commencement or continuation of proceedings in another country was tantamount to interference with the jurisdiction of the foreign court and, so far as the Convention was concerned, incompatible with the principle that, consistently with the necessity for mutual trust between the legal systems of the contracting states that underpinned the convention, the jurisdiction of a court could not be reviewed by a court in another contracting state other than in exceptional circumstances.

It was, therefore, clear from *Gasser* that the Convention was no respecter of exclusive jurisdiction clauses. The *lis pendens* rule took precedence. And it was clear from *Turner* that the English courts could not issue anti-suit injunctions to protect proceedings properly brought in England and Wales from abusive actions brought in the rest of Europe.

So how does this jurisprudence apply to arbitrations? Arbitration seemed to have been excluded from the scope of the Convention and Regulation No 44/2001: see Article 1(2)(d). On the face of it, therefore, there was nothing to stop an English court issuing an anti-suit injunction to enjoin a contracting party from issuing torpedo proceedings arguably in breach of an arbitration clause. This wider

---

[10] C-159/02 *Turner v Grovit* [2005] 1 AC 101.

view accorded with that expressed by the UK at the time of its accession. The opposing narrower view was that there was nothing to stop arbitration agreements being undermined in the same way as exclusive jurisdiction clauses had been. The issue of the scope of the exception of arbitrations was resolved by the ECJ on a reference by the House of Lords in the *West Tankers* case in 2009.[11] The narrow approach to the arbitration exception favoured by the original signatories was held to be correct.

The specific issue in *West Tankers* was whether an anti-suit injunction could be issued in order to protect English arbitration proceedings arising from a tanker collision in Italy. The charterparty was governed by English law and contained a clause providing for arbitration in London. West Tankers Inc (the claimant) commenced arbitration proceedings in London. The defendant issued separate proceedings in Italy against the claimant. The question in both proceedings was essentially the same. West Tankers Inc, which had commenced the arbitration proceedings, applied for an anti-suit injunction to protect them by stopping the Italian proceedings. The High Court granted the relief sought by the claimant. On appeal, the House of Lords referred to the ECJ for a preliminary ruling on the question whether an anti-suit injunction granted in order to give effect to an arbitration agreement was consistent with Regulation 44/2001. The ECJ held that it was incompatible with the Regulation for a court of a Member State to make an order restraining a person from commencing or continuing with proceedings before the courts of another Member State on the ground that such proceedings would be contrary to an arbitration agreement. The reasoning was that, in the dispute before the Italian court, the subject-matter of the defendant's claim for damages fell within the scope of Regulation 44/2001, and not the arbitration. The existence and applicability of the arbitration clause merely constituted a preliminary issue which the court seised of the matter had to decide when considering whether it had jurisdiction. The Italian proceedings came within the scope of the Regulation given their subject matter. Any question of the applicability of the arbitration exception to the Regulation was, therefore, one on which the Italian court could rule. In essence the situation was the same as it was for exclusive jurisdiction clauses. The consequence was inevitable: logic prohibited the use of anti-suit

---

[11] *West Tankers Inc v Alliance SpA* [2009] 1 AC 1138.

injunctions, which were again criticised as running contrary to the development of mutual trust between Regulation States.[12]

In the result, as a consequence of *Gasser*, *Turner* and *West Tankers*, a situation had arisen whereby contracting parties could evade their contractual obligations both as to forum of choice and arbitration by issuing torpedo actions. Contracting parties could no longer rely on the prospect that, having agreed to arbitrate their disputes, they could look forward to a cost-effective and speedy form of dispute resolution. Arbitration had in effect become subject to the cost and delays of legal proceedings. From West Tankers' perspective, the European court's judgment meant that they might obtain an arbitral award in England in their favour, but would then be subjected to litigation all over again in respect of the same issue, but this time in Italy.

THE GREEN PAPER AND THE RECAST REGULATION

In 2009 (the year in which the *West Tankers* decision was given), the European Commission published a Green Paper which contained a review of the 2001 Regulation.[13] Unsurprisingly both the operation of the *lis pendens* rule and the relationship between the Regulation and arbitration formed part of the discussion. In respect of the former, four options for reform were canvassed: releasing the court designated in a choice of jurisdiction agreement from the obligation to stay proceedings where it was the court second seised; giving the designated court priority to determine issues concerning jurisdiction; suspending the lis pendens rule when there are proceedings on the merits in one jurisdiction and parallel proceedings for declaratory relief in another jurisdiction; and finally, providing a power to award damages for litigating in breach of a choice of jurisdiction agreement. The problem of torpedo actions was to be dealt with one way or the other.

When it came to arbitration, the Green Paper took a less sanguine view than had been taken in 1979. The seemingly simple exclusion of arbitration was said to be difficult. The problem of parallel

---

[12] For an overview see A Ippolito and M Adler-Nissen, 'West Tankers revisited: has the new Brussels I Regulation brought anti-suit injunctions back into the procedural armoury?' (2013) 79(2) *Arbitration* 158.

[13] Green Paper on the Review of Council Regulation (EC) No 44/2001 on jurisdiction and the recognition and enforcement of judgments in civil and commercial matters, COM(2009) 175 final.

proceedings dealing with the same issues was particularly acute.[14] A number of potential reforms were suggested, ranging from the removal or partial removal of the arbitration exclusion, to the provision of special jurisdictional rules that would confer exclusive jurisdiction on the courts of Regulation States that were designated as the place of arbitration, to the introduction of a rule rendering unenforceable a court judgment reached in parallel proceedings where there was an arbitral award enforceable under the New York Convention.[15] The reintroduction of the anti-suit injunction was not seriously considered. The bold proposals to bring arbitration within the scope of the Regulation did not, however, survive scrutiny. The majority of the national reports considered by the Commission's Study Group on the proposed reform opposed these proposals, not least because they said that any extension would undermine the efficacy of the New York Convention.[16]

Following the Study Group's report, further work was done. This resulted in a fully fleshed out proposal from the Commission in 2010 that in my view correctly noted the vexatious effect of parallel proceedings and made the point that they undermined the utility of arbitration proceedings. The Commission proposed that arbitration should be brought within the scope of the Regulation, but only to a limited extent. A specific rule was to be introduced, which would put an end to parallel proceedings by giving priority to the courts of the Regulation State of the seat of the arbitration or to the arbitral tribunal.[17] The courts of any other Regulation State would have to stay any proceedings before them as soon as either of the former was seised of the matter. The torpedo would thus be defused just as it would be so far as exclusive jurisdiction clauses were concerned. That was the suggestion, and you might have thought it was a good one.

---

[14] Green Paper at 8.

[15] Green Paper at 8–9.

[16] For a summary of views see B Hess, T Pfeiffer, and P Schlosser, *Report on the Application of Regulation Brussels I in the Member States*, Study JLS/C4/2005/03, 52ff, available at ec.europa.eu/civiljustice/news/docs/study_application_brussels_1_en.pdf.

[17] Proposal for a Regulation of the European Parliament and of the Council on jurisdiction and the recognition and enforcement of judgments in civil and commercial matters (Recast) COM (2010) 748 final 2010/0383 (COD) (Brussels, 14.12.2010) at 5, 9 and see draft recital 11 and 20, draft art 29(4) 'Where the agreed or designated seat of an arbitration is in a Member State, the courts of another Member State whose jurisdiction is contested on the basis of an arbitration agreement shall stay proceedings once the courts of the Member State where the seat of the arbitration is located or the arbitral tribunal have been seised of proceedings to determine, as their main object or as an incidental question, the existence, validity or effects of that arbitration agreement.'

As I have already mentioned, what finally emerged was the recast Regulation 1215/2012. The Italian torpedo, in so far as parallel proceedings in breach of exclusive jurisdiction clauses was concerned, was effectively destroyed by the new Regulation's recital 19 and Articles 29–34. Those new provisions give precedence to the courts of the chosen jurisdiction. Other jurisdictions must stay any proceedings commenced before their courts until the court chosen by the contracting parties declares it has no jurisdiction.

Arbitration did not fare so well. It was not to receive the same protection as exclusive jurisdiction clauses. The difference in treatment between exclusive jurisdiction clauses and arbitration clauses is surprising. One would have thought that contractual autonomy would have led to the same outcome in the two cases. If the principle of mutual trust between Regulation states was paramount, surely it should have carried the same weight in both cases. Upholding a contractual bargain as to where and by what means a dispute is to be determined by staying proceedings issued in breach of the bargain ought to be clear, simple and easy to apply. It also has the benefit of providing effective protection to one party against wasteful, costly and vexatious litigation by the other whose object is to undermine the integrity of the agreed dispute resolution process. The Regulation states went down this route in upholding exclusive jurisdiction clauses, but did so only to a limited extent in relation to arbitration clauses.

Arbitration was not to be brought within the recast Regulation. An opportunity was, therefore, missed to make a real improvement. Rather than provide a clear means by which the integrity of arbitration clauses could be protected, a minimalist approach was adopted. There were to be no substantive changes regarding arbitration. The recast Regulation would do no more than re-assert the exclusion of arbitration from it by the retention of Article 1.2(d) (which explicitly states that the Regulation does not apply to arbitration) and a new recital 12. I feel constrained to say that this recital is not expressed in language of crystal clarity. In view of its importance, I propose to read it out:

> This Regulation should not apply to arbitration. Nothing in this Regulation should prevent the courts of a Member State, when seised of an action in a matter in respect of which the parties have entered into an arbitration agreement, from referring the parties to arbitration, from staying or dismissing the proceedings, or from examining whether the arbitration agreement is null and void, inoperative or incapable of being performed, in accordance with their national law.

A ruling given by a court of a Member State as to whether or not an arbitration agreement is null and void, inoperative or incapable of being performed should not be subject to the rules of recognition and enforcement laid down in this Regulation, regardless of whether the court decided on this as a principal issue or as an incidental question.

On the other hand, where a court of a Member State, exercising jurisdiction under this Regulation or under national law, has determined that an arbitration agreement is null and void, inoperative or incapable of being performed, this should not preclude that court's judgment on the substance of the matter from being recognised or, as the case may be, enforced in accordance with this Regulation. This should be without prejudice to the competence of the courts of the Member States to decide on the recognition and enforcement of arbitral awards in accordance with the Convention on the Recognition and Enforcement of Foreign Arbitral Awards, done at New York on 10 June 1958 ('the 1958 New York Convention'), which takes precedence over this Regulation.

This Regulation should not apply to any action or ancillary proceedings relating to, in particular, the establishment of an arbitral tribunal, the powers of arbitrators, the conduct of an arbitration procedure or any other aspects of such a procedure, nor to any action or judgment concerning the annulment, review, appeal, recognition or enforcement of an arbitral award.

The first issue that arises is one that does not go to the substantive terms of the recast Regulation, but rather to the issue of when it comes into force. It was published in December 2012. It does not, however, become operative until 10 January 2015.[18] It is, of course, not unusual for legislation to come into force at a point in time after its enactment. But it is perhaps less common for legislation that purports to remedy an obvious identified defect to sit on the books for such a long period of time before it becomes operative. While there may be good reasons for delay regarding the recast Regulation's other provisions—and on that point I say nothing—it is difficult to see what justification there is for such a delay regarding arbitration.

All that the delay in commencement appears to do is give an extended period of grace—if it that is the right way to put it—to those who wish to abuse the present position. That is hardly ideal from the perspective of those who believe that international arbitration provides a more economic, efficient and less technical approach to dispute resolution than litigation in the courts perhaps allows. This defect is, fortunately, time-limited. But the *substantive* issues that

---

[18] Articles 75 and 76 take effect in January 2014.

arise concerning the recast Regulation's approach to arbitration are not. The first and perhaps most important such issue is that of how the recast Regulation deals with the problem of parallel proceedings. To what degree does it torpedo the torpedo? The answer is not entirely straightforward.

It could be said that the recast Regulation has taken the sting out of the torpedo, as Ippolito and Adler-Nissen have suggested.[19] In itself this is not the most ringing of endorsements, but it is better than nothing. At best it seems that, if recital 12 does its job, it will ensure that a torpedo action will not be able to stop arbitral proceedings in their tracks. It does not, however, put a stop to abusive legal proceedings whose object is to frustrate the proper conduct of an arbitration. It does not prevent a contracting party from commencing such proceedings, obtaining a declaration that an arbitration clause is invalid and then going on to obtain a judgment on the substantive merits in a jurisdiction other than that agreed as the seat of the arbitration. Nor does it put an end to the possibility that a contractual dispute results in competing arbitral and court awards.

At its highest, recital 12 protects the integrity of arbitration clauses in the following way. Assume that a torpedo action is launched seeking a declaration that the arbitration clause is invalid. Under the present regime, by reason of the court first seised rule, the party wishing to rely on the clause cannot bring proceedings in the seat of arbitration supportive of the arbitral process. It seems that this will not be the case under the recast Regulation. The opening two paragraphs of recital 12 permit parallel legal proceedings to be pursued. They appear to allow the courts of the seat of arbitration to support the arbitral process notwithstanding an adverse decision on the validity of the arbitration clause from the court seised of the torpedo action. According to the recital, any decision made in the torpedo action as to the validity of the clause falls outside the Regulation and is a matter for the law of the seat of arbitration to determine. Assuming a prior positive judgment from the seat of the arbitration, it is difficult to envisage how the judgment from the torpedo action could be enforced. In the words of Ippolito and Adler-Nissen,

> The beneficial effect of these [aspects of recital 12] is that while parallel court proceedings may still be brought in foreign courts, such proceedings will not prevent arbitral proceedings from commencing or continuing with support from the courts of the seat.[20]

[19] Ippolito and Adler-Nissen, 160.
[20] Ippolito and Adler-Nissen, 168.

Let us pause here for a moment. It is a clear benefit of the reforms that torpedo actions will no longer prevent arbitrations taking place. For supporters of the arbitral process that is a benefit to be welcomed. But how much of a benefit is it? Two major problems remain as a result of the possibility that torpedo actions can still be pursued in parallel to the arbitral process. First, one contracting party can still commence a torpedo action and involve the other party in costly, time-consuming duplicative legal proceedings. The scope remains for a party to indulge in the cynically obstructive conduct which brought the torpedo action into disrepute. Some of the victims of such behaviour may not have the financial muscle to withstand the loss of cash flow that it may engender; others may give up pursuing their contractual rights in despair, because they cannot afford the cost of battling on a second front with the prospect of victory receding, possibly years into the future. These are serious concerns.

But there is a second problem. The fact that arbitral and legal proceedings may be pursued in parallel gives rise to the possibility that competing inconsistent decisions may be produced. An arbitral award may be made in favour of one party. The court proceedings may result in a decision in favour of the other party. This leaves the unsatisfactory situation that the arbitral award could be subject to enforcement under the New York Convention, while the substantive judgment of the court would be subject to enforcement under the recast Regulation: a situation no better than we had in the nineteenth century, when the common law and equity courts could and did reach contrary decisions on the same cause of action.

One possible answer to this problem is that, since recital 12 of the recast Regulation acknowledges the primacy of the New York Convention, the conflict between the arbitral award and the court decision should be resolved in favour of the former. Unfortunately, it is not clear that this is the effect of the recast Regulation: it does not provide any guidance as to how the courts of Member States should resolve such issues. Equally, it is unclear whether the existence of an adverse court decision on the merits may form the basis of a refusal to enforce the arbitral award under the New York Convention on public policy grounds under article VI of that Convention. Would enforcement violate a fundamental value or principle of justice to satisfy a public policy refusal, as Hay has suggested?[21] Much will depend on the circumstances, and different approaches may be taken in different Member States.

---

[21] P Hay, 'Notes on the European Union's Brussels-I "Recast" Regulation—An American Perspective' (2013) 1 *The European Legal Forum* 7.

There are other problems too. Suppose that one court decides that an arbitration agreement is invalid, and goes on to give judgment on the substance of the dispute; but the arbitrators disagree and they proceed to give a contradictory award on the substance of the dispute. A court in a third Regulation state will be faced with two conflicting decisions, both potentially entitled to recognition and enforcement, namely the judgment under the Regulation and the award under the New York Convention. As Clifford Chance point out in their briefing note of January 2013, recital 12 suggests that this third court must reach its own conclusion as to whether the arbitration agreement is null and void, inoperative or incapable of being performed for the purposes of the New York Convention. If it decides that the arbitration clause is invalid, all that remains is the court judgment; but if the court decides that the arbitration clause is valid, perhaps the arbitral award takes priority because of the precedence given to the New York Convention. Ultimately, the Court of Justice of the EU will have to decide which decision carries the day.

CONCLUSION

The recast Regulation has certainly made significant improvements, but these are mainly confined to giving proper effect to exclusive jurisdiction clauses. A great opportunity was lost to do the same in relation to upholding and giving full effect to arbitration clauses. The torpedo action will still have the power to undermine the arbitral process. The justification for doing so seems to be rooted in the desire of the Member States to proclaim their trust in each other. If that is indeed the justification, it seems to me that the maintaining of that laudable principle is too high a price to pay in this particular context. As I have sought to explain, the price is increased cost and complexity of litigation accompanied by the vice of potentially conflicting decisions on the same issues by different tribunals. I use the word 'vice' advisedly. Contentious proceedings, whether arbitral or in court, are costly. They should be a last resort when all attempts at alternative means of resolution have failed. If parties are driven to arbitrate (or litigate), they should at least know that the process on which they are embarking is an effective method of resolving their dispute. From the perspective of contracting parties, it is difficult to think of any reason which can justify a process which sanctions parallel proceedings on the same issue with the attendant costs and delays, not to mention the possibility of contrary conclusion.

To these obvious disbenefits there should be added the uncertainty as to enforcement of judgments to which I have just referred.

It appears to be certain that it will take a considerable time and a degree of jurisprudence from the court in Luxembourg before these, and no doubt other, issues are resolved. Perhaps it is fortunate that the recast Regulation will not come into force until 2015. Let us hope that during the next two years some at least of the problems to which I have referred may be tackled and resolved.

This takes me back to where I started: the *Law Quarterly Review* article and its account of the merits of arbitration. The problem with the recast Regulation is that, as I have sought to explain, it diminishes the utility of this vital method of dispute resolution in cases where there is a European dimension. What benefit is there if a contracting party has an arbitral award in its favour, but has also had to be involved in legal proceedings in another jurisdiction? Arbitration is said to be expeditious where the law is slow, cheap where the law is costly, and simple where the law is technical. But the recast Regulation does not seem to promote those advantages. Quite the contrary. There is a real danger that contracting parties may choose to forgo arbitration where legal proceedings are commenced in breach of an arbitration clause, rather than incur the cost of two sets of proceedings and run the risk of competing awards and the potential uncertainty of enforcement? Would it not have been better if arbitration agreements had been treated as being analogous to exclusive jurisdiction clauses?

This raises a final consideration, which I intend to leave you with. From its origin in 1965 the Regulation was intended to increase legal certainty, to increase mutual trust between the member states and further the development of the internal market. The first and last of those aims go hand-in-hand, as they both focus as much on the users of the market as they do on the member states. Without adequate protection of the arbitral process legal certainty is undermined, as is the proper functioning of the internal market. If we are to further these objectives, more substantive steps are likely to have to be taken than those set out in the recast Regulation. Might it be time for us all to consider the prospect of a short EU instrument dedicated to protecting the integrity of the arbitral process from abusive conduct so that contract parties are properly held to their agreements, and to the benefits of arbitration?[22]

---

[22] For a similar suggestion, although one focused on further reform of the recast Regulation, see NA Dowers and D Holloway, 'Brussels I Recast Passed' (2013) 16(2) *International Arbitration Law Review* N-18, N-21.

Part V

Personal

28

*School Speech Day**

W HEN I GREW up in Leeds in the 1950s, it was a black and grimy city. No financial services then; no posh shops, no Harvey Nicks; no smart restaurants. Just honest pubs (not of the gastro variety) and fish and chip shops and factories where people made things. Leeds was proud of the success of the Yorkshire cricket team and Leeds United at soccer. We did not play soccer at Leeds Grammar School for Boys. Instead, we played the gentlemen's game of rugby union. Soccer was not called 'the beautiful game' in those days.

This magnificent building was built between 1853 and 1858. It is huge in size and flamboyant in the detail of its design and decoration. It matched the mood of the mid-Victorian era when the breasts of the citizens of the country, county and city were bursting with confidence and pride. The building served to house various council offices and to act as the new courtroom facility for the city. It continued to house the law courts until that awful red brick building was opened in the 1970s round the corner.

It occupies a very special place in my heart. As I was growing up, I used to come to concerts here on Saturday nights with my parents. My brother and I used to sit behind the timpani in the orchestra rises. And then once a year, there was the Speech Day. I cannot pretend that I can recall any scintillating or riveting speech. In fact, I can recall nothing whatever about any of the speeches. I suspect that the main hope was that they would not go on for too long. I recently met one of my school contemporaries who went on to have an unblemished career as a solicitor in Leeds. He told me that one year he was so bored by the speeches that he started stuffing the vents of the organ pipes with programmes. He did not tell me what effect this had on the quality of the sound emitted by the organ, and I hope that that you will not be inspired by this bit of school history to do something similar today.

* Prize-giving Speech at Grammar School at Leeds Town Hall, 2011.

Later, when I was reading for the Bar, I would come here from time to time to watch the great advocates of the day performing in what were still known as the Assize courts. I was drawn to the murder trials, incredulous that people who looked so ordinary in a courtroom could do such terrible things to each other in their lives outside.

My first personal brush with the Law arose in a rather strange way. I had parked my father's car in a side street near the University and went to the Library to do some work. No yellow lines were marked on the road and no parking restrictions were indicated. On returning to the car, I discovered that I had been summonsed to appear before the magistrates on a charge of obstructing the highway. I was outraged and was determined to contest this monstrous charge. Surely the law could not be so unfair and, yes, stupid. The fateful day duly arrived. There was I standing nervously outside the courtroom in this very building where we are now. The rather nice police prosecutor came up to me and asked if I was still bent on fighting the case. I said that I was. He then asked me if I was aware of a court decision whose name he gave to me. He gently suggested that I read the decision in the Law Reports and then reflect on my position. With a sense of foreboding, I went off to the library. I started to read the law report and with that sickening feeling that we have all experienced in the pit of the stomach when we suddenly discover some disaster, I realised that I had no defence. I returned to the court with my tail between my legs, apologised to everyone for wasting their time and pleaded guilty. No doubt, the magistrates thought that I was a rather naive and over-enthusiastic student. They imposed the minimum possible fine.

I learnt two important lessons from that experience. First, always do your homework and come to any test (whatever it is) fully prepared. Second, always be polite and try so far as possible not to allow yourself to be tempted into confrontation and aggression. As a barrister, I always found that my most successful cross-examinations were conducted gently and with as much charm as I could muster. People lower their guard when treated in this way. An aggressive cross-examination is far more likely to be met with an unyielding response. I am sure that I would have been fined more heavily if I had behaved in a cocksure and arrogant way.

You will be relieved to know that I do not intend to deliver a sermon. But I do want to say a few words about ambition. When harnessed in a sensible and realistic way, I think that ambition is a force for good. But all-consuming and unrealistic ambition can be damaging, if not destructive. We all have skills and talents and I think that everyone should be encouraged to make the most of what they have, but in a sensible and realistic way. I was passionate about cricket when I was a teenager. I practised constantly in the nets at school and endlessly with my brother in our back yard at home. Sadly, my talent was no match for my passion. One day, I was selected to play for the Colts XI against Drax Grammar School. My father bought me some gleaming white new kit. I was terribly excited. We travelled to Drax. I was no 5. Unfortunately, the other side had a demon swing bowler. Our first three wickets fell within no time. In I marched to face this bowler. I had never seen anything like it. So prodigious was his swing that I missed the first four balls, but by some miracle they also missed the wicket. In fact, I was nowhere near the ball on any occasion. I also missed the fifth ball, but this time ... well, you've guessed it. That awful death rattle.

I still recall the humiliation. Many times, I have relived this match in my mind, changing the facts exorbitantly, so that I scored a century, took many wickets as well as some blinding catches. But I never played for the school again. I had to accept my limitations.

So what did I do? Well, after a classics degree at Oxford I went to the Bar in London and practised mainly in the field of construction and engineering law. That was very surprising to those who knew me, because I am not practical and not interested in technical things. But that was the direction in which the Chambers of which I was a member went and I joined in. I just got on with being a barrister. For many years, it never crossed my mind that one day I might become a judge. But one day, I was asked by the Lord Chancellor if I would like to be a high court judge and I said yes. There were no competitions in those days. I have learnt that life sometimes takes you where you never planned to go. And that applies to your personal life too. A chance meeting and you fall in love and your life is changed forever.

So I became a judge, successively a High Court Judge, a judge of the Court of Appeal and some 18 months ago a Justice of the Supreme Court. The work has been immensely varied and utterly fascinating. The Law affects the lives of every one of us. It includes criminal cases of the kind that obsess the tabloid press; family cases; commercial and tax cases; accident, libel, privacy and intellectual property cases and many others besides. In the Supreme Court, we spend a lot of our time dealing with human rights cases and disputes between the citizen and the State. I thought that I would spend a very few minutes talking about the work that we do in the Supreme Court, because it is an important feature of our national life and, although its work is open to view, who we are and what we do are still enveloped to some extent in mystery.

The court is in Parliament Square opposite Big Ben. Anyone can walk through our doors and can sit in on an appeal and see what goes on. I would encourage all of you on your next visit to London to come and see us. You will be most welcome. I assure you that everyone is very friendly. The proceedings are also televised on a Sky TV Channel. We hear cases which raise points of general public importance. Some of the most difficult cases are ones where we have to decide whether a government decision is unlawful. Occasionally, when we say that what the government has decided to do is unlawful, Ministers become very frustrated and complain about these unelected and unaccountable judges making it impossible to govern the country. It is also not uncommon for us to be heavily criticised by the Press. We simply have to put up with that and just get on with the next case. We can't answer back. So the job is demanding and carries huge responsibilities, because we are the final court of appeal. It is a far cry from my first appearance before the Leeds magistrates in this wonderful building all those years ago.

I was at Leeds Grammar School in the 1950s. Our links with Leeds Girls' High School were minimal, and corporal punishment (both by teachers and school prefects) was rife. Despite these relics of the nineteenth century, I received an excellent education for which I remain very grateful to this day. I visited the Grammar School at Leeds earlier today and spoke to some of the senior students about the Law. I recall when I was in the 6th form being addressed by a visiting High Court Judge and being excited by what he said about the Law. I hope that I aroused a degree of excitement in some of the students I met today. I was hugely impressed by their enthusiasm and brightness as I was by the remarkable quality of the facilities.

Although I have lived in London for some 45 years now, my Yorkshire roots remain strong. I still miss the Dales. You should all count yourselves as fortunate to have grown up in this part of the country and to have been educated at such a fine school.

It is time I stopped talking and got down to the serious business of the day. There seem to be a lot of prizes to get through.

29

*How My Classical Education Has Affected My Life**

L IKE DAVID COPPERFIELD, I propose to start at the beginning. I was born in Leeds. My father showed no signs of knowing any Latin, although I suspect that he must have learnt some of the rudiments in the early years of the twentieth century; so far as I know, he had never studied Greek. My mother, who was educated at a German-speaking school in Sofia, Bulgaria, was able to recite a sentence or two from one of Cicero's Catiline speeches. I remember that she pronounced Cicero as 'Tsitsero', and patientia as 'patsientsia'. These were not particularly auspicious parental acorns from which a classical oak tree might emerge. I was sent to the local preparatory school. There, incredibly as it must now appear, I started to learn Latin at the age of about five. My classical studies (I use the term loosely) comprised, in the main, daily recitations in unison of declensions and conjugations of some of the leading nouns and verbs.

At the age of eight, I went to Leeds Grammar School. There I started Latin from scratch all over again. The same old declensions and conjugations, but now these were occasionally laced with the odd short sentence about military manoeuvres. When I was 13, I started studying ancient Greek. From then on, it seemed that I was inexorably destined for the Classical Sixth form, where, in addition to Latin and Greek, I studied Ancient History. I eventually won a scholarship to read law at Wadham College, Oxford.

For the most part, the subjects were taught at school in a most unimaginative way. If you had a good memory and a reasonably clear mind, you could perform well, and earn much praise from teachers and parents alike. There was, however, one teacher who did have a wonderful ability to inspire. He certainly aroused a love of Latin

---

* Speech at inaugural meeting of Legal Group of Classics for All in March 2015.

and Greek in me. His name was Tom Beckett, otherwise known as 'Froggy'. He enthused me, in particular, as I recall, with a love for some of the Greek tragedies, and for Latin poetry. I have a specific recollection of a certain ardour for the love poems of Catullus. There was another teacher, who had an unhealthy interest in young boys. He concentrated on erotic passages in the poetry of Horace, and was at great pains to explain to us what they meant and in some detail. Much time, however, was spent translating difficult English prose and verse into passable Latin and Greek prose and verse, as well as in the daunting business of performing translations (unseen) from Latin and Greek into English. I was certainly no budding Sophocles or Virgil.

On my arrival at Wadham, I was summoned to see the Warden, Sir Maurice Bowra. He advised me to read Honour Mods in Classics. His simple argument was that, if I intended to spend my working life in the Law, there would be plenty of time to learn about the Law later on. The young in those days did not argue with those in authority, and I accepted his advice without demur. The result of my doing so was that I became a barrister knowing very little law indeed, and, no doubt to the chagrin of some of my clients, I had to learn on the job. But to revert to Oxford, I completed the Mods and the Greats courses, and enjoyed both very much indeed. I do not regret that I did not study law, although I do not doubt that, at least in my early years at the Bar, I would have had a better grasp of legal principles if I had studied law than I did have.

I enjoyed immersing myself in the texts of the Greek and Roman writers. I had my doubts about the usefulness of studying the contributions of different scholars to the textual criticism of a word here, and a phrase there. There was a good deal of rote learning in this part of the course. I refined such skills as I possessed in the art of translating from Greek and Latin to English, and became reasonably competent at it. I greatly enjoyed the Ancient History; the philosophy less so. I was uncomfortable with the combination of Plato and Aristotle on the one hand, and the Oxford school of linguistic analysis on the other. So far as I could tell, the rigours of linguistic analysis did little more than make me aware of the need to think about the way in which we use language, but it did not enlighten me about real solutions to any of the fundamental problems that have engaged the attention of philosophers for centuries.

As I approached the end of my career at Oxford, I began to ponder what I wanted to do with my life. I had so enjoyed, in particular, Ancient History, that I was seriously tempted to explore the possibility of becoming an academic classicist. Eventually, I decided to revert to the Law.

I do not propose to give you an account of my career first as a barrister, and later as a judge. Well, what influence, if any, has my classical education had on my career? Over the past century at least, a disproportionately large number of barristers and judges have had an intensive classical education. The traditional route for entry into the profession was classics via public school and Oxbridge. In recent years, the proportion has declined, but there are still a fair few of us. But it is worth asking why so many classicists have been successful in the Law and have achieved high judicial office. Part of the answer, I am sure, is simply that 40 years ago, clever pupils who were not scientists were strongly encouraged to take the classics route. What were such pupils to do when they emerged from many years of Latin, Greek and Ancient History? If they decided not to become a professional classicist, then the Law was an obvious potential suitable candidate. It is worth recording what Sir Hugo said to the young Daniel Deronda shortly before Daniel went up to Cambridge. He said:

> ... I should like you to do yourself credit, but for God's sake don't come out as a superior expensive kind of idiot, like young Brecon, who got a Double First, and has been learning to knit braces ever since. What I wish you to get is a passport in life. I don't go against our university system: we want a little disinterested culture to make head against cotton and capital, especially in the House; My Greek has all evaporated: if I had to construe a verse on a sudden, I should get an apoplectic fit. But it formed my taste. I daresay my English is the better for it.

Here, there seems to be a rather grudging acceptance of the possibility that a classical education can be of some benefit even to someone who does not become a Don. In this passage, he raises, albeit fleetingly, the question: what direct and tangible benefit does a classical education confer on a person? In what ways can a grounding in Latin and Greek and classical civilisation enhance a person's prospects of earning a living, or generally improve the quality of his or her life?

I shall concentrate on its influence on my work as a lawyer. What skills does a good lawyer need to possess? When Mr Micawber was studying the Law, David Copperfield asked him how he was getting on:

> 'My dear Copperfield', he replied, 'To a man possessed of the higher imaginative powers, the objection to legal studies is the amount of detail

which they involve. Even in our professional correspondence', said Mr Micawber, glancing at some letters he was writing, 'the mind is not at liberty to soar to any exalted form of expression. Still it is a great pursuit. A great pursuit.'

Charles Dickens was no great lover of lawyers, but in my view the words he put into the mouth of Mr Micawber do encapsulate some, but only some, of the essential qualities of a good lawyer. An able lawyer certainly needs to have a clear analytical mind, to have a good understanding of language, and to be able to express himself with clarity and accuracy. As Mr Micawber says, there is often a great deal of detail to sift and classify. It is necessary at all times to keep an eye on the wood. It is true that the trees and the small bushes cannot be ignored, since the detail may be of critical importance. But it is vital never to lose sight of the overall objective. So Mr Micawber is right when he says that flights of fancy have little place in the Law. Someone who arrives at solutions by instinct alone is unlikely to be a good lawyer.

But I think that two important qualifications need to be made to Mr Micawber's observations. First, he is wrong to imply that what is required of a good lawyer is nothing more than a process of mechanistic, computer-like analysis. Law is not a science. This is because so much of it involves the meaning of words. It is surprising how often a document or a statutory provision is, at least arguably, capable of more than one meaning. When that happens, it will frequently be a matter of judgement to determine which is the better interpretation. But the process of interpretation must start, where it has always started, with a consideration of what the words mean. If, however, the literal interpretation is inconsistent with the plain intention of the draftsman, then it will have to give way.

The second qualification that I wish to make to the words of Mr Micawber concerns the language used by lawyers to express themselves. It is not always true to say that lawyers cannot resort to some 'exalted form of expression'. Certainly, lawyers should not indulge in loose, inaccurate language. Although purple passages of high-blown language are currently out of fashion, some of the finest prose ever written in the English language is to be found in the judgments of our greatest judges. It may be full of vivid imagery, but none the worse for that.

I am in no doubt that my classical education has helped me to analyse and understand the language used by others, and I hope also that I am able to express myself clearly and accurately. Of course, I cannot say that my analytical and linguistic skills would have been any different if I had had a different form of education. But I am sure that all those years of translating Latin and Greek into English and vice versa have left their mark. I am very sensitive to the way in which people use words, and I try to ensure that what I write is succinct, free from ambiguity and other uncertainty, and that it accurately reflects what I want to say. I have a real abhorrence of fudge and prolixity, and I suspect that this owes much to my Latin and Greek.

But I do not wish to give the impression that, so far as I am concerned, the only benefit of studying Latin and Greek has been to sharpen my ability to analyse language and (I hope) to express myself with accuracy and clarity. I think that Greek and Latin literature have also made me sensitive to language in a more general and less prosaic sense. There is much that is beautiful and elegant in Greek and Latin verse and prose. Although I do not think that I am capable of writing particularly elegant English prose, I think that I can recognise and appreciate good English, and I believe that, to some extent at least, this is as a result of my classical education.

I have concentrated on the effect of my classical education on me as a lawyer. I fear that, rather like Sir Hugo, my Greek and Latin have largely evaporated, and I too might have an apoplectic fit if I had now to translate a Shakespeare sonnet into Greek iambics or Latin hexameters. To be required now to do this in an examination would be a nightmare of serious proportions. I find it difficult to believe that this was something that I was able to do so many years ago. I did try to read book 6 of Thucydides when we were at Sicily a few years ago, but I was heavily dependent on the Loeb translation. I suspect that, with a great deal of effort, I would be able to retrieve something of what I once knew. Of one thing I am in no doubt: I was very privileged to have a thorough classical education, and I am grateful to Sir Maurice Bowra for the wise advice that he gave me.

I am delighted to be able to associate myself with Classics in Schools. The revival of Classics in schools is a cause for celebration. But much work remains to be done.

It gives me great pleasure to propose a toast to 'the Classics'.

30

*Valedictory**

THIS IS A very emotional moment in my life. There has been little time for reflection as I have rushed around doing one thing and another. But I have thought how lucky I have been to live in this great country. I wonder what my father's parents would have made of today. They came from Lithuania at the turn of the twentieth century. They were both 19 years of age. They had had little education and had little money. They were hoping to go to the US, but could not afford to get any further than Leeds. And my mother came from Bulgaria in 1939 at a time when most people in this country had probably not even heard of the place. Her mother spent six months in Bergen Belsen in 1944, something that she could hardly ever bring herself to talk about. I wonder what she would have made of today too. I keenly regret that my parents are not here today. Even at my age, I would have liked to bring them my achievements for their approval.

It is on an occasion like this that I feel a deep gratitude to this tolerant country for allowing my forebears to settle here and giving me and my family the opportunity to flourish here. I fervently hope that the events of recent weeks have not put that tolerance at risk. I am fearful that it is being put under strain by the xenophobia and dangerous forces of hate that have been unleashed in some quarters. I have faith in the fair-mindedness of the British people and believe that their tolerance will continue to shine through. But as a fall-back position (and it is always good to have a fall-back position) I may have an escape route. I think that, thanks to my mother, I may be entitled to apply for a Bulgarian passport.

I can still think of no better place to live than in this country. I am proud to have been able to give something back to it. Maintaining the Rule of Law is as important as it has ever been. Perhaps even more so today, as the executive arrogates to itself more and more

* Court of the Lord Chief Justice in July 2016.

powers. I hope that I have been able to make a modest contribution to maintaining the Rule of Law in my 23 years as a judge. I have been hugely privileged to have had a wonderful career.

There is so much that I shall miss about the RCJ. I confess that I shall not miss the endless meetings. We are in the grip of an epidemic of meetings to which there appears to be no known antidote. But I shall greatly miss the people who work here. Everyone is so friendly and helpful. I wondered what it would be like to be in charge of the Court of Appeal. I confess that I had a certain sense of fore-boding when I faced the serried ranks of 38 colleagues at my first plenary meeting some four years ago. I had been warned that they were independent-minded and could be difficult. I need not have worried. I could not have wished for a more supportive and colle-giate group of people. The work is hard and there has been the odd complaint. But overall, it has been a great and happy experience.

I cannot possibly mention all the people whom I would like to thank, including the staff who have worked so hard to support me and make the place function and all the clerks who have looked after me. But I must mention Peter Farr, my private secretary. He is the embodiment of wisdom and good judgement. He has become a good friend in whom I confide everything, well almost everything. Inevitably, there have been times when the going has been a little rough. Peter has always been there to calm me down and keep the show on the road. He is one of the kindest persons I have ever met.

Of my judicial colleagues, I must mention Martin Moore-Bick who has been a wonderful Vice-President of the Court of Appeal Civil Division. I have been able to delegate so much to him in the knowledge that he has an unerring feel for the right answer. He has taken a great weight off my shoulders. Michael Briggs has been my Deputy Head of Civil Justice and done great work to alleviate the pressures facing the Court of Appeal. He is a man of vision and drive who has helped me enormously in so many ways. And my thanks also go to their predecessors Maurice Kay and Stephen Richards for all their work.

I must also thank David Neuberger, who is a wonderful President of the Supreme Court. He has encouraged and supported me over the past few years in more ways than I can say. And I am grateful to him for many hours of delectable gossip, which is very necessary to keep one sane.

Finally, of the currently serving judges, John Thomas. We have worked together very closely for the last three years. I can say with-out fear of contradiction that he is a great Chief Justice. A reformer of real vision and a man of terrifying energy who keeps telling me that he is slowing down and like the rest of us not getting any younger. He has given me tremendous support in all that I have tried to do since becoming Master of the Rolls. For this I shall always be grateful.

I would also like to thank Igor Judge who was Lord Chief Justice during my first year as Master of the Rolls. It was Igor who first suggested that I should apply to be Master of the Rolls. I thought he must be joking. I told him that I was far too old. He brushed that objection aside with that combination of charm and firmness that brooks no opposition. Of course, he said, I was of exactly the right age. I am grateful to him for planting the idea in my mind.

I have left the hardest bit to the end. I have made many decisions in my life, but far and away the best and most important was to ask Jackie to marry me all those years ago. I knew she was the girl for me almost immediately and we were engaged within a few weeks. My professional life has been very exciting and stimulating. But I have been happiest when in her company, just doing the simplest of things. She has been my rock of support and my life mate. I have been so fortunate. And so fortunate to have a wonderful family, all here today. One of my grandsons has said that Grandpa has an interesting job and Grandma just tags along. How cruel children can be. Anyway, it's not true: I mean the bit about tagging along.

I do not intend to retire to cultivate my garden. I plan to be quite busy. But I do hope to be able to spend more time with her.

I am astonished and humbled by how many have come to say good bye today. I thank you all so much.

Part VI

Epilogue

31

*Changes in the Law in the Last 50 Years**

I T IS ALWAYS a great pleasure to come back to Leeds. I left for
London almost 50 years ago to make my way in the world. Leeds
has changed so much since I left and so has the Law and the legal
profession. The city is barely recognisable as the grubby (but fiercely
proud) place in which I grew up. The area round the River Aire
was considered to be a dangerous no-go area into which respectable people did not venture. It was certainly not a place to locate
smart offices or posh restaurants. Indeed, I don't think there were
any posh restaurants in those days. There were posh shops, but they
were nowhere near the River Aire or where Harvey Nicks now is;
the John Lewis store was not even a twinkle in anyone's eye; the site
now occupied by the arts centre was occupied by the largest council housing estate in Europe (the famous Quarry Hill flats). The city
had a famous and highly successful football team. That is another
change. The big civil trials were held in the Assize courts and conducted in uncomfortable, but rather grand courts in the Town Hall
(where the magistrates' courts were also accommodated). As you
know, in the 1970s the assize courts were replaced by the less than
wonderful building that now stands close to the Town Hall, which
no-one seems to like and whose future I suspect is in doubt.

This prestigious lecture series was established in memory of a
remarkable lawyer, John Munkman. He practised at the Bar here in
Leeds. He never took Silk. But he left his mark on the Law in a very
effective and enduring way. He was a prolific writer of seriously
important legal textbooks. He is perhaps best known for his seminal
books on *Damages for Personal Injury and Death* and on *Employer's
Liability*. These are both areas of the law which affect the lives of
huge numbers of ordinary people and which are far more difficult

---

* Munkman Lecture, 23 March 2017.

than fancy commercial lawyers would allow. Munkman had an ability to explain the principles in a clear manner which was readily understandable even to a first year law student. In 1950 he also wrote a book on the *Law of Quasi-Contract* (what we now call restitution). As if that were not enough, in 1951 he wrote a book called *The Technique of Advocacy* too. He died in 2000. I am truly sorry that I never had the good fortune to meet him.

My purpose this evening is not to muse nostalgically in a self-indulgent way about the world of 50 years ago. Rather, it is to describe objectively some of the changes that have taken place in the legal profession and the Law during my adult life. Sometimes, it is salutary to pause for breath, look back and see what has happened. As we shall see, the changes have been truly breathtaking.

I shall start with the legal profession. I shall concentrate on the Bar and Bench because that is what I know about. I have the added excuse that John Munkman was a barrister. In the late 1960s, there were about 2,000 barristers. There are now more than 12,000. There were very few women barristers and the majority of them practised in criminal and family law. A specialist female civil barrister was something of a collector's item. Most barristers' clerks (and most male barristers) regarded women as ill-suited to the profession. They were too emotional; they lacked gravitas; they lacked credibility in the eyes of their (mainly male) clients; and of the few who, despite these perceived disadvantages, managed to build up a practice, most would leave to start a family. From the clerks' point of view, this was inconvenient to say the least.

How this has changed. There are now outstanding women barristers in all areas of the law. As many women as men are now entering the profession. The male bastion has been well and truly stormed. It is still tough for a woman with young children. But in some ways it is easier for a young female barrister than a young female solicitor, particularly one who practises in civil law, where so much work can now be done at home with the aid of electronic communication.

The maximum size of Chambers tended to be about 12 to 15 barristers when I started at the Bar. There are 130 barristers in 39 Essex Chambers, the Chambers to which I have returned. Many sets have well over 50 barristers. Most (if not all) of them are now run as large state of the art businesses. Many occupy modern offices. A far cry from the Dickensian rooms in which barristers used to work 50 years ago. When I started, computers and electronic communication did not exist. All records were kept manually. Unthinkable today.

And how the barrister's clerk has changed. When I started, clerks were all men. Not so today. Almost invariably, they had left school at the age of 16. Even in the best Chambers, much of their business was done by wily chatting up of legal executives over a pint in the pub. Some of that may still go on. But not in the best Chambers. The senior clerk managed the Chambers. In effect, he was the chief executive, although not in name. Most of the senior clerks of 50 years ago would not have had the skills to manage a large complex business. That is precisely what the senior clerk or chief executive of a large set of Chambers does today.

In the late 1960s, many barristers wore bowler hats and pinstripe trousers and carried beautifully furled black umbrellas. Women were not allowed to wear trousers. All suits had to be charcoal and men had to wear waistcoats. Some judges refused to hear from barristers who were not properly dressed.

A barrister had to pay a pupillage fee of £50 for six months' pupillage. This was no different in principle from the fee that articled clerks had to pay solicitors and accountants for their articles. Chambers did not offer scholarships. Nowadays, nobody charges for a pupillage and Chambers are required to make scholarship awards. The result has been a huge reduction in the number of pupillages that are available. Provided that you had a decent CV and looked respectable and behaved decently, you were likely to get a pupillage at the drop of a hat. There was no formal process whatsoever. Whether a barrister took on a pupil was a personal matter for him; it was of no concern to the other members of Chambers. How different from the stressful experience that the young have to undergo today.

So pupillage was something of a free for all. Pupillage was entirely unregulated by the profession and uncontrolled in most—if not all—cases by the Chambers themselves. The profession was riddled with what now seem to be extraordinary restrictive practices. Most barristers' clerks were paid 10 per cent of the barristers' gross fees. Even in those days, when Chambers were so much smaller than they are today, the result was that some clerks became seriously rich, far richer than many, and in some cases, than most of their barristers. Junior barristers always received two thirds of the QC's fee. Thus a junior was often paid more when led than he would have been for doing the same work on his own. A QC always had to have a junior with him. QCs could not be briefed on their own. Nor could they be instructed to draft pleadings or write opinions, regardless of what the client wanted and was willing to pay. The interests of the client did not come into the picture. And somehow, the fee charged by a barrister was usually the same as that charged by his opponent. This was the product of a surreptitious clerk-to-clerk telephone conversation before fees were negotiated.

No set of Chambers was permitted to have more than two QCs in it. And when a barrister from out of London took Silk, he had to move to Chambers in London even though the bulk of his work continued to be on circuit.

Advertising was not permitted. It was condemned as 'touting' and was contrary to the professional rules of conduct. I am not sure whether holding a seminar in Chambers to which actual or potential clients were invited would have been acceptable. I suspect not. There is no doubt that much of the networking that is routinely done today would have been frowned upon and considered to be a breach of professional standards; and therefore a reportable offence.

Gradually, all of these Byzantine practices faded away. To modern eyes, some of them are shocking, others just peculiar. All of them would be indefensible today as being grossly anti-competitive.

Appointments to Silk have also undergone a major change. These appointments used to be made by the Lord Chancellor after taking secret soundings, mainly from a small number of senior judges. A negative response from a very senior judge would usually be fatal to the prospects of even a very successful junior taking Silk. Happily this kind of black-balling is now a thing of the past. The appointments are now dealt with by a body (QC) which operates under the aegis of the profession. Silk is granted on application. The application process is elaborate, complex and stressful. But at least it is fair. The days of black-balling have gone.

I have concentrated on the Bar because that was my profession. The solicitors' profession has also changed hugely. Fifty years ago, there was no such thing as a limited liability partnership. And firms could not have more than 20 partners. So the risk of unlimited liability was borne by a small number of partners. Today, there are limited liability partnerships with unlimited numbers of partners. This is the result of the amalgamation of practices and the emergence of massive firms with hundreds of partners employing thousands of people. It has also led to the globalisation of firms of solicitors with the large firms having offices both in this country and in major international centres around the world. The technological changes to which I have referred have affected the solicitors' profession at least as much as the Bar, if not more so.

Time does not permit me to do more than mention the Legal Services Board, the Bar Standards Board and the Solicitors Regulation Authority, which did not exist 50 years ago. These bodies regulate the professions in a way that would have been unthinkable when I stated at the Bar.

It is time to move on from the professions. I want to say a few words about judges. First, the changes to the manner of judicial appointments. The arrival of the Judicial Appointments Commission has made a huge change to the *process* of judicial appointment. Appointment is made only from those who apply. The days of the tap on the shoulder by the Lord Chancellor have gone and gone forever. Every appointment is made by open competition. For the highest courts, the applications are considered by a panel of five (three lay and two judicial). There is usually a sifting process followed by an interview of the shortlisted candidates. It is very time-consuming for the panel and very stressful for the candidates. When this system was introduced, it was said by many that no barrister would be willing to subject himself or herself to the process of applications and interviews. It would be demeaning. It would become known who had applied and failed. In the event, there has been no shortage of applicants for the posts of circuit and district judges. But it is undeniably the case that more top QCs are refusing to apply to become High Court Judges than refused the offer of an appointment even 20 years ago (the so-called 'refuseniks'). There are probably several reasons for this, but I doubt whether the application process is one of them.

There were very few women judges 50 years ago and hardly any at High Court level and none above. When the revolutionary step was taken of appointing the first female justice to the Court of Appeal, what to call her proved to be a real challenge to our male-dominated system. Elizabeth Butler-Sloss was initially styled 'Lord Justice Butler-Sloss'. It took some time before something was done about this absurdity. It was eventually abandoned in favour of 'Lady Justice Butler-Sloss'. There were a few female judges at the lower levels, but very few overall. Now there are about 20 per cent in the High Court and the Court of Appeal, and a higher percentage than that in the lower courts. There is still a long way to go, but progress is being made.

Before I come to some of the huge changes that have occurred in our substantive law, I want to touch on three other developments of importance. First, the change in the role of the Lord Chancellor.

Until the passing of the Constitutional Reform Act 2005, the Lord Chancellor (who held an ancient office of great constitutional significance) was a member of the Executive, the Legislature (by virtue of being a member of the House of Lords) and the Head of the Judiciary (although he rarely sat as a judge). By convention, he was always a lawyer and an elder statesman who was not on his way up the greasy pole in politics. Therefore, he could and did discharge fearlessly one of his most important roles, which was to defend the independence of the judges, and in particular defend them from unfair and unjustified attacks by the government and the media. The effect of the 2005 Act was that the Lord Chancellor no longer had to be a lawyer. The last three Lord Chancellors have not been lawyers. They have all been ambitious young politicians on their way up. It is understandable that they do not wish to upset the Prime Minister or any other senior member of government. The judges are now less well protected from unwarranted attacks than they were before the reform. In my view, this is convincingly demonstrated by the woefully inadequate response of the current Lord Chancellor to the 'enemies of the people' attack by some of the Press to the High Court ruling in the Brexit case.

The second important development to which I wish to refer is the creation of the Supreme Court. As from October 2009, it replaced the Appellate Committee of the House of Lords as the highest court in the UK. I think it most unlikely that the decisions of the Supreme Court are any different from what they would have been if the Appellate Committee had continued to exist. No doubt, the court is evolving the law in response to various forces at work in our society. It was ever thus. I do not believe that the fact that the Supreme Court has come into being is, of itself, relevant to how that court is developing our law. As I see it, the principal reason for creating the Supreme Court was the desire to formalise the separation of powers between the Executive, the Legislature and the Judiciary although, in practice but not in form, that separation had always been scrupulously respected by the Appellate Committee. Having said that, I do think that appearances matter. In any event, the changes have not merely been formal and cosmetic. The Supreme Court is far more visible than its predecessor was. It is housed in a beautiful building in Parliament Square which is easily accessible to the public. The public (especially the young public) visit the court in droves. The Appellate Committee sat in a committee room which, even for the advocates who were appearing in an appeal, was difficult to find. The work of the Appellate Committee was something of a mystery to most citizens. Proceedings in the Supreme Court are live-streamed. Its judgments are summarised in (usually) accessible press summaries. In short, large sections of the public now have a fairly good idea of what our highest court does. That must be a good thing.

The third development that I want to touch on is not a good thing. It concerns the massive curtailment of access to justice that has occurred in the last few years. 50 years ago, legal aid was available (subject to means and merits tests) in most areas of the law. How different things are today when (again subject to means and merits tests) legal aid is still available for criminal cases (though less generously than used to be the case); is available in certain areas of civil law (but not for the bulk of civil litigation); but is not available at all for family disputes. Alternative ways of funding litigation (including conditional fee agreements) have been introduced. The complexity of the new schemes was such that it gave rise to a great deal of litigation itself. Although the new funding arrangements did lead to many litigants being represented, the withdrawal of legal aid also resulted in a huge rise in the numbers of litigants-in-person. This has posed considerable problems for the litigants themselves, the lawyers who represent opposing parties and for the judges.

The slashing of legal aid has been a consequence of the reduction in funds granted to the Ministry of Justice. The MoJ is not protected from the cuts that have been repeatedly demanded by the Treasury in recent years. A few years ago, the responsibility for the prisons was transferred from the Home Office to the MoJ. The justice system therefore now has to compete with prisons for the money. With prisons full to bursting point, it is no surprise that the justice system comes off second best. In my view, it is no exaggeration to say that the justice system is being starved of funds.

Another recent MoJ initiative has been the introduction of a massive increase in court fees. This was an ill-considered attempt to raise some money for the Department. All the signs are that this has had a seriously adverse effect on access to justice for all but the wealthy and the very poor (who do not have to pay). Many people who are no more than comfortably off and many small- and medium-size enterprises can no longer afford even to issue proceedings. This will encourage would-be litigants to find alternatives to litigation to resolve their disputes. Fifty years ago, alternative dispute resolution (ADR) was unknown as a concept. Mediators did not exist. Early neutral evaluation was also unknown. The current trend to promote these alternatives to litigation is now clear for all to see. I suspect that in 50 years from now, the courts will rarely be used for private law litigation. They will be used largely to resolve claims against the state. I shall not be around to see whether this bold prediction is borne out by events.

It is time that I moved away from the system and said a few words about changes in the law itself. There have been some dramatic changes in the last 50 years. The first half of the twentieth century was a period of relative stability in the law. Let us consider what has happened in the last 50 years or so. Family law (including the law relating to children) has changed out of all recognition. Contested divorces were not uncommon 50 years ago. Today they are a rarity. A spouse who petitioned for a divorce had to seek the discretion of the court if he or she had committed adultery. There were common law defences such as connivance and condonation which, if proved, would be a bar to the grant of relief. The grounds of divorce were different. Most important, the question of who was the guilty party was important for the resolution of claims for financial relief. That has all changed, although the law relating to financial relief still seems to be complex and unpredictable. As regards children, the law is now clear. Whether the issue arises in the context of a divorce or of whether a child should be placed in the care of a local authority, it is the welfare of the child and the promotion of his or her interests that has now been established as the determinant factor. This welcome clarification has been a crucial change in the law relating to children.

Criminal law (including sentencing) has become far more complicated than it was 50 years ago. Substantive criminal law has been the subject of a massive amount of legislation. Take sexual offences as an example. I believe that 50 years ago, sexual offences were dealt with in a single chapter in *Archbold*. Now there is at least one massive textbook devoted entirely to sexual offences. And the latest supplement of that book is itself a massive tome. Many sexual offences have been added to the statute book. There has also been a huge increase in the number of statutory offences generally. Sexual offending is now prosecuted far more than it used to be. Many circuit judges spend most of their time trying sex cases.

Until about 50 years ago, there was no attempt to provide sentencing guidance to judges. The traditional view was that nothing should be done to interfere with the freedom of the judge to exercise his (it usually was 'his') judgment as he saw fit. The result was chaos, incoherence and inconsistency. Things started to improve when the Lord Chief Justice started to give so-called 'guideline judgments' in which he gave sentencing guidance for certain types of offence. Much later, the Sentencing Guidelines Council (now the Sentencing Council) was established under the chairmanship of a judge of the Court of Appeal to promulgate sophisticated and detailed sentencing guidelines for a huge range of offences. This has made a big difference and has reduced inconsistency in sentencing to a considerable extent.

Another significant change is that we now demand far higher standards of fairness and competence from trial judges than we used to do 50 years ago. The judges used to receive no training whatsoever. The big change occurred when the Judicial Studies Board, or JSB as it was called (now the Judicial College), was established. There was much opposition to the idea of judicial training from many of the more senior judges. Any attempt to train the judges was considered by many of them to pose a threat to their judicial independence. Anyway, the judges were all so brilliant that they did not need any training. The arrogance of such attitudes is breathtaking to modern eyes. These attitudes were not shared by the younger judges, especially those (like me) who had had no experience of criminal law and the criminal courts. The JSB introduced compulsory induction and continuation training courses which were largely run by the judges themselves. Excellent written materials were produced, including the invaluable *Handbook* which contained tips as to how to sum up and deal with issues that frequently cropped up in a criminal trial.

I believe that, with a few exceptions, judges now conduct trials more fairly than they used to do. There are probably a number of reasons for this welcome change. First, I think that most modern judges regard themselves as public servants doing an important job in the public interest. Humility was not the hallmark of the judge in days gone by. I would not claim that all judges in the twenty-first century are paragons of humility. But I do believe that judges today have a better understanding than some of their predecessors of the importance of acting fairly. The training that they receive must have contributed to this. Secondly, the duty of any decision-maker in whatever context to act fairly has been clearly articulated and explained in many cases both here and abroad. As a matter of law, it occupies centre stage in our justice system. A verdict in a criminal trial (and a decision in a civil trial) that has been arrived at unfairly will often be quashed or set aside as unlawful. Thirdly, since the introduction of the power to order a retrial following the quashing of a conviction on appeal, the Court of Appeal Criminal Division has been more willing to allow an appeal on the ground that the defendant did not receive a fair trial. Trial judges now know that if they overstep the bounds of fair conduct, a conviction may be quashed. Trial judges do not like their decisions to be overturned on appeal, especially if the reason for the success on appeal is that they conducted the hearing unfairly. I acknowledge that, even today, there are some judges who like to put the boot in. The wily ones will sum up heavily in favour of a conviction, lacing their tendentious summary of the evidence with a healthy scattering of 'you may think that … but, of course, it is a matter for you, members of the jury'. Appellate judges are not fooled by such attempts to mask their unfair behaviour.

There has been a great deal of activity in the field of the law of criminal procedure in recent times. The changes are too many to enumerate. They include the establishing of a Criminal Procedure Committee through which many criminal procedure rules have been introduced to streamline the trial process. An important reform has been to allow the court in defined circumstances to order a retrial following an acquittal.

Nor should I overlook the Criminal Cases Review Commission (CCRC) which was established in the mid-1990s to investigate cases of suspected miscarriages of justice. The cases investigated were ones where the criminal justice system had run its course. In an appropriate case, the CCRC could refer the case to the CACD for reconsideration. This was an important safeguard inspired by some notorious miscarriages of justice that occurred in the 1970s.

Before I leave criminal justice, I must mention the fact that the death penalty was abolished in 1965 and the last death penalty was executed in August 1964. The death penalty is not the subject of discussion these days. There is no clamour for its reintroduction. But I sometimes wonder what the outcome of a referendum on the death penalty would be. Although it is no longer a live issue, the abolition of the death penalty shortly before I started to practise at the Bar was a momentous change in our law.

I turn to judicial review. Although the famous case of *Associated Provincial Picture Houses Ltd v Wednesbury Corpn*[1] was decided as long ago as in 1947, judicial review was still in its infancy 50 years ago. The grounds on which a public law challenge to a decision could be made were narrowly interpreted by the courts. The nomenclature of the grounds of relief was antiquated and off-putting: *certiorari* and *mandamus*. There were some landmark decisions of the House

---

[1] *Associated Provincial Picture Houses Ltd v Wednesbury Corpn* [1948] 1 KB 223 (CA).

of Lords in the 1960s such as *Anisminic Ltd v Foreign Compensation Commission*[2] (1968) which moved the law along. But comparatively few lawyers practised in the field of public law at that time. Since then the principles have been developed and refined and, to the dismay of the government, there has been an explosion of litigation in this field. I have little doubt that, even without the influence of EU law and the Human Rights Act 1998 (the 1998 Act), there would have been increasing resort to the courts by persons bringing public law claims. Fifty years ago, there was no Administrative Court. But there was something called the Crown Office List of the Queen's Bench Division. Very few judges were ticketed to hear cases in that List because there was not much work. Now most of the Queen's Bench Division judges sit in the Administrative Court deciding public law cases. Leaving aside the judges of the Commercial Court, the Chancery Division and the Technology and Construction Court, few private law cases are heard by High Court Judges.

Although the UK ratified the European Convention on Human Rights in 1951, the Convention did not become part of our domestic law until the 1998 Act came into force in January 2000. This Act has had a dramatic effect on our law, although perhaps not too many cases would have been decided differently on an application of the common law. That may in part be because the common law evolves and, in developing it, our judges have responded to and reflected the Convention and the jurisprudence of the Strasbourg court. These days, our courts are bombarded with citation of Strasbourg case-law in any case where it is even remotely relevant.

There are undoubtedly differences between Convention law and our common law. These can lead to different results on the same facts. A good illustration of this is to be found in the case of *Smith and Grady v UK*[3] (the gay servicemen case). Mr Smith brought a judicial review claim against the Ministry of Defence challenging its decision to discharge him from the Royal Navy on the grounds of his homosexuality. His claim was dismissed by our courts in 1996 on the grounds that the decision to discharge him was not unreasonable in the *Wednesbury* sense or unlawful in any other way recognised by our common law. The claim could not be advanced as a complaint of breach of the right to respect for private life under Article 8 of the Convention, because the Convention was not part of our law at the time. The case went to Strasbourg and the claim succeeded.

---

[2] *Anisminic Ltd v Foreign Compensation Commission* [1969] 2 AC 147 (HL).
[3] *Smith and Grady v UK* [1999] ECHR 72 (ECtHR).

The ECtHR held that the discharge from the Royal Navy was in breach of Article 8. The claim would, of course, have succeeded in our courts after the enactment of the 1998 Act and the consequent incorporation of the Convention into our domestic law.

Where decisions and policies are challenged in legal proceedings on the grounds that they infringe one or more of the rights protected by the Convention, their lawfulness is judged, inter alia, by whether the decisions or policies are proportionate. Proportionality is a European concept which has no part to play in our common law jurisprudence. Indeed, thus far, attempts in common law cases to unseat the test of *Wednesbury* unreasonableness and replace it with the more sophisticated test of proportionality have failed in our courts. The concept of proportionality is routinely applied in cases which concern issues of EU law or claims for breach of the Convention. Fifty years ago, our judges would have had no idea of what proportionality meant or how to apply it. Today, aided by the jurisprudence of the courts in Strasbourg and Luxembourg, not to mention the courts of civil jurisdictions, our judges have become familiar with the concept and how to apply it.

The influence of EU law has been great since the UK joined the EU and became subject to EU law on 1 January 1973. In the case of *Bulmer v Bollinger*,[4] Lord Denning MR famously said of the treaty by which the UK became bound by EU law: 'it flows into the estuaries and up the rivers. It cannot be held back'. Characteristic Lord Denning prose and a wonderful metaphor. It captured the imagination at the time, but I doubt whether many thought that what he said was more than colourful hype. At the time, that might well have been a fair assessment. But how right Lord Denning has proved to be. He may be forgiven for not having foreseen the possibility of Brexit. But Brexit was the only way of escaping from the tentacles EU law.

It is strange that, for a long time, the critics of the European influence on our law and the perceived loss of UK sovereignty concentrated their fire-power on the European Convention on Human Rights and the decisions of the Strasbourg court rather than EU law and the decisions of the Luxembourg court. They conveniently overlooked the fact that the brilliantly drafted 1998 Act did not make the decisions of that court binding on our courts. It merely required our courts (by section 2(1)(a)) to 'take into account' any relevant Strasbourg

---

[4] *Bulmer (HP) Ltd v J Bollinger SA* [1974] Ch 401 (CA).

jurisprudence. That is not, however, to say that this jurisprudence has not influenced the development of our law. It has done so to a very significant degree.

But when it comes to issues which come within the scope of EU law, our courts are obliged to apply that law and to follow (and not merely take into account) any relevant jurisprudence of the Luxembourg court. The significance of this unequivocal obligation has only recently dawned on critics of Europe (including Eurosceptics within the government). The clamour to withdraw from the Convention has become muted of late and has given way to the demand to withdraw from the EU and from the jurisdiction of the Luxembourg court. The reach of EU law has continued to expand massively in recent years. When it was largely focused on economic issues such as, for example, competition, patents and consumer protection, oddly it was not seen by its critics as a threat to the sovereignty of Parliament and the jurisdiction of our courts. But EU law now regulates an ever increasing number of areas of our lives. It is true that most of it has been transposed into our domestic law by regulations. But make no mistake: it is in substance EU law. Since the domestic regulations are intended to reflect the parent EU instrument, our courts interpret them so as to accord with the true meaning of the EU instrument. And if the instrument has been interpreted by the Luxembourg court, then our courts interpret them in accordance with that interpretation. EU law now regulates large swathes of our national life. Environmental protection is largely the product of EU law. Employment law is now largely regulated by EU law. The modern law relating to discrimination is largely the product of the EU. And the same can be said of many other areas of social and economic life. But it does not stop there. The law of asylum is now the subject of EU law. Even human rights ever since the EU signed up to the Convention.[5]

This is not the place to go into the details of the extent to which our law is now governed (or at least influenced) first by the laws promulgated by Brussels and interpreted by Luxembourg and secondly by the Convention as it has been interpreted by the Strasbourg court. The important point is that these developments represent a sea-change in our law. It is one that the judges who dispensed justice in the first half of the twentieth century would not have

---

[5] It should be noted that even though the EU is obliged to accede to the Convention, it has not yet acceded to it.

foreseen and which, I suspect, many if not most of them would have found seriously objectionable.

In the last 50 years, there has been a great deal of social and economic legislation whose effect has been to make huge changes to our law. Until the 1970s, discriminatory behaviour was largely uncontrolled by the law. Discrimination, which was unfair and caused great harm and suffering to vulnerable members of society, went unremarked. There was no legal mechanism for preventing it or compensating those who were victims of it. But since the 1970s, there has been a plethora of legislation which has made specific types of discriminatory behaviour unlawful. The Equal Pay Act 1963 was the first such major piece of legislation. It was followed by other hugely important statutes such as the Race Relations Act 1965; the Sex Discrimination Act 1975; the Disability Discrimination Act 1995; and the Equality Acts of 2006 and 2010. It is difficult to exaggerate the effect that these statutes have had in influencing social attitudes and behaviour. Discrimination law is particularly complex and difficult. It has given rise to a great deal of litigation both here and abroad. The principles and their application are still being worked out.

Time does not permit me to discuss (even in the barest outline) all the many other changes in our law that have taken place in the last 50 years. I have touched on the influence of the EU in areas such as competition, patent law and consumer protection. There has been a veritable explosion of legislation in these and other areas. All of it has had to be interpreted and explained by the courts here and abroad. There has also been much important legislation that does not bear the footprint of Brussels at all. To take but one example, the Unfair Contract Terms Act 1977 provided protection to consumers against unfair contractual terms. This was an important erosion of the old common law principle of *caveat emptor.*

So far I have said nothing about civil procedure. By the late twentieth century, the cost and delays of civil litigation had become scandalous. In the 1990s Lord Woolf produced a report which led to the making of the Civil Procedure Rules (CPR). The aim of the Woolf reforms was to make litigation more efficient and less costly. The basic principle was that the judges were to control the pace and complexity of litigation. These reforms have improved the efficiency and speed with which cases were managed and tried. But the cost of litigation (including in particular the cost of disclosure of documents) remained as high as it had ever been. Lord Justice Jackson had another go at tackling costs. Most of his recommendations were incorporated into the CPR. One of his more controversial recommendations was that there should be costs budgets in most cases. I mention these changes not in order to make a value judgment about them, but to draw attention to them as yet further evidence of the massive changes to our system of justice that have occurred during my professional life.

Occasionally it is salutary to stand back from the detail of what one is doing and consider it in a wider historical context. For almost 50 years, I engaged in the practice of the law, first at the Bar and then as a judge. The purpose of this lecture is not to express a value judgment about the particular changes that I have described. It is only by setting out in one place some of the changes that have taken place (and there are many to which I have not referred) that it is possible to see just how many hugely significant changes there have been. One tends to think of the Law as something of a slow-moving tanker. I hope this lecture has shown that it has been racing along during the last half century or so. As for the future, who can tell? There are no signs that things are slowing down at the present time.

Index